THE WINES OF GERMANY

THE CLASSIC WINE LIBRARY
Editorial board: Sarah Jane Evans MW,
Richard Mayson and James Tidwell MS

There is something uniquely satisfying about a good wine book, preferably read with a glass of the said wine in hand. The Classic Wine Library is a series of wine books written by authors who are both knowledgeable and passionate about their subject. Each title in The Classic Wine Library covers a wine region, country or type and together the books are designed to form a comprehensive guide to the world of wine as well as an enjoyable read, appealing to wine professionals, wine lovers, tourists, armchair travellers and wine trade students alike.

Port and the Douro, Richard Mayson
Cognac: The story of the world's greatest brandy, Nicholas Faith
Sherry, Julian Jeffs
Madeira: The islands and their wines, Richard Mayson
The wines of Austria, Stephen Brook
Biodynamic wine, Monty Waldin
The story of champagne, Nicholas Faith
The wines of Faugères, Rosemary George MW
Côte d'Or: The wines and winemakers of the heart of Burgundy, Raymond Blake
The wines of Canada, Rod Phillips
Rosé: Understanding the pink wine revolution, Elizabeth Gabay MW
Amarone and the fine wines of Verona, Michael Garner
The wines of Greece, Konstantinos Lazarakis MW
Wines of the Languedoc, Rosemary George MW
The wines of northern Spain, Sarah Jane Evans MW
The wines of New Zealand, Rebecca Gibb MW
The wines of Bulgaria, Romania and Moldova, Caroline Gilby MW
Sake and the wines of Japan, Anthony Rose
The wines of Great Britain, Stephen Skelton MW
The wines of Chablis and the Grand Auxerrois, Rosemary George MW
The wines of Germany, Anne Krebiehl MW

THE WINES OF GERMANY

ANNE KREBIEHL MW

ACADEMIE DU VIN LIBRARY

German-born but London-based, Anne Krebiehl MW is a freelance wine writer and lecturer. She is the contributing editor for Austria, Alsace, Burgundy and England for *US Wine Enthusiast* and also writes for trade and consumer wine publications such as *The World of Fine Wine*, *Decanter*, *The Buyer*, *Falstaff* and *Vinum*. She lectures, consults and judges at international wine competitions and is a panel chair at the International Wine Challenge. She completed her WSET Diploma in 2010 and was admitted to the Institute of Masters of Wine in September 2014. Anne has helped to harvest and make wine in New Zealand, Germany and Italy.

To all the women who matter – Anna, Marianne, Martina, Irene, Louise and Astrid – with love.

'Frauen, die den frischen, herben Wein lieben, sind köstliche Naturkinder, mit denen durch Wald und Flur zu streifen eine Lust ist. Sie lieben Das Echte und Klare.'

Rudi vom Endt, *So du zum Weine gehst …*

Copyright © Anne Krebiehl, 2019, 2024

The right of Anne Krebiehl to be identified as the author of this book has been asserted in accordance with the Copyright, Designs and Patents Act 1988.

First published in 2019 by Infinite Ideas Limited
This edition published 2024 by Académie du Vin Library Ltd
academieduvinlibrary.com

All rights reserved. Except for the quotation of small passages for the purposes of criticism or review, no part of this publication may be reproduced, stored in a retrieval system or transmitted in any form or by any means, electronic, mechanical, photocopying, recording, scanning or otherwise, except under the terms of the Copyright, Designs and Patents Act 1988 or under the terms of a licence issued by the Copyright Licensing Agency Ltd, 90 Tottenham Court Road, London W1T 4LP, UK, without the permission in writing of the publisher.

A CIP catalogue record for this book is available from the British Library
ISBN 978–1–913141–55–4

Brand and product names are trademarks or registered trademarks of their respective owners.

Front cover: Rhine valley, castle Katz in autumn, Germany © Germany Images David Crossland/Alamy Stock Photo
Back cover photo courtesy of Wines of Germany
Photo page 144 courtesy of Johannes Leitz
Maps by Darren Lingard from source maps courtesy of Wines of Germany
Graph on page 14 courtesy of Wines of Germany
Colour photograph of Riesling grapes, courtesy of Ralf Kaiser.
All other colour photographs courtesy of Wines of Germany.

Printed in the U.S.A.

CONTENTS

Thank yous	ix
Maps	xi
Introduction	1
1. History	3
2. German wine law – a perpetual palimpsest	9
3. Riesling – 'life is hard enough, let us drink light wine'	25
4. Spätburgunder – the late bloomer	31
5. Sekt – *méthode allemande*	35
6. Climate change – a blessing and a challenge	41
7. Ahr valley – the Pinot canyon	47
8. Baden – degrees of diversity	59
9. Franken – non-Baroque splendour	85
10. Hessische Bergstrasse – awakening beauty	107
11. Mittelrhein – castles, cherries, nymphs and Riesling	111
12. Mosel – a cosmos unto itself	117
13. Nahe – triumph at last	151
14. Pfalz – sunny abundance	165
15. Rheingau – from monks to meritocracy	189

16. Rheinhessen – more than a sea of vines　217

17. Saale-Unstrut and Sachsen – additions from
　　another Germany　245

18. Württemberg – southern promise　259

Glossary　283

Bibliography　287

Index　295

THANK YOUS

Heartfelt thanks go to everyone who helped me along the way. To all the *Winzerinnen* and *Winzer* who so kindly gave their time to explain, answer my questions and show me around. Some of them also fed me and their generosity and kindness is deeply appreciated. Thank you to Janek Schumann MW, Sonja Ostermayer at Rheinhessenwein e.V.; Gillian Bals and Ulrike Siegrist at Sektkellerei Kupferberg; Selina Fritsch at Verband Deutscher Sektkellereien e.V.; Herrn Tuma at Naumburger Weinbaugesellschaft; Geoff Taylor; Patrick Heitmann at KHS GmbH; Frau Fritzges and Frau Diehl at the Ministerium für Wirtschaft, Verkehr, Landwirtschaft und Weinbau Rheinland-Pfalz; Klaus Schneider and Christian Schwörer at Deutscher Weinbauverband e.V.; Wolfgang Janssen and Gerhard Lux at Deutscher Wetterdienst; Petra Teberelli at Stadtarchiv Bingen; Paul Gieler at Ahrwein e.V.; Thomas Hagenbucher at Baden-Württembergischer Genossenschaftsverband e.V., Jesko Graf zu Dohna at Fürstlich Castellsches Domänenamt; Dieter Greiner at Kloster Eberbach; Stefan Doktor at Schloss Johannisberg; Professor Roger Brett Boulton at UC Davis; Professor Dr Hans Schultz at Universität Geisenheim; Professor Dr Ulrich Fischer at Weincampus Neustadt and Dr Daniel Deckers at the Frankfurter Allgemeine Zeitung for sharing and providing so much invaluable information.

Thank you to Sandra Warzeschka at Gebietsweinwerbung Saale-Unstrut; Sandy Prüger at Weinbauverband Sachsen e.V. and Ansgar Schmitz at Moselwein e.V. for helping to organize my travel. A huge thank you to Steffen Schindler and Ernst Büscher at the German Wine Institute: without their support in terms of travel cost this entire undertaking would have been impossible. I thank Ralf Kaiser for one of the best photographs of Riesling ever. Last but certainly not least I thank Robin Navrozov, Sebastian Thomas and above all Andrew Neather for proofreading various chapters. To you all: *Herzlichsten Dank*.

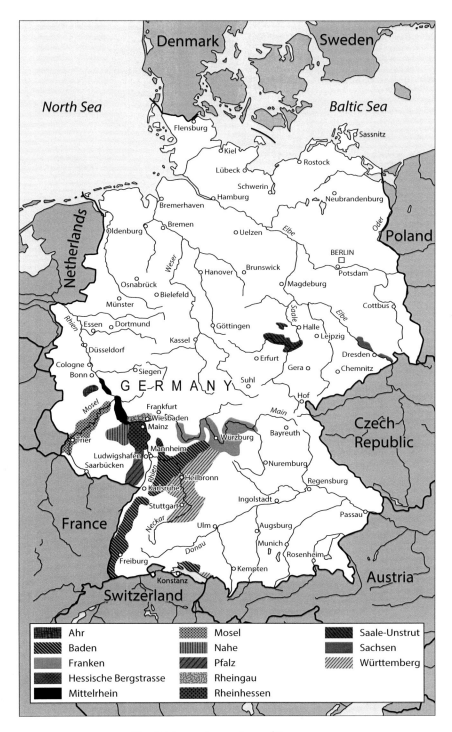

The thirteen wine regions of Germany

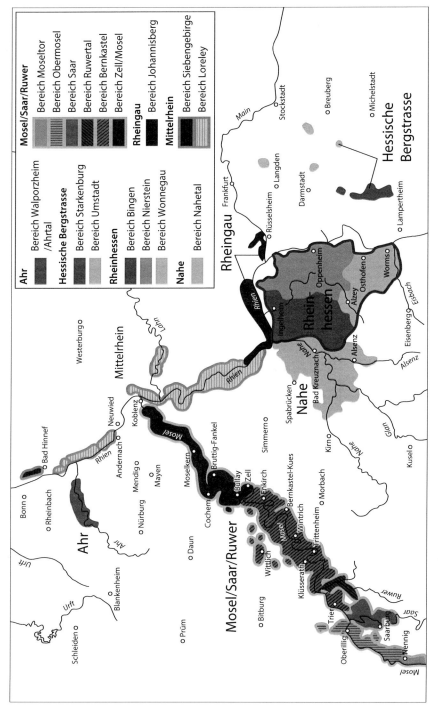

Ahr, Mosel, Mittelrhein, Nahe, Rheingau, Rheinhessen and Hessische Bergstrasse in detail

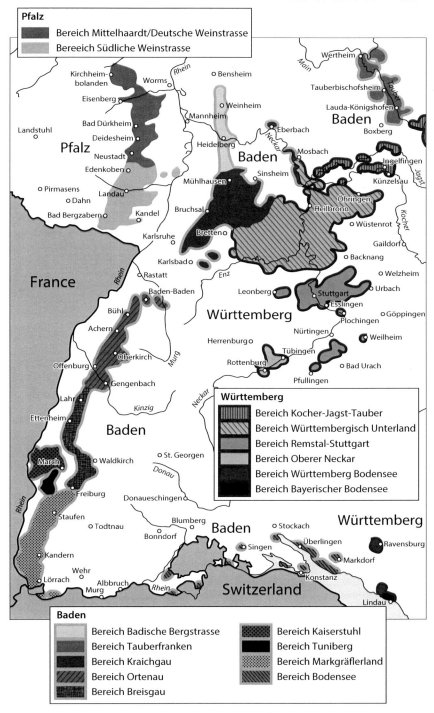

Pfalz, Baden and Württemberg in detail

Saale-Unstrut and Sachsen in detail

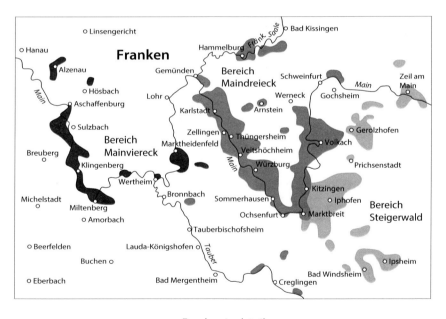

Franken in detail

INTRODUCTION

Squeezing all of Germany between the two covers of a wine book was a formidable task. The singularities of each region could easily fill separate books, but I hope I have done Germany justice. There are just so many sources, so many details, so many stories. But while this book necessarily leaves a lot to be said, it is also an opportunity to step back and give an overview of its thirteen wine regions; to look at German wine, place it in the context of its history and see how far this wine country at the very heart of Europe has come. It is an opportunity to explain why some regions are very well known and others are not. Are there gaps? Certainly, the subject is just too vast. Is this comprehensive? No, it can only ever be a sketch, but I hope it will give readers the appetite to delve deeper, to explore, to taste and above all visit.

During my research, I drove through Mosel mist, Dresden snow and Baden sunshine. I took ferries across the Rhine, Main and Elbe. While clocking up the miles in my trusty old Volvo, I had the opportunity to appreciate variations not only in climate and geography but also the cultural diversity of Germany. This diversity is what I hope to convey. Throughout all this, one thing has become clear: it is only now that Germany is emerging from the convulsions of the twentieth century to become its true self and allow the uniqueness of its vineyards and diverse landscapes to take centre stage. The wines bear witness to that.

With 102,592 hectares of vineyard, Germany is the fourteenth largest wine-producing country in the world. It has thirteen wine regions across four degrees of latitude – from 47.5°N in Baden to 51.5°N in Saale-Unstrut – which lie mainly along various rivers: Rhine, Main, Neckar, Mosel, Saar, Ruwer, Nahe, Ahr, Elbe, Saale and Unstrut.

Topography is as important as geology as the often steep slopes created by these rivers enable grapes to ripen in a formerly marginal climate. Climate change has transformed German viticulture and today more than a third of its hectarage is planted to red grape varieties. With 11,767 hectares of Pinot Noir, aka Spätburgunder, Germany is now the world's third-largest producer of this variety – a remarkable success story and a fascinating addition to the world's Pinot pantheon. Despite climate change, vintage variation remains a firm feature in German wine. With 23,809 hectares, Germany is the world's largest, most important and diverse grower of Riesling. The many faces of German Riesling, grown across all thirteen regions, are of infinite variety and nuance – they defy description. While Riesling is grown around the globe, it reaches its most thrilling, diverse, alluring, unique and spine-tingling expressions in Germany. Above all, Germany is home to a diverse, creative, dynamic and evolving group of winemakers who constantly hone and redefine what authentic German wine culture is.

The book starts with a look at the origins and history of winemaking in Germany and continues with a chapter on German wine law. Deeply aware how confusing German wine law can be, I have tried to explain it by charting its evolution. This is followed by chapters on Germany's signature grape Riesling, its most important red grape variety, Spätburgunder, a chapter on the literally effervescent category of Sekt, or sparkling wine, and finally a chapter on the opportunity and challenge that is climate change. Following that, each region, with a selection of producers, is profiled.

There are just under 16,000 wine estates in Germany's fragmented wine industry. Necessarily, a selection had to be made. The idea was to show a good cross-section in each region, with a focus on leading lights with international presence and more recent, up-and-coming estates which represent the future. The scope and volume of this book made this selection difficult. Everywhere I look there are more estates worthy of inclusion. Do the profiled estates constitute a recommendation? Absolutely. Are there many more which would have merited mention? Definitely. My regret is that I could not visit and profile them all.

It is my hope that this book will be your travelling companion on your own vinous forays to a country I love very much.

Anne Krebiehl MW, London, June 2019

1
HISTORY

So manifold, so regional and so diverse is the history of German wine that this chapter, necessarily, is a broad sweep. More detail can be found in each of the regional chapters. The following serves to set the scene, showing how integral viticulture once was, the vast extent it reached and how geography, trade, conflict and climate have shaped German wine.

ORIGINS AND MIDDLE AGES

The origins of German viticulture can be traced to the Romans, especially in the Mosel where pollen dating suggests the presence of *Vitis vinifera* around AD 150. Whether the Celts before them already cultivated the vine is unclear. While remains of Roman press houses have been found in the Mosel, Rheinhessen, Mittelrhein and the Pfalz, there is sparse evidence for other German regions. In any case, by the fourth century, viticulture was well established along the Mosel and the left bank of the Rhine. German viticulture survived the dark ages. During the early Middle Ages the ongoing spread of Christianity required sacramental wine, while honest work needed both sustenance and the relative hygiene wine could offer. As Roman rule gave way to that of the Merovingians and Carolingians, it spread to the right bank of the Rhine. This was first documented in a gift deed from 638 by King Dagobert, last of the Merovingian kings. Viticulture spread further under the Carolingians, whose rule culminated in Charlemagne (742–814). After conquering the Saxons and Langobards, Charlemagne, then King of Franks, was crowned emperor in Rome on Christmas Day of the year 800.

His coronation laid the foundation of what, over the following centuries, gradually became the Holy Roman Empire of the German Nation: a patchwork of duchies, electorates, principalities and free imperial cities. This *Kleinstaaterei* with its countless jurisdictions, tariffs and measuring units would last until 1806 – before going down with barely a whimper. Note that Charlemagne's was the first *Reich*, or empire. The second was Bismarck's *Deutsches Reich* under Prussian auspices, founded in 1871. This was followed by the infamous Third, supposedly 'eternal', *Reich*; Germany's darkest and most destructive. But back to Charlemagne. His Frankish empire spanned what is now Germany, the Netherlands, France and parts of Italy. One of Charlemagne's laws, *Capitulare de villis*, neatly laid out how royal and all dependent estates were to be managed. Ten of the 70 paragraphs mention wine, illustrating how well-established and important viticulture was[1]. Wine was thus part and parcel of life, as were beer, cider and perry.

The Carolingians also saw it as a duty to spread the Christian faith. Kloster (abbey) Prüm was founded in 721, Kloster Fulda in 744, Kloster Lorsch in 764 – all with substantial vineyard holdings far and wide. Viticulture spread with the monastic orders, first Benedictines, then Cistercians, who required wine for the sacrament and as nourishment for their communities. As worldly powers sought to secure eternal salvation by donating possessions and lesser mortals by joining an order, two elements combined: land and labour. The rapid expansion of especially Cistercian endeavours, propelled by the Cluniac Reform, coincided with the Medieval Warm Period (approximately 950–1250). Not only did monastic settlements proliferate, so did their vineyards. Countless site names still bear witness to this monastic past. In 1136 Kloster Eberbach in the Rheingau was founded as a filiation of Clairvaux. Its abbot, Bernard of Clairvaux (1090–1153), became the most influential of all Cistercians: by the time of his death 344 Cistercian monasteries had been founded in Europe. As these monasteries grew, their networks spread, with affiliated granges, or farmsteads.

The vine thus spread far and wide, as far north and east as Silesia;

---

1 It notes: 'our stewards shall take charge of our vineyards in their districts, and see that they are properly worked; and let them put the wine into good vessels, and take particular care that no loss is incurred in shipping it … that the wine-presses on our estates shall be kept in good order. And the stewards are to see to it that no one dares to crush the grapes with his feet, but that everything is clean … that wine is to be transported in good barrels rather than in skins.' Annual statements were to be made, of the income from vineyards and of the income from those 'who pay their dues in wine.'

indeed German viticulture never reached the same extent again. By now wine was not only sacrament, drink and nutrition, it was also a precious good to be traded profitably. Kloster Eberbach, for instance, had its own fleet to ship wine upstream on the Rhine to Cologne, *the* wine trade hub of the Middle Ages, where they had several cellars. The twelfth century also saw the gradual formation of the Hanseatic League, a trading association of cities on the Rhine, the North Sea and the Baltic. This trading empire made Rhine wine – then anything grown along the Rhine – famous in the Middle Ages.

CONFLICT AND CONTRACTION

As the climate cooled from the mid-thirteenth century onwards, viticulture contracted in the marginal areas in the north and east. As the use of hops in brewing gradually spread, beer became more stable, and possibly tasted better than some local wine. Increasing tax burdens hampered wine trade. But it was war that dealt the most severe blows to viticulture in the sixteenth and seventeenth centuries. The *Bauernkrieg*, or Peasants' Revolt, of 1525 was brutally put down and soon religious strife replaced feudal injustice as the main *casus belli*. The Reformation, its touchpaper lit by Martin Luther in 1517, set off more than a century of conflicts between Catholics and Protestants. Its bloody culmination was the Thirty Years' War, between 1618 and 1648. Germany had never seen such devastation. Marauding troops on all sides destroyed, killed and pillaged. By 1648 murder, pestilence and famine had slashed the population from seventeen to ten million. In some areas no farmers were left to till land or tend vineyards. But the Holy Roman Empire muddled on, its various powers engaging or getting caught up in various conflicts, especially along the Rhine, the constantly contested natural border between France and Germany.

A NEW EUROPEAN ORDER AND THE 'LONG NINETEENTH CENTURY'

Napoleon's pan-European warfare brought lasting change. In 1792 he first occupied then annexed all German territories on the left bank of the Rhine, turning them into *départements* of his republic in 1798. For ordinary folk this was a blessing, as feudal order was replaced by the *Code Civil*, spelling out civic rights for the first time. Napoleon dissolved monasteries, secularized aristocratic and ecclesiastical estates and auctioned them off. Today's wine regions of Pfalz, Rheinhessen, Nahe, Mosel, Saar, Ruwer and Ahr were now under French rule, and ownership structures changed fundamentally. This prompted the redistribution, in 1803, of what was left of the Holy Roman Empire to compensate German aristocrats for their territorial losses west of the Rhine. There had been 314 'statelets' in the Holy Roman Empire; now there were just 39. After the dissolution of the Holy Roman Empire in 1806, these 39 states formed the *Deutscher Bund*, or German Confederation.

After Napoleon's final defeat, a new European power balance was brokered during the Vienna Congress of 1815. At the time, field blends dominated and German viticulture throughout the country was still at the mercy of wildly varying vintages and yields. In the Rheingau, Riesling started to take hold in a handful of aristocratic estates whose owners could afford to pay increasing attention to selective harvesting. This established a new paradigm of quality and Rhine Riesling, especially Rheingau Riesling, fetched ever higher prices. The nineteenth century saw much progress: local viticultural associations were founded, along with viticultural colleges. Winemaking increasingly benefited from scientific understanding and official support measures aiming to improve viticulture. A proper wine industry was forming with its own wine publications.

From the mid-nineteenth century onwards, Prussia was in the ascendancy. Its victories in the Austro–Prussian war of 1866 and the Franco–Prussian War of 1870–71 led to the creation of the *Deutsches Reich*, or German Empire, in 1871. By now Mosel Riesling had become fashionable. In the late nineteenth century the scourges of downy and powdery mildew, followed by phylloxera, prompted the establishment of further state-owned model estates and schools to serve as research stations; the Prussian state domaines, above all, set new standards. Yet German viticulture with its fragmented ownership structures was in dire straits. Despite these difficulties, German Rieslings from Rhein and Mosel reached their zenith: by the turn of the twentieth century they were amongst the most expensive and sought-after wines in the world.

THE TUMULTUOUS TWENTIETH CENTURY

Riesling's golden age, as well as that of the German Empire, ended with the First World War. After 1918 a defeated Germany faced the punitive conditions of the Versailles Treaty and the political instability of the Weimar Republic. Viticulture struggled: its profitable export markets had collapsed. Prohibition was enforced in the United States from 1920, the Bolsheviks ruled Russia and Britain was no longer keen on German wine. The hyperinflation of 1924 and the world economic crisis of 1929, along with poor vintages, set the scene for more misery, and paved the way for National Socialism. The new Nazi regime of 1933 lost no time in establishing a centralized authority governing all aspects of agriculture and viticulture: the *Reichsnährstand*, with its horrendous slogan '*Blut und Boden*', blood and soil. Wine as an expression of national identity and pride was an ideal vehicle for Nazi propaganda and a source of precious foreign currency. The Nazis both ruthlessly and efficiently implemented the viticultural improvement measures that their Prussian-led predecessors had not been able to push through: they banned hybrid varieties, which had become popular in southern Germany after phylloxera, and restricted plantings to quality varieties and suitable sites. Jewish wine merchants were initially slandered and later banned from wine auctions. Later, relentless discrimination ended in their persecution, deportation and mass murder. That German-Jewish merchants like O.W. Loeb, Fritz Hallgarten and Peter Sichel[2] were key to the post-war revival of German wine on the international stage is possibly the most touching episode in German wine history. At the very least this darkest and most shameful chapter of German history is taught unflinchingly to every schoolchild today.

By the end of the Second World War Germany was on its knees. But viticulture muddled on. With the *Wirtschaftswunder*, or economic miracle, of the 1950s a different spirit took over. What had once been the putative *Volk der Dichter und Denker*, a people of poets and thinkers, now became a nation of engineers and technocrats. Progress, rationalization and technical prowess became the driving forces of German viticulture, a story told in Chapter 2. It is only today that Germany is emerging from the long shadow cast by the twentieth century.

2 O.W. Loeb dedicated his book on the Moselle 'to the memory of Sigmund Loeb (1859–1950), President of the Moselle Trade Association from 1903–1930'.

2

GERMAN WINE LAW – A PERPETUAL PALIMPSEST

Germany is a wine country at the heart of Europe. It used to be at the northern limit of viticulture and its wine culture was thus defined by the ability to ripen grapes. For this reason German wine law differs substantially from that of other European countries. With its scale of *Prädikate*, from *Kabinett, Spätlese, Auslese, Beerenauslese* and *Trockenbeerenauslese* to *Eiswein*, Germany's complex wine law is confusing even to German speakers. The only way to understand it is in the context of its history, taking Riesling, ripeness, climate, tradition and site classification into consideration. This rather intricate chapter, in connection with Chapters 3, 12 and 15, explains why Germany has such a baffling and now outdated wine law.

RIESLING AND THE DEVELOPMENT OF PRÄDIKATE

During the course of the eighteenth century, Riesling emerged as a quality variety in the Rheingau. Wealthy estates owned the best sites, where Riesling ripened in good years. Exceptional years made late harvests possible, a process and style which had been discovered in 1775 when the idea of late and selective harvesting took hold. By 1788, late and selective harvesting was officially recommended for the Rheingau and became the foundation of its reputation. The different stages of partial or full botrytis infection were known and aimed for – and vinified separately. Access to markets that paid commensurate prices compensated for the inherent risks of late harvesting and mono-varietal planting. Winemaking included the practice of racking the barrels several times from the spring following harvest until the autumn, sometimes over several years. To ensure cashflow even in low-yielding years, keeping the best of these wines for years had given rise to so-called *Cabinet* cellars, small, separate cellars for these special reserves. These wines became known as '*Cabinet*' wines. In the late nineteenth century the *Prädikat* scale was calibrated further to denote distinct botrytized styles like *Beerenauslese* (BA), *Edelbeerenauslese*[3] and *Trockenbeerenauslese*[4] (TBA). Across the Rhine in Bingen, coincidence had led to the first *Eiswein* in 1829[5]. Meanwhile, the term *Auslese* was further defined by the attributes *feine, feinste, hochfeine, hochfeinste*, i.e. fine, finest, very fine, supremely fine.

Thus the terms *Spätlese, Auslese, Eiswein* and *Cabinet*, coined in eighteenth century Rheingau, gained currency and became a mark of quality. By the early twentieth century *Prädikate* had become accepted terms that denoted style and quality. Their use was restricted chiefly to Riesling (sometimes Traminer) from the *Edelweinbaugebiete*, or noble wine districts, of Rheingau, Rheinhessen, Mosel/Saar/Ruwer and Rheinpfalz[6]. The term *Cabinet* was used almost exclusively in the Rheingau. These wines were amongst the most expensive in the world. Their stratospheric prices were backed by quality which had its foundation in single varietal plantings of Riesling in the best sites, harvested with stringent selection.

THE NATURREIN PRINCIPLE, THE VDNV AND THE FIRST GERMAN WINE LAWS

In pre-climate change Germany, achieving such quality was only possible in the best sites. Riesling would not ripen in lesser sites[7] and

3 *Edelbeerenauslese* denoted a style between *Beerenauslese* (BA) and *Trockenbeerenauslese* (TBA).

4 In 1893 Kloster Eberbach first used the term TBA for a fully botrytized wine. In the Mosel, which had adopted the *Prädikat* terms, the first TBA was not achieved until 1921.

5 Kloster Eberbach harvested its first *Eiswein* in 1835 in the Steinberg; Schloss Johannisberg in 1858.

6 Other German wines, with the exception of Steinwein from Würzburg, did not play a role in this luxury market.

7 In 1867 Friedrich Wilhelm Dünkelberg wrote: 'The preferred cultivation of Riesling is characteristic for the Rheingau, its late-ripening grapes are essential for … long-lived wines, even though they won't ripen sufficiently in weaker vintages and result in a sour beverage.'

could only be made into a drinkable wine by 'gallization' (see Chapter 12), a process developed in the 1830s and popularized in the 1850s. This meant enriching musts not with dry sugar but with sugar solution, which had the added benefit of diluting acid. Initially intended for poor *Winzer* (wine growers) with lesser sites, gallization was also used by unscrupulous merchants to stretch weak, insipid musts and 'faked' wines were rife. Thus, the principle of *Naturwein*, of naturally ripened, unadulterated wine, bottled at the estate, was born. A Mosel guidebook from 1869 contains a whole chapter on *Reinheit*, or purity, while an English book from 1875 describes 'gallization' in unflattering terms. Germany thus felt the need to regulate the wine market and the first German wine law of the unified *Reich* was passed in 1892. It permitted both dry enrichment and gallization, as did the wine law from 1909. But the latter restricted the use of all quality- and purity-denoting terms, including *Prädikate* and *Cabinet*, to *Naturwein*. Naturally the owners of the best sites, who made *Naturweine* and sold them at auctions, wanted to protect their privilege. In the late nineteenth and early twentieth centuries they formed regional associations, before founding the *Verband Deutscher Naturweinversteigerer*, or VDNV, the Association of German *Naturwein* Auctioneers, in 1910. Estate bottling of estate-grown wines was one of their central, quality-guaranteeing tenets.

THE ENDURING WINE LAW OF 1930

A new wine law, passed in 1930, aimed to define the 1909 terms better. Two points are notable. First, gallization continued to be legal but was restricted to 25 per cent of total wine volume, as the process had been used to stretch wine with sugar water. Second, it defined the labelling of wine origin but watered down the use of site names. A wine could be named after a certain site even if it was not grown there, so long as it was 'similar in kind', 'equivalent in value', from a 'neighbouring' or 'nearby' vineyard. It also said that origin could be stated so long as at least two-thirds of the wine originated there. These points were the beginning of a slippery slope. While the Nazis governed viticulture with various ordinances via the *Reichsnährstand* from 1933 onwards, they did not change this law. Neither did the *Bundesrepublik*, or Federal Republic, after 1949. In 1958 an amendment reinforced these trends: planting restrictions put in place by the Nazis in 1937 were lifted, so vines could now be planted in 'unsuitable' sites while gallization was still allowed

– in a climate where grapes struggled to ripen even in good sites. More and more thin, gallized yet anaemic wines came to market. The dilemma was nomenclature: while enriched wines were barred from using the prestigious terms associated with *Naturwein*, they could be labelled by site, variety and vintage. The ordinary consumer was none the wiser. The fudging of definitions of origin ensured two things: various wines rode piggy-back on famous site names without originating there; and cross-regional blends were rife: slightly riper Südpfalz wines went by the tank load to be blended and labelled – legally – as Mosel. Viticultural progress, mineral fertilizers and agrochemicals had increased yields and grapes were made into increasingly manipulated wines. German wine started to get a bad name. At the German Wine Congress of 1960, Dr Albert Bürklin, a VDNV member, deplored the 'poor musts from unsuitable varieties on unsuitable soils.' A scathing article in the influential political weekly *Der Spiegel* in 1961 pilloried the German wine industry, forcing wine minister Oscar Stübinger to admit that, 'According to an international standard only 10 per cent of German wine would count as top class.' With the signing of the Treaty of Rome in 1957[8], European integration loomed, meaning Germany needed to bring its wine laws in line with the rest of Europe. The wine law from 1930 was effectively in force until 1969, and the new law was supposed to remedy all its faults.

THE 1971 WINE LAW: UNINTENDED CONSEQUENCES

The new wine law was passed in 1969 and updated in 1971. This is the law – with various amendments since – that is still in force today. Its four-tier quality categories are: *Deutscher Wein*, *Landwein*, *Qualitätswein* and *Prädikatswein* (see graph, page 14). Since the law sets such low standards for *Qualitätswein*, the bottom two categories are rarely used and most German wine today is made in the two categories of *Qualitätswein* (formerly *Qualitätswein bestimmter Anbaugebiete* or QbA) and *Prädikatswein* (formerly Qualitätswein mit Prädikat or QmP). The distinction between the two – and this is the hangover from the *Naturwein* idea of the past, is that *Qualitätswein* allows enrichment while *Prädikatswein* does not. Only a look at historic German wine law explains this distinction. On this basis, the ability to achieve ripeness was and is still

---

[8] This created the European Economic Community, the European Union's precursor.

central to the law, even though it rode roughshod over tradition. On the one hand, everything was 'quality wine', on the other the time-honoured *Prädikate* of *Spätlese, Auslese, BA* and *TBA*, once restricted to the best single-site Rieslings, were now applicable to any non-enriched wine so long as it reached a minimum must weight. Each *Prädikat* had a defined minimum Oechsle level according to region. Using *Prädikate* to denote different styles of selectively harvested Riesling had made sense. Applying them to every grape variety across Germany did not. Grauburgunder from Baden or Kerner from Rheinhessen now could be *Kabinette* or *Auslesen* if they reached the requisite degree of Oechsle. The ancient term *Cabinet*, once reserved for the finest, oldest, most precious Riesling, was misappropriated into *Kabinett* to represent the bottom rung of the *Prädikate*. Any terms formerly associated with *Naturwein* (*naturrein, natur, Gewächs, Wachstum*) and the term itself were scrapped. The idea of quality was now linked to ripeness alone and measured in Oechsle. *Prädikat* wines, once the pinnacle of German wine culture, could now be made in a former potato field. That varieties like Müller-Thurgau or newer crossings[9] could easily reach *Prädikat* levels in lesser sites was ignored.

Table 1: Minimum must weights converted to potential per cent abv[10]

	Min. degree Oechsle	Potential per cent abv	Brix
Qualitätswein	55–72	7.3–9.6	13.6–17.5
Kabinett	70–85	9.3–11.4	17–20.5
Spätlese	80–95	10.7–12.9	19.3–22.7
Auslese	88–105	11.9–14.3	21.1–24.9
Eiswein/Beerenauslese	110–128	15–17.6	25.9–29.7
Trockenbeerenauslese	150–154	20.9–21.5	34.3–35.1

At the time, these levels were realistic minimums and did not need upper limits as the climate was much cooler than today. As the table above shows, grapes reaching must weights of 70° Oechsle, i.e. a potential alcohol level of 9.3% were considered *eigenständig*, i.e. they could be made into an unchaptalized, stable wine. The ripeness ladder of the *Prädikate* implied that riper is always better and that a *Kabinett* had to be cheaper than *Auslese*. To this day, some wine schools teach it as a scale of quality rather than of ripeness.

---

9 Like Huxelrebe, permitted for planting in 1968, Kerner, permitted in 1969 and Bacchus, permitted in 1972.

10 Conversion source: www.musther.net/vinocalc.html#sgconversion

When *Kabinett* wines are hailed as a 'German classic' today it is important to note that this wine style – as it exists today – is not even fifty years old.

Strikingly, the law always included the category of table wine, i.e. *Tischwein*, which became *Tafelwein*, and is now *Landwein*. But when standards are so low that any ordinary, regional wine can reach *Qualitätswein* status, why use a lower category? In 2017 only 2.1 per cent of German wine was designated as *Deutscher Wein* or *Landwein*. In a poor vintage like 1972 *Tafelwein* was up to 16 per cent of production, but in good years, like 1976, this went down to zero.

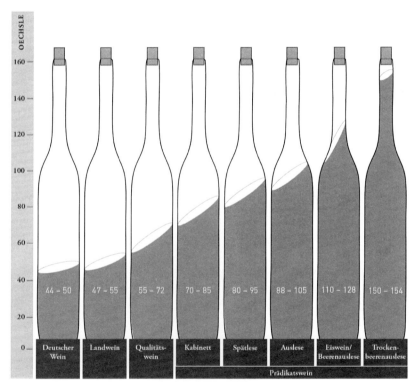

Minimum starting must weights

EINZELLAGEN AND GROSSLAGEN: SHIFTING SHAPES

In line with the rest of Europe, German law now restricted stated origin to the growing region, which ended cross-regional blends. Yet, within each region, it once more fudged the definition of origin. The law distinguished between *Einzellagen* (single sites) and *Grosslagen* (collective sites). The trouble with *Einzellagen* was that they had to be at least 5 hectares in size. Each wine commune had to delineate its *Einzellagen*, a task executed with varying degrees of scrupulousness. Some really believed that enlarging sites would translate into marketability, others clung to the historic outlines of sites. Some went to court to prevent iconic sites being enlarged; the Bernkasteler Doctor site being a prime example. In effect, lesser vineyards were subsumed into enlarged *Einzellagen* to take advantage of celebrated names while other site names disappeared altogether. To list all these sites, a *Weinbergsrolle*, or vineyard register, was created. It whittled approximately 30,000 site names, similar to French *lieux dits*, down to a mere 2,658[11]. While German site nomenclature needed some decluttering, this exercise was brutal. Some sites were enlarged 'beyond recognition' – depending on who lobbied harder and had more say. Note that this was a delineation, a definition of the outlines of a site, not a classification into quality categories.

By now, a large part of Germany's fragmented wine industry was organized into cooperatives which had invested in modern cellars with the capacity to make vast amounts of wine. People sincerely believed in rationalized methods and technical progress where wines from relatively large areas could me made into a homogenized wine. This was the motivation behind the creation of *Grosslagen*, or collective sites. They were thought of as a huge improvement on the cross-regional blends of the past. In that sense, the idea was not bad, even logical. What amounted to legalized fraud, however, was nomenclature. *Grosslagen* adopted the naming tradition of *Einzellagen*, which combines village and site – without having to state that they were a *Grosslage*. There was no way a consumer could tell apart Piesporter Goldtröpfchen, an *Einzellage* of 66 hectares and Piesporter Michelsberg, a *Grosslage* of 1,106 hectares, which is bigger than some German regions. Helmut Dönnhoff, winemaker from the Nahe, who worked on the site delineations of his village, calls this law 'a paragraph of consumer deception'.

DECLINE AND RENEWAL

The intention of the law had been egalitarian. Dönnhoff remembers the strong anti-establishment sentiments of 1968 which swept through

---

11 Others put this number at 36,000, e.g. Anon., 'Immer wieder anders sein', *Der Spiegel*, no. 5/1971.

France and Germany: 'The desire to break old structures was extreme. The great sites were in the hands of a privileged few and they were not the majority.' The law had wanted to end the privileges of the old elite estates and pull an extremely fragmented producer base into the market economy of the twentieth century. Yet it could not help itself. It appropriated and misappropriated old terms to ride on the coattails of exactly the glory it tried to abolish. The result was the gradual devaluation of *Prädikate*, of site names and eventually of German wine. First the national then the international market was destroyed. Price pressure was immense and the 1980s were rocked by scandal: *Prädikatsweine*, especially *Spätlesen*, were faked with added sugar, which resulted in gallization finally being outlawed in 1984. In 1985 Germany had its own version of Austria's glycol scandal and any remaining consumer confidence was lost. Those estates which honestly made good, unadulterated wine suffered as much as the fakers. It took a generation to recover from this damage but it was at this low point that a new quality movement was born.

Table 2: Comparison of quality categories

Deutscher Wein	Landwein	Qualitätswein	Prädikatswein
100 per cent grapes from German vineyards	85 per cent grapes from a Landwein region	100 per cent grapes from a specified wine-growing region	
Minimum starting must weight (° Oechsle)			
44–50	47–55	55–72	70–154
Enrichment permitted			Not permitted
subject to food law regulations		subject to official quality-control testing	
Minimum existing alcohol (% abv)			
8.5		7.0	5.5 (as of BA category)
Total alcohol content (% abv)			
maximum 15			
Permitted styles of sweetness			
all	trocken, halbtrocken*	all	

*also lieblich (mild) and süss (sweet) in the Landwein regions of Rhein, Oberrhein, Rhein-Neckar and Neckar

In 1984 the Charta movement was founded in the Rheingau, promoting dry wine from single sites. Across other regions, pioneering *Winzer* formed various quality-oriented groups, or left co-ops to start on a quality path. In 1994 the ProWein wine fair was held for the first time, in Düsseldorf, and the first ever annual wine guide of the modern era, *Gault Millau Weinführer* was published. All this added up to a new focus on quality which slowly turned German wine culture around in spite of the existing law. It also coincided with climate change, without which the quality we encounter in Germany today would not have been possible. Its impact cannot be overstated.

Since 1971, there have been several amendments to the law, but it has never changed fundamentally. It failed to take into account new varieties, such as Huxelrebe, Kerner and Bacchus, that clocked up sugar easily; and it never addressed the absurdity of *Grosslagen* – which was also down to lack of political will on the part of complicit politicians. In 2007 the terms *Qualitätswein bestimmter Anbaugebiete* and *Qualitätswein mit Prädikat* were amended to *Qualitätswein* and *Prädikatswein*. In 2009 it brought both *Qualitätswein* and *Prädikatswein* into the European designations of protected origin.

Table 3: International equivalents

France	Germany	Italy
Designations for Landwein		
Indication géographique protégée (IGP)	Geschützte Geografische Angabe	Indicazione geografica protetta (IGP)
Designations for *Qualitätswein* and *Prädikatswein*		
Appellation d'origine protegée (AOP)	Geschützte Ursprungsbezeichnung	Denominazione di origine protetta (DOP)

CLASSIFICATION AND THE VDP

In a cool climate, which Germany had until the 1990s, site selection was key to ripening grapes and achieving quality. Locals always knew where the best sites were, whether they were clearly delineated or not. As territories changed hands in the nineteenth century, vineyards in the areas that produced the most expensive wines, i.e. Rheingau, Mosel-Saar-Ruwer and Pfalz, were of great interest to the authorities as a source of taxation. The Prussians to whom most of the areas on the left bank of the Rhine fell in 1815, including the Mosel, established a taxation system in the 1820s. Bavaria, to which the Pfalz had fallen in 1815, also commissioned a land classification in 1828. Based on the site evaluations of Mosel, Saar and Ruwer vineyards conducted by the Prussian tax authorities between 1816 and 1832, the Prussians published a vineyard map in 1868 for the district of Trier, grading vineyards into three classes. But the Rheingau, just after falling to Prussia in 1866, pipped them at the post by publishing its own map in 1867. Compiled by one Dr Dünkelberg, it is not known what he based his classification on, but it was the first German map of classified vineyards. Classification continued and a new map for the Rheingau was published in 1885, for the Nahe in 1901, Mittelrhein in 1902 and Ahr/Upper Mittelrhein in 1904.

By the time the 1971 wine law had made such a hash of sites, these classifications had almost been forgotten. The 1984-founded Charta group in the Rheingau was the first to remember and started classifying the Rheingau vineyards of its members in 1987, creating the concept of *Erste Lagen*, or *premiers crus*. This group had a crossover with the *Verband Deutscher Prädikatsweingüter*, or VDP. The VDP was born out of the 1910-founded *Verband Deutscher Naturweinversteigerer*, which had renamed itself in 1971. In 1991 it finally rallied with a stringent set of production rules – many members who had become lazy left while new ones joined. Inspired by Charta and German history, the VDP spent the 1990s thrashing out its approaches to classification and resolved in 1998 to classify all the vineyards of its members, often based on the historical classification maps. Work started and in 2002 the first *Grosse Gewächse*, or GGs, were released: dry wines made from classic varieties according to stringent regulations from single sites classified as *Grosse Lage*. This was a breakthrough for Germany and the model became successful. In 2012 the VDP approved its quality pyramid of *Gutswein–Ortswein–Lagenwein*, i.e. estate wine, village wine and single-site wine. This simple pyramid has since been adopted by many non-VDP estates, too. *Prädikate* are still used by the VDP but are restricted to residually sweet wines. Its dry wines and all GGs are labelled *Qualitätswein* rather than *Prädikatswein*. Their classification is private and operates within the existing law but this also means that some of the best German wines are not categorized in its highest legally defined category. The VDP's 195 members only farm 5 per cent of Germany's wine hectarage but their actions have had a big impact on the way German wine is perceived in the world.

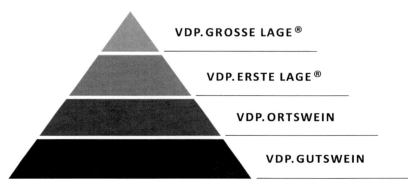

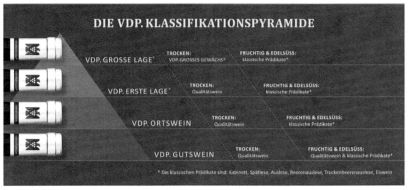

Justified criticism has been levelled at the VDP for classifying so many sites as *Grosse Lage*, when many of them might be better off as *Erste Lage*. There has also been more recent criticism for allowing *Gewanne*, or parcel names, within a classified site, creating renewed confusion. Steffen Christmann, current VDP chairman, is aware of this, saying: 'We do not claim to have completed a classification – not in either direction: no classified site has the claim to remain so forever. By the same token, a currently unclassified vineyard is not excluded from the possibility of being classified in the future. We are entering into a process now where we once again investigate the quality of each site in depth. This is a phase of self-reflection.'

To a degree, there is a conflict between classification and *Prädikate*. Classification is about provenance only, about delineating a site. *Prädikate* are about a wine style – but linked to climate. Helmut Dönnhoff encapsulates both ideas: 'A classification is the protection of a landscape; and landscape needs advocates. A classification is not a wine competition, either, but the protection of a site name that evolved over centuries. *Prädikate* originated in an era when no classification existed, but where people knew in which vineyards grapes would ripen naturally. The history of classification is the history of Riesling.'

SWEETNESS IN WINE – THE GERMAN CURSE

In the past, sweetness was prized. Only good years, favourable conditions and great sites would yield grapes so concentrated that the wine could not complete fermentation and remain sweet. Selective harvesting and separate vinification of these different selections increased the likelihood of obtaining a sweet wine, but nature still held the key – sweet wines were precious and rare. Most wines were dry, or off-dry: only natural yeasts were available, cellars were cold and fermentation could not be controlled. While repeated racking removed lees, it did not remove yeast and with changing temperatures in the cellar, most fermentable sugars must have been consumed. In 1893 Conrad Schmitt, a chemist, analysed 52 Rheingau *Cabinet* wines from the vintages 1706–1880 and published the results. In 2011 these results were checked for plausibility and republished. They show residual sugar levels between 0.71 grams per litre and 7.06 grams per litre; total acidity levels between 5.73 grams per litre and 7.92 grams per litre, alcohol levels between 4.71 and 11.61% abv and sulphur dioxide levels between 59 milligrams per litre and 260 milligrams per litre. So these wines were dry. Nobly sweet wines were an exception.

Florian Lauer, winemaker in the Saar, says: 'People often ask me what classic Saar wine is. I then ask what kind of period they refer to: 1880 to 1920 or post-1950? In the earlier period the wines had about 11% abv and 12–15 grams per litre of sugar, had possibly undergone malolactic fermentation during long lees ageing and tasted dry. That was the classic style; they may even have been drier than that.' Stopping fermentation had only been possible by moving barrels to a cooler part of the cellar, racking early and filtering (non-sterile) in spring and again before bottling – but the danger of refermentation remained. Cold cellars and natural yeasts often resulted in residually sweet wines in spring, but they would continue fermenting as the cellar warmed up again. Egon Müller points out how easy it is to stop a ferment with sulphur dioxide when pH levels are very low. Ernie Loosen adds that in the past, sulphuring was only possible by burning sulphur wicks inside the barrel.

This began to change with technological innovation and shifted the focus from vineyard to cellar, enabling wine styles that became a caricature. The Seitz company in Bad Kreuznach invented sterile filtration in 1913 but due to the First World War could not develop a marketable filter for the wine industry until 1926. This invention meant that fermentations could now be stopped at a desired point to leave residual sugar in the wine by removing yeast. But sterile filtration requires sterile equipment – and the technique of sterile bottling was not widely mastered until the 1950s. Prestigious estates like Joh. Jos. Prüm worked with such filters to preserve the precious, natural sweetness of their *Auslesen*. But as historian John Winthrop Haeger notes: 'Sterile bottling was rare until the 1960s'. By then sterile filtration equipment had become more affordable and another technique emerged that only worked in tandem with sterile filtration. With cultured yeast now available, it was easier to let a wine ferment to dryness and adjust its sweetness later with *Süssreserve* – sweet, unfermented grape must – and sterile-filter it just before bottling.

But the law placed limits on sweetness. In January 1958 a *Restzuckerbegrenzung*, or cap on residual sugar, was introduced that applied to all wines apart from *Auslesen*, *Beerenauslesen* and *Trockenbeerenauslesen*: unfermented sugar was capped at one quarter of existing alcohol. This meant that:

> A wine with 87 grams per litre of alcohol, equal to 11% abv, can have no more than 21.75 grams per litre of residual sweetness – whether enriched or not.

Depending on acid and grape variety, this tasted either dryish, off-dry or sweet. Less than ten years later, in March 1965, this cap was increased to one third of existing alcohol.

> A wine with 87 grams per litre of alcohol, equal to 11% abv, can have no more than 29 grams per litre of residual sweetness – whether enriched or not.

It is unclear why the 1958 cap was introduced. Because wines were too sweet? But it shows that the real sweet sins of German wine did not happen until later. By 1965 the cap was already loosened, by 1969 it was abolished for QmP, paving the way for sweeter styles – in effect creating the style that became known as *Kabinett* – while remaining in place for QbA. Crucially, in 1971 the federal law devolved regulation of the residual sugar cap for QbA to the federal states. The State of Rheinland-Pfalz, in which Pfalz, Rheinhessen, Mosel-Saar-Ruwer, Mittelrhein, Ahr and Nahe are located, set the QbA residual sugar cap as follows[12]:

Wine type	Ratio between alcohol (g/l) and residual sugar (g/l)
Red wine – all varieties, all regions	3:1
Riesling from Ahr, Mittelrhein, Mosel-Saar-Ruwer and Nahe excluding Bereich Süd	2:1
All other grape varieties of these regions	3:1
Riesling from Rheinpfalz, Rheinhessen and Bereich Süd Nahe	2.5:1
All other grape varieties of these regions	3:1

Even these caps were removed by the Federal State of Rheinland-Pfalz 1982 – probably under lobby pressure. When little had stood in the way of sweetness since 1971, nothing did in 1982 – at least not in the Rheinland-Pfalz wine regions. Other states exercised restraint. At that time, wines that were actually dry were so unusual they were marketed as *Diabetikerweine*, wine for diabetics. Today the tide has turned and *trocken*, defined as containing a maximum of 9 grams per litre of residual sweetness, is the rule. In the 2017 vintage, 30.17% of wines were sweet. The second half of the twentieth century thus created the *Zerrbild*, or distorted image, of the magnificent, noble Riesling grape that persists to this day.

PRÄDIKATE TODAY

With climate change, restricting *Prädikate* to residually sweet wines, as the VDP does, makes sense, at least outside the coolest regions of Mosel and Nahe. Steffen Christmann, of Weingut Christmann in the Pfalz, says, 'Before 1971, the difference between the entry level and the best wine of the estate was 40° Oechsle. Entry level wine was harvested at

---

12 Source: Erste Landesverordnung zur Durchführung des Weingesetzes vom 12 August 1971, Gesetz- und Verordnungsblatt für das Land Rheinland-Pfalz.

75° Oechsle, the best at up to 95° Oechsle, above that were sweet *Auslesen* and *Beerenauslesen*. There were 7–8° Oechsle between each *Prädikat*. This was a difference in ripeness that was extremely noticeable. Today, in our estate, it is often the case that there is no difference in Oechsle between the *Gutswein* and *Grosses Gewächs*, so I cannot grade according to must weight.'

Today it is no longer difficult to reach the minimum Oechsle levels set in 1971, neither have maximum levels ever been introduced, which would guarantee a wine style related to ripeness. In effect, most *Kabinette* today are *Spätlesen*, in warm years even *Auslesen*. Style, rather than must weight, is the decisive factor today – and consumers are more confused than ever. Some estates' *Kabinette* have 25 grams per litre of residual sugar, other estates' 30, 40 or 60. Neither are *Prädikate* used widely outside of Mosel, Saar and Ruwer, where they are still important. In Rheingau, Mittelrhein and Nahe they have tradition but are no longer central. The removal of residual sugar restrictions by Rheinland-Pfalz in 1971 created what is today seen as an iconic German style: *Kabinett*. It works because Riesling has killer acid, but Oechsle levels have shifted. Hanno Zilliken, winemaker in the Saar, says, 'Climate change forced us to apply the yardstick differently.' He says that in some warmer years almost all wines reach *Spätlese* levels according to the legal definition: 'If we acted according to the minimum Oechsle levels of the law, there would be no *Kabinette* in some years.' Thus, harvest point becomes the deciding factor. Florian Lauer, winemaker in the Saar, says that he handles *Prädikate* thus, '*Kabinett* are ripe grapes, *Spätlese* are overripe grapes, *Auslese* grapes are botrytized. With increasing botrytis infection you have BA and TBA – that is ver y simple.' His approach makes sense and results in clearly delineated wine styles – regardless of Oechsle.

In an ideal world one would restrict the use of *Prädikate* to Riesling and the coolest regions, impose maximum Oechsle levels to create stylistic clarity and apply a new name to nobly sweet wines from other grape varieties and regions. But that is probably pie in the sky.

IN CONCLUSION

The 1971 law is a relic from pre-climate change Germany, a palimpsest that preserves and perverts tradition in equal measure. Its greatest weakness is that it tries to have one law for a vastly diverse wine country without making quality transparent for the consumer. It is a muddled, complicated beast. In a country that prides itself so much on its *Reinheitsgebot*, or purity law, for beer, this lax attitude to wine is puzzling, to say the least.

In April 2018, Klaus Schneider, president of the *Deutscher Weinbauverband*, the German Wine Growers' Association, announced that the wine law was under review, that a change 'towards a provenance-based quality system' was under way, citing how climate change had invalidated many principles of the 1971 law. The idea is *Je enger die Herkunft, desto höher das Qualitätsversprechen*, or 'the smaller the designated origin, the higher the promise of quality'. In effect, this is the hierarchy already practised by the VDP and many other estates. Christian Schwörer, general secretary of the *Deutscher Weinbauverband*, explains that the move to a provenance-based model would have a separate set of increasingly stringent rules for region, district, village and single site. The federal law would provide the framework, the local grower associations would determine the criteria. This idea meets with both approval and opposition. *Prädikate* would fall into a category of 'traditional terms', and Schwörer mooted that they could be 'reformed' and defined so they have value once again. He speaks of transition periods and gradual change. It will take years but I wish him and his colleagues luck. German wine law needs to be simplified. The adoption of the term Rheingau Grosses Gewächs (RGG) in 2019 for the 2018 vintage (see page 193) and the movement of Maxime Herkunft Rheinhessen (see page 219) show that real change is afoot.

3
RIESLING – 'LIFE IS HARD ENOUGH, LET US DRINK LIGHT WINE'

Nobody knows exactly when or where Riesling originated. We do know that Riesling is ancient, that it has a parent–offspring relationship with Gouais Blanc, this most promiscuous of European grapes, and a possible sibling relationship with Savagnin Blanc. There are numerous theories but historian John Winthrop Haeger has done thorough detective work. He concludes that, 'it is in north-eastern France and astride the linguistic divide [between France and Germany] that both Gouais and Savagnin show the greatest genetic diversity and the most numerous surviving progeny, which makes that area the most likely candidate for Riesling's birthplace.' Haeger also cautions against pouncing on the first documented mention of Riesling in 1435, or later mentions in 1464 and 1490; simply because neither spelling nor ampelography were reliable then. Notwithstanding all these valid question marks, Riesling emerged as a quality variety in Germany over the course of a few centuries. Much is made of two key dates: the Prince-Abbot of Fulda's order in 1720/21 to plant Schloss Johannisberg's vineyards in the Rheingau to Riesling, and Clemens Wenceslaus Elector of Trier's 1787 edict to replace the lesser varieties of the Mosel vineyards with Riesling and other quality varieties. Whether all of Schloss Johannisberg was planted exclusively to Riesling is doubtful and we know that the 1787 edict was never fully implemented – but these dates set important markers in Germany's Riesling history. Riesling was also favoured in earlier instances: in 1669 Freiherr von Leyen ordered the planting of 200 Riesling vines per annum in his Nahe vineyards; in 1688 the clearing of a hillside in Langenlonsheim (Nahe) was permitted on the condition that only Riesling be planted; a 1697 ordinance restricts plantings in the Bingener Scharlachberg to Riesling. In 1780 new plantings in Bechtheim (Rheinhessen) are restricted to Riesling and Traminer. Thus, by the late eighteenth century, Riesling clearly had a reputation for quality. By the late nineteenth century it had reached glory: the world's most expensive white wines were Rhine and Mosel Rieslings. Elsewhere monovarietal plantings were rare, as was quality viticulture. Riesling's attributes, as we know them today, made it eminently suitable for Germany. Riesling can thrive in cool climates and requires minimum growing season temperatures of 13–15°C. Its hard wood makes it particularly hardy in cold winters while its late-budding habit helps it to avoid spring frosts. It requires good exposure to ripen fully but prefers poor soils. It is more drought resistant than other varieties – in short, it thrives where others struggle. This is the case especially on steep slopes. Riesling's mid- to late-ripening habit takes advantage of the longer autumn day-length in higher latitudes. Northerly Riesling is proof that it is light, not heat, that ripens grapes. Light enables photosynthesis while raised temperature increases the metabolic rate of vines. When summer heat has passed and autumns are sunny but cooler, the long ripening with slow sugar accumulation and acid retention enables the synthesis of aromatic compounds and their precursors. These processes are heightened in Germany's cool but sunny Saar, Ruwer, Mosel and Nahe valleys, where Germany's most distinctive Rieslings grow. It is this combination of inherent lightness and aromatic depth that has always marked Riesling out. Its aromatic spectrum is wide and changes with the degree of ripeness. As regards climate, Riesling can thrive in cool climates but has proved itself adaptable to higher average temperatures, both in Germany and in warmer Riesling regions of the world, albeit expressing a different wine style.

FLAVOUR AND ACID

Two groups of organic compounds are greatly responsible for Riesling's varietal aromas: terpenes and norisoprenoids. Both are bound by sugars in grape juice but set free during fermentation. Norisoprenoids like β-damascenone and β-ionone are key to varietal character. Terpenes, amply present in nature, like citronellol, geraniol, nerol, hotrienol and linalool, variously give citrus, fruit, floral and spice notes to Riesling. Terpenes are also responsible for the headiness of Muscat and Gewürztraminer, but Riesling has them in lesser concentrations. As Haeger puts it, 'Riesling occupies a sweet spot in this complex aromatic space. It is blessed with enough terpenes and norisoprenoids to be both interesting and distinctive, and enough variety of terpenes to display a wide range of aromatic personalities.' The fact that terpenes can be both free and bound explains the wide aromatic spectrum, depending on the individual aroma composition of a wine. It may also explain the changing aromas of Riesling as it ages. However, where Riesling really stands apart is in its acidity. Where other white grape varieties can have total acidity levels (measured in tartaric acid) of between 4 and 6 grams per litre, Riesling regularly clocks up 7–9 grams per litre and can even go beyond 10 grams per litre and still make a balanced wine. It is likely that our personal predilections for acidity determine whether we become Riesling fans or not. To me, acidity in wine acts like bright light: it pulls everything into sharp focus and illuminates every nuance of flavour, creating precision and clarity. Or as Egon Müller puts it, 'Acidity is what turns Riesling into Riesling. You have to have acidity, otherwise the wine is not good.'

THE MINERALITY TRAP

That Rieslings taste so different even when harvested from adjoining plots is down to a complex matrix of viticultural and oenological conditions. Soil composition, water availability, planting density, rootstock and scion, training, canopy management and harvest point already offer vast permutations of flavour. Oenological practices add another layer of possibility: destemming, crushing fruit or not, skin contact, pressing regimen, settling and clarification of must, yeast, fermentation vessel, temperature as well as cellar temperature all have bearings on how aromas express themselves. Yet Riesling is often described as 'mineral', a semantically treacherous term that implies a direct link between stony soils and perceived flavours. Rieslings from limestone or sandstone, slate or basalt, granite or rhyolite express very different aromas while still preserving the varietal signature of Riesling. But it is simplistic to think that these are the aromas of the soils themselves – plant metabolism is too complex. That different soils, together with numerous other variables – notably water availability – result in different flavours is not in doubt. Even soil colour reflecting sunlight radiation into the canopy affects enzymatic processes within the grape which in turn affect flavour. 'There is however no direct proven link between the soil composition and the taste of a wine although there are some correlations,' notes Geisenheim's president Professor Dr Hans Schultz, drawing on recent research.

ACID AND SUGAR

Whether bone-dry, lusciously sweet or anywhere in between, Riesling can make balanced and compelling wines. This is not down to sugar alone but to acidity, which balances the sweetness. It is wrong to look at sugar levels in isolation when both acidity *and* sugar levels are significant. A Pinot Gris at 4.5 grams per litre acidity and 4.5 grams per litre residual sugar is starting to cloy. A Riesling at 7.5 grams per litre acidity and 4.5 grams per litre sugar comes across as dry. The same Riesling at 7.5 grams per litre sugar would still taste almost dry. Residual sugar occurs mostly as fructose, because yeasts prefer to metabolize glucose. When exploring perceived sweetness–sourness interactions, Zamora *et al.* found that 'the suppressive effect of tartaric acid on fructose sweetness is stronger than the suppressive effect of fructose on tartaric acid sourness.' It must also be noted that in very small quantities, sugar does not act as a sweetener but as a flavour enhancer of fruit – a fact also evident in side-by-side comparisons of dosaged and non-dosaged Champagnes. This explains why Riesling can take a certain amount of residual sugar and still taste dry. The sensory perception of sweetness and acidity in wine is very complex and not fully understood. Alcohol as well as acid-buffering potassium have an effect. This is indirectly linked to the pH of wines, which in cool-climate Rieslings can be very low. Some winemakers insist that low pH changes the perception of acidity, others refute that pH affects the perception of sweetness or acidity. Context is everything: 'Sugar is a substance you can measure, but sweetness is a human sensation – they are just not entirely related,' another scientist, Clark Smith, says. Whatever your flavour preference is, inherent acidity means that Riesling can be made successfully in a wide spectrum of wine styles. Working towards a desired wine style starts in the vineyard. While certain sites will, for example, favour the development of botrytis, other factors like ventilation and soil moisture also play a role, as does planting density, yield, training, sun exposure, canopy height and management. These are decisive factors. Aiming for *Kabinett* as opposed to *Grosses Gewächs*, encouraging botrytis infection or not, demands different viticultural approaches.

TDN – THE FAMOUS PETROL AROMA

Riesling is often associated with one particularly pungent aroma compound: TDN or 1,1,6-trimethyl-1,2-dihydronaphthaline. The perception threshold for this norisoprenoid is just 2 micrograms per litre. High temperatures, berry exposure to sun and vine stress from drought, heat and nutrient deficiency during the growing season will increase the production of non-volatile TDN precursors. These form both free and bound TDN in the finished wine. TDN is more common in Rieslings from riper years or warm climates. Synthesis of TDN is also influenced by Riesling genetics and pressing regimen. Winemakers are wise to this and protect their grapes from sunlight with shaded canopies. Professor Dr Ulrich Fischer of Weincampus Neustadt explains the TDN life cycle in Riesling thus: bound aroma compounds are released during fermentation and ageing. If TDN is present, it will become more intense with time, as bound TDN is released. At the same time free TDN dissipates, so wine is in a constant state of flux. Over time, most wines reach a peak and stay stable for years, until TDN levels recede again as free TDN is dissipated and the reserves of bound TDN are used up. The storage temperature of bottled wine also has an influence on the release of bound TDN: at 7°C less than 2 micrograms per litre is converted; at 15°C less than 8 micrograms per litre, at 25°C less than 30 micrograms per litre. Fischer also compared TDN in Australian and German Rieslings. While some Australian Rieslings show very low TDN readings of as little as 2 micrograms per litre, the lowest median values of 36 micrograms per litre were observed in Adelaide Hills Riesling. Notably, this rather low reading for Australia is still higher than any TDN level measured in 27 vintages ranging from 1959 to 2010 in aged Riesling wines from the Staatsweingut mit Johannitergut in the Pfalz. Here the highest reading was 19 micrograms per litre for the warm 2005 vintage. This may well be down to the fact that solar radiation is weaker in autumn, when Riesling ripens. It is my experience that many people misidentify mature Riesling aromas – often heady like chamomile tincture – as TDN. Not every mature Riesling has that petrol smell.

4

SPÄTBURGUNDER – THE LATE BLOOMER

Spätburgunder, the German name for Pinot Noir, has a long history in Germany – but one lacking in detail. Its widespread success is recent and unquestionably linked to climate change. The early mentions we have of its presence, such as 1318 at Kloster Salem and 1335 at Affental, both in Baden, then in 1442 and 1470 in the Rheingau, are not reliable, since spelling, nomenclature and ampelography were patchy at the time. The much-vaunted mention in 884 is apocryphal – even if Charlemagne's great-grandson did have red vines from France planted in Bodman on Lake Constance, we have no proof they were Spätburgunder. There has always been a desire to link Spätburgunder's arrival in Germany to the Cistercians who, coming from Burgundy, spread viticulture with every one of their settlements – but there is no proof of that, plausible as it may be. Yet various Spätburgunder synonyms crop up in historic records. In a treatise on red winemaking from 1856, Johann Philipp Bronner names many: from Klebrot via Clävner, to Arbst and Malterdinger, even Schwarzer Riesling – but are they really all Spätburgunder? In any case, Spätburgunder's historic presence in Germany was always confined to small pockets, and never of more than local importance. Only one Spätburgunder attained something of a reputation and that was Assmannshäuser. At the western end of the Rheingau, the Assmannshäuser Höllenberg, a steep, south-south-west facing site of mica schist in a lateral valley of the Rhine is probably Germany's most iconic Spätburgunder vineyard. The site was first mentioned in 1108 but it is not clear when it was planted to Spätburgunder. From 1803 it belonged to the Ducal Domaine of Nassau and fell to the Prussians in 1866, who established one of their state domaines there. The State Domaine's Spätburgunders from the Höllenberg are the only German red wines to appear with any regularity in wine menus of the nineteenth and early twentieth centuries; where other Spätburgunders were listed, too, from Ingelheim (Rheinhessen), Dürkheim (Pfalz), Walporzheim (Ahr), Assmannshäuser was always the most expensive. A 'Red Hock' also appears on an 1896 wine list of London merchant Berry Bros & Co., costing the same as Volnay and Léoville. In 1925, just 2.5 per cent of German vineyards were planted to Spätburgunder but the variety was considered important enough to be included in clonal trials at the State Domaine in Assmannshausen in 1927. Clonal selection resumed after the Second World War in the research stations in Geisenheim and Freiburg. In 1957, Frank Schoonmaker describes Germany's foremost Spätburgunders from Ahr and Assmannshäuser thus: 'both wines, at their very summit of excellence, are like rather light and common wines from one of the less famous communes of the Burgundian Côte d'Or, or like a good Burgundy from an off year.' Clearly it was still too cold for Pinot Noir in Germany. In 1964, there were just 1,839 hectares of Spätburgunder in Germany, most of them in Baden (1,516 hectares) and the Ahr (103 hectares). Co-ops in both regions routinely thermo-vinified their Spätburgunder into fruit-driven, light reds for regional consumption – often with residual sweetness. It took some brave souls to look beyond the status quo of the dire 1970s and '80s, but the time was ripe. Tentative beginnings stirred in diverse regions. The scientifically minded looked at climate and soil data, those who had tasted red Burgundy began to experiment, some vaguely remembered talk of past glory, others just had their hearts and minds set on the best quality for the prime grape in their region. Thus, very slowly, a band of determined winemakers turned their attention to planting, growing, and making quality Spätburgunder. To them it seemed odd that in a climate by now so similar to Burgundy's Spätburgunder should be so different from its admired French brother. In the mid- to late-1980s some pioneers set to work and a whole number of factors coincided: immense viticultural progress combined with climate change meant ripe, red grapes; an uncompromising drive for quality meant drastically reduced yields; training, international outlook and experience meant new red-wine expertise in a predominantly white wine producing country; a resurgence of German wine in the home market meant that the necessary work in the vineyard was compensated by price. Above all, those pioneers realized that the only way to compete was on quality. Spätburgunder plantings doubled from 1990 to 2010. Interestingly, this was a pan-German tipping point: in Baden, Ahr, Pfalz, Rheingau and Franken winemakers made waves with this new, old grape. German-selected, small-berried, loose-clustered clones that had been selected for quality rather than yield were released in 1999 and 2001. In 2017, Germany had 11,767 hectares of Spätburgunder – the world's third largest hectarage after France and the US.

Germany's Spätburgunder landscape is diverse, both climatically and geologically: Spätburgunder grows across four degrees of latitude, in every German region and on soils as diverse as limestone, slate, basalt, sandstone, schist, granite, *Keuper* and loess.

Stylistically, Spätburgunder has evolved, too, even in this short time. Paul Fürst, winemaker in Franken, and one of Germany's Pinot pioneers says, 'It is a blessing, and people have now understood, that finesse trumps power. Of course, we initially extracted too much, we were doing things which we did not readily understand, which we weren't that good at yet. We tried to go for power when attributes like elegance, finesse and crystalline purity are so prized and so hard to achieve. This is what we have the natural conditions for, what we are working on, what people have now realized and what is being implemented on a broad scale.' His colleague Hansjörg Rebholz from the Pfalz echoes this: 'Along with a few other parts of the world we [in Germany] can produce cool, red fruit with Spätburgunder: coolness, elegance, depth endowed with the generosity of Pinot. But coolness is the magic term. Coolness means elegance, length, structure. And we have all learned a lot in the meantime.'

These days a younger generation is at the helm, honing their own, even more slender version of this grape. They know that absolute quality is possible, their endeavour is to define what Spätburgunder actually is. Benedikt Baltes in Franken takes his cue not from Burgundy but from Spätburgunder's white counterpart, Riesling, when he says:

> *I have learned at least, at least, as much about Spätburgunder from Riesling estates as I have from top Pinot estates. Look at Riesling, there are powerful Rieslings, even some that are opulent, which never saw fermentation on skins. How then should a long fermentation on skins produce a very elegant wine? And vice versa, is a Spätburgunder puny*

because of too little skin contact? Then there is the concept of finesse and aligning the entire winemaking process to it. Spätburgunder has such a different tannin structure from other red varieties and my winemaking aligns more and more with white wine: good pH, fine extraction, reductive methods. That is what I have learned. German Riesling is a fine wine with moderate alcohol, its long ripening period affords it enormous saltiness. It has an autonomous identity. Working out that identity is what is happening to Spätburgunder now.

Julian Huber from Baden says, 'I think it's only just begun. I think we have firmly arrived in the German market with Spätburgunder. Internationally it only starts properly now. We work with incredible precision; we question everything and that takes us forward.' Julia Bertram, one of the newest winemakers in the Ahr, says, 'There is no more interesting time for Spätburgunder than right now.' So watch out for German Pinot, it's the late bloomer that turned into a wondrous flower.

German rosé wines

Germany has many terms to describe rosé wines. *Weissherbst*, literally 'white harvest', is an old-fashioned term for rosé. There is a tradition of co-fermenting red and white grapes to obtain a pale pink wine; these wines are known as *Rotling*. In Württemberg *Rotling* is called *Schillerwein*, in Sachsen *Schieler* and in Baden there is a special designation of *Badisch Rotgold* to denote a co-ferment of Spät- and Grauburgunder with a larger proportion of the latter. The legally undefined term *blanc de noirs* has become fashionable for white wines made from various red grapes.

5
SEKT – MÉTHODE ALLEMANDE

What is Sekt? The term simply means sparkling wine in German. For the longest time, it covered a multitude of sins, namely the millions of bottles of indifferent, mass-produced, fizzy plonk the Germans make and drink every year as the world's most enthusiastic consumers of sparkling wine. Yet Sekt has an illustrious history – it died an ignoble death but is now being reborn.

Shakespeare, or rather his German translators, are responsible for the term 'Sekt'. They translated 'sack', then a term for Sherry, as 'Sect'. In 1825, when a celebrated actor went for a glass of sparkling wine while still caught in his role as Falstaff, he demanded: 'Bringe er mit Sekt, Schurke!', or 'Give me a cup of sack, rogue!' – and the connection between Sekt and fizz was made. The date is interesting, since Georg Christian von Kessler founded Germany's first Sekt house in Esslingen in 1826. He had joined Veuve Clicquot-Ponsardin in Reims in 1806 as a clerk – since he had worked in Mainz, which was French at the time, the move to Reims was not outlandish. (Incidentally, a few years later another boy from Mainz would move to Reims: his name was Joseph Krug, but that is another story.) Kessler moved up quickly and became the widow's business partner. He experimented with making his own sparkling wine in Germany for a while and set up his business in Esslingen. But he was not alone. Everywhere around him experimentation was rife since sparkling wine, especially Champagne, was all the rage. An exciting luxury product, it represented a way of adding value to the light-bodied, high-acid wines that were the mainstay of German viticulture at the time. A German manual on the production of sparkling wines from 1842 states: 'For more than a quarter of a century Germany has endeavoured to emulate French Champagne.' This was at a time when the Champenois themselves were still perfecting their methods. From the 1830s onwards, numerous *Sektfabriken*, or Sekt factories, were founded and their produce found a ready market – at home often shamelessly labelled 'Champagne', and abroad as 'Sparkling Hock', 'Sparkling Moselle' or even 'Sparkling Neckar'. A trade directory of the German wine industry from 1889 lists 121 *Sektfabriken*, but it is not clear whether this list is complete. It includes names like Deinhard, Henkell, Kupferberg, Kessler, Söhnlein – all famous in their day, some still existing to this day, albeit as producers of tank-fermented, high-volume Sekts. The German catalogue for the Paris World Exhibition in 1900 notes the rapid growth of the industry, stating annual bottle production of a quarter million for 1840, 1.25 million for 1850, four million in 1878, six million in 1886, approximately nine million in 1892 and assuming a total annual production of 12 million bottles for 1900. In the late nineteenth and early twentieth century German Sekt is listed separately from Champagne on wine menus and trade lists, the German products not quite reaching the French prices.

Yet Sekt was prestigious business: in 1870 the English crown princess Alice, daughter of Queen Victoria, visited the Kupferberg cellars in Mainz and in 1876, the Rheingold brand was launched by JJ Söhnlein at the first ever Bayreuther Festspiele, named in honour of Richard Wagner. The illustrations and posters created from the 1880s until the First World War to advertise Sekt charted the new art of marketing and brand building – and set a new and unprecedented standard for advertising budgets. But where money is made, taxation follows. In 1902 the first *Sektsteuer*, or Sekt tax, was introduced. It was quickly dubbed *Flottensteuer* as Kaiser Wilhelm II used the proceeds to finance his navy and build the Kiel Canal. In 1909 this became a *Staffelsteuer*, a tax staggered according to bottle price. This was poison for the burgeoning industry: it favoured the production of cheaper Sekt, gradually destroyed the high end of the market and thus turned the tide in favour of Champagne. The year 1918 saw the territorial loss of Lorraine, where much base wine had been sourced, the prohibition of the term 'Champagne' for German Sekt in the Versailles Treaty, and the collapse of export markets. Before the First World War Germany had exported 1.5 million bottles of Sekt but by 1924 this had fallen to 240,000 bottles. It was only after the Second World War that the German Sekt industry slowly started to recover. The introduction by Henkell and Kessler in the 1950s of affordable, small quarter bottles called 'Pikkolo' or 'Piccolo' popularized and democratized Sekt, once the preserve of the rich. Demand rose and soon enough the big *Sektfabriken* invested in vast tanks, moving from bottle fermentation to the tank-fermented Charmat method in the 1960s. Progress spelled the beginning of the end of traditional method, quality Sekt. Tax and law once again were key: due to a law from 1902, until 1971 Sekt production was restricted to *Sektkellereien* – almost all of whom moved towards tank-fermentation – and the art of bottle-fermentation was almost lost. Initially base wines were still sourced in Germany but price pressures meant that the big houses began to source base wines from across Europe turning them into vast amounts of off-dry, easy, fizzy, tank-fermented Sekt. The term was devalued and became a byword for plonk – which did not stop the Germans from drinking it. While the restriction on Sekt production was lifted in 1971, enabling *Winzer* and co-ops to produce Sekt, it was not until 1988, when the law allowed that *Winzer* could hold untaxed Sekt in bond in their own cellars, that making traditional method Sekt became more than a mere experiment. For some it became a serious sideline, for others their main business. It took another decade for the terms *Winzersekt* and later *Crémant* to be defined in German law.

Here is an overview that shows the increasing quality standards for the different terms:

Schaumwein, *or sparkling wine*
- Can be made from red or white grape varieties
- Can be made by any production method but cannot name the method on the label
- Min. 8.5% abv
- Min. 3.0 bar pressure

Sekt
- Can be made from red and white grape varieties
- Must be made by second fermentation either in tank or bottle and can state the method on the label.
- Tank-fermented Sekt must spend at least 90 days on lees; for tanks equipped with mixing paddles 30 days are sufficient
- Bottle-fermented Sekt must spend at least 9 months on lees, transfer method is allowed.

- Min. 9% abv
- Min. 3.5 bar pressure

Deutscher Sekt
- As for Sekt above, but in addition base wines must be German.

Sekt b.A. (bestimmter Anbaugebiete)
- As Deutscher Sekt, but base wines must be from one of the 13 German wine regions.

Winzersekt
- Must be from one of the 13 regions
- Must be made by the traditional method, from 100 per cent estate-grown fruit
- Must state grape variety and vintage (min. 85 per cent from that year or grape)

Crémant – *reserved for Sekt b.A.:*
- If white grapes are used they must be whole-bunch-pressed, with a maximum yield of 100 litres of must from 150 kilograms of grapes
- Must be made by the traditional method, with a minimum of 9 months lees ageing
- Max. 15 grams per litre of dosage

While both *Crémant* and *Winzersekt* offer a legal framework for great Sekt, initially a 'base wine culture' was missing. Sekt was a contingency product for wines from cooler sites, in cooler vintages or from younger vines – these base wines were slender and brisk but did not really have base wine parameters of acidity and pH, that is, slender still wines were used as base wines. Over the past decade this has changed dramatically. Quality producers of Sekt now set out to make base wines: this begins in the vineyard with the right site, yield and canopy management decisions. This has given top-ranking German Sekts a tremendous boost.

In 2018, the VDP published its own statute for Sekt. It follows the regulation for *Winzersekt*, is made from hand-harvested, whole-bunch-pressed, 100 per cent estate-grown, regional grape varieties and underlies yield restrictions and pressing regimens. *Ortssekt* (village Sekt) must spend a minimum of 15 months on lees; *Lagensekt*, from a single site classified as *Erste* or *Grosse Lage,* must spend a minimum of 36 months on lees. It must be stressed that the sites classified by the VDP as *Erste* or *Grosse Lage* for still wine are not necessarily the best sites for sparkling base wine, but hopefully the VDP Sekt Statute will evolve.

Germany's climate and growing methods make it possible to produce sparkling wines with no or very low dosage. There is an increasing number of zero dosage and extra brut Sekts (0–6 grams per litre), while most are brut (up to 12 grams per litre). Note that for sparkling wine the legal definition of *trocken* is different: for Sekt this means 17–35 grams per litre, while *halbtrocken* denotes 33–50 grams per litre of dosage.

Germany's unique selling point in the sparkling wine market is *Rieslingsekt*. Its inherent freshness and lightness make Riesling eminently suitable as a sparkling wine base. Its aromatic spectrum can result in very perfumed wines that are fundamentally different from Pinot- and Chardonnay-based Sekts. 'Riesling is a unique grape variety,' says Mathieu Kauffmann, former chef-de-cave at Champagne Bollinger and now cellarmaster at Reichsrat von Buhl in the Pfalz. '*Rieslingsekt* is in a class of its own with its balance of fruit, acidity, minerality and length. I think the potential for *Rieslingsekt* is tremendous – also for single-site wines. I think a lot about the possibilities of *Rieslingsekt*. It is a German concept that cannot be copied.' Stylistically there are two avenues: a certain old-school style that favours mature, evolved Riesling fruit in all its facets, another that favours autolytic expression. The difference between them is style, not quality. The varietal nature of *Rieslingsekt* is sometimes enhanced by a dosage of mature, sweet, still Riesling, adding fruity allure – still resulting in a brut Sekt, but with more pronounced varietal character.

Even now, when the Sekt renaissance is only just getting under way, there is a broad spectrum of styles with producers working to a very different standard than they did a decade ago. We have much to look forward to as many supreme Sekts are already bottled, maturing on their lees in cold cellars to be disgorged in the early 2020s. For now, the proportion of fine Sekt is still dwarfed by the production of the big, tank-fermented Sekt brands, but Germany looks to an effervescent future. The best is yet to come.

6

CLIMATE CHANGE – A BLESSING AND A CHALLENGE

As things stand today, German viticulture has mostly benefited from climate change – which in these latitudes has been significant. Climate change is responsible for Germany's recent success with Spätburgunder and for the sylistic evolution of dry Riesling. In living memory, unripe vintages with forbidding acid levels were a reality, with grapes struggling to ripen fully. The last horror vintages for Riesling were 1980, 1984 and 1987, with acidity levels of up to 20 grams per litre. The fact that grapes now ripen reliably in every vintage is a welcome development. This is not to say that climate change does not pose very real challenges; on the contrary, the changing climate requires rethinking and adaptation. Its effects go well beyond rising ambient temperatures: spring frosts, extreme weather events and unpredictable, shifting weather patterns have real impact.

Professor Dr Hans Schultz, climate specialist and president of Hochschule Geisenheim, outlined the current situation in Germany. In a 2014 lecture, Schultz noted that average potential alcohol levels in the period from 1994 to 2013 rose by approximately 26 per cent compared to the period 1970–1986. Over the same period, total acidity levels decreased from 15.5 grams per litre to an average of 9 grams per litre[13]. According to the Intergovernmental Panel on Climate Change average temperatures are expected to increase by at least 1.5°C by 2050. Schultz explains

---

13 Expressed as tartaric acid equivalent.

that this figure is a planetary average and that Germany, at higher latitudes, 'will feel these temperature changes more.' He continues:

> *Analysis of wine growing regions, no matter where, shows the same tendency, whether in Australia, the US or Armenia. We can observe that there is a distinct change since about 1980. This is not only down to external factors like CO_2, but also to more stringent environmental regulations which led to less air pollution and therefore stronger radiation which has fuelled the effect. This phase from about the 1980s onwards is referred to as 'global brightening'. All wine regions are affected in terms of temperature, at varying levels of course. But temperature is the lesser problem. The actual problem is the unpredictable distribution of precipitation. In physics, one degree Celsius of increased ambient temperature equals 7 per cent more evaporation – and all of that must come down again. If we assume two degrees of warming, we are looking at 14 per cent more evaporation. This is more extreme on steep slopes, so steep sites will face more challenges.*

Schultz notes that soil temperatures have also changed:

> *Soil temperatures have a considerable effect on the release of nitrogen and organic matter. The so-called Potsdam Zeitreihe begins in 1889 and has continually measured soil temperatures from a reference point in Potsdam to a depth of 12 metres. This clearly shows that the warming of soil temperatures was stronger than that of air temperatures. Gauging the effect this has on micro-organisms and the rhizosphere is difficult. There is no real data either. But this relatively unique time series shows clearly that things have changed. All this has to be viewed very carefully. There always have been and there always will be variations but observations and the data we have show that warming is faster in the northern than in the southern hemisphere due to greater landmass.*

What about the 'greening' effect of more carbon dioxide within the atmosphere? 'This is difficult to judge because there is too little data. Viticulture poses many questions: what happens to microorganisms in the soil, what to those at the surface? Do wine constituents change, what about water availability? What about carbon dioxide concentration in concert with other climatic observations like insects or vine diseases? These are all questions we are not yet able to answer,' he cautions. Schultz, however, does not want to be alarmist. 'We are not a coral reef,' he says, meaning that viticulture is not completely at the mercy of the environment. 'We can do everything in our power to delay ripeness.' This also includes different criteria in clonal selection: where previously criteria included sugar accumulation, they now include acid retention and slower ripening. Schultz notes that a lot is yet to be done on rootstock research.

German viticulture for the past 150 years has been all about achieving ripeness. Every aspect of viticulture was geared towards ripening grapes fully: pruning, yield, canopy height and management as well as timing of harvest. Schultz suggests dialling back these measures. He cites lower canopies with reduced leaf surface for photosynthesis and fine-tuned canopy management. While viticulture is key, he also sees further possibilities in oenology, like employing yeast strains which convert sugar into less alcohol. Regarding Riesling, he notes that it thrives in a wide spectrum of climates. In order to preserve a wine style, 'we have to think of measures that dial ripening back. We also must question our approaches: how do I manage change? Do I need irrigation? Do we need to change environmental laws? Do we need to build water reservoirs? And, and, and …'.

Kai Schaetzel of Weingut Schaetzel, Rheinhessen, with vineyards in the exposed and sunny Roter Hang, farms according to a new paradigm. His approach counters the view that Germany is getting too hot for certain wine styles and underlines the quality of the best sites. His explanation is worth quoting at length:

> *Viticulture always means adaption. In the past you could not take for granted that grapes would ripen and could be made into a stable wine. Thus our grandparents trained their vineyards to capture as much sunlight as possible to speed up the ripening process. Today we can work to slow ripening, that is our job. We are shapers and cultivators, not victims. Over the past decade climate change has provided us with a great playground that allows us to reorientate, to adapt. Much has happened that is a cause for joy rather than a cause for grubbing up Riesling and replacing it with Cabernet Sauvignon. Our wine style changed. Our alcohol levels came down from 13 per cent to 11 per cent for dry wines and our pH values are back down to 2.8 – because we listened and stopped doing what used to be necessary in a cooler climate. We use shade, we changed the fruit–leaf ratio, we changed our harvest points; there are so many aspects to address.*
>
> *The first thing we did was to decelerate the vineyard by removing energy. There used to be 2 metre high canopies to collect as much*

energy as possible, but we no longer need that. Today our canopies measure just 1.4 metres but are allowed to overgrow to create shade. This way we achieve a different grape skin structure, phenolics which are not created by sunburnt grape skins but by fruit grown in the shade in a hot vineyard. In the past there would be a harvest pass to cut out weaker grapes so the remaining ones would concentrate more – today we do the opposite. The best grapes are harvested first because they ripen first; the tiny, millerandaged[14]*, golden grapes. If we left them on the vine, the grape skins would lose structure and, talking about dry wines or Kabinett, we would lose the soul of Riesling. We need healthy, crunchy skins to have stability and a cool tannic structure. This is labour-intensive but we harvest exactly at the point where the grapes are about to turn golden. This approach also puts paid to botrytis since the grapes never get to this point where they might turn into raisins. We [Germans] have always been aware that each vine has such a wide spectrum of ripening processes. This is how the German model of Prädikate was developed in the first place, to exploit the different levels of botrytis infection. But now we have turned selection on its head.*

The most interesting thing about this is that these methods work best in warm vineyards. Here we can harvest physiologically ripe grapes early. One could argue that it is simple to make 'cooler' wines by harvesting earlier but unripe grapes never yielded delicious wines – neither will they in the future. We need physiological ripeness and the best sites, the warmer spots, the steep slopes are physiologically at a different level. This is fascinating and counterintuitive, but it works. That typical German picture of a Winzer measuring sugar levels with a refractometer in the vineyard is disappearing. Analysis today is all about pH. It governs what we do in the vineyard, it is the most stabilizing factor that allows us to work with less sulphur dioxide. In the past higher Oechsle were prized; higher must weight meant a higher Prädikat. When the paradigm changed from residually sweet to dry wines we clung to the same parameters. But Germany can remain relevant. Perfect adaptation to our climate and to the best sites creates limitation. This leads to value because it is not replicable.

While climate change poses real challenges, viticulture must change along with it.

---

14 Bunches of grapes where not every berry was fertilized during flowering, leading to small berries with no or fewer seeds.

Table 4: Comparative data

Region	Commune	Annual average temperature 1981–2010 in °C*	Annual average temperature 1961–1990 in °C**	Annual average rainfall 1981–2010 in mm*	Annual average sunshine 1981–2010 in hrs*	Annual average sunshine 1961–1990 in hrs*
Mittelrhein	Bacharach	10.3	10	559	1566	1530
Rheingau	Eltville	10.4	10.6	609	1587	1603
Rheinhessen	Bingen	10.7	—	578	1595	
Rheinhessen	Nierstein	10.7	—	578	1595	
Rheinhessen	Worms	10.8	10.4	603	1643	
Mosel	Winningen	10.6	—	663	1492	
Mosel	Traben-Trarbach	10.3	10.1	674	1490	1358
Saar	Wiltingen	9.9	—	813	1547	
Ruwer	Mertesdorf	9.7	9.9	814	1555	1265
Nahe	Bad Kreuznach	10.5	9.5	508	1544	1512
Ahr	Bad Neuenahr	10.4	9.8	646	1492	1390
Pfalz	Neustadt	10.8	10.4	579	1688	1800
Pfalz	Landau	10.6	—	692	1686	
Baden	Bruchsal	10.7	10.3	753	1686	1691
Baden	Baden Baden	10.3	—	1259	1598	
Baden	Freiburg	11.3	10.1	953	1761	1739
Württemberg	Stuttgart	10.7	—	712	1723	
Württemberg	Heilbronn	10.5	9.6	744	1656	1638
Franken	Würzburg	9.9	9.1	649	1622	1565
Franken	Miltenberg	9.8	9.2	740	1602	
Sachsen	Meissen	9.7	8.9	586	1636	1570
Saale-Unstrut	Naumburg	9.6	9.1	571	1637	1600

* Source: Deutscher Wetterdienst, 2019
** Source: Weinatlas Deutschland, published 2007 – data sourced from Deutscher Wetterdienst and Wetterwarte Würzburg

7

AHR VALLEY – THE PINOT CANYON

'The Ahr is a little river that tumbles down out of the Eifel hills to join the Rhine some fifteen miles south of Bonn,' wrote Frank Schoonmaker in 1957. 'It is safe to say that few people outside Germany have ever heard of it,' he continued. How things have changed. Today the Ahr is synonymous with Spätburgunder and was a region that pioneered German red wine on the international stage. This does not seem to add up on paper: a red wine region at a latitude of 50.3°N? Yet topography, soil and climate make it possible. Protected by the Eifel mountains and situated along the southern edge of the Cologne Bay, the area benefits from the Atlantic influence of the Gulf Stream. Geologically it is part of the Rhenish Massif with its Devonian slate and greywacke formations, which are exposed in the steep vineyards, weathered to varying degrees and partially covered with loess, loam and sand in their lower parts. Distension of one of these Devonian folds, the so-called Ahr saddle, led to weaknesses along its ridge and millions of years later the Ahr ground its way along these fissures. This also explains the spa and mineral springs in Bad Neuenahr, later intensified by Tertiary volcanic activity. The Ahr runs from west to east for just 85 kilometres. During its last 25-kilometre stretch from Altenahr to Heimersheim, just 7 kilometres before it joins the Rhine at Remagen, it creates a Pinot canyon of rare beauty. It meanders and curves to create south-facing slopes. Some are precipitously steep and vineyard terraces of single-staked Spätburgunder are perched at vertigo-inducing heights, supported by drystone walls. The narrowest, most dramatic part of the valley is the western end from Alternahr to Marienthal. It gradually opens up in Bad Neuenahr towards the Rhine plain and the Heimersheimer Landskrone, a freestanding volcanic elevation. In the Ahr 83.2 per cent of vineyards are planted to red varieties: no other German wine region has a higher proportion of red grapes.

Sources vary when it comes to dating the beginnings of viticulture: some take Roman villas in the area as circumstantial evidence for Roman viticulture, others think that viticulture began with the Merovingians. The first documented mention of vineyards is in 893 in connection with the Benedictine Abbey of Prüm. From then on viticulture is well documented, especially as property of various Cologne churches and religious orders. The creation of terraces is documented for the twelfth century. Various sources suggest that Spätburgunder came to the Ahr valley after the Thirty Years' War in replanting efforts, but there is scant evidence. The term '*Bleichert*', referring to pale red wine, effectively a *vin gris*, appears time and again in old Ahr records, but there is no proof that this was made from Spätburgunder. The first properly documented mention dates to 1788 when an Ahrweiler official applies to the archbishop of Cologne for permission to plant the '*Rothe Burgundertraube*'. But wherever there is Spätburgunder there are legends. There is a specific Spätburgunder clone that was isolated in the Ahr, still known as Kastenholz. Even Geisenheim's own clonal manual states that Benedictine monks at Kornelimünster, just south of Aachen, had sourced the vines directly from Burgundy to plant them at Castle Kastenholz. Geisenheim studies confirm great similarities to French clonal material – but the Burgundian connection, however plausible, remains conjecture. The truth, if records survived and indeed contain that information, slumbers in some archive – a definite case of 'had we but world enough and time'.

Lying to the left of the Rhine, the area was occupied by Napoleon's troops from 1794 and later became part of the *Département Rhin-et-Moselle*. After the Corsican's defeat in 1815 it fell to Prussia. Vineyards grew steadily as the region benefited from protective tariffs. This had a sudden end in 1833 when Prussia joined the *Deutscher Zollverein*, a tariff union which exposed the wines to heavy competition. Poverty ensued and led to 'mass emigration' in the 1840s and the foundation of *Winzergenossenschaften*, or cooperatives. The co-op in Mayschoß, founded in 1868, is the oldest German co-op still in existence[15]. As an interesting

---

15 Earlier co-ops were founded in Württemberg in the 1850s.

aside, 'red grapes from the best sites in the Ahr' were used for early Sekt experiments by Carl Tesche of Koblenz in 1834. Vineyards expanded and by 1910 there were 1009 hectares. In fact, viticulture must have been profitable enough to warrant the clearing and even blasting of hillsides to create new vineyards, as a series of 1928 photos show (below, top). The same series shows the crushing of grapes in a hand-cranked mill and fermentation on skins in open wooden *cuves* and cement vats (below, bottom). The same process was described in 1900, so clearly by then there was a tradition of quality Spätburgunder.

The years following the Second World War were unkind to the Ahr, and thin, off-dry Spätburgunders were made to please masses of weekend travellers for whom the valley was a cheap tourist destination. By 1953 the vineyard had shrunk to 610 hectares, by 1964 to 444 hectares, not reaching the 500 hectare mark again until 1995. By the mid-1980s time was ripe for change. Winemakers like Werner Näkel, Gerhard Stodden and the Adeneuer brothers knew that better quality was possible. 'My father kept visiting Burgundy in the late 1980s,' remembers Alexander Stodden. That's just what Werner Näkel had done. In 1985 Stodden had his big *Fuder* barrels shaved on the inside to experiment with wood ageing, Näkel used his first small 228-litre *pièce* barrel in the same year. That was the game changer. Others soon followed and Ahr Spätburgunder began its renaissance. This coincided with a fashion for big reds which the warm, steep slate vineyards made possible. Alcohol levels of 14 per cent or even 14.5% abv were easy to clock up, so initially the wines were rather powerful as well as extracted. Over the past decade, however, elegance has returned, at least for the top producers. Canopy management and harvest point are key: the best sites used to be harvested last, now they are picked first. Right now, talented newcomers like Julia Bertram are developing an even more contemporary style.

Administratively, there is one *Bereich*, one *Grosslage* and 43 *Einzellagen*. In 2017 there were 561 hectares in total of which 365 hectares were Spätburgunder, 46 hectares Riesling and 35 hectares Frühburgunder.

Weingut J.J. Adeneuer
Bad Neuenahr-Ahrweiler
www. adeneuer.de

While the family can look back on 500 years of winemaking, beginnings were not easy for Marc and Frank Adeneuer. After the death of their father when they were both small children, their aunt ran the estate until the brothers could take the reins in the early 1980. This is when they started making dry wines. In the 1990s they achieved success with powerful, concentrated wines. Marc Adeneuer's candour is exemplary when he explains how everything changed after 2012: 'As of 2013 everything is in a purist style,' he says. This means freshness above all. He and his brother had set their course towards quality when they began; now they are redefining what Spätburgunder really is, and freshness trumps all else. With their site cuveés Adeneuer No. 1 and No. 2 – from *Erste* and *Grosse Lage* sites with only a small portion of new wood, they bring two exceptionally good value wines to market, whose slender, savoury scentedness – think rosehip and iron oxide – gives you a glimpse of what is in store from their *Grosses Gewächs*. Their treasure is the tiny Walporzheimer Gärkammer (situated within the Kräuterberg), just 0.67 hectares of terraced slate and greywacke, that has been their *monopole* since 1713. Here there are 60- to 80-year-old vines of the local Kastenholz clone. VDP member estate.

Try: Spätburgunder No. 1 for dangerously seductive aromatics.

Weingut Julia Bertram
Dernau
www.juliabertram.de

Julia Bertram is one half of Germany's Pinot power couple, being married to Benedikt Baltes, who makes Spätburgunder in Franken. Julia's family has always had vines but this *Weingut* is her own project, which she founded in 2014 – with 1.5 hectares from her family that used to go to the co-op. Now she farms 4.5 hectares over 54 different parcels which she either owns or leases. Her sites are in the Marienthaler Trotzenberg, Mayschosser Mönchberg, Ahrweiler Rosenthal, Dernauer Goldkaul and Ahrweiler Forstberg with some Frühburgunder on the Neuenahrer Sonnenberg. 'Freshness, acidity, structure and pH are now the most important thing,' she says, and her transparent, poetic Spätburgunders express this most eloquently. She has started conversion to organic farming, a challenge in her ultra-steep sites. 'I realize that Germany is perceived as the land of Riesling but Spätburgunder is the *non plus ultra*,' she says. Her entry level Spätburgunder is called Handwerk, i.e. craft. Her *blanc de noirs* still wine is fermentend in 30 per cent wood, 70 per cent stainless steel. The red Spätburgunder is vivid, tart and ideal for being chilled in summer. Upwards from there, her village and single site wines embody Germany's new Pinot paradigm in their firmness, transparency, elegance and silkiness. If you want any of these wines make sure you are on the mailing list. A future star.

Try: Dernauer Goldkaul for one of those heart-stopping Pinot moments.

Weingut Burggarten
Heppingen
www.weingut-burggarten.de

The estate lies at the foot of the Landskrone mountain, a distinctive remnant of volcanic activity. Its entire southern slope is planted to vines and divided into the Burggarten and Landskrone sites. The Schäfer family owns parcels in the Burggarten as well as in the Schieferlay, Sonnenberg and Kräuterberg. Of their 16 hectare portfolio 95 per cent is on classified sites. It was just after the 1970s *Flurbereinigung* that Paul Schäfer bought many of these prime sites. The wine estate, however, was not founded until 1989. Before that all the grapes went to the local co-op. Sixty per cent of production is Spätburgunder, 10 per cent Frühburgunder and just 10 per cent is Riesling. Today Paul Schäfer junior, who trained in the Ahr, Mosel and South Africa, makes the wines while his brother Heiko looks after the vineyards; brother Andreas runs the adjacent hotel Weinquartier. The entire family steers a firm quality course. Freshness and elegance are to the fore. Paul wants 'a certain coolness' of this northerly but climatically favoured region to show in his wines. He uses 228-, 300- and 500-litre barrels to let fruit and sites speak. The single site wines need time, so do the magnums which are a speciality here. VDP member estate.

Try: an older vintage of Walporzheimer Kräutergarten – but let it breathe.

Weingut Deutzerhof Crossmann-Hehle
Mayschoß
www.deutzerhof.de

The Deutzerhof estate looks right onto the majestic Mönchberg, an awe-inspiring, terraced greywacke site as concave as an amphitheatre that rises to 220 metres. It is down to Hans-Jörg Lüchau that Deutzerhof made it through a tumultuous decade that saw both Johannes and Wolfgang Hehle pass away. Lüchau started as a *stagiare* in 2001 and quickly became Wolfgang Hehle's right-hand man. Hehle had been amongst Ahr's quality pioneers and got his first barrique in 1989, winning the German *Rotweinpreis*, then Germany's greatest accolade for red wine, in 1992 – which created 'quite a bit of hype,' Lüchau says. He underlines how much has changed in the Ahr when he recalls that grapes were harvested well into November in the early 2000s to reach 14.5% abv. Today he is more concerned about preserving acid. His portfolio covers the entire region: from the Altenahrer Eck (steep slate and greywacke up to 250 metres) to the Heimersheimer Landskrone (basalt, up to 120 metres). He has a total of 7 hectares and farms 80 per cent Spätburgunder, 10 per cent Frühburgunder amd 10 per cent Riesling, with a little Dornfelder and Chardonnay. Lüchau also guards treasure: one of the Mönchberg terraces holds a parcel of Portugieser planted in 1928. These 90-year-old vines bring forth a Pinot-esque wine with a fine, floral scent and a slender, gentle presence. Deutzerhof's Spätburgunder Ortswein is a classic of the genre. The Frühburgunder is spicy and peppery, the Mönchberg GG is rounded and cherry-ish. VDP member estate.

Try: Caspar Spätburgunder for effortless elegance and freshness.

Frühburgunder

Also known as Pinot Noir Précoce, Frühburgunder is a mutation of Spätburgunder that ripens earlier (*früh* = early; *spät* = late). Nobody quite knows where or when the mutation happened as there are accounts of Précoce in both France and Germany. It used to be popular in the Ahr, Ingelheim (Rheinhessen) and in Franken, at a time when the climate was much cooler and Frühburgunder brought decent must weights and more bearable acidity than Spätburgunder. However, every producer who works with the grape uses the same adjective to describe it: 'brutal'. The grapes are very sensitive and can rot from one day to the next while yields are usually modest. Frühburgunder is thus demanding and frustrating in equal measure. Yet its wines can have the most beguiling scent. It is not always possible to tell them apart from their sibling Spätburgunder in the finished wine. For those who grow and make it, it clearly is a labour of love. In the Ahr it is now planted as a quality variety in sites that used to be planted to the lesser Portugieser. In 2017 there were 246 hectares of Frühburgunder in Germany. It is also planted increasingly in English vineyards where it is well-suited to the climate.

Weingut Josten & Klein
Bad Neuenahr-Walporzheim
www.josten-klein.com

Marc Josten has caught the slow boat – but in the best possible sense. It was in 2011 that this aspiring youngster founded this brand-new *Weingut* with his childhood friend Torsten Klein. Both had parents who grew grapes as a supplementary income to sell to the local cooperative. Josten and Klein started a youth initiative within the co-op but soon realized that they had bigger dreams. Josten had also started buying up fallow vineyards in the Mittelrhein – a mere 30 kilometres away – in Leutesdorf: steep sites of slate, unsung but precious. So the pair started with their parents' vineyards in the Ahr valley and the new Mittelrhein sites which needed recultivating. Since Klein moved away in late 2017, Josten is now in sole charge of his 8 hectares and has decided to give the wines more time and to release later. The wines are all the better for it. All of the Ahr Pinots and most of the Mittelrhein whites are matured in oak, and even barrel-aged Grauburgunder has welcome bite and backbone here; each of the Rieslings shows its own personality. That Josten is inspired is evident in his oak-aged Sauvignon Blanc 'Glanzstück' which he planted on steep slate in Leutesdorf. His Spätburgunders are of purity and well-judged slenderness. They have innate brilliance. He's one to watch.

Try: Spätburgunder Mayschoß Laacherberg for evocative aromatics.

Weingut H.J. Kreuzberg
Dernau
www.weingut-kreuzberg.de

The estate was founded in 1953. The idea was to leave the co-op, bottle the wine from the one hectare and sell it at a *Strausswirtschaft* to the tourists who streamed into the pretty valley on weekends. This proved to be a good decision: by 1960 there were 2 hectares of vines. Prompted by a family crisis, Ludwig Kreuzberg, a trained engineer and former chimney sweep, took over in 1994 when there were 3.2 hectares. 'It was learning by doing,' he admits now, but he had expanded the estate to 8.5 hectares by 1999. Since then the size has not changed but the parcels have. They are all in excellent sites like the Dernauer Hardtberg and Pfarrwingert, Marienthaler Trotzenberg and Walporzheimer Alte Lay. In 2013 Ludwig's childhood friend Frank Josten joined the estate and together they make up the management and sales team. The wine is now made by consultant Albert Schamaun who consulted from 2008 until 2014 when he came on board fully. Kreuzberg credits him with a leap in quality. The wines have sinuous elegance and bright freshness. They also have a knack for Frühburgunder: its customary plushness is met with bite here. Lovely and great value. VDP member estate.

Try: Spätburgunder Silberberg for structure and finesse.

Weingut Meyer-Näkel
Dernau
www.meyer-naekel.de

Werner Näkel, who has done so much to put the Ahr on the map, has given the reins of his winery to his talented daughters Meike and Dörte.

Both trained at the best estates in Germany (Knipser, Heger, Fürst) and further afield in Burgundy, Portugal, South Africa and New Zealand. This shows how much has changed in just one generation. Näkel senior would have loved to train as a *Winzer* but that was not deemed sensible in the late 1970s, so he trained as a teacher instead. He never entered the classroom, because he needed to take over the 1.5 hectares at home in 1982. 'When our father started, the Ahr was *not* known for premium wine,' Meike says. 'Nobody knew any of the site names, so he called his Spätburgunder "Blauschiefer", or blue slate.' Things could not be more different today. The names Dernauer Pfarrwingert (steep, south-facing greywacke and slate) and Walporzheimer Kräuterberg (steep, terraced, south-facing greywacke and slate) now signal this estate and the region. Meike joined the estate in 2005, Dörte in 2008, and the sisters make a more slender style than their father, which suits these savoury, smoky Spätburgunders very well. All the fruit is destemmed and cold-soaked before fermentation; wines in the the top range ferment spontaneously. The wines then mature in 228-litre barrels, the GGs for 18 months, the *Guts-* and *Ortsweine* for about 10 months. Of their total 23 hectares, 14 hectares are on steep slopes. Spätburgunder accounts for 78 per cent of their plantings, 10 per cent is Frühburgunder and the rest is Riesling, Pinot Blanc, Dornfelder and Cabernet Sauvignon. Plaudits go to the family for restoring numerous drystone walls. VDP member estate.

Try: Spätburgunder Ortswein, Blauschiefer for scented purity.

Weingut Erwin Riske
Dernau
www.weingut-riske.de

Volker Riske has just been joined by his son Jan in this 100-year-old estate. Jan Riske trained with Stodden, in New Zealand and at Geisenheim. Since 2007 the estate has also farmed 3 hectares in Leutesdorf (Mittelrhein), where 50-year-old Riesling thrives along with Weissburgunder and Sauvignon Blanc on steep slate slopes. In their 5 hectare Ahr vineyards from Rech to Bad Neuenahr they grow 80 per cent Spätburgunder, complemented by Frühburgunder, Portugieser and a little Dornfelder. Volker Riske remembers what huge changes the early 1990s wrought: he made Spätburgunder with 30 grams per litre residual sweetness and only one dry wine. Changing style meant losing customers. Today they only make dry wines; as Volker says, 'It was missionary work.' Father and son are a solid team and Jan wants to push boundaries – in both directions. He says his heart beats for top Pinot but he also understands fun: a stainless steel fermented Spätburgunder, made to be served chilled, is a huge hit at their *Strausswirtschaft* in summer. Their single site Pinots are scented, fresh and evocative.

Try: Spätburgunder Dernauer Pfarrwingert for elderberry aromatics.

Weingut Paul Schumacher
Bad Neuenahr-Ahrweiler
www.weingut-ps.de

While Paul Schumacher is an Ahr local he, unusually, did not grow up on a *Weingut*. Yet he knew he wanted to become a *Winzer*. He trained locally and became manager of a local cooperative before working as a consultant and running a wine lab. In 2008 he bought his current home and started with 0.8 hectares of vineyard, which he has slowly grown to 5 hectares: four in the Ahr, one in Leutesdorf/Mittelrhein. 'I could make wine the way I wanted,' he says, referring to his individualistic, snappy, translucent style. Right from the start he worked with French *pièces* but he has dialled his use of new oak right back to let fruit and soil speak all the more clearly. He does his own thing and delivers very unusual Spätburgunders which take a while to come round. They start off in the most tender fashion only to deliver a killer blow of concentrated Pinot-ness on the finish. His sites are in the Ahrweiler Rosenthal, Walporzheimer Kräuterberg and Marienthaler Trotzenberg. From a special parcel of very small-berried Pinot in the Rosenthal he makes a separate wine called Magna Essencia which only comes in a magnum. An ideal destination for Pinot-fanatics. Good value.

Try: Spätburgunder Marienthaler Trotzenberg

Rotweingut Jean Stodden
Rech
www.stodden.de

The Stoddens, who have made wine since 1578, call themselves *das Rotweingut*, the red wine estate. Alexander Stodden, who also has stints in South Africa and Oregon under his belt, started working with his pioneering father Gerhard in 2006 and took over the reins in 2013. He proudly says, 'Neither my father nor I ever planted a white vine.' His father grubbed up Riesling vineyards in order to plant Spätburgunder. Today their 9 hectares are planted to 92 per cent Spätburgunder, 5 per cent Frühburgunder and a small amount of old-vine Riesling. Six of those 9 hectares are in GG sites: the Neuenahrer Sonnenberg, Mayschosser Mönchberg and his calling card, Recher Herrenberg. His own massal selection of old vine material is in the process of being certified as the Stodden selection by Hermann Jostock (of St Urbanshof nursery in Leiwen, Mosel) in order to preserve this old genetic material. Fruit selection is stringent and all grapes are destemmed before a cold soak. Both cultured and spontaneous yeasts are employed for fermentation in open *cuves* before maturation in 228-litre barrels. Stodden also remembers the 'Oechsle-fetishism' of the past but has completely changed his game. He says he made the wines a little more 'approachable' and modestly says that his own style is only 'crystallizing now'. The wines used to border on the sumptuous but now are smoky and elegant and notable for their silky tannins. They age beautifully. VDP member estate.

Try: Spätburgunder Recher Herrenberg Alte Reben – a treasure, and cultural monument to 90-year-old vines.

8

BADEN – DEGREES OF DIVERSITY

In Baden's deep south you see its riches illustrated perfectly: feathery fields of asparagus on the Rhine plain, vines in the foothills and finally the dark conifers of the Black Forest; its woods teeming with game, its icy brooks with trout. Ernest Hemingway once came to fish,[16] and tranquillity and beauty are still a draw. Baden, in Germany's sunny south-west, spans two degrees of latitude. Its northernmost *Bereich* of Tauberfranken sits at 49.5°N, its most southerly tip in Weil am Rhein on the Swiss border at 47.5°N. Apart from outposts on Lake Constance and said Tauberfranken, it is a narrow band running between the Rhine and Black Forest. Across the Rhine in France are the peaks of the Vosges and the vineyards of Alsace. Geologically, the Upper Rhine Rift is key. Around 30 million years ago tectonic movements created a fissure which widened into a wedge-shaped trough. It sank further as its margins were pushed upwards with their different strata. This created the plain of the Upper Rhine Valley, the Black Forest on the German and the Vosges on the French side. The fissured surface broke into plates that were folded up to create the foothills of the Black Forest. Different geological strata now reach the surface and you find both Triassic and Jurassic limestone, granite, sandstone and loess as well as volcanic formations in the Kaiserstuhl, an extinct volcano on the Rhine plain. Some formations have weathered, others have been covered by wind-blown loess. Warm air enters from the south through the Belfort Gap, creating very favourable conditions in the Upper Rhine Valley. Baden

---

16 Hemingway stayed in 1922 and wrote about it in *The Snows of Kilimanjaro*.

gets more rain than its French mirror image Alsace, and cool Black Forest air descends at night. Climatically, Baden is the only German region classed as EU growing zone B, the same as Austria, Alsace and Champagne, but whether that still makes sense is questionable. Today, Baden is often painted as a Pinot-paradise but with few exceptions, its history of quality winemaking is relatively recent. For the longest time history and politics conspired against it.

One historian put it aptly: as 'a smaller mirror image of the Holy Roman Empire, Baden was the result of splintering German history'. Parts of what is Baden today belonged to the Habsburg empire as *Vorderösterreich*, to the Duchy of Württemberg, to church states, other minor principalities and free imperial cities. Even the house of Baden itself was split into Baden-Baden and Baden-Durlach until 1771. This meant conflict instead of continuity. Documented viticulture begins in the sixth century. The bishoprics of Constance, Basel, Strasbourg, Speyer, Worms, Mainz and Würzburg all owned land here, as did the abbeys of Sankt Gallen, Einsiedeln, Andlau and Beuron, and viticulture spread. Baden's viticulture reached its zenith with flourishing vines and markets in the sixteenth century. The Thirty Years' War dealt a particularly cruel blow to the south-west. What pillaging soldiers did not destroy, epidemics and pestilence did. The population was decimated and there was little reprieve as conflicts[17] continued to whirl through Germany's south-west, trailing misery in their wake. Not that this prevented the absolutist margraves from embarking on grand projects: the line of Baden-Baden built its own version of Versailles in Rastatt; Baden-Durlach conceived the fan-shaped city of Karlsruhe. Viticulture survived and slowly recovered, as did the population, as farmers from Switzerland and further afield settled.

Finally, one progressive luminary tried to make a difference: Margrave Carl Friedrich von Baden (Durlach line, 1728–1811). He confined viticulture to south-facing slopes and discouraged vineyards on frost-prone plains. He introduced Gutedel to the Markgräflerland in 1780 and had Baden's first single-varietal vineyard planted to Riesling on the Klingelberg beneath his Castle, Staufenberg, in Durbach in 1782. Carl Friedrich's biggest achievement, applauded across Europe, was the abolition of serfdom in 1783. He was Baden's '*aufgeklärter Absolutist*', or enlightened despot. While the Rhine had been other regions' route to market,

---

17 The Dutch War (1672–8), the War of the Palatinate Succession (1688–97) and the War of the Spanish Succession (1701–14).

the fact that its upper reaches in Baden were not fully navigable hindered trade. It often flooded and changed course and was not navigable all the way to Basel until 1876[18]. Only the best wines travelled. Baden became a Grand Duchy in 1806 but viticulture contracted: the tithe system was abolished in 1833 and joining the Zollverein, or customs union, in 1835 exposed wines to competition from imports. The only wines that had a reputation beyond the region were Markgräfler and possibly Affenthaler. Germany's official catalogue for the Paris World Exhibition in 1900 dedicates just one short paragraph to the region and notes that Baden makes 'some very good, but also extraordinarily cheap white and red wines,' remarking that Kaiserstuhl, Markgräfler and Affenthal have some reputation. Even in 1925 over a fifth of Baden's vineyard was planted to Elbling, just under a fifth to Gutedel, another fifth to mixed whites, 13 per cent to Riesling, 4.7 per cent to Silvaner and 8.6 per cent to Spätburgunder. By 1964 there were 7,607 hectares in total, with more Müller-Thurgau than Spätburgunder, more Gutedel than Grauburgunder and more Silvaner than Riesling. The first cooperative in Baden was founded in Hagnau on Lake Constance in 1881, with many more following in the early twentieth century. Initially a boon for the poverty-stricken farmers with their fragmented holdings, co-ops have now come to dominate the scene: 67.3 per cent of Baden's vineyard was farmed by cooperative members in 2018. But Baden is alive: all the top estates now have talented, internationally experienced and determined youngsters at the helm, honing contemporary styles of Spät- and Grauburgunder. Joachim Heger makes a valid point on Baden Riesling: 'Our Rieslings are often shoved into a box as being too fat, too rounded, too broad but people forget that not even 20 kilometres away, across the border in Alsace, some of the world's greatest Rieslings grow.' Then there is the ever-growing *Landwein* movement (see box, page 82). If you had an idea of Baden wine, forget it now. Baden, at least in its leading estates, has turned over a new leaf.

Administratively, there are nine *Bereiche*, 16 *Grosslagen* and 306 *Einzellagen*. In 2017 there were 15,834 hectares of which 5,432 hectares were Spätburgunder, 2,432 hectares Müller-Thurgau, 2,079 hectares Grauburgunder, 1,519 hectares Weissburgunder, 1,104 hectares Gutedel and 1,051 hectares Riesling. Since Baden is so diverse here is a summary of its nine *Bereiche*, from north to south:

[18] Johann Gottfried Tulla was tasked with 'rectifying' its course, starting in 1817, but the monumental engineering feat was not completed until 1876.

Tauberfranken (616 hectares)[19]

The Tauber valley straddles three administrative wine regions: Franken, Württemberg and Baden. The Baden part, along the Tauber valley from Bad Mergentheim to Reicholzheim, is a vinous little island that likes to call itself 'Baden's cool climate'. Its soils are Triassic *Buntsandstein* and *Muschelkalk* and a speciality is Schwarzriesling, aka Pinot Meunier, vinified as red wine.

Badische Bergstrasse (386 hectares) and Kraichgau (1.155 hectares)

The Badische Bergstrasse consists of the vineyards around Heidelberg. Soils are Triassic *Buntsandstein* and *Muschelkalk*. The Kraichgau covers the scattered vineyards between Wiesloch and Pforzheim where loess soils dominate. In both cases the wines are mostly of local importance.

Ortenau (2,705 hectares)

Running from Baden-Baden to Offenburg, this is a picturesque region of vineyards against the backdrop of the Black Forest. Vines flourish in the lateral valleys of Acher, Rench, Durbach and Kinzig that emerge from the Black Forest. Granitic soils predominate, often on steep slopes. Ever since the margrave had vines planted in 1782, this has been Baden's Riesling district but the wines are nowhere near as well-known as they should be. Sometimes Riesling is still referred to as Klingelberger. In Baden-Baden there are some volcanic porphyry soils around the Yberg.

Breisgau (1,592 hectares)

The Breisgau covers a large area from Lahr to Freiburg. Formerly considered a little too cool for top wines, this is fundamentally different today when the cold down winds from the Black Forest are a boon. The folding up of geological strata during the Upper Rhine Rift means that both Jurassic and Triassic formations (e.g. Hecklinger Schlossberg) come to the surface here, but loess is also common.

Tuniberg (1,066 hectares)

Between Kaiserstuhl and Markgräflerland and west of Freiburg, the Tuniberg is a loess-covered Jurassic limestone bench where Pinot varieties thrive.

---

19 Figures from Badischer Weinbauverband for 2018 – hence the discrepancy with the Baden figures from Deutscher Wein Statistik for 2017.

Kaiserstuhl (4,1042 hectares)

This volcanic outcrop sits between Vosges and the Black Forest in the Rhine plain. Its highest elevation, the Totenkopf, at a mere 557 metres nonetheless affords panoramic views to either of these mountain ranges and the Rhine. Some parts of the Kaiserstuhl are covered in metre-deep layers of loess, in other parts the varied volcanic geology comes to light with tephrite, phonolithe and limburgite. Vast 'monster' terraces, as the locals call them, have been dug in the loess during rather too thorough *Flurbereinigung* in the 1960s (see box, page 144). The combination of particularly mild climate and fertile loess might make you think that this has always been a little paradise but in fact it was 'the poorhouse' of Baden. It is thought that the vineyard close to the Burkheimer Schloss was the first Kaiserstuhl vineyard on volcanic soil, planted in 1781. It was not until a doctor, Ernst Georg Lydtin, bought land in Ihringen that the first vines were planted in the Winklerberg, in 1815. This was followed by the efforts of Johann Baptist Hau who planted various noble varieties in 1822, including Spätburgunder amongst others. The brothers Blankenhorn, who planted in Ihringen in 1844 after blasting bits off the Winklerberg, used Riesling and Traminer sourced in Deidesheim and Spätburgunder from Clos Vougeot. But as Konrad Salwey reports, red wines were still a prized rarity in the 1950s and '60s. Co-ops only sold red wine to customers who would also buy sufficient quantities of white. The predominance of Spätburgunder is thus rather recent.

Markgräflerland (3,205 hectares)

This sunny, southernmost tip of Baden borders France and Switzerland and runs from Freiburg to Basel. Loam and loess soils predominate but Jurassic limestone also crops up. Its Markgräfler wines, based on Gutedel that was introduced here in 1780, were famed for ageing well and developing a pronounced bouquet. This area is cooler than the Kaiserstuhl due to cool Black Forest winds. The peaks also catch the clouds so there is sufficient rainfall. Even in hot, dry years like 2018 dry stress is only a problem for newly planted vines.

Bodensee (631 hectares)

These are the vineyards from Überlingen to Lindau on the northern shore of Lake Constance (Bodensee in German) and the island of Reichenau. The lake, with its thermic stability, is what makes viticulture possible here. The vineyards reach up to 500 metres and white wines predominate on the moraine soils. There is some documentation that Charles the Fat (839–888), great-grandson of Charlemagne, had vines planted in his *Königsweingarten* in Bodmann on Lake Constance in 881 or 884. This seems to be the base for the legend that this may have been Spätburgunder as the vines apparently came from Burgundy. There is no proof for this whatsoever but that did not prevent its repetition *ad nauseam* as the earliest instance of Pinot Noir in Germany. It was in Hagnau on Lake Constance that Baden's first co-op was founded, in 1881.

BADISCHE BERGSTRASSE

Weingut Seeger
Leimen
www.seegerweingut.de

Thomas Seeger, the thirteenth generation of his family to make wine here, near Heidelberg in Baden's far north, had no desire at all to become a *Winzer*. He hated having to help in the vineyards as a child and wanted to study medicine – but it was hard getting a place at university. So wine it was to be – and good teachers gave him so much love for the subject that he ended up going to Geisenheim. He made his first wine at home in 1984 and has since become a master of oak. Seeger's 10 hectares of vineyards are on the *Muschelkalk* and loess soils of Leimener Oberklamm and Spermen and in the Heidelberger Herrenberg. His wines pack away new oak – Grau- and Spätburgunder are especially surprising in this respect. Apart from Pinot varieties he also grows Sauvignon Blanc, aromatic and creamily smooth, and Blaufränkisch, aka Lemberger. VDP member estate.

Try: Grauburgunder Oberklamm for precision and well-honed freshness.

ORTENAU

Weingut Kopp
Sinzheim
www.weingut-kopp.com

Johannes Kopp had a tough start to his wine career: at 22 he had to take over after the sudden death of his father. Kopp senior had founded the estate in 1996 with 2 hectares of vines and taken it to 17 hectares by 2012. He had initially trained as a mechanic but retrained with Bernhard Huber in order to run his own *Weingut*. His son valiantly took over and now farms a total of 31 hectares. They are in Varnhalt and Sinzheim and cover loess, granite, clay and porphyry. His holdings also include 4.5 hectares of old Riesling vines on *Buntsandstein* from the former Abbey Fremersberg. Johannes loves Spätburgunder and plants his new vineyards to relative high density. The next step is to convert to organic farming. Mineral fertilizers and herbicides are already a no-no. As of 2017 Kopp has also been part of a winemaking project in South Africa where he loves working with Chenin Blanc and Sauvignon Blanc. Johannes Kopp certainly has a special touch: each site has personality, each wine brilliance and purity. Both Riesling and Spätburgunder stand out. He knows what he wants and what he has to do to get it. This is a great mix of genius and determination. We will hear a lot more from him. Great value.

Try: Spätburgunder Roter Porphyr and Riesling Feigenwäldchen for sheer brilliance.

Weingut Alexander Laible
Durbach
www.weingut-alexanderlaible.de

Alexander is the younger son of Andreas Laible (see over). He founded his estate in 2007 when the opportunity arose to lease 6 hectares of vines. His love for Riesling is evident, not only in the fact that he worked in the Mosel. Despite being based in Durbach, his vineyards are further afield. Further south in Lahr, where all his Pinot varieties are, his sites are loess-covered *Muschelkalk*; further north in Sinzheim his Riesling is on calcareous marl. He has 13 hectares in total, 40 per cent of which are Riesling, 10 per cent Sauvignon Blanc and the rest Pinot varieties, Chardonnay and a little Scheurebe and Blaufränkisch. Wine ferments are spontaneous and mostly in stainless steel – the tanks are all in a large former bakery that he fashioned into a winery. His wines have a fruity brilliance and squeaky-clean concentration but are also brimful of Baden sunshine.

Try: Riesling Alte Reben for tangerine gorgeousness.

Weingut Andreas Laible
Durbach
www.weingut-laible.de

The granitic soils of the Durbacher Plauelrain, a south-south-east facing steep slope in the Durbachtal, a lateral valley of the Black Forest opening to the Rhine plain, have long been synonymous with Riesling. Likewise the Schlossberg, on which Margrave Carl Friedrich von Baden had the first single-varietal vineyard planted in 1782. Few have worked as diligently to express a place as Andreas Laible senior on this hillside of granite with traces of porphyry and agate. Today his son Andreas Christian runs the estate. He joined in 1999 after a stint with Bründlmayer in Austria. Half of the 7.5 hectares are planted to their own massal selections of Riesling but there is also a colourful palette of other varieties – from Traminer via Muskateller to Scheurebe. The Rieslings are vinified in stainless steel but get long lees ageing. They are rounded but fresh. VDP member estate.

Try: Achat Durbacher Plauelrain Riesling Trocken, for body and texture.

Weingut Sven Nieger
www.sven-nieger.de

All of Sven Nieger's wines start with U: his Rieslings are called *Unbeschwert* (carefree); *Ungeschminkt* (without make-up); *Unbestechlich* (incorruptible); *Ungezähmt* (untamed) and Underdog. Nieger did not come from a wine background but nonetheless ended up studying oenology at Geisenheim. While holding down a full-time job in the Pfalz, he started his own project in Baden on the side. He started out with just 0.2 hectares in 2011. By 2013 he had 3 hectares and started running his estate full time; today he has 12 hectares. Of these, 70 per cent are planted to Riesling, 15 per cent to Spätburgunder and, since he loves to try new things, he has just planted some Chenin Blanc. There also is a tiny bit of Scheurebe and Bacchus. His sites are in the Mauerberg (granite), Klosterbergfelsen (granite with porphyry) and Stich den Buben (*Buntsandstein*). He admits that he is still in a formative period but as of 2015 he has declared all his wines as *Landwein*, so he is not steering a conventional course. His Rieslings are sunny but taut; some are heady with hayflower and apple and show pronounced saltiness. In the cellar anything goes: whole-bunch pressing and skin contact, spontaneous ferments and extended lees ageing. The wines are juicy, moreish, salty and original.

Try: Riesling Unbestechlich for textured, ultra-lemony freshness.

Weingut Schloss Neuweier
www.weingut-schloss-neuweier.de

Schlossberg, the terraced Mauerberg and Goldenes Loch are further evidence, if it were needed, that Riesling and granite go well together. The formations here include arkose, a kind of sandstone, as well as porphyry. Records at this historic estate, where Riesling has been grown since the late eighteenth century, show that viticulture goes back to at least the twelfth century. In 2012 the estate was bought by the Schätzle family. Robert Schätzle is an intellectual and obsessive winemaker. He trained with Zind-Humbrecht and Kreydenweiss in Alsace and worked for Heger and Keller in Baden and Clos du Val in Napa after training in Bordeaux. He treasures this trinity of vineyards. 'Riesling from granite is like a tonic,' Schätzle says. Riesling is whole-bunch pressed, gets no skin contact but is fermented with a portion of whole berries. There are also vineyards in the Heiligenstein (granite), where he farms Spätburgunder. He has a total of 16 hectares of which 85 per cent are Riesling. The Rieslings are zesty, taut wonders of exquisite, stony intensity and slenderness. The Spätburgunders are darkly aromatic and taut. VDP member estate.

Try: any Riesling at all.

BREISGAU

Weingut Enderle & Moll
Münchweier
www.enderle-moll.de

Sven Enderle and Florian Moll made natural wines *avant la lettre*. With backgrounds in teacher training and social sciences neither was predestined for wine but both somehow wanted to train as *Winzer* which is how they met in 2003. In 2005 they farmed two parcels of vineyard for an elderly owner and this sparked their idea of a project. In 2007 they founded their tiny winery, making wine in a former potato cellar. By sheer fluke a friend of theirs took their wine to Chambers Street Wines in Manhattan and the rest is history. Not a single bottle was sold in Germany. To this day they export almost all their wine. 'It started in a crazy fashion and continues that way,' says Sven. Nothing went to their heads.

Their premises are still rented, low-key and low-tech, there definitely is no tasting room or anything swish. You see the cellar and you know that low intervention means just that. 'Right from the start we kept white wines on their skins for eight days. We had never even heard of orange wine but we had been to the Jura. A grape has a skin and that has a function, no?' questions Enderle. They own 2.5 hectares of the 7 hectares from which they make wine and farm organically (though they are not certified). They make Müller-Thurgau, Auxerrois and Grauburgunder but predominantly Spätburgunder which is sold under the labels Liaison, Buntsandstein and Muschelkalk. Austrian star cooper Stockinger was so impressed with their wines, he gifted them a large, oval barrel. The wines have real bite, are whole-bunch fermented and show vivid expression. Enderle and Moll may have cult status but they remain refreshingly unpretentious. In a beautiful touch, their old-fashioned label as well as every cork displays their motto: *Rien sans peine*. One-hundred per cent *Landwein*.

Try: Spätburgunder Buntsandstein for grip and purest cherry.

Weingut Bernhard Huber
Malterdingen
www.weingut-huber.com

The term 'Malterdinger' used to be a synonym for Spätburgunder. The fact that the village of Malterdingen is once again on the world Pinot map is due to the visionary Bernhard Huber. A trip to Burgundy and the parallels of climate and soil had a decisive impact on the young winemaker, who decided to leave the co-op in 1987 to make his own wine. His first Spätburgunder received immediate acclaim. Huber never stopped fine-tuning and the most elegant Spätburgunders emerged and turned him into a leading light of Germany's Spätburgunder revolution. By the time of his premature death in 2014, Bernhard's wines had taken their rightful place alongside the world's best. His son Julian is a worthy successor. He studied in Geisenheim and trained in Württemberg, Burgundy and South Africa. He has the same understatement and modesty as his father, the same quiet love for the vineyards whose names had already slipped into obscurity before Bernhard demonstrated their real potential. Today there are 30 hectares but Julian wants to go back to 25 hectares and concentrate solely on Spätburgunder and Chardonnay. His sites are in the steep, exposed and sunny Hecklinger Schlossberg (weathered *Muschelkalk*), Bombacher Sonnenhalde (south-west facing

Muschelkalk) and Malterdinger Bienenberg with the wondrous parcel that is Wildenstein (a reddish, iron-rich weathered *Muschelkalk* slope facing south-south-east, with a view of the Black Forest). Cistercian monks had already cultivated vines there, as noted in the *Tennenbacher Güterbuch*, a charter of land. High-density planting is the rule with 11,000–14,000 vines per hectare but Julian also stresses the significance of the massal selections that his father began. Julian's wines are more crystalline and slender than his father's, and slightly less extracted. There have always been proportions of whole-bunch and all the Pinots are luminous, pure and elegant. The Schlossberg more energetic, the Wildenstein scented. Every Pinot-lover should know this address. VDP member estate.

Try: anything at all – look out for library releases.

Shelter Winery
Kenzingen
www.shelterwinery.de

An English name in deepest Breisgau? And why shelter? Simply because Silke Wolf and Hansbert Espe made their first wine in the 1950s missile shelter of a Canadian airforce base. Neither of them is from a wine family but both found their way to wine and Geisenheim which is where they met. It was in 2003 that they took on their first 1.5 hectares of vineyard as a hobby. But then 'we wanted to become a proper *Weingut*,' they say, almost in unison. Today they have 5 hectares in 13 parcels across the Malterdinger Bienenberg, Bombacher Sommerhalde, Hecklinger Schlossberg, Nordweiler Herrenberg and Kenzinger Hummelberg. They grow 95 per cent Spätburgunder and 5 per cent Chardonnay and have now moved into a purpose-built winery in Kenzingen. Their wines are honest and elegant. A single, old parcel of Spätburgunder, just a few rows of vines, bottled separately, sets a new standard.

Try: Spätburgunder N114 for structure and finesse.

Weingut Wöhrle
Lahr
www.woehre-wein.de

Despite being this far north in Baden, Lahr still falls under Breisgau. This estate started its life in 1979 when Markus Wöhrle's parents Hans and Monika leased 8 hectares of vineyards from the municipal Weingut in Lahr with south-facing sites on the Schutterlindenberg, a loess-covered

Buntsandstein outcrop at the foot of the Black Forest. These are Gottesacker, Kirchgasse, Herrentisch and Kronenbühl. They all benefit from the cool winds that descend from the Black Forest at night which used to mean a struggle for ripeness but is a bonus now. The Wöhrles immediately converted their leased vineyards to organics and were certified in 1991. In 1997 they were able to buy the estate. Their son Markus studied at Geisenheim and worked in the Pfalz before taking the reins at home in 2002. These days there are 15 hectares. Seventy per cent are white and mostly Weiss- and Grauburgunder with a little Chardonnay and Auxerrois. All the red is Spätburgunder. Wöhrle manages to raise Weissburgunder to its greatest heights. He employs skin contact and ferments spontaneously in 225- to 800-litre barrels to create wines of utter brilliance. They are pristine, creamy and yet totally zesty. The Grauburgunders come with more substance but still make a virtue of this focused style. VDP member estate.

Try: Weissburgunder Herrentisch for chiselled precision.

KAISERSTUHL

Weingut Bercher
Burkheim
www.weingutbercher.de

Cousins Arne and Martin Bercher run the estate today. Viticulture has been in the family since 1475 but the Berchers only came to Baden from Switzerland after the Thirty Years' War, to repopulate the devastated area. Their house, in the centre of picturesque Burkheim, was built in 1756 and Berchers have made wine here ever since. Martin Bercher looks after the vineyards while Arne makes the wine. They have 25 hectares in Burkheim, Sasbach and Jechtingen. Spätburgunder is the most important variety, followed by Grau- and Weissburgunder, a little Riesling, 'as a hobby', and Chardonnay. The interplay between volcanic (Haslen and Kesselberg) and loess sites (Schlossgarten) illustrates the Kaiserstuhl beautifully. Arne likens his task to that of a stonemason – revealing a true picture of the site by the wine he crafts. Addressing the style proliferated by the co-ops he says: 'This means the Kaiserstuhl is not opulent and fat. It means that Kaiserstuhl can present elegance – without denying its provenance.' Each wine has a sense of place. Weissburgunder is particularly notable in its herbal creaminess and elegance. But the Berchers have long cocked a snook at preconceived ideas of unbounded heat in the Kaiserstuhl. They have made their own Sekt for more than 30 years from two dedicated plots of Chardonnay and Spätburgunder. It is creamy and bone-dry. VDP member estate.

Try: Pinot extra brut for creamy Baden freshness.

Weingut Dr Heger
Ihringen
www.heger-weine.de

Joachim Heger's grandfather, the doctor in the family, founded the *Weingut* in 1935. Joachim almost went down the medical route himself, but life conspired to make him study oenology instead. He took over at home in 1986 and has seen the Kaiserstuhl go through immense change. He and his wife Silvia have kept pace: horse Willi ploughs the vineyards and the wines are a model of elegance. The Spätburgunders have astonishing florality – not an easy feat with such an extreme vineyard as the Ihringer Winklerberg, a terraced, south-facing site of weathered tephrite: 'It will always be a site that brings very fine wines of infinite layers,' Heger says. Viticulture is a careful calibration of high-density planting, shaded rows and micromanaged canopies. The different parcels in the Winklerberg are called Häusleboden, Gras im Ofen and Rappenecker. He also has a slice of the Achkarrer Schlossberg. Apart from Spätburgunder he also grows Grau- and Weissburgunder, Riesling and a most beguiling, scented, dry Muskateller from the oldest vines in Baden – they were planted in 1951. The Spätburgunder vines in the Achkarrer Schlossberg are from 1963. Joachim, with a southern, self-deprecating wit, plays down his expertise but it is evident in his wines that he has never stopped questioning his every thought and deed. Those who insist that the Winklerberg is getting too hot for Spätburgunder should be served a Heger wine. The Hegers also have a line of wines made from bought-in grapes, sold under the Weinhaus Heger label. The future is assured: daughter Rebecca is poised to join him for the next harvest. VDP member estate.

Try: Spätburgunder Vorderer Winklerberg GG for scent and sinuousness.

Weingut Holger Koch
Bickensohl
www.weingut-holger-koch.de

Gabriele and Holger Koch have created a remarkable boutique winery by sticking to their purist aims and setting their sights quite literally high. The *Weingut* itself, founded in 2001 from the three hectares of vines his parents farmed for the co-op, is at 300 metres and the vineyards are at 350–400 metres. They farm 8 hectares of vines and their most prized site for Spätburgunder is the Halbuck at 370 metres, at the foot of the Totenkopf peak. Koch loves that this volcanic site with a thin loess cover is constantly exposed to the breeze. New plantings are also up high, like the Rischbühl and the Bitzenberg. Koch, who trained with Stephan Neipperg in St Emilion before a stint as cellarmaster for Franz Keller, has a policy of only planting French clonal material and has slowly made his name with tender, expressive and firm Spätburgunders – he prefers the French name – that really stood out in the Kaiserstuhl. People did not expect such elegance and tenderness. His Weissburgunders are like veils of freshness; his Grauburgunder has lovely structure from partial skin fermentation. The entry-level Spätburgunder is a pure, snappy delight. The wines higher up the scale really need bottle age to shine but totally warrant the patience. Holger and Gabriele do not want to expand, they want to be as exacting as possible. This means small, allocated volumes. Snap them up.

Try: Spätburgunder Kaiserstuhl for raspberry-scented gorgeousness.

Weingut Salwey
Oberrotweil
www.salwey.de

Konrad Salwey is one of those quiet types whose easy smile and manner belie his seriousness of purpose. He trained in Germany, Burgundy and Alsace and studied at Geisenheim before joining his father at home in 2002. Wolf Dietrich Salwey, who tragically died in a car crash in 2011, was a pioneer. He made his wines dry and sold 100 per cent whole-bunch fermented Spätburgunder when nobody in Germany had heard of it. He was also one of the first to use barriques, in the late 1980s. The fact that Sandi Benzarti, originally a car mechanic from North Africa, has advanced to the role of cellarmaster since he started work here in 1981 tells you all you need to know about this family. Today there are 22 hectares of vineyards, mostly in the west of the Kaiserstuhl. Among them are gems like the Eichberg (volcanic ash on basalt with a thin loess cover), the Kirchberg (volcanic rock with calcareous veins) and Henkenberg (volcanic rock with inclusions of black melanite). Of his 22 hectares, 17 are in classified *Grosse Lagen*. Reds have portions of whole-bunch, get cold soaks, are fermented spontaneously and mature in *pièces* made of local Kaiserstuhl oak. They are sinuous, bright, elegant and long-lived. Weiss- and Grauburgunder are increasingly matured in large barrels – this is Grauburgunder but not as you know it: snappy, taut, energetic, electric. 'I do not want mellow, powerful stuff, I want wine I can drink,' Salwey says. But his thinking goes further: 'The sites are what always remains. With Grau- and Weissburgunder and Chardonnay we have three varieties that are not that different and all three are helpful in depicting a site. So why am I making three wines from one site when in fact what I should be making is Kirchberg? I want to show that site.' This is the exciting direction of travel. He also experiments with extended barrel ageing over a number of years, but no wines have been released yet. 'We have lost the time factor,' says Konrad and says that his white wine ideas owe as much to Champagne as to Rioja. Watch this space. All the estate-grown wines have the coat of arms, the wines from bought-in fruit come with a falcon on the label. VDP member estate.

Try: Weissburgunder Henkenberg GG for conifer-scented loveliness.

Weingut Reinhold & Cornelia Schneider
Endingen
www.weingutschneider.com

Although the Schneider family dealt in timber for a long time, vines were always part of their set-up. It was in 1981 that Reinhold and Cornelia left the co-op and set up their own *Weingut*. Bit by bit they increased their holdings but also exchanged lesser for better sites. The 7 hectares today are in Endingen, in sites like Diel (loess), Schönenberg (tephrite), Engelsberg (a plateau with clay soils) and Floh (a plateau with deep loess soils). Son Alexander joined in 2002 after training with Friedrich Becker in the Pfalz. Fifty per cent of plantings are Spätburgunder, the rest is Chardonnay, Grau- and Weissburgunder, Silvaner, Auxerrois and Sauvignon Blanc. Alexander likes to start ferments with a *pied de cuve* and still clings to the *Prädikat* system. His wines get lots of time on their gross lees. They are bone-dry, creamy and rounded but also have backbone and freshness. The Spätburgunder, with some whole-bunch, is aged in large barrels. Great value.

Try: Spätburgunder Engelsberg for clear, pristine cherry and raspberry.

Weingut Schwarzer Adler – Franz Keller
Oberbergen
www.franz-keller.de

The Schwarzer Adler is an institution. There has been an inn on this site since the sixteenth century and the tradition lives on with three different restaurants, one of which has held a Michelin star continually since 1969. The Keller family have owned it since the late nineteenth century and have turned the estate into a multi-faceted business. They are agents for the best Bordeaux and Burgundy domaines with a depth of vintages stretching into the decades, while current boss, Fritz Keller who has been in charge since the mid-1980s, is also chairman of the Freiburg SC football club.

Vines were always part of the deal but Fritz's maverick father Franz Keller insisted on making his own wines rather than bringing them to the co-op and sold them at his inn – while his wife Irma achieved that Michelin star in the kitchen. Just as Franz went against the grain with his bone-dry wines when the rest of the Kaiserstuhl almost drowned in sweetness, so his son went against all snobbery when he agreed to make wines for a discount supermarket project – from bought-in fruit. He simply called it his 'Bauhaus' project, a wine for everyman. Fritz has had his share of *Tafelwein*, i.e. of being refused an *Amtliche Prüfnummer*, especially when he started vinifying Grauburgunder in new wood in the late 1980s. A new winery was finished in 2013 as the old facilities in the centre of Oberbergen had outgrown their capacity. The new building just outside the village merges into the vineyard. It houses a state-of-the art winery, office, shop and restaurant. As much as tradition may inform the Schwarzer Adler, Fritz Keller has always looked to the future, as businessman and *Winzer*. There always is a new project, a new challenge.

Their vineyards include Achkarrer Schlossberg, Oberrotweiler Kirchberg and Eichberg, Jechtinger Enselberg and Oberbergener Pulverbuck, Leh and Kähner. But this is a big business with 60 hectares of vines. Since 2016 Fritz has been joined in the winery by his eldest son Friedrich, who trained with Heger, in Switzerland and Burgundy and finished Geisenheim in 2015. He has room to manoeuvre and freedom to realize his own ideas. Since his arrival a whole new taut and purist touch inhabits the wines. The plans are to plant more in higher altitudes, like the Steinriese site, especially Chardonnay. Father and son say that the role of Chardonnay will increase but their core focus is on

Spät-, Weiss- and Grauburgunder. Coming from a family of restaurateurs Fritz says that making wine for the table remains the 'supreme discipline'. The wines bear this out – as does the food – be it haute cuisine or exquisitely executed Baden specialities. Then as now it is a destination: 'vaut le détour'. VDP member estate.

Try: Spätburgunder Achkarrer Schlossberg for savoury redcurrant seamlessness and poise.

MARKGRÄFLERLAND

Weingut Blankenhorn
Schliengen
www.gutedel.de

When Martin Männer, a lawyer, bought the Blankenhorn estate in 2014 it was in order to see through a process from start to finish. When he met Yvonne Keßler, an oenologist running a wine lab in the Pfalz, love struck. She began consulting on winemaking in 2015 and took over as winemaker in 2017. Since late 2018 she has been supported by Markus Weickert, who looks after vineyard and general management. Keßler, Männer and Weickert are a dynamic trio engaged in understanding their sites and honing their approach. That also means doing justice to the 1980s-planted Cabernet Sauvignon and Merlot vines they inherited from the previous owner, even grafting over some Spätburgunder and Gutedel vines to these varieties, which really ripen here, while planting more Spätburgunder vines higher up in cooler reaches. Gutedel is also getting attention with lower yields and fermentation and maturation in oak. A new cellar is being built – laying the groundwork for their future, with a deliberately contemporary and international outlook. Keßler has wrought quite a shift already with her vivid Spätburgunder that shows lovely structure and purity of fruit. All their sites are close to the estate; the Sonnenstück, of calcareous marl with a loess cover, looks west toward the Rhine plain, the Himmelberg is just above it, the Ölacker has more limestone, and in a lateral valley is the south-south-west facing Mauchener Halde. The very latest is a Gutedel *pét nat*. VDP member estate.

Try: Gutedel 'Courage' for nutty, long-lived lightness.

Gutedel

It was the enlightened Margrave Carl Friedrich von Baden (1728–1811) who introduced Gutedel to the Markgräflerland in 1780 with cuttings brought from Vevey on Lake Geneva. This white grape is known as Chasselas in Switzerland and Fendant in France. In the past, the wines were aged for a long time so they would develop their famous 'bouquet' of tertiary flavours. Henry Vizetelly reported tasting a 107-year-old wine in 1875, 'which had preserved its vinous character'. In fact, a Markgräfler wine from 1928 was more expensive than Graacher Himmelreich – but cheaper than Ürziger Würzgarten – on the wine menu for the Graf Zeppelin airship's round-the-world voyage in 1929. Thus, Gutedel had reputation, quality and achieved commensurate prices. That all changed in the second half of the twentieth century. At a time when local, obscure varieties were not really valued, Gutedel with its generous yields was ideal for churning out neutral wine by the gallon. What once was an esteemed wine became a workhorse grape. But Gutedel has new proponents: 'A different way is possible,' says Philipp Rieger at Weingut Rieger in Buggingen, who wrote his Geisenheim thesis on the subject. Made from low yields at full ripeness with skin contact, fermented bone-dry, matured in wood and kept on lees, Gutedel becomes a textured, almost emollient, creamy, age-worthy wine. Rieger's 10-year-old Gutedel is fresh, waxy, bright and youthful. Hanspeter Ziereisen who used to hate Gutedel has rediscovered the variety for himself and grows it on Jurassic limestone. He says emphatically, 'A great variety was turned into a crap variety and had an image of guzzling wine imposed on it. But Gutedel can do so much more. Even at full ripeness it has just 11.5–12% abv and you get a real mouthful of wine. 'This ability to ripen without clocking up too much sugar and yet presenting a full-bodied wine is a boon. But it means that lots of early-harvested Gutedel is chaptalized and churned out as plonk, with a little Sauvignon Blanc added for aroma to make it less banal. Felix Scherer of Scherer & Zimmer in Bad Krotzingen says that the cooperatives to this day 'ride roughshod over Gutedel's real potential'. The Ziereisens broke the mould when they launched Gutedel Jaspis Alte Reben Zehn hoch Vier in 2011 at €125 ($140) – it is from densely planted Gutedel vines in pure limestone rock.

Weingut Jürgen von der Mark
Bad Bellingen
www.weingutvondermark.de

That Jürgen von der Mark is a man possessed is evident in his pristine, unusual, individual wines. Born in Bonn, he swiped a bottle of wine from his father's cellar as a teenager and became wine obsessed. His law studies were soon dismissed for a *Winzerlehre*, followed by Geisenheim and a career in international wine sales. It was love that made him move in 1994 to Baden, where he first set up as a consultant, helped along by the fact that he became an MW in 1996. Being able to lease a very good vineyard in 2003 prompted his *Weingut*. He started with just four barrels of Spätburgunder and has since worked to perfect his vision – always questioning, always evolving. Today he has 4 hectares of vineyards, 55 per cent Spätburgunder and 45 per cent whites. Of particular note in the whites is an age-worthy, touching Sauvignon Blanc and a recently-planted *Gemischter Satz* called Diebskinzig, featuring unusual varieties like Orleans, Petit Manseng and Grünfränkisch along with the main varieties Pinot Blanc, Pinot Gris and Chardonnay. His vineyards are all in the Tuniberg, a Jurassic limestone bench just south of the Kaiserstuhl, covered in loess. His top wines, resulting from the most stringent selection, are all named after songs. These, he says, 'express their gender and temperament' and range from rock to opera. All his Spätburgunders are scented and touching, some are poetic, others dramatic – all have personality. Pinot lovers will be smitten.

Try: Sauvignon Blanc Rastlose Liebe and any of the 'song' wines.

Weingut Rieger
Buggingen-Betberg
www.weingutrieger.de

Most of Philipp Rieger's 14 hectares of vineyards are in a radius of 500 metres of his winery in the loess-loam dominated Maltesergarten site. His parents gradually moved their 7 hectares away from the co-op and started bottling their own wines from 2 hectares in 1985. Rieger knew he wanted to follow in their footsteps, joining the estate in 2005 when it had 10 hectares. He started converting the farming to organics which eventually led to a biodynamic certification in 2010. 'My aim was growth and to become an established, top quality estate of the Markgräflerland with a young team,' he says. While he farms various white varieties and 28 per cent Spätburgunder, he wants to make his name with both Gutedel and a Bordeaux-style blend. Both stand out: Rieger wrote his thesis on spontaneous ferment and wood maturation of Gutedel – but his flagship wine is called Chasselas (Gutedel's Swiss name) because the local name, in his opinion, is tainted with a low-quality image. It is, like all his wines, about texture. His Bordeaux blend of Merlot and Cabernet Sauvignon is lifted and beautiful. His top wines, made from his oldest vines, are called SR Alte Rebe – these are exquisite value.

Try: Chasselas SR Alte Rebe for creaminess and subtlety.

Weingut Scherer-Zimmer
Bad Krozingen
schererzimmer.jimdofree.com

Felix Scherer and Michael Zimmer may look like hipsters, beards and all, but there is nothing pretentious or affected about them – on the contrary. They started their estate on a shoestring, fashioning an old pigsty into a cellar. Scherer grew up in the Markgräflerland on his parents' asparagus farm and met Zimmer, a Berliner, when they both did their *Winzerlehre* in Freiburg. Scherer followed this with Geisenheim while Zimmer worked for a year in New Zealand. Neither of them set out with high-minded ideas and there is something refreshing about their honesty and sense of fun. 'The style has found us,' Zimmer says about the easy-drinking, but strait-laced, dry wines which are made with cultured yeasts in stainless steel – at least for the entry-level. They started with 2 hectares, and now have 2.5 hectares on heavy loess-loam sites. They have farmed organically since 2013. One third of production is Spätburgunder, alongside Weiss- and Grauburgunder and Gutedel. It is with Gutedel that they are experimenting: spontaneous ferments and skin-contact show us where they are heading. They want to grow but also hold on to their ideals – and are clearly too sensible to overstretch themselves. They make *Landwein* only and bring energy, drive and fun to the scene.

Try: Gutedel MG, for skin-fermented saltiness.

Weingut Claus Schneider
Weil am Rhein
www.schneiderweingut.de

The Schlipf vineyard straddles the Swiss–German border, looking south-south-west towards the Rhine. Its name is derived from its heavy, calcareous loam soils, which have a tendency to slide. Parts are very steep and viticulture has been documented here for centuries. On the German side, in Weil am Rhein, it is farmed by the Schneider family. On the slope of the Tüllinger Berg the vineyard abuts and continues as the named sites Haltinger Stiege and Ötlinger Sonnhole. Here the soils are less calcareous. Johannes Schneider, a chemistry graduate with experience from

Alsace and Burgundy, has just been joined by his brother Christoph in running their parental estate. The youngsters grow predominantly Spätburgunder, supplemented by Weiss- and Grauburgunder, Chardonnay and Gutedel. Their aim is to reflect the difference of these sites and to do so particularly with Gutedel and Spätburgunder. Right now they have 18 hectares and want to stay at this size: 'We want to be able to do it all ourselves – we want a human scale,' says Johannes. The whites have inherent freshness and bite, there is a lovely skin-fermented Gutedel called 'L'Ambré' while the Spätburgunders attest to Johannes' talent in expressing elegance and nuance. The top-range wines, denoted by three stars, need bottle age. Look out for late releases and watch what these talented brothers do next. They've only just begun.

Try: a mature Pinot Noir Drei Sterne.

Weingut Wasenhaus
Staufen
www.wasenhaus.de

Christoph Wolber and Alexander Götze are the new faces of Baden. There is a little cult already about the minuscule quantities of wine they make from barely 2 hectares. Upon arrival you find a picture-book pony farm called 'Wasenhof' set in idyllic fields, but that is just Christoph Wolber's childhood home. The wine is made in a rented, old cellar in the village. Wolber studied agriculture in Vienna, then set off for Burgundy in 2013, where he worked for Anne-Claude Leflaive and Comte Armand. This is where he met Alexander Götze, currently still installed at Domaine de Montille. In 2016 they resolved to start their own project and Wolber got his hands on parcels in the loam-covered limestone of the Ehrenstetter Ölberg and the Alter Ölberg, the same mountain, just that the latter looks east and south-east to the wooded peaks of the brooding Black Forest while the former faces south. This is where their Möhlin wines are from, named after the brook beside the vineyard. They also have a parcel in the Kirchhofener Kirchberg where the Spätburgunder is called Bellen and the Chardonnay, Filzen. They also make creamy, slender Weissburgunder in the Achkarrer Schlossberg and more Spätburgunder in the Jechtiner Eichert – the wine is called Vulkan. Since they make *Landwein*, they are not allowed to use site names. They farm organically but are not certified. Their methods are simple: whole-bunch spontaneous ferments for the reds, basket pressed and aged in used barrels from their Burgundian friends.

Reds and whites stay on gross lees until bottling. Care, love and fun all speak equally. All their wines are marked with distinct, snappy freshness, purity and poise.

Try: Spätburgunder Bellen and Weissburgunder Möhlin for new visions of Baden.

Weingut Fritz Waßmer
Bad Krotzingen
www.weingutfritzwassmer.de

Fritz Waßmer is Martin's older brother (see below) and is at least as smitten with wine. Driven by utter curiosity from an early age, he never stopped learning, gaining qualification upon qualification, travelling the world and its wine regions with his strawberry and Christmas tree farming business. In 1998 he started planting vineyards with a focus in the Breisgau, building an enviable portfolio of sites: Bombacher Sommerhalde, Staufener Schlossberg, Kenzinger Roter Berg and, in the Kaiserstuhl, Achkarrer Schlossberg. His curiosity and spirit is evident in the fact that Viognier, Cabernet Franc and Merlot thrive alongside Spätburgunder, which clearly has stolen his heart. Structure, a certain prowess and power characterize these elegant wines. A Spätburgunder obsession seems to run in the Waßmer family. The Kenzinger Roter Berg (*Muschelkalk* and red sandstone on top of calcareous marl) is creamy but grippy while the Herbolzheimer Kaiserberg, a well-ventilated slope of loess-loam on calcareous marl atop slate and granite – which he considers his best site – is floral, fine and sumptuous. 'The grapes are treated as though they were precious pearls,' he says. These wines need bottle age but are full of structure and promise.

Try: Herbolzheimer Kaiserberg Spätburgunder for concentration and floral finesse.

Weingut Martin Waßmer
Bad Krotzingen
www.weingut-wassmer.de

It simply is astonishing what Martin Waßmer has achieved in just 22 short years. It was only in 1997 that he made his first wines – having trained as a chef and established himself as a strawberry and asparagus farmer. He blames 'a certain hankering after great Burgundy' for what has no doubt been a painstaking, yet eventually successful, quest. He started with just 0.5 hectares and farms 37 hectares of vines today – on choice sites like the Dottinger Castellberg (terraced by Margrave Carl Friedrich von Baden in the eighteenth century), a steep, south-facing limestone site and listed landmark where viticulture has been documented for 1,200 years. Spätburgunder and Chardonnay are densely planted here, where no mechanization is possible. The Ehrenstetter Ölberg is a declared nature reserve of *Muschelkalk,* while the Schlatter Maltesergarten is dominated by calcareous loam and loess. Ninety-five per cent of his sites are in the Markgräflerland; only the Glottertäler Roter Bur of weathered gneiss at up to 500 metres is in the Breisgau. The top wines, coded 'SW' and 'GC', are of exquisite elegance and superlative freshness. While no effort is spared, the wines seem effortless, elegant, convincing, timeless – each with its own personality. Whole bunch ferments in the Pinots lend structure and savouriness. He also makes some of the best German Chardonnay – also from the Castellberg – scented, bright, fresh and chalky. His traditional method Sekts are lovely, too. Yet Waßmer remains modest, anxious almost, to get the very best out of the sites he is so devoted to. You sense quiet but burning passion – and the result is in the glass. Quite simply world class.

Try: any top Spätburgunder and Castellberg Chardonnay, for real poise.

Weingut Ziereisen
Efringen-Kirchen
www.weingut-ziereisen.de

Edeltraud – just Edel to her friends – and Hanspeter Ziereisen are as original as their wines. It is hard to imagine two less conventional or more authentic people. They just do their thing – and magic happens. Deeply rooted in their culture, they manage to express a bold and authentic vision of Markgräflerland. Their 20 hectares of vines grow on the Efringer Ölberg, a south-facing 360-metre elevation of Jurassic limestone with inclusions of jasper (*Jaspis* in German) and a thin cover of loess. On clear days you can see the Bernese Oberland from its plateau: France is just 2 kilometres to the west, Switzerland 15 kilometres to the south. The Ziereisens grow Gutedel, Grauburgunder, Weissburgunder, Spätburgunder and Syrah. There are some old vines, Spätburgunder from 1958, for instance. Newer parcels are densely planted: Syrah with 14,000 vines per hectare and Gutedel at 10,000 vines per hectare. There also is a small vineyard in the foothills of the Black Forest where Pinot is grown on iron-rich soil. The top wines from old vines are called Jaspis

– and like all the wines are declared as *Landwein*. The Ziereisens are the founders of the Baden *Landwein* movement (see box, below). Some of the whites in the vaulted cellar (which dates from 1734) are under flor but stonkingly fresh; they are textured and salty, yeasty and alive. It is with Spätburgunder that they very deservedly made their name after founding their wine estate in 1991. Others would have rested on their laurels but the Ziereisens pushed further. Edel says that making good wine comes from drinking good wine – from curiosity, and they drank widely: 'Textbook winemaking was never our thing.' Now they have arrived at completely individual, authentic and mind-boggling visions of Gutedel, Weissburgunder, Grauburgunder and Silvaner – alongside the reds. One Gutedel is made in an amphora buried in the vineyard; a Chardonnay is matured on aged yeast and a wine made from a secondary crop of Grauburgunder combined with other whites has been aged without sulphur since 2007. It tastes like Sherry on speed. Somehow all this crazy stuff works. A new cellar with a quirky sound installation is just outside the village. Painstaking work in the vineyards is the key – what happens in the cellar is anarchic, devil-may-care but also visionary – fed as much by curiosity as by courage and experience. Their entry-level wines remain ridiculously good value – like the Heugumber ('grasshopper') Gutedel. The Ziereisens and their wines are a real experience.

Try: anything at all!

Baden's *Landwein* movement

With a history of peasant revolts, Badeners have form when it comes to counterculture. So it is no surprise that a protest movement is under way today. It pits itself against the overly conventional strictures of the *Amtliche Prüfung* in Baden, where each wine to be sold as *Qualitätswein* must pass a sensory test that deems it typical. This is the case across Germany but it seems to be particularly onerous in Baden. Here officials are accused of protecting the rather boring, neutral styles made by the co-ops. A wine that is turned down by the panel must thus be declassified as *Landwein*, which is not allowed to state a site on the label. Likewise, a *Winzer* can classify his wine as *Landwein* and it is no longer required to have an AP number. One winemaker says Baden seems to be stuck 'in a rather narrow habit that leaves little room for stylistic expression.' Another reports that a bone-dry rosé was turned down for being 'atypical'. Hanspeter Ziereisen, who has declared some of his wines as *Landwein* since 2004 and now makes 100 per cent *Landwein*, says: 'The crux is the corset of the *Amtliche Prüfung* and the enforced conformity. They have never tasted what is made across the world and therein lies the problem of Baden. They are all sitting on a treasure chest and not even one of them is trying to look for the key. Baden can do so much more.' This prompted him to start the first annual *Landweinmarkt* in Müllheim in 2016, in which only estates producing 100 per cent *Landwein* may participate. Each year there are a few more *Winzer*. Some winemakers who make both *Qualitätswein* and *Landwein* say that there also is a divisive, polemical component to the *Landwein* movement, at a time when the Markgräflerland and Baden should pull together. For Ziereisen, 'it is simply a statement for Baden: that things can be done differently. Not everything that is presented at the *Landweinmarkt* is world class but at least it has the courage to be different.'

9

FRANKEN – NON-BAROQUE SPLENDOUR

Franken's extended wine lands have a pulsating centre in Würzburg. A UNESCO World Heritage Site since 1981, Würzburg attracts more visitors for its splendid Baroque architecture than for its wine. Two ancient charitable foundations and an even older state domaine, all three with historic cellars, have their headquarters here. The Staatlicher Hofkeller, Bürgerspital and Juliusspital have made or traded in wine almost since their respective foundations in 1128, 1316 and 1576. Vines and the typical Franconian bottle, the round-bellied *Bocksbeutel* (see box, page 88), are never out of sight in this town. Würzburg's famous Stein vineyard is even more noticeable and spectacular. This south-facing, steep slope of *Muschelkalk* dominates and partly frames the town, which lies snugly in an S-shaped bend of the Main river. But Franken boasts many spectacular vineyards besides the Würzburger Stein: Homburger Kallmuth, Escherndorfer Lump and Kingenberger Schlossberg. They, like most Franken vineyards, have two things in common: their Triassic origin (see box, page 271) and the looping bends of the river Main. Most Franken vineyards are on one or more of the strata of the so-called *Schichtstufenlandschaft*, or 'tiered layer landscape' of *Buntsandstein*, *Muschelkalk* and *Keuper* through which the Main river ground its way two million years ago. On its east–west course through Franken it stays just below the fiftieth degree of latitude, before joining the Rhine at Mainz-Kostheim. In the south, Franken extends to the Tauber valley with a few vinous outposts, bordering Baden and Württemberg. Franken is protected by the Rhön and Steigerwald ranges from north and east winds. In Franken's west, known as the Mainviereck, or Main rectangle, red *Buntsandstein* dominates; in Franken's heartland, the Maindreieck, or Main triangle, *Muschelkalk* dominates and in the east the *Keuper* of the Steigerwald, a low mountain range further from the river, takes over. These are Franken's three districts (*Bereiche*); their geological communality quite neat for Germany. Franken can be a geological picture book. Driving north on the B27 from Würzburg along the river Main you can see the impressive *Muschelkalk* rocks towering to your right. Just a few moments later you spot terraced vineyards with *Buntsandstein* walls: a smooth transition from cream-coloured to red within a few metres. Driving along the Main from Wertheim to Klingenberg, the red of the *Buntsandstein* quarries and castles shines from afar. But you might have seen it elsewhere, too. Both Wiesbaden Hauptbahnhof and the former Weinhandlung Borchardt in Berlin, a restaurant today, were built with red Franken sandstone.

The earliest records of Franken viticulture fall into the Carolingian era and go hand in hand with monastic settlements. The Benedictine Abbeys of Fulda, founded in 744, and Münsterschwarzach, founded in 780, as well as the Cistercian Ebrach Abbey, founded in 1127, are important. Viticulture in Franken was so widespread that in 1500 there were an estimated 570 hectares of vineyards in Würzburg and more than 40,000 hectares in all of Franken. The river Main was the transport route in both directions. Records of precise loading fees and taxes in Miltenberg, Wertheim and Kitzingen document lively trade. Politically, the area that is Franken today was not a unit but splintered into secular and ecclesiastical territories. The west of Franken, today's Mainviereck, was part of the Electorate of Mainz and adopted the invented name of 'Churfranken' in 2007 to underline its distinct history. In central Franken the *Hochstift*, or bishopric, of Würzburg held sway until its dissolution in 1803. It was a stronghold of Catholicism, evident in its Counter-Reformational fervour and countless witch trials. Over the centuries, wine from the Würzburger Stein attained fame: Johann Wolfgang von Goethe hailed 'Würzburger' his favourite, while 'Steinwein' was famous enough to be faked. Henry Vizetelly in his 1875 tome *The Wines of the World* noted that 'genuine Stein of a good vintage is a potent beverage of singular vigour and fire, utterly different from the feeble growths largely palmed off for it. Of a splendid gold colour, with no kind of harshness, but a considerable amount of mellowness, combined with great consistency, finesse, and aroma …' The term 'Steinwein', however, was also used as a generic term for Franken wine. Viticulture had contracted since the seventeenth century. Conflict, especially the devastation of the Thirty Years' War, and cooler climate were to blame. Later came mildew and phylloxera. Statistics show a dramatic decline in the vineyard area: 9,818 hectares for 1878; 7,733 for 1900; 4,126 in 1914 and 2,657 in 1952. In 1964 there were 2,203 hectares, but from 1972 to 1979 there was a jump from 2,897 hectares to 4,303 hectares. This might have been down to *fränkisch trocken*, a properly dry style of wine that Franken adhered to when the rest of Germany was favouring sweetness.

The varietal statistics are also enlightening. For many, Franken is synonymous with Silvaner (see box, page 96), that subtle grape variety which reaches its apotheosis here. Despite fluctuations in the total hectarage of Franken in the second half of the twentieth century, Silvaner remained at a relatively constant 1,250 hectares until the early 2000s, although it stood at 1,493 hectares in 2017 – albeit still below Müller-Thurgau at 1,593 hectares. It is also notable that in Franken there is more Bacchus (754 hectares) than Riesling (333.4 hectares). For red varieties, you are likely to come across the rather unfortunately named Domina, a 1927 crossing of Spätburgunder and Portugieser. It covers 322 hectares and the less said about it the better. Spätburgunder takes up just 276 hectares but reaches sublime expression here, especially in the *Buntsandstein* slopes of Klingenberg and Bürgstadt. A little treasure, the old autochthonous variety of Tauberschwarz, of which just 12 hectares are planted, shows unique expression in the Tauber valley (see Weingut Hofmann, Röttingen). Harking back to history, the planting of *Alter Fränkischer Satz*, or old Franconian field blend, has also become popular again. Franken wines – Silvaner, Riesling and Spätburgunder above all – are rarely loud. They are subtle and nuanced and therein lies their disarming and enduring beauty. Often slender, they convince with depth rather than power and are, just like the landscape, illustrative of the soils. In this respect they are the perfect counterpoint to the ornate splendour and gilded frills of Würzburg's celebrated Baroque.

Administratively Franken may have been a part of Bavaria since 1802, but there is nothing Bavarian about this region or its people. Every Franconian will attest to this. There is a distinct identity with distinct dialects. If you look carefully, their emblem, a red and white zigzag shield known as the *Fränkischer Rechen*, or Franconian rake, pops up everywhere. There are three *Bereiche* in Franken, 23 *Grosslagen* and 216 *Einzellagen*. In 2017 there were a total of 6,204 hectares of vineyards with Müller-Thurgau, Silvaner and Bacchus taking the top spots.

> ### Bocksbeutel
>
> This is the round-bellied, squat bottle in which so much Franken wine is sold. The oldest depiction of a *Bocksbeutel* is thought to be in a 1576 stone relief by Hans Rodlein at Würzburg's Juliusspital. This historic bottle shape, once far more widespread, is now under EU protection and its use is restricted to Franconia and a tiny part of Baden. It made history, however, as one of the earliest original bottlings in the world. In a drive to guarantee authenticity of its oft-copied wines, the city council of Würzburg, which ran the Bürgerspital, decreed in 1726 that all its wines thenceforth would only be sold in sealed *Bocksbeutels*. Look out for the dinky, handbag-sized 0.2-litre *Bocksbeutel* as well as magnums.

MAINDREIECK

Weingut Bickel-Stumpf
Frickenhausen
www.bickel-stumpf.de

Frickenhausen is a well-preserved little jewel of a town with ramparts, turrets and the famous Frickenhäuser Kapellensteige, a cobbled, walled path that leads into the vineyards, past a chapel, seamed by wayside shrines. Here the Main loop flows from east to west and creates directly south-facing vineyards. The other jewel is Weingut Bickel-Stumpf. Marriage meant the fusion of two wine families, with *Muschelkalk* sites around Frickenhausen and *Buntsandstein* sites in Thüngersheim. The vineyards are 35 kilometres apart, and while logistics were difficult in the 1970s when Carmen Bickel and Reimund Stumpf decided that they would farm both their families' sites, today it represents an opportunity to express different soils. Tasting side by side is eye-opening: the stony linearity of Silvaner on *Buntsandstein*, its slender creaminess on limestone. Siblings Melanie and Matthias run the estate today but their father insisted on planting a vineyard of *Alter Fränkischer Satz*, a field blend of different Silvaners, Elbling, Traminer, Muskateller and Gutedel, on the Kapellenberg. The wine is scented, fresh and spicy. All their wines have a gorgeous purity and vitality. There is also a creamy, classy Sekt. Silvaner plays first fiddle, followed by Riesling. VDP member estate.

Try: Silvaner Rothlauf GG and Mönchshof GG for sheer contrast.

Bürgerspital zum Heiligen Geist
Würzburg
www.buergerspital.de

In 1316 the Würzburg citizen Johannes von Steren left an estate to the town in order to turn it into a shelter for the sick. It has been a municipal foundation ever since and has been called 'Bürgerspital', or citizens' hospital, since the sixteenth century. Today it is a huge complex that provides both medical and residential geriatric care but the *Weingut* is still a central part. Over the years, the foundation was endowed with numerous vineyards and now has 120 hectares with sizeable plots in Würzburg, Randersacker, Thüngersheim and Veitshöchstheim. In Würzburg there is the Pfaffenberg, the Innere Leiste and the Stein, with some separate parcels like the particularly steep Hagemann, or their *monopole* of Stein-Harfe. Director Robert Haller, who has ushered in a wonderfully clear-cut style, notes how much the soil structure varies, even within the *Muschelkalk* of the Stein. In the vast cellars 160 large 5,000-litre barrels are used every year. Skin contact is employed, as is long sedimentation and clarified must; fermentation is spontaneous and for most site-specific wines happens in large, old barrels. Only Chardonnay, Spätburgunder and Blaufränkisch age in barrique. The last remaining bottle of 1540 Stein-Wein is also on show in the cellar. The wines are whistle-clean and wonderfully expressive. Ten-year-old dry *Kabinett* wines brim with youthful vigour in both Riesling and Silvaner. Stein-Harfe Silvaner is savoury and herbal, shimmering with yarrow, dandelion and hayflowers – and while fruit expression changes with vintage, those savoury aromas remain. Riesling from the Randersackerer Teufelskeller, exceptionally fermented in stainless steel, is a jolt of thrilling finesse. The Riesling from the Hagemann parcel in the Stein is a marvel of tautness. A distinct signature runs through the wines: they are clear, precise and linear. There is a lovely Weinstube and a shop. VDP member estate.

Try: Silvaner Steinharfe GG for limestone, lemon and concentration.

Sektkellerei Höfer
Würzburg
www.hoefersekt.de

Carsten Höfer is a modest man. Before turning his attention to making his own exquisite Sekts, he built a service business from scratch, turning the base wines of many renowned Franken wineries into Sekt – lending his expertise and providing all the facilities for making sparkling wine.

Having made Sekt for other people for such a long time, Höfer has now started making his own traditional method sparkling wines. Housed in a former brewery, his naturally cool 12-metre-deep cellar, hewn into Würzburg's *Muschelkalk*, is part of the appeal: thousands of bottles mature slowly here before being riddled and disgorged. Made from base wines in specifically chosen vineyards, these Sekts have elegance and real depth, low sulphur levels, restrained dosage and a very creamy mousse. Höfer has been hiding his light under a bushel but his Sekts will speak for him.

Try: Pinot Brut for dry, creamy finesse.

Juliusspital
Würzburg
www.juliusspital.de

Founded in 1576 by Prince-Bishop Julius Echter as a charitable foundation to tend to the old, the sick and the needy, the Juliusspital today is a hospital, nursing home and palliative care centre. The *Weingut* is still a central part of it and makes its old motto – 'every sip a good deed' – ring true. With 180 hectares of vines in Würzburg and across Franken Juliusspital is Germany's second largest wine estate and largest grower of Silvaner, with 70 hectares of Franken's signature grape. An enviable portfolio is a roll-call of premium sites including the Würzburer Stein and Innere Leiste, Iphöfer Julius-Echter-Berg, Randersacker Pfülben, Bürgstadter Mainhölle and Escherndorfer Lump. They cover all the Franconian Trias formations of *Muschelkalk*, *Buntsandstein* and *Keuper*. Astonishingly, all fruit is still vinified in central Würzburg, where the historic cellars underneath the princely palace are still in use. Equally astonishing is the care lavished on the wine: it would be easy to trade on goodwill, branding and tradition but cellarmaster Nikolas Frauer, who arrived in 2011, has higher ideals. Since 2013 all *Erste* and *Grosse Lagen* wines have been fermented spontaneously and the soft-pruning methods of Simonit & Sirch have been adopted. A clean-cut, vivid style runs from *Gutswein* to *Grosses Gewächs* with impressive site expression throughout the *Erste Lagen*. The Silvaners, depending on site and soil, show aromas of lemon balm, nettle, blackberry leaf and yarrow. They make a virtue of Franconian dryness, slenderness and freshness. As the motto suggests, drinking them is a charitable act. VDP member estate.

Try: Silvaner Rödelseer Küchenmeister for vivid, citrussy saltiness.

Ökologischer Land- & Weinbau Krämer
Auernhofen
www.kraemer-oeko-logisch.de

The Krämers farm 75 hectares of arable land on top of their 4 hectares of vines – all certified organic. It is not easy to combine sugarbeet, wheat and maize with vines, but you feel that Stephan Krämer's heart is totally in it. Viticulture became part of the farming mix in the mid-1980s when vineyards in the Tauber valley were recultivated. Today Krämer's vineyards are in Tauberzell and Röttingen where *Muschelkalk* has graphite and quartz veins. Krämer trained with Wittmann, amongst others, and has steadily honed his winemaking to emerge with his very own style. As of 2013 all wines have been fermented spontaneously and he has consistently experimented with on-skin and intracellular ferments with whole berries. The wines are fermented in large, old barrels and in stainless steel. He uses as little sulphur dioxide as possible and makes *pét nats* as well. His wines are bone-dry, vivid, textured and bright. The Silvaner Alte Reben, from 50-year-old vines in Röttingen is harmonious, creamy, pure and thrilling. The Rieslings are juicy and taut. Great value.

Try: Silvaner Alte Reben.

Weingut Rudolf May
Retzstadt
www.weingut-may.de

Rudolf May's wines are a study in subtlety. Since founding his estate in 1987 he has amassed a 15 hectares portfolio of choice sites. His parents used to deliver the grapes from their 1.5 hectares to the co-op. While May had trained to be a *Winzer*, he did not take over at home but worked as a scientist at the Bavarian Landesanstalt, conducting viticultural trials for 19 years. This stood him in good stead for developing a clear focus when he decided he wanted to be his own boss: Silvaner from steep sites and old vines. Indeed, 70 per cent of production is Silvaner; there is Spätburgunder too and a tiny smattering of other grapes. His vineyards are on the river Main and in lateral valleys at altitudes of up to 300 metres. Several of them were grafted over from other varieties to Silvaner in order to preserve their precious root structure. Any new plantings are high density. His two GGs are Retzstadter Himmelspfad (*Muschelkalk*, fully south-facing and very steep) and Thüngersheimer Rothlauf (*Muschelkalk* and *Buntsandstein*) – he grows exclusively Silvaner in both. His wines are very exacting, bone-dry, almost austere. The most stringent selection allows for all this clarity. The wines are fermented spontaneously and remain on their gross lees until bottling. Certain parcels, like 'Der Schäfer' and Himmelspfad, are always fermented and aged in *Stückfässer*, while the Rothlauf GG is in concrete egg, tonneau and stainless steel. This is a most subtle Silvaner: quiet and understated but utterly disarming in its clarity and honesty. The Spätburgunders show a similar style: crisp, elegant and aromatic. Lay these wines down. The Silvaners become ever more themselves and a 2008 Spätburgunder tasted in 2019 had barely started developing. A new winery was built just outside the village in 1998 and the conversion to organic certification was begun in 2016. May's children are set to continue – not only in the winery but also in May's quest: 'Right now Silvaner is not hip, but we're working on it,' he jokes. VDP member estate.

Try: a mature Rothlauf Silvaner.

Weingut Rothe
Nordheim
www.weingut-rothe.de

In the thirty-odd years since Manfred Rothe, a former chef, made the decision to take over the farming of his ailing in-laws' vineyards, he has been a pioneer time and again. He could not countenance farming unless it was organic, so the conversion took place in 1982/3 when this was still far from mainstream. He also decided right from the start that he would use neither site names nor *Prädikate*, another brave step at the time. The estate was properly founded in 1999 and while his in-laws had only ever had Silvaner in their 1.3 hectares, he planted fungal-resistant varieties like Muscaris and Helios. Today he farms 14 hectares in Nordheim, Sommerach, Escherndorf and Astheim, some of it leased, some of it owned. He became a pioneer in Nordheim again in 2010 by skin-fermenting Silvaner, and in 2013 by vinifying Silvaner in a Georgian *kvevri*. His wines are highly original. There is an entry-level of easy 'bio' wines, but when it comes to Silvaner, we see the variety transformed, by skin-ferment (the Indigenius line) and/or *kvevri*, into elegant, individual and subtle wines. A blend of Grauburgunder, Muscaris and Helios also works beautifully in *kvevri*, benefiting in phenolics and aromatics from the thicker skins of these new varieties. It is beautiful when local and global cultures meld so seamlessly and in such down-to-earth fashion.

Try: KVEVRI weiß for savoury earthiness.

Weingut Horst Sauer
Escherndorf
www.weingut-horst-sauer.de

Horst Sauer's favourite word is 'precision'. Everything he says, thinks and does comes back to this. He loved to go out to the vineyards as a child – he'd come home from school and go find his father in the vines. It was this love and need to see something through from start to finish that made him leave the co-op as early as 1977 and found his estate with just 1.5 hectares. Once he knew his daughter Sandra would join him, he realized more vineyards made sense, doubling the size of the estate in the past decade. Sandra, a Geisenheim graduate with Australian experience, joined in 2005. Today they have 18.5 hectares, most of these in Escherndorf. Sauer's prime site is the majestic, south-facing Escherndorfer Lump which forms an impressive amphitheatre around a loop of the river Main. *Muschelkalk* is covered in a thick layer of loam and loess which helps with water retention on this steep site. The river intensifies the heat in summer and some parcels closer to the water are predestined for botrytis. Sauer makes both exquisite dry and nobly sweet wines here. 'This vineyard is incredibly powerful. Budbreak comes early, quality is always possible here. The real art is to rein in the power of this site, to make sure the wines remain fine and filigree,' he says, knowing that he has mastered this art completely and obsessively. Nothing is left to chance – and he is so in tune with his vineyard and vines that he feels they know what his vision for their fruit is. When discussing quality he says, 'You have to have your feet firmly on home ground, but your head needs to be in the world.' He knows what level the game is at. His *Ortswein* is textbook Silvaner, herbal with yarrow and hay, his *Erste Lagen* in Riesling and Silvaner show concentration and citric purity. His GGs are statuesque but slender monuments to the Franconian expression of these varieties: the Silvaner is creamy, concentrated, bone-dry but buffered in all its linearity; the Riesling is full of smoky, lemony, arrow-like thrill – and both are far too cheap for what they are. Experiencing the wines, you understand what he means by 'precision'. His TBAs are of such concentration, vividness and purity – they have captured all the brilliant energy of that sunny river loop; they are like elixirs of sunshine. Prepare to be wowed. VDP member estate.

Try: Silvaner Escherndorfer Lump for suspended precision with notions of greengage and apricot.

Staatlicher Hofkeller
Würzburg
www.hofkeller.de

This is the oldest of Würzburg's three ancient wine institutions. Founded as a monastery in 1128 when it was first endowed with vineyards by bishop Embricho, this estate with holdings across Franken has made wine ever since, albeit in different incarnations. Over time, it morphed into the *Fürstbischöflicher Hofkeller*, i.e. the cellar of the prince bishop, then it became the Königlich Bayrischer Hofkeller, i.e. the royal Bavarian court cellar and now it is the Staatlicher Hofkeller and belongs to the Federal State of Bavaria. New management was installed in 2018 and big plans are afoot. Thilo Heuft, the new director, reports a 'backlog' of investment but he and the new oenologist Stefan Schäfer look forward to realizing their ambitious plans. A new winery is mooted – somewhere in the vineyards – but right now all the work is still done in the historic cellars of the *Residenz*, one of the architectural Baroque splendours of Würzburg. The impressive 110-hectare portfolio includes plots in Würzburg, Randersacker, Grosheubach, Marktheidenfeld, Iphofen and Dorfprozelten. The offer of wines is broad, from very simple, fruity wines up to *Grosse Gewächse*. It will be interesting to see how Heuft and Schäfer interpret their potential. The cellars are open for visiting and there is a full programme of tastings. VDP member estate.

Try: Würzburger Ortswein Riesling for strait-laced refreshment.

Winzerhof Stahl
Auernhofen
www.winzerhof-stahl.de

Christian Stahl is the first proper *Winzer* in his family. Here in Auernhofen, the southern tip of the Maindreieck, quite a distance from the Main and much closer to the river Tauber, phylloxera had spelled the end of viticulture. In the 1980s, Stahl's parents who farmed cattle here, took advantage of an EU recultivation programme and started planting a vineyard in the Tauber valley. Christian, who also moonlights as a chef, then decided on winemaking rather than farming and started making the wines. He has done so since 2000, while training in Franken, Rheingau and Geisenheim. Today he owns and leases 30 hectares of vineyards, 6 hectares of which are in the cool, quiet Tauber valley. The Taubenzeller Hasennestle is a steep site of *Muschelkalk* and it is here that he made his name with premium Müller-Thurgau – something nobody had done before. His other sites are in Randersacker and Sulzfeld, where Silvaner takes precedence. His winemaking has evolved and he has increasingly been using wood for vinification. His entry-level wines are steely, clear-cut and bright; his wood-fermented wines are fresh, creamy and elegant. Scheurebe, Sauvignon Blanc and Chardonnay receive as much attention as Silvaner and Müller-Thurgau. Everything is whistle-clean.

Try: Fass 500 Sauvignon Blanc, for creamy finesse and depth.

Weingut am Stein
Würzburg
www.weingut-am-stein.de

Built within the Stein vineyard, the contemporary winery of Weingut am Stein is striking – but so are the wines. Sandra and Ludwig Knoll have built a winery entirely in tune with their vision: the lines of the concrete are as sleek as their wines. The estate, initially in Würzburg's centre, was founded in 1890 as a cooperage and moved to its current location in 1980. The Knolls took over from Ludwig's parents in 1990, converting the farming first to organics then to biodynamics. They built the modern winery in 2005 and added an impressive new cellar in 2015. Today they farm almost 40 hectares of vineyards, mostly in the Stettener Stein, but also in the Würzburger Stein, the Innere Leiste and the Randersacker Sonnenstuhl. Twenty-five kilometres north of Würzburg, the Stettener Stein vineyard sits atop 80-metre-steep walls of so-called *Schaumkalk*, porous cellular limestone, where it steeply rises another 130 metres, facing south-south-west. Its soils are poor and stony. More than a third of the Knolls' production is Silvaner, a quarter is Riesling, another quarter Pinot varieties. They are supported in their work by Breton dwarf sheep and chickens that roam the vineyard. Ludwig Knoll makes the wines and ferments spontaneously wherever possible: stainless steel, various sizes of wood, concrete eggs and amphorae all figure in the winemaking. 'Mouthfeel, texture and savouriness, not fruit, are paramount,' Ludwig says. Wines stay on their gross lees for almost a year, but all have a sinuous, snappy slenderness. The Silvaners have hay-flower and herb aromas, the Rieslings are vivid with citrus – all is purity and poise. A new series of *pét nats* has just come out under the name pure&naked. VDP member estate.

Try: Vinz Alte Reben Silvaner for peppery, herbal savouriness and concentration.

Silvaner

Silvaner and Franken, Franken and Silvaner, they just go together. It is here that the variety reaches sublime expression and is as much a transmitter of soils as Riesling. But it is a subtle variety. As Robert Haller of Würzburg's Bürgerspital says: 'Silvaner is love at second sight.' In its youth it shows tender, herbal notes of chervil and hayflowers, in its maturity there is often a vegetal savouriness reminiscent of salsify and white asparagus. It shows lovely creaminess on *Muschelkalk* and stony tautness on *Buntsandstein*. If treated with respect it makes age-worthy, unusual wines. It has less acidity and fruitiness than Riesling – its charms are subtle. Silvaner maestro Horst Sauer says yields are key to quality as Silvaner can also be a high-cropping workhorse grape.

One particular arrival of Silvaner in Franken is well-documented. The devastation of the Thirty Years' War had led to a contraction of viticulture which was now concentrated on the most suitable sites. Silvaner, then still called Österreicher, or 'Austrian', had started standing out for its reliability. Six Silvaner vines were planted in 1659 to replace vines that had died in the Reitsteig vineyard of Graf Wolfgang Georg I zu Castell-Remlingen. The record from 5th April 1659 is still at the Fürstlich Castellsches Domänenamt and Silvaner is still planted there. The fact that Silvaner vines cost twice the price of others is also documented as more vines were planted shortly after. But it was not only in the tiny Castell principality that Silvaner was planted. Abbot Alberich Degen at the Ebrach Cistercian Abbey was the first to have Silvaner planted in Würzburg, listing it as part of its vast holdings in 1665. Whether the Ebrach Cistercians or Graf Castell were the first to plant is neither here nor there, it was first documented at Castell. Whether planted as a single variety or as part of a field blend or both, the Cistercians at Ebrach spread it. This may also explain the name Österreicher: the abbey had connections to Cistercian abbeys in Austria. DNA profiling has shown that Silvaner is a natural cross of Savagnin and Österreichisch Weiss that happened more than 500 years ago, so this is a plausible theory of how Silvaner came to Franken and Germany.

Silvaner conquered Germany with great success. References to Österreicher and Silvaner crop up consistently in historic records. It was a variety that thrived in the cool German climate and that growers could always rely on. Manfred Rothe of Weingut Rothe remembers his grandmother saying: 'Silvaner has never let us down'. Even after poor flowering, even with disease pressure, there was still something to harvest. It was so successful that in 1925 Silvaner represented 39 per cent of German plantings. Its popularity only waned with the advent

> of the new crossings in the post-war years. In 1964 Silvaner was still the most planted variety in Germany with 18,781 hectares, compared to 17,083 hectares of Riesling, much of it in Rheinhessen and Pfalz. In 2017 there were 4,853 hectares of Silvaner in Germany, representing 4.7 per cent of Germany's vineyard.
>
> Philipp Luckert of Zehnthof Luckert points out that there are different strains of Silvaner. While the law makes no distinction between Gelber and Grüner Silvaner, the latter is more common as it gives higher yields. Gelber Silvaner has smaller, golden berries which have more aromatic, complex flavours. Roter Silvaner has pink skins, like Pinot Gris, is aromatic and has slightly higher acid, while Blauer Silvaner has red grapes. Silvaner has also left a genetic legacy. It is the parent of Bacchus, Regent, Rieslaner and Morio-Muskat – but not as so often repeated, of Scheurebe.

Weingut Stefan Vetter
Karlstadt
www.vetter-wein.de

Nicht mehr aber auch nicht weniger (not more, but no less, either) is the statement on Stefan Vetter's labels. He does not hail from a winemaking family, yet he trained to be a *Winzer* and studied International Wine Business in Geisenheim. After stints in Australia and the Mosel he started working for Hans and Anita Nittnaus in Austria's Burgenland and this set him on the trail of biodynamics. An advert in the local paper in 2009 looking for someone to take over a small 1958-planted Silvaner vineyard in the Casteller Kirchberg (*Keuper*) made him return home and start his own estate. He went down the natural wine route, and now farms 3.5 hectares in Castell as well as in the Gambacher Kalbenstein, a mix of *Buntsandstein* and *Muschelkalk*. Seventy per cent of vines are Silvaner (which he spells Sylvaner), the rest is Müller-Thurgau, Riesling and a little Spätburgunder. The grapes are harvested when they are just ripe, whole-bunch-pressed and fermented spontaneously in barrel. They stay for at least a year on gross lees and have their first small addition of sulphur dioxide just before bottling. True to the words on the label, the wines are ultra-light but pure, salty, yeasty and thrillingly dry. The alcohol levels are moderate but the wines age beautifully. Vetter wants substance without weight, and is far removed from chasing fashion fads. 'The way I make these wines is present, but it does not dominate,' he says.

Try: Sylvaner Schale, Stiel und Stengel, skin-fermented but exquisitely light.

Zehnthof Luckert
Sulzfeld am Main
www.weingut-zehnthof.de

Sulzfeld am Main is yet another of those small, bijou Franken wine towns with its own ramparts. The Luckert winery is housed in a 1558-built *Zehnthof*, or tithe house, in its historic centre. Philipp Luckert who came on board in 2005 now makes the wines. He trained with Fürst, Christmann, Hirtzberger in Austria and Wittmann before and after studying in Geisenheim. His grandparents founded the winery in 1961, although viticulture had been practised for centuries; his father and uncle, Wolfgang and Ulrich, are still involved. Ninety per cent of production is white and the focus is clearly on Silvaner. The 10 per cent reds are Früh- and Spätburgunder. Their 17 hectares of vineyards are both on the Main, which flows from north to south here, and a little further up on a plateau. Their *Grosse Lage* is Maustal, a steep south-south-east facing *Muschelkalk* site with very little topsoil that looks towards the Main. Their two *Erste Lagen* are Berg I, terraced and looking south-east directly on the Main, also on *Muschelkalk*, and Sonnenberg, on a plateau of up to 270 metres with *Lettenkeuper* on top of *Muschelkalk*. The Luckerts have farmed organically since 2008 and were certified in 2013. They have also preserved a complete treasure in their Creutz site. The small plot of 1870-planted, ungrafted Silvaner is probably the oldest Silvaner in Germany and sits in a back garden within a residential area. The village encroached on the vineyard and the vines were already cut off, but then the Luckerts saved the site before the roots were grubbed up. They grew a new cane and nursed the vines back into fruiting. The wine is an experience of completeness, creaminess, concentration and fluidity. Across the board the Luckert wines have a rare luminosity and gentleness. There is something quiet about them that gets under your skin. Large, used wood is the rule, as is spontaneous fermentation. The Silvaners are defined by scentedness, and are slender and bone-dry. The Spätburgunder is pure and fresh. There is a light touch and rare talent here. VDP member estate.

Try: Silvaner Maustal GG for lemony, chalky, salty precision.

STEIGERWALD

Fürstlich Castellsches Domänenamt
Castell
www.castell.de

You simply breathe history in the little village of Castell on the fringes of the Steigerwald. Everything here is dominated by the Fürstliches Domänenamt, the princely estate, where Fürst Ferdinand zu Castell-Castell oversees his family's agriculture, forestry and wealth-management businesses and even runs a private bank alongside the wine estate. The Castells, who have made wine here since 1224, can trace their history back to 1091. Their little principality was one of the tiny states that made up the Holy Roman Empire. It had just 10,000 inhabitants when it was dissolved in 1806 and the family lost its political power. The current *Fürst*, who took over from his father in 1996, represents the twenty-sixth generation of his family to make wine here. 'This was entrusted to me in order to hand it over to the next generation. My aim is that it will be bigger, more beautiful and efficient when I hand it over than when it was handed to me,' he says. The family archives contain one entire kilometre of files, amongst them the documents that trace the first plantings of Silvaner in Germany, which happened here in 1659 (see box on page 96). They own 70 hectares of vineyards around Castell and have seven *monopole* sites. Reitsteig, Schlossberg and Hohnart were named as early as 1266. The soils are all Triassic formations of *Gipskeuper*, with some alabaster in the Schlossberg, and *Schilfsandstein*. Silvaner makes up more than 40 per cent of plantings, followed by Müller-Thurgau, Riesling, Bacchus and Pinot varieties along with a little Portugieser and Domina. They also buy grapes from the 25 hectares of the local co-op which they run on behalf of about 50 owners and which is sold under a separate label. The wines are aged in *Stück* and *Doppelstück* barrels made from the oak in their own forests. Oenologist Peter Geil makes the wines, which are expressive in terms of variety and site. Instead of looking back over centuries of tradition, the entire outfit is firmly in the present, looking towards the future. Their clever and contemporary marketing, featuring family portraits of historic Castell women, is only one element of this. The wines are good value and there is a year-round programme of events. VDP member estate.

Try: Silvaner Hohnart Erste Lage for creaminess and delicate herbal notions.

Weingut Wilhelm Meuschel
Kitzingen
www.weingut-meuschel.de

Lukas Herrmann has his work cut out. This once grand and important estate and royal warrant holder in Kitzingen – formerly an important wine trade centre – was bought by a team of investors in January 2019. Herrmann had come on board in August 2018, just in time for the early harvest, and must now bring this rather run-down business into the twenty-first century. The purpose-built winery from 1906 has impressive cellars, ample space and huge potential, as well as 5.7 hectares of its own vineyards. These are on the south-facing Kitzinger Wilhelmsberg, a *Muschelkalk* site. It will take time and money to get this 'rough diamond', as Herrmann calls it, back into shape. Herrmann, who has high-volume experience under his belt from Marlborough in New Zealand, now needs to oversee renovations, manage the vineyards, make and market the wines and define a new style. For now the wines – Silvaner, Riesling, Bacchus and Müller-Thurgau are clean-cut. Herrmann loves Sekt and has already made some base wine. Stay tuned.

Try: one of the Sekts, once they are ready.

Weingut Wirsching
Iphofen
www.wirsching.de

With 90 hectares of vineyards this is Franken's biggest privately owned *Weingut*. The Wirsching family has made wine since 1630 but it was Hans and Heinrich Wirsching in the post-war years who started accumulating the family's holdings around their home village of Iphofen. Their chief site is the Julius-Echter-Berg, named after Würzburg's Prince-Bishop Julius Echter who founded the Juliusspital in 1579. It is a majestic, south-facing slope on one of the western foothills of the Steigerwald, rising to 380 metres, forested at the top. Its *Keuper* soils also have traces of *Schilfsandstein*. The Wirschings also farm the Kronberg (*Gipskeuper*, up to 380 metres) and Kalb (*Gipskeuper*, up to 405 metres) vineyards in Iphofen. The Wirsching range is vast and a visit to the beautiful, well-preserved little town is recommended. With 40 per cent of plantings, Silvaner plays the biggest role here, followed by Riesling, Scheurebe, Weiss- and Spätburgunder. Winemaker Dr Klaus-Peter Heigel says that there are no recipes: there is stainless steel and wood, both cultured and spontaneous yeast. Heigel also experiments with microferments to see how his precious Silvaner reacts to being skin-fermented at different ripeness levels. The Silvaners are slender, dry, juicy and creamy – and above all excellent value. The Wirschings also run a fine line in nobly sweet wines. VDP member estate.

Try: Scheurebe Alte Reben (planted in 1952).

MAINVIERECK AND CHURFRANKEN

Weingut Benedikt Baltes
Klingenberg
www.weingut-benedikt-baltes.de

Benedikt Baltes is a force of nature. His fearless can-do attitude must run in his family since his great-grandfather was a founding member and chairman of one of Germany's oldest co-ops. Born and bred in the Ahr valley, he has now transplanted to Franken, where in 2010 he bought the then almost defunct municipal estate Weingut der Stadt Klingenberg together with an investor. Since then he has steadily honed his thoughts and his style. Today he is undoubtedly amongst the vanguard of Spätburgunder producers, making wine of purity, tension and elegance. There is no preconceived notion he does not challenge. Ripeness? Trellising? Sustainability? He seems to relish challenges, and is actively experimenting, testing, pushing boundaries to see what will work. Refreshingly, he takes setbacks on the chin – stepping away from received ideas has its price, and he is happy to pay it. Breton dwarf sheep roam the vineyards, acting as weeders and fertilizers.

Baltes trained with the Adeneuer brothers in the Ahr, then in Austria, Hungary and Portugal. He farms 11 hectares in Klingenberg, Bürgstadt and Großheubach. Conversion to organics started in 2015 and certification came in 2018 but biodynamic practices are now employed. Since most vineyards are steep and mechanization is impossible he is the rare *Winzer* without a tractor. Spätburgunder is his main concern, vinified spontaneously, with partial whole bunch, and aged for 18 months in German 300-litre barrels and larger oak formats. The wines are slender but profound, aromatic and pure. Spätburgunder is also made into most intriguing and unusual *blanc de noirs* which, when mature, could pass for aged Chablis. Unusually there also are minuscule quantities of graphite-scented Cabernet Franc sourced from a historic field blend on the Schlossberg and dreamy, floral Portugieser from 1940-planted vines. Baltes is married to Julia Bertram, making them Germany's future Pinot power couple. VDP member estate.

Try: Klingenberger Spätburgunder for a slender, red-fruited thrill.

Sekt Burkhardt-Schür
Bürgstadt
www.burkhardtschuer.de

This is one of the most promising new German Sekt estates. Right from the start in 2012 when Laura Burkhardt and Sebastian Schür made the first base wines for their newly founded estate, they aimed for the best Sekt. Their first release was not until 2018. The couple met in Geisenheim and their ideas of quality match: Burkhardt worked in sales and was familiar with many Grower Champagnes; Schür is the viticulturist at Paul Fürst – so finesse, elegance and quality came naturally. They restrict themselves to Spätburgunder, Chardonnay and Pinot Meunier. 'We wanted to make artisanal Sekt from different sites,' Burkhardt explains. They source their base wines most carefully. The Chardonnay, almost counterintuitively, comes from a loess-covered volcanic parcel in Oberrotweil am Kaiserstuhl, the Pinot Meunier from *Muschelkalk* in the Tauber Valley and the Spätburgunder from the *Buntsandstein* of Bürgstadt and the gneiss of Glottertal. The couple monitor the farming and turn the grapes into base wines at the Fürst winery. Just 50 per cent of juice is used and is fermented spontaneously in used barriques or *Doppelstück*. Most undergo malolactic fermentation. They stay on their gross lees until the following August, when they are bottled and stay on tirage for at least 48 months. Dosage is between zero and 4 grams per litre. Production is still small, but their careful, slow and uncompromising approach is to be applauded. The wines age in a beautiful old cellar of the local red sandstone. The raw Sekts, disgorged *à la volée*, there and then, are vivid, creamy and taut. They have a purity and poise that captivates the senses and appeals to lovers of traditional method sparkling wine. Many bottles are still slumbering for lees ageing up to 60 months. It is their down-to-earth nature that allows them to fly so high.

Try: any of their Sekts at all!

Weingut Rudolf Fürst
Bürgstadt
www.weingut-rudolf-fuerst.de

Paul Fürst is one of Germany's true Pinot pioneers. Modest about his towering achievements, he reports humbly of his exacting, uncompromising quest for quality. Back in 1971 it was an unusual move to go far afield to be apprenticed but Paul Fürst decided to train at Schloss Johannisberg, Rheingau. 'It was an elite estate,' he says and credits the mature and often very old Riesling wines he was allowed to taste there with setting him on the path of pursuing the same world-class status for Spätburgunder. Every production parameter was questioned, as he learned, travelled and experimented to emerge as Germany's finest Spätburgunder producer. The poor sandstone soils lend a transparency 'that forgives not a single mistake in viticulture, but they also have the potential for the greatest finesse,' Paul says. In 2017 his son Sebastian formally took over, having joined his father in 2007. Sebastian, equally modest, has inherited Paul's magic touch and continues to fine-tune. The Geisenheim graduate trained in Germany, Alsace, South Africa and at several addresses in Burgundy.

Father and son farm 20 hectares, which include the Bürgstadter Centgrafenberg, the fillet piece of which, Hundsrück (with poorer soils), is a south-facing slope in a lateral valley of the Main river and since 2004 also the Klingenberger Schlossberg. The Schlossberg, first documented in 1261, is a dramatic, terraced, steep site of hot days and cold nights. The Fürsts have planted very high-density vineyards and spare no effort whatsoever in tending these vines – mechanization is impossible. The Spätburgunders astonish with their ethereal transparency and a fine-boned structure that belies their beautiful depth. These wines age effortlessly – as a vertical of Centgrafenberg going back to 1990 proved. Hundsrück has quiet power, Centgrafenberg has cool, peppery spice, Schlossberg has herbal savour. Whole bunch vinification figures in various proportions, up to 100 per cent. 'This green [the stems] later lends sweetness and power,' Paul Fürst says. However, Spätburgunder's earlier-ripening cousin with identical DNA, Frühburgunder (see box, page 53), gets equal top billing here. There is also fine, super-slender, dry Riesling while Chardonnay and Weissburgunder grown in Astheim (Volkach) are increasingly important, too. It is down to Paul Fürst that these sandstone sites in Bürgstadt and Klingenberg, so perfectly suited to this variety, are monuments to Spätburgunder culture today. Pinot lovers should make the pilgrimage. VDP member estate.

Try: Bürgstadter Berg Spätburgunder, the village wine, which already spells purity, tension and elegance.

Weingut Fürst Löwenstein
Grossheubach
www.loewenstein.de

Erbprinzessin Stefanie zu Löwenstein, a pediatric surgeon, took on the running of the estate after the tragic death of her husband in an accident in 2010. The land includes several thousand hectares of forest as well as the wine estate, with sites in both Rheingau and Franken. A new winery, built in 2010, in the vaulted former stables of the Baroque Schloss in Grossheubach, means that production is now here. The Löwensteins have owned one of Franken's – and Germany's – most iconic vineyards since 1611. Erbprinzessin Stefanie aptly calls it 'Franken's Uluru': the Homburger Kallmuth is a majestic site. Its steep terraces induce vertigo, its spectacular situation, hugging a west-facing curve of the river Main, inspires awe. Its base is of *Buntsandstein*, the upper reaches have *Muschelkalk*. Owned for centuries by the Augustine monks of Stift Triefenstein, Kallmuth was first documented in 1136. By the seventeenth century its wines enjoyed fame well beyond Franconia. Silvaner has been documented in the Kallmuth since 1702. Since 2016 the wines have been made by Peter Arnold, a local winemaker who wrote his thesis on the Kallmuth before working in South Africa and Spain and returning to Germany. 'It is a privilege to work here,' he says. 'The character of this vineyard is best expressed in Silvaner.' He is right – even though the Rieslings are equally compelling. These are the leading varieties but there is also Sauvignon Blanc and some Spätburgunder. The wines are bright, clear and, since Arnold's arrival, have lovely tension. VDP member estate.

Try: Kallmuth Silvaner 'S' for salty, juicy precision; Silvaner Kallmuth Asphodill for smoke and stone.

TAUBERTAL

Weingut Familie Hofmann
Röttingen
www.weinguthofmann.com

In this remote, southern tip of Franken in the Tauber valley, Jürgen Hofmann is guardian of an ancient, autochthonous variety called Tauberschwarz. The variety was first mentioned in 1726 and its genetic origins are not yet identified. There are just 12 hectares of it left in Tauberfranken and Hofmann farms 1.4 hectares of them. While the family had grown vines for generations, it was his father Alois who started making the wines himself in 1991 with just 1.3 hectares. Today Jürgen, who trained with Paul Fürst and took over in the late 1990s, farms 9 hectares of vines and almost all of them are in the Röttinger Feuerstein vineyard, a south-facing slope of *Muschelkalk* with quartz veins. More than 60 per cent of plantings are white, with Silvaner and Riesling taking the top spots – the Silvaner Drei Sterne, from vines planted in 1969, is particularly finely textured. But Tauberschwarz is where Hofmann's heart really is. This quiet, understated winemaker really pushes the variety to its limit. The vines are grown on the Röttinger Feuerstein, which in the early nineteenth century was almost completely planted to this old variety, also a part of many field blends. It needs poor, stony soils and was thought to be extinct by the 1950s. But an old vineyard was discovered and vines were propagated. While Tauberschwarz has a reputation for 'light reds', here they come with subtle power and endurance. Low yields and vinification in oak give them structure. A slight floral overtone hovers above the aromatic mulberry notes, while silky tannins leave real impression. That such a poetic variety is given centre-stage here should be shouted from the rooftops. But Jürgen Hofmann is far too modest to do that. So here is my shout on his behalf. The wines are incredible value.

Try: Tauberschwarz 'R' for silky, aromatic depth.

10

HESSISCHE BERGSTRASSE – AWAKENING BEAUTY

This little region on the right bank of the Rhine in Hessen derives its name, literally 'mountain road', from an ancient Roman trade road that circumvented the marshy, soggy Rhine plain. It starts at Baden's northern border and is in fact the continuation of the Badische Bergstrasse, one of Baden's northerly *Bereiche*. It is so small that it does not quite run from Heidelberg to Darmstadt but stops short at Seeheim-Jugenheim. The region benefits from the mild climate of the Rhine valley and enjoys the protection of the Odenwald, a low mountain range, whose western slopes constitute the vineyards. Formed by the Upper Rhine Rift (see p.59), its granitic subsoils are mostly covered in loess and loam and only exposed in a few places. Most vineyards are thus on loess and loess-loam. Around Heppenheim there is some Triassic *Buntsandstein*. The Hessische Bergstrasse also seems to be the last German region still in a *Dornröschenschlaf*, the deep slumber of Grimm's Sleeping Beauty fairy tale. The local co-op, Bergsträsser Winzer e.G., with its 399 members farms 264 hectares or 57 per cent of vineyards. They offer a bewildering array of wines from various varieties – valiantly trying to be all things to all people. However, one winemaker with backing from a local industrialist has planted the first tender kisses of awakening on this region. By specializing in Sekt he has put the Bergstrasse back on the map with a bang.

Administratively there are two *Bereiche*, three *Grosslagen* and 23 *Einzellagen*. In 2017 there were 462 hectares of which 197 hectares were Riesling, 51 hectares Grauburgunder and 48 hectares Spätburgunder.

Griesel & Compagnie
Bensheim
www.griesel-sekt.de

Right from the start Niko Brandner was given free rein to make Sekt according to his ideas. It was in 2013 that the local industrialist couple Jürgen Streit and Petra Greißl-Streit bought the former premises of the former Hessian State Domaine in central Bensheim, with its beautiful vaulted cellar. They named the estate Griesel & Compagnie after the street it stood in, Grieselstrasse, and had the inspired idea to hire Niko Brandner straight from college to develop a new brand of premium, artisanal German Sekt. Brandner rose to the occasion magnificently. With singular focus and initially bought-in grapes he set about making remarkable bubbles. The first releases in 2015 immediately won plaudits and demonstrated an already elegant style, which he continues to refine. Today there are 7.5 hectares of vineyards around Bensheim that provide the Riesling, Chardonnay and Pinot varieties for the base wines. They are fermented spontaneously in small and large wood and steel and stay on their fine lees for around 10 months before tirage. All wines have a minimum of 16 months' lees ageing, while the top range has 36 months on lees – and there are bottles in reserve. Elegance, purity and freshness are key but more is to come. Brandner has started a *reserve perpetuelle* and is honing his style. We should all raise our glass to the Streit family and to Brandner for giving this region new impetus.

Try: Rosé Extra Brut 'Prestige' for creaminess, elegance and bite.

Schloss Schönberg
Bensheim
www.schloss-schoenberg.de

By installing the young Rabea Trautmann as winemaker here, the Streits (see above), who started the estate in 2016, have replicated the successful recipe of Griesel & Compagnie: hire energetic, youthful talent and give them scope, means and space to express their ideas. Trautmann, who studied landscape architecture and found her way into wine by chance, sees her job, encompassing viticulture and winemaking, as a 'brilliant challenge'. For now, basic orientation and replanting are the chief concerns of this young estate. Its 6.5 hectares are in the Schönberger Herrnwingert, Auerbacher Fürstenlager and Auerbacher Höllberg. It is Trautmann's intention to keep the old Riesling vines while top-grafting is planned for existing other varieties. The desired focus will be on Pinot varieties. Wines for now are fermented in the Griesel cellar, both in stainless steel and in wood. Trautmann makes bone-dry, whistle-clean styles but is full of ideas. A Riesling *solera* was started and holds wines from 2016, 2017 and 2018, so exciting times are ahead. The name-giving Schloss, an imposing edifice on a picturesque promontory just outside Bensheim, is in the process of being renovated and will house the winery in the future.

Try: Weissburgunder Ortswein for exquisitely lean concentration.

11

MITTELRHEIN – CASTLES, CHERRIES, NYMPHS AND RIESLING

Is there any other stretch of river with so many castles pitched so precipitously on steep slate cliffs as this narrow section of the Rhine from Bingen to Bonn? The area is so exceptional that the 65-kilometre long Rhine Gorge has been a UNESCO World Heritage Site since 2002. Forty castles and castle ruins grace the river and it is here that the idea of *Rheinromantik* was born. Poets and thinkers like Schlegel, Goethe, Hölderlin and Kleist visited and reported. J.M.W. Turner came here to paint. The wild-romantic landscape thus became a firm stop on the European Grand Tour. Above all it was the legend of a Rhine nymph that captured the imagination. There are various versions of the tale, but the most famous is told in Heinrich Heine's popular verse from 1822, set to an evocative melody by Friedrich Silcher. Lovely Lorelei sits on her rock, combing her golden hair and singing. She is so resplendent and spell-binding that poor Rhine skippers perish in the rapids, overcome with 'wild woe'. The other versions are no better: the girl always spells ruin, never the men. A particularly steep slate cliff at a dangerous riverbend near Sankt Goarshausen is still called Lorelei and attracts many visitors. The remarkable landscape was created as the Rhine was forced to cut through the rising Devonian and Carboniferous formations (slate, greywacke) of the Rhenish Massif in the Quaternary period. The region covers either bank of the Rhine and continues beyond Koblenz all the way to the southern outskirts of Bonn. For such a long stretch of river the region is surprisingly small and has just 469 hectares of vineyard, most of them on steep slopes. As Peter Jost of Weingut Toni Jost says: 'The entire Mittelrhein has less hectarage than some wine villages in Rheinhessen or Pfalz.' There are two very different wine styles depending on whether the vineyards are in a cool, lateral valley, such as Bacharach or Sankt Goar or on the warm Rheinfront, like Boppard and Spay. Further north towards Bonn the soils get heavier but the wines cooler. As it happens, a number of Ahr estates also farm this northern part of Mittelrhein. The region often falls by the wayside and is forgotten amongst the larger more famous areas, but there is much to discover.

Mittelrhein viticulture has Roman origins and was firmly established by Carolingian times by monastic settlements which cleared land for the planting of vines. Abbeys in Trier and Cologne owned many vineyards here. Bacharach, a well-preserved medieval town with picture perfect half-timbered houses, was an important reloading point on the Rhine. Until it could be blasted away with explosives in the nineteenth century, a quartzite reef near Bingen made the Rhine unnavigable for larger vessels, so reloading from larger to smaller vessels and vice versa happened here. It explains the wealth of the town with its impressive buildings and gates. Like other wine regions on the left Rhine bank, the western part of the Mittelrhein became French in 1798 following Napoleon's occupation in 1794. Koblenz, or Coblence, at the confluence of Rhein and Mosel, became the capital of the Département Rhin-et-Moselle. This meant the end of feudal rule, the introduction of the *Code Civil* and the secularization of church estates – and fundamental changes in ownership structures. In Koblenz, for instance, 207 citizens bought 540 *biens nationaux*. Evidently the French inspired a fashion for fizz, for Koblenz achieved significance as the seat of various *Sektkellereien*, like Deinhard or Tesche & Co. Cooperation and exchange with Champagne was lively. In 1828 Remy Auguste Ruinart, of the Champagne house, married a daughter of Karl Anton Tesche who had founded his *Sektkellerei* in 1834. The famous house of Deinhard, which set up as a wine merchant in 1794, before becoming a Sekt producer in 1843, did a lot to popularize 'Hock' and later 'Moselle' in export markets. By 1856 no other German town had as many Sekt producers as Koblenz. The cool lateral valleys around Bacharach and St Goar were traditionally sources for Sekt base wine. As phylloxera hit in the late nineteenth century Mittelrhein farmers switched crops. There had already been a tradition of growing cherries in the warm slate soils and as early as the 1830s they were exported as far afield as England. Phylloxera meant that cherries now took advantage of the sunshine and almost usurped the vine. In 1964 there were 870 hectares of vines in the Mittelrhein. Today there are just 469 hectares. That 309 hectares of those are planted to Riesling is a clear statement for quality: there are few superfluous vineyards with inferior varieties – there may only be 45 hectares of Mittelrhein Spätburgunder but we know that where Riesling thrives its red counterpart also makes compelling wines. There are also 24 hectares of Müller-Thurgau.

Administratively there are two *Bereiche*, ten *Grosslagen* and 111 *Einzellagen*.

Weingut Fritz Bastian
Bacharach
www.weingut-bastian-bacharach.de

Both opera and an island figure in this 300-year-old *Weingut*. Located right on Bacharach's cobbled market square, Fritz Bastian keeps a small vinothèque. He is a trained opera singer, a career he combines with winemaking. 'I still feel like I lead a life between two spheres but at least now there is structure,' he says. Bastian also is the owner of a Rhine island and grows wine on its sandy soils, which sit atop a slate bank. He calls it the Bastian Riesling Insel but its proper name is Heyles'en Werth. He has 8.5 hectares of vineyards in sites like the Bacharacher Wolfshöhle and Posten, as well as the Steeger St Jost. Eighty per cent of plantings are Riesling, complemented by some Scheurebe, Spätburgunder and Portugieser. His zesty Rieslings are particularly lovely with bottle age. VDP member estate.

Try: The off-dry island wine, of course, and the snappy, dry Alde Fritz Riesling.

Weingut Toni Jost
Bacharach
www.toni-jost.de

Peter Jost was one of the quality motors of the Mittelrhein. His daughter Cecilia, the seventh generation, runs the estate today. She joined the estate in 2008 after finishing at Geisenheim and farms 15 hectares of vines, both in Walluf in the Rheingau and in Bacharach in the Mittelrhein. Her chief site and *monopole* is the Bacharacher Hahn, a south-south-east facing steep slope that turns from the Leimbach valley towards the Rhine. Its Devonian slate soils warm up and make for a spicy, zesty, ripe citrus-fruited Riesling. Rieslings are mostly made in stainless steel with minimal use of wood. On the lower part of the slope Cecilia grows impressive and exquisitely fresh Spätburgunder. In view of climate change she and her family have also started recultivating a terrace above the Hahn vineyard in Bacharach, abandoned in the 1980s. The so-called Mathiasweingarten lies 100 metres higher, also south-facing and on Devonian slate, and brings perfectly ripe grapes at a modest 12% abv. With such talent for Spätburgunder and dry Riesling it is easy to forget the *Prädikat* styles but a ten-year-old Spätlese blew me away. VDP member estate.

Try: Riesling Devon 'S' Trocken for snappy, slatey, zesty fun.

Weingut Matthias Müller
Spay
www.weingut-matthiasmueller.de

Today, Marianne and Matthias Müller are joined by their sons Johannes and Christoph. Johannes, who came on board in 2015 after Geisenheim and stints in the Nahe and Alto Adige, is an articulate and forward-looking winemaker. The family has farmed the slopes of the Bopparder Hamm since 1678, in the past growing cherries as well as grapes. Their parcels are in the Feuerlay, Mandelstein, Ohlenberg and Rabenlay. The Bopparder Hamm, on an S-shaped bend of the Rhine, is a massive slope, fully Rhine- and south-facing that brings forth powerful wines. They are juicy with stone fruit flavours but also toned. Johannes aptly describes this as 'deliberate freshness, a certain extract, a certain fullness and also "*Wonne*",' a term that translates as joy, delight or pleasure. There is a 'special edition' series called MM, which stands for Matthias and Marianne; these are the top wines alongside the GG. The Ohlenberg MM Riesling, in its lusciously ripe but precise and dry style is reminiscent of the Austrian Rieslings grown on the Danube – such is the power of the Rhine on the fiftieth parallel. More emblematic of the house style is the Feuerlay MM: zesty, stony, slatey and chiselled. All the Rieslings are made in stainless steel and are fermented both with cultured yeast and spontaneously. Riesling (85 per cent) is complemented by Weiss- and Grauburgunder, which are vinified in wood. Ridiculously good value. VDP member estate.

Try: Feuerlay Riesling for slate and savour.

Weingut Philipps-Mühle
Sankt Goar
www.philipps-muehle.de

Thomas and Martin Philipps grew up in this mill which has stood here, in the narrow Gründelbach valley, since 1265. Their family has been here since 1881, and it was in use until 2015 when their father, one of the last artisan millers, retired. Unusually, the brothers are the first generation of their family to grow and make wine. This valley had 10 hectares of vines in the 1960s but by 2000 all had been given up. It was in 2005 that they started recultivating a steep 0.3-hectare plot. Today they have 3.5 hectares, all on hair-raisingly steep sites like the St Goarer Ameisenberg and Frohwingert, with another 3 hectares in Oberwesel. Ninety per cent of plantings are Riesling, 10 per cent Müller-Thurgau. The brothers use 100 per cent stainless steel for their zesty, clean Riesling. Great value.

Try: St Goarer Frohwingert Riesling for herbal zestiness.

Weingut Ratzenberger
Bacharach
www.weingut-ratzenberger.de

Joachim Ratzenberger, whose family bought the estate in 1956, loves the relative isolation of his vineyards in the quiet, narrow Steeg valley to the west of Bacharach. This is where he farms the Bacharacher Wolfshöhle and the Steeger St Jost. Both are south-facing, very steep sites of Devonian slate. He is proud that his ecological approach means even heavy rains do not cause erosion. Some of his Riesling vines are more than 60 years old. He has just bought a 10 hectares swathe of vineyards in the next valley further south which is less narrow, and its vineyard, Oberdiebacher Fürstenberg, is slightly less steep. The entire slope had terraces dredged in what Ratzenberger calls a future vision of steep slope viticulture. This happened in collaboration with Geisenheim University and is a biodiversity project called 'Bioquis'. Wild flowers and herbs naturally at home in such environments thrive alongside the vines and attract beneficial wildlife. He owns 28 hectares of vineyards, 22 hectares of which are currently under vine. But Ratzenberger has more up his sleeve: his family have made their own hand-riddled Sekt since 1987. The base wines are grown on blue slate at an altitude between 170–240 metres and are harvested last. This means they are particularly expressive and fruity and create a very different but totally compelling style of Riesling Sekt. The product of long lees ageing, usually 4 years, they age extremely well. The still Rieslings are whistle-clean and have a savoury herbal and citrus perfume. There are also tiny quantities of cool, smoky, transparent Spätburgunder. All the wines are great value. VDP member estate.

Try: Vintage Riesling Sekt.

Weingut Weingart
Spay
www.weingut-weingart.de

Florian Weingart has fulfilled his dream with a new, modern, circular winery at the foot of the Bopparder Hamm. He always knew he wanted to be a *Winzer* but rejected the business model of his father. He wanted to focus on quality and so managed slowly to assemble 11 contiguous hectares in the eastern part of the Bopparder Hamm, where the Rhine makes an S-bend and creates a fully south-facing slope of Devonian slate with pumice veins. His sites are in the parcels Engelstein, Ohlenberg and Feuerlay, where he grows 83 per cent Riesling and 17 per cent Spätburgunder. In a philosophical essay on 'anarchistic' wine he explains his approach: his awe in the face of nature, his recognition of wine as a cultural phenomenon. He is unusual in sticking to the *Prädikate* but tasting his wines you see where he's coming from. A *Spätlese feinherb* Riesling from the Engelstein is scalpel sharp and utterly taut, a *Kabinett* is smoky and gorgeous. Aged *Auslesen* are like balm. These are unusual wines from an unusual man. Raise your glass to this free-thinker. Great value.

Try: any of his vivid Kabinett Rieslings.

12

MOSEL – A COSMOS UNTO ITSELF

Not only are the valleys of Mosel, Saar and Ruwer unique; they seem like a different universe. Here, grape, climate, soil and topography combine in such a fashion that the ancient contract between humans and vine, between sweat and fruit, is driven to its extreme. It is here that the greatest effort leads to the greatest lightness; that Riesling climaxes with absolute transparency, exactitude and expression. Nowhere else is it more apparent that it is light, not heat, that ripens grapes. Take the legendary south-facing Scharzhofberg in Wiltingen. You climb to its ridge and look at the shrub on its shaded, north-facing side: barely an apple would ripen there.

Until 2007 the Mosel region was still called 'Mosel-Saar-Ruwer', also crediting the valleys of the smaller tributaries. These subregions now go under the Mosel umbrella but are as distinct as ever. This region covers the final, brief stretches of three river valleys: the Mosel on its meandering path before it joins the Rhine at Koblenz, the Saar and Ruwer before they run into the Mosel at Konz and Trier, respectively. While the river Mosel rises in the French Vosges mountains and flows north past Metz and Schengen, the German wine region begins at the Luxembourg border. This is the relatively unknown Obermosel where Elbling and white Pinot varieties on Triassic formations dominate. What is commonly understood to be the Mosel region proper begins in Trier and follows the snaking river bends which take 237 kilometres to cover the 96 kilometre distance to Koblenz. By grinding its way into the 400-million-year-old sediments of the Rhenish Slate Massif between 15 and 2.5 million years ago, the river created this spectacular topography, curve by winding curve. The Mittelmosel, where all the most famous vineyards are, runs from Trier to Briedel. Its villages from south to north read like a wine menu: Leiwen, Piesport, Braunberg, Bernkastel, Graach, Wehlen, Traben-Trarbach and Enkirch. Driving along the Mosel in this narrow valley is confusing: the road follows the river but on alternating banks, so after one or two loops and bridges you lose all sense of direction. However, driving early in the morning allows you to see how the rising sun hits some knolls and slopes first, some dells and troughs later. At dusk some parcels are still sunlit while others have been shaded since noon. This mix of exposure, gradient, relative distance to the river and altitude already accounts for many differences in the wine. Add elements like varying subsoils, vine genetics, viticulture and winemaking and you have a perfect matrix of infinite possibility. This alone inspires awe, let alone the vertigo-inducing steepness of the rocky vineyards. The experience is much enhanced by the white lettering proclaiming the famous vineyard names from afar.

The stretch of river from Zell to Koblenz is called Terrassenmosel as the valley becomes a little warmer but much steeper, so vineyards are usually terraced. This is where Germany's, and possibly Europe's, steepest vineyard is, the Bremmer Calmont. The Mosel is of course synonymous with slate but there are variations of it as well as other formations. The fact that the Germans like to use the term *Schiefer*, or slate, freely causes much confusion so caution is advised. The oldest formations are Devonian shales, or *Tonschiefer*. Depending on colour they are named *Blauschiefer* or *Grauschiefer* and are the dominant formation in all three valleys. The same era also left some quartzite, especially in the Terrassenmosel as well as volcanic diabase in the Saar. The Permian era left rhyolite, red with iron oxide, which is often called *Rotschiefer*; the Ürziger Würzgarten is famous for it. All these formations are weathered to varying degrees; some are so fine you can crumble them in your hand. The dialect word '*Lay*' means slate, explaining why this term crops up in so many vineyard names. In the Ruwer valley, just outside Trier, vines are more difficult to spot because the vineyards are choice, south-facing, singular slopes not on the Ruwer itself but on tiny tributaries, like Eitelsbach, Weschbach or Kundelbach. They are at slightly higher altitude and don't benefit from the moderating effect of a sufficiently large body of water, so they are cooler than the Mosel valley. The same is true for the Saar, which is altogether more spacious, more remote and wilder.

Merely its last 25 kilometres from just south of Serrig to its confluence with the Mosel at Konz constitute its world wine fame. Few vineyards are directly on the Saar and rise to 300 metres and beyond, both accounting for their coolness. These slopes are much more exposed to the elements. You realize how marginal the area is when you spot signs for the *Viezstrasse*, or cider route, which also is a speciality here. Saar vineyards are monumental in a different way from those in the Mosel. The good distances between them, their relative isolation and altitude seem to afford them lofty majesty and grandeur that underscores their individuality. The mere mention of sites like Kanzemer Altenberg, Ockfener Bockstein, Saarbuger Rausch, Ayler Kupp and Scharzhofberg will send shivers of pleasure down the spines of Riesling lovers.

But history also plays its part. Neither poetry nor artefacts leave any doubt that viticulture has been a central part of Mosel life since at least Roman times. The Mosel's 'rising, natural theatre of vines' was described as early as the fourth century by Roman poet Ausonius, who had been summoned to Trier, or *Augusta Treverorum*, an important Roman settlement and garrison, to teach the sons of Emperor Valentinian. Remnants of Roman wine presses in Piesport and Braunberg bear witness to active, early wine culture. After the invasion of the Franks, Trier emerged as an early centre of Christianity whose archbishops united worldly and ecclesiastic powers, expanded their territory and rose to become powerful electors in the twelfth century. The electorate of Kurtrier was an important church state and wine was central to its economy as countless records document: vineyards are named, *Fuders* bought and sold, trade regulated, and prices listed. In the tumultuous centuries surrounding the Thirty Years' War, conflict was never far away, but viticulture, then still dominated by Elbling and field blends, always revived. In 1787 Elector Clemens Wenceslaus decreed that within the coming seven years all lesser varieties were to be grubbed up and replaced with quality vines like Riesling. Much is made of this famous edict but as later records show, it was never fully put into practice, especially since the French occupation of the left bank of the Rhine disrupted the political order once and for all. As one writer noted, the entire Mosel, 'from its source to its confluence with the Rhine, became a French river.' The area of Mosel, Ruwer and Saar which Napoleon's troops had occupied since 1794 became the French Département de la Sarre in 1797. Secularization followed, as did the *Code Civil*, and former church possessions were sold off. Estates like Scharzhofberg and Maximin Grünhaus can trace their history to these transactions. It is believed that almost half of all vineyards changed hands at that time, a cataclysmic upheaval after centuries of feudalism.

By 1815 however, with Napoleon defeated, the area fell to Prussia. An initial period of prosperity was swiftly followed by disaster: the scrapping of protective tariffs combined with poor harvests spelled hunger and misery. The poverty he encountered among Mosel *Winzer* moved a young Karl Marx to pen several articles railing against Prussian injustice. Around the same time another social reformer, Ludwig Gall, introduced the idea of *Nassverbesserung*, literally 'wet improvement'. Based on the ideas of Jean Antoine Chaptal in France, who had introduced 'chaptalization', i.e. the enrichment of musts with sugar, Gall's idea was the improvement of musts with sugar solution (sugar dissolved in water) which killed two birds with one stone: it enriched must and diluted acidity. *Nassverbesserung* thus made unpalatable, sour wine at least drinkable and therefore marketable. Needless to say, the method was and remained controversial, but became so widespread that *gallisieren* entered the vocabulary – no doubt the practice also helped to entrench the *naturrein* principle of unadulterated wine firmly in the German wine psyche. Yet this western backwater of Prussia remained desperately poor. Landowners with other income streams could survive, but for farmers especially reliant on viticulture in this narrow valley without much space for other arable crops, each vintage spelled either feast or famine. The Mosel flooded at regular intervals, too, creating more misery. If you look carefully you can see the high-water marks of past floods on doorways and bridges. Thorough as ever, the Prussians commissioned their cadastral inspector and tax councillor Franz Josef Clotten to create a vineyard site classification. Based on the site evaluations of Mosel, Saar and Ruwer vineyards conducted by the Prussian tax authorities between 1816 and 1832, this map was published in 1868 and graded vineyards into three classes. The best vineyards – mostly the same as today – were marked out in dark red and not only served tax purposes but also became a handy guide for wine merchants. A string of good vintages in the 1860s meant that Mosel wines were going up in the world. Geopolitically, Europe was changing, too. Prussia was in the ascendant, threatening the carefully calibrated European power balance of the Vienna Congress. France declared war in July 1870 and by February 1871 the Prussians were victorious. While the Franco–Prussian War set the scene for the creation of the *Deutsches Reich* in 1871, it also emphasized the strategic importance of the Mosel region. This formerly French and remote province now received a railway line that connected Berlin, Koblenz, Trier and Metz in the newly annexed region of Lothringen/Lorraine. Steamships had already eased transport, but the Mosel then was not navigable year round. Trains meant that wines could now go to market easily. Indeed, if you look closely at old Mosel labels you will see an unusual number of steamboats or locomotives signalling ready transport links. By the 1870s Mosel wines started to become highly fashionable. The English writer Henry Vizetelly described them in 1875 as lacking 'the robustness of their brethren of the Rhine' but noted that they were 'at any rate light and delicate, and possessed of a fresh and at times even a decided flavour, rendering them highly palatable.' While Rhine wines were drunk with bottle age, Mosel wines were drunk young. The wine chapter in the official catalogue of the *Deutsches Reich* for the 1900 World Exhibition in Paris gives a nod to this fashion by describing Mosel and Saar wines as 'by now popular'. It was their marked difference to the revered, mature Rhine wines that set them apart. Conscious of the need to support the populace of a border region, in 1896 the government in Berlin started founding not one but three *Staatsdomänen*, or state domains, in Avelsbach, Serrig and Wiltingen: this way the state could benefit from the profitable wine business while also providing research and teaching centres serving as model domaines for best practice.

It was also in the nineteenth century that Riesling's predominance was cemented in the Mosel. In 1845, Servatius Muhl reports lots of field blends in Saar and Mosel, noting Kleinberger, i.e. Elbling, and a hotchpotch of varieties. He notes that Elbling is often co-planted with Riesling, quoting the local wisdom: 'Kleinberger brings much wine, Riesling makes it good.' He also remarks that Riesling is planted in some places where it will not ripen in weak and average years. Fifty-three years later in 1898, Koch and Stephanus note that as a development of the past 20 years Riesling had become the predominant variety – but they also point out that in lesser sites Riesling is mixed with Silvaner, Pinot varieties and Traminer. Occasionally there are references to red wine – made from Spätburgunder and Portugieser. They also emphasize the viticultural progress. It was at that time that several harvest passes were made in the best Riesling vineyards, and grapes of the same ripeness were fermented to create different wine styles. Mosel wine was thus at its zenith at the turn of the century – and would remain so until the First World War. In this golden age these wines were amongst the most expensive and desirable in the world. The decades that followed the war were marked by difficulty. The tough conditions of the Versailles Treaty, the economic crisis and inflation of 1929, the ascent of Nazi Germany that ended in devastation, loss, and misery. Yet, when German chancellor Konrad Adenauer negotiated the release of the last German prisoners of war still captive in the Soviet Union with Nikita Khrushchev in 1955, he took precious Berncasteler Doctor Riesling from the 1950 vintage with him.

Recovery was slow in the immediate post-war years, but vineyard expansion was rampant from the 1960s to the 1980s. The fact that *Nassverbesserung*, that relic of the nineteenth century, was still allowed, coupled with the 1971 invention of *Grosslagen*, or collective sites, meant that much Mosel wine became a parody of itself. One of the most grotesque examples of a *Grosslage* is the Piesporter Michelsberg, or PiMi in bulk wine circles, with 1,106 hectares – larger than some German wine regions! The figures tell the story: in 1879 there were 6,144 hectares in the Mosel, of which 42 per cent were Riesling; by 1906 there were 7,484 hectares of which 88 per cent were Riesling. In 1964 there were 9,835 hectares of which 79 per cent were Riesling; in 1979 there were 12,298 hectares, of which 58 per cent were Riesling and 22 per cent Müller-Thurgau. All this rode on the coat-tails of former glory and culminated in the 1980s when several scandals broke: amongst them that of inverted sugar syrup in 1980, which centred on the Mosel, where sugar was used to create fake *Prädikat*-level wines from poor wines, and the diethylene glycol scandal of 1985, where this substance was added to wines to mimic the viscous mouthfeel of rich, sweet wine. Domestic and export markets collapsed and even blameless estates suffered. The region's reputation lay in tatters. Various parcels on the steep slopes fell fallow.

It took the Mosel until the turn of the millennium to start recovering. Climate change has helped: 'Mosel, Saar and Ruwer have benefited because there are no more sour wines. Viticulture is much better today. We want to maintain the delicacy, the positive lightness. Vineyards which used to be abandoned because they were too cool are being recultivated, we go higher up, we go into the lateral valleys,' explains Johannes Selbach of Selbach-Oster. And now Spätburgunder is also winning plaudits. The past twenty years have seen a flowering of quality where old vineyards and vines are valued; where young winemakers invest their futures in this region; where visionaries like Ernie Loosen, Markus Molitor and Roman Niewodniczanski of van Volxem created a dynamo effect with their respective investments and achievements; where arch traditionalists like Egon Müller, Maximin Grünhaus and Joh. Jos. Prüm hold fast to their historic values. Once again Germany and the world are conscious of the uniqueness of Riesling that can be achieved here. The slopes are still as steep, but the counsel from an old book, 'that no bread in Germany is earned harder, nor sliced more frugally, than in the Mosel,' is thankfully consigned to history – even though the wines are far too cheap across the board for the effort that goes into growing them. It is a delicious contradiction that such monumental effort should lead to such weightlessness and delicacy. Today the stylistic spectrum of Riesling in this region alone is mind-blowing. If you wonder about the differences between Mosel and Saar Riesling, here are the opinions of two experts. Nik Weis of St Urbanshof says that 'the particular conditions of the Mosel are even more heightened in the Saar,' while Hanno Zilliken of Forstmeister Geltz Zilliken notes: 'The difference between Mosel and Saar is the different weighting of constituents. A Mosel Riesling is carried by its fruit accompanied by acidity. A Saar Riesling is carried by its acidic structure accompanied by fruit.' Fans should not miss two annual events: Mythos Mosel and Saar Riesling Sommer which draw an enthusiastic and young crowd.

Administratively, there are six *Bereiche*, 19 *Grosslagen* and 524 *Einzellagen* – many of them so legendary that it would take another book to profile them. Today there are a sensible 8,770 hectares of vines which comprise 5,393 hectares of Riesling, 979 hectares of Müller-Thurgau, 487 hectares of Elbling and 400 hectares of Spätburgunder.

Slate

Schiefer, the German term for slate, is an umbrella term and the cause of much confusion. Its various forms are translated as slate, shale or schist. Geology makes a fundamental distinction between three rock types: igneous, formed from magma; metamorphic, altered by heat or pressure; and sedimentary, formed by erosion or deposition. Slates are a foliated, fine-grained, metamorphic group of rocks. German slate formations date to the Devonian (420–360 million years ago) and Carboniferous (360–300 million years ago) periods and are weathered to varying degrees. Winemakers use the term freely so proceed with caution. Slate is free-draining and its dark colour helps to retain heat – both aspects help vines to ripen their grapes.

TERRASSENMOSEL

Weingut Heymann-Löwenstein
Winningen
www.hl.wine

Cornelia and Reinhard Löwenstein founded their estate in 1980. Despite a 500-year-long family tradition in wine, Löwenstein had set his sights on a doctorate in politics. But the vines called and with little money they started their own *Weingut* in order to pursue a historic Riesling style that was perceived as heretic at the time. 'We want no *Kabinett*, no *Spätlese*, or whatever else is classed as "classic". This only works if your classics begin in the 1970s,' he explains. In order to be able to use less sulphur dioxide, he started fermenting his Rieslings as dry as possible, initially (in the early 1980s) with the help of cultured yeasts. Since the mid-1980s ferments have been spontaneous. He distinguishes between *konsequent durchgegoren* and *konsequent trocken*, i.e. he fermented the wines as far as they would go and accepted if there was residual sweetness left. So the wines were more or less dry. As of 1989 *Fuder* were reintroduced and today wines are fermented in both steel and wood. 'In the 1980s many people, even friends, shook their heads,' he remembers. It turned out that Löwenstein was ahead of his time. Now the tide has turned. Despite being a VDP member, he speaks of his steep, terraced sites Uhlen and Röttgen as *grands crus*, a concept he has used since the early 1990s. 'All our *premiers crus* go into the Schieferterrassen wine,' he says. These days he is supported by Kathi Starker and Diego Rias, two young, talented and energetic oenologists. The south-south-west facing Uhlen is of grey slate with high fossil limestone content and iron-rich, sandy slate. The south-south-east facing Röttgen has a different kind of slate. The wines reflect the juicy fruit of the warmer Terrassenmosel. Daughter Sarah is poised to take over. A new winery building, their 'Kubus', quotes Pablo Neruda's 'Ode to Wine' in lovely metal letters. VDP member estate.

Try: Winninger Uhlen Blaufüßer Lay for lovely slate notes.

Weingut Knebel
Winningen
www.weingut-knebel.de

Matthias Knebel took over his parental estate in 2004 while still at Geisenheim. He graduated in 2008 and has since worked on farming his 8 hectares, of which 6.5 hectares are in steep, terraced sites, with as much respect for the environment as possible. He is a quiet and thoughtful winemaker, aiming to streamline the relative generosity of the milder Terrassenmosel into finesse. Scrupulous selection is key to the precision of his dry wines. Skin contact and spontaneous ferments along with extended lees ageing lend substance. He has parcels in Röttgen and Uhlen and manages to bottle wines of wonderful depth and purity. The wines really are too cheap for the back-breaking work they entail. VDP member estate.

Try: Riesling von den Terrassen „R" for zesty substance.

Materne & Schmitt
Winningen
www.materne-schmitt.de

Rebecca Materne and Janina Schmitt are personifications of girl power. The two youngsters, neither from a wine producing region, met while studying oenology at Geisenheim. Stints in the Mosel followed but after graduating in 2008 they initially went their separate ways to get international experience. In 2011 they decided to set up on their own in the Mosel: 'For us the Riesling here is simply special,' they say. 'The fact that everything is done by hand fascinated us; we have no choice in the steep slopes but to handle each vine.' They founded their estate in 2012 and went full-time in 2013/14. Initially they leased just 0.5 hectares, now they lease 3.5 hectares in 35 different parcels. Their aim is to reflect vintage and provenance while honing their dry style. In 2018 they were able to move to larger premises with a proper cellar. They make three village wines from Winningen, Kobern and Lehmen and three single-site wines from Lehmener Lay and Ausoniusstein and Winninger Hamm. Their entry-level Riesling is called Wunschkind. Their wines have substance and wonderful stoniness. These girls deserve every success.

Try: Winninger Hamm for tangerine and slate notes.

MITTELMOSEL

Weingut Clemens Busch
Pünderich
clemens-busch.de

Rita and Clemens Busch were pioneers when they converted their vineyards to organics in 1985 – a risky and difficult undertaking in the cool, damp pre-climate change Mosel. Since 2007 they have been certified biodynamic and have arrived at a style of utter, stony depth and salty expression. Of the 16 hectares of vineyards, their main holding is in the Pündericher Marienberg, which changes from grey, weathered slate to blue and red slate over the course of 700 metres along the Mosel. The varying parcels Fahrlay (blue slate), Falkenlay (grey slate) and Rothenpfad (red slate) express their differences beautifully and make for a fascinating side-by-side comparison. It was Clemens Busch who recultivated parcels in the Rothenpfad that had been fallow for 30 years because access was so difficult. Today the vineyard just across the river, reflected in the Mosel, provides a glorious and idyllic panorama. There is only Riesling (apart from a tiny bit of Spätburgunder for Sekt) and vines are on single stakes as Clemens believes that this gives him more even growth and ripeness with relatively little botrytis. Ferments are spontaneous in *Fuder* and the wines mature on their gross lees. Depending on the vintage, the entire gamut of styles is made but it is dry, unusually savoury wines that the Busches are famous for. The wines take their time to unfold but often show wonderfully herbal notes. Son Johannes is now also on board. VDP member estate.

Try: Marienburg Kabinett for explosive liveliness and fireworks of flavour.

Weingut Heinrichshof
Zeltingen
www.weingut-heinrichshof.de

Brothers Peter and Ulrich Griebeler decided to jack in their respective, almost corporate, wine careers in order to focus on their parental estate. They, the eleventh generation, took over in 2014 and extended their holdings from 3 hectares to 7.5 hectares. Their sites are in Zeltingen in the Himmelreich, the Schlossberg, and their top site, Sonnenuhr. Riesling accounts for 85 per cent of production, and there are small amounts of Pinot Blanc, Spätburgunder and Sauvignon Blanc. Their dry, snappy, bright and vivid Rieslings are making their names, especially in export markets. 'If you want to make good dry wine in the Mosel you have to work in the vineyard,' Peter says about their fine-tuned approach to canopy management. He is as quiet as his wines but as convincing. There are no frills here, what you get is honest and pure. The wines have ripeness and lightness in equal measure. A particular parcel in the Zeltinger Sonnenuhr called Rothlay is vinified separately and shows the brothers' talent for sinuous expression: there is a floral touch, lovely tension and utter balance. Seek them out. They are shy but totally worth it – and as so many in the Mosel far too good value.

Try: Riesling Sonnenuhr Rothlay for aromatic beauty.

Weingut Immich-Batterieberg
Enkirch
www.batterieberg.com

The little angels on the label who shoot a Riesling-bottle-shaped cannon might seem incongruous at first. But then you learn that the Batterieberg in Enkirch was created by blasting the rock with dynamite from 1841–45. This happened under the auspices of the Immich family, who owned the estate until 1989 when a consortium of investors took over. In 2009 new owners installed the experienced and talented oenologist and consultant Gernot Kollmann as a winemaker. Anything high-tech is anathema and the wines ferment spontaneously, sometimes after skin contact, in various sizes of old barrels. There are 9 hectares of old vines on single stakes in the steep sites of Batterieberg, Ellergrub, Zeppwingert and Steffensberg, all farmed without herbicide or mineral fertilizer. The wines are wonderfully transparent and clear, yet savoury and spicy. A Sekt, Jour Fixe, brimming with apple freshness, is made from 70-year-old vines and one of the entry-level wines is called Detonation. An original approach with much clarity.

Try: Enkircher Ellergrub for vivid transparency.

Weingut Sybille Kuntz
Lieser
www.sybillekunz.de

Sybille Kuntz's 17 hectares of Riesling vineyards are spread across more than 100 parcels. Seven hectares are in the Niederberger Helden and a further 7 hectares are in the Lieser Schlossberg. She, with her husband Markus Kuntz-Riedlin, is the sixth generation in her family to farm here. Sybille has made the wines since 1984 and wanted purity above all – aiming to make the opposite of the then prevalent, sweetish style. She had just 2.5 hectares then but with sheer determination she expanded her holding. Today the farming is organic which, Kuntz says, is made possible by the small caterpillar machines available now that don't compact the soil. She has worked towards organics since 1990 and became certified in 2010. Biodynamic certification followed in 2016. Ferments are spontaneous and in stainless steel; the wines stay on their gross lees until spring of the following year. While her wines state *Prädikat* levels, they have nothing in common with the styles usually understood under these terms: they are dry and have much substance. They don't immediately say 'Mosel' but have a distinct, structured, concentrated style which is particularly suited to the table.

Try: a mature Spätlese trocken for herbal savour and spicy substance.

Weingut Loersch
Leiwen-Zummet
www.weingut-loersch.de

Alexander Loersch is one of the quieter young stars of the Mosel. He joined his parents' estate in 2002 and took over fully in 2009, nowadays farming 7 hectares of Riesling, mostly in Trittenheim. One of his great achievements is the recultivation of fallow parcels in the upper part of the Trittenheimer Apotheke, known as Vogelsangterassen. 'I found these terraces fascinating and knew what quality they could bring,' he says. 'Sixty- to eighty-year-old vines were overgrown with bramble and shrub. It took two years for them to fruit again. But since then we've always harvested beautiful, tiny little grapes from the old vines up there.' Vinification is in stainless steel and *Fuder* and the wines are vivid, slender and classic.

Try: Trittenheimer Apotheke Riesling Vogelsang for weightless, expressive fruit.

Weingut Dr Loosen
Bernkastel-Kues
www.drloosen.com

Few people have done as much to revive the reputation of German Riesling as Ernie Loosen aka 'Mr Riesling'. The ebullient and articulate winery owner took over his family's estate in 1987 and has since built an enviable business. Refreshingly opinionated and energetic, he collaborates with winemakers in Australia, Oregon and Washington and always seems to be in some airport or other on his tireless travels. Yet his team, above all cellarmaster Bernhard Schug, who has worked at Ernie's side since 1988, manage to deliver great wines from a 22-hectare portfolio of historic sites including Erdener Prälat and Treppchen, Ürziger Würzgarten, Wehlener Sonnenuhr, Bernkasteler Lay and Graacher

Himmelreich. Loosen also worked to return to the dry styles that his grandfather had made, which all mature in large, old *Fuder*. Yet off-dry and sweet *Prädikate* are not neglected either. What is most impressive is Ernie's enduring curiosity: he still experiments, he still tries out new things every year. His estate-grown 'Blue Slate' and 'Red Slate' labels are perfect entry-level wines and great ambassadors for Germany. His top single-vineyard wines are up there with the best. His non-estate grown wines under the Dr. L Riesling label have spread the taste of Mosel slate far and wide in an affordable, approachable manner. VDP member estate.

Try: Ürziger Würzgarten Alte Reben GG for peachy spice.

Weingut Melsheimer
Reil
www.melsheimer-riesling.de

From his ancient dingy, dark and dripping cellar Thorsten Melsheimer brings forth luminous, fresh and expressive wines. As cramped as the tiny *Weingut* is in the confines of Reil, as glorious, precipitous and idyllic are his vineyards. In spring they are covered with tiny, sweet and aroma-laden wild strawberries because nobody has sprayed any herbicides here since 1995. When Thorsten took over at home in 1994 he started conversion to organics and as of 2013 has been certified biodynamic. Melsheimer is a man who simply does his own thing. He makes far too many wines for his 12 hectares, feeling he needs to do justice to every parcel and experiment with unusual styles. He is more relaxed about this than his distributors, who simply have to wait until the various wines are ready. In May 2018 the 2017 wines were still fermenting happily away in that cool, damp cellar. The *Fuders* are old and one Riesling, called Lentum, fermented for four years before being bottled at a smooth, light 10.5% abv. All his vineyards are within two kilometres of home in the Reiler Mullay-Hofberg, Goldlay and Burger Hahnenschrittchen. Ninety-nine per cent are planted to Riesling, with just one per cent of Spätburgunder, which makes its way into a most unusual but delicious Sekt blend of fifty–fifty Riesling and Spätburgunder. Bubbles are an important part of the business with *pét nat* and Sekt representing 20 per cent of production and natural no-sulphur wines another 20 per cent. It was not easy for this Geisenheimer to leave the textbook behind but tasting widely helped. There is nothing of the hipster about him. He acts out of conviction and made his first unsulphured wine in 2011. On another level his wines just go to show what creative heights Riesling is capable of. You get the feeling that it is Melsheimer's experience and intuition that allows him to tread such an individual path. There is something calm and centred about him and his peace expresses itself in his utterly disarming wines. A true original, and again far too good value.

Try: Cuvée Prestige Brut Nature for elegant thrill, Vade Retro Riesling for a different take.

Weingut Markus Molitor
Bernkastel-Wehlen
www.markusmolitor.com

Over the past 35 years, Markus Molitor has created one of Germany's biggest privately-owned estates. Starting out at the age of 20 in 1984 with just 3 hectares of vineyards, he now owns 100 hectares in all the best Mosel sites. What is far more remarkable, however, is that Molitor still makes all the wine himself with such exacting focus that they reach new heights every year. Only a man possessed could accomplish this. His motto is 'perfection in the vineyard, selection in the cellar.' He wants his Rieslings to be 'clear as a mountain stream, sharp as a Japanese sword.' To achieve this, a crew of up to 80 full-time staff works in the vineyards, rising to 100 at harvest. The grapes are crushed, receive skin contact and are pressed in a gentle basket press. Ferments are spontaneous and absolutely no botrytis is tolerated for the dry wines. Maturation is in old *Fuder* and bottling happens in late summer of the following year. What sets the Molitor wines apart is the absolute attention to even the minutest detail. Molitor himself emphasizes that it is his ability to select exactly the fruit needed for each style, from dry, to deliriously, nobly sweet, across his vast holdings. Nothing is left to chance. Half of his production is dry and the wines are colour-coded: white stands for dry, green for off-dry, gold for nobly sweet. Molitor has also been a pioneer in recultivating vineyards in abandoned lateral valleys and at higher altitudes. This allows him to harvest expressive, slowly but fully ripened, healthy grapes that will make a dry *Kabinett* with moderate alcohol. He loves the idea of expressing Riesling in all its myriad facets and does so with almost unparalleled clarity. The vineyards on the Klosterberg surrounding the beautifully renovated Haus Klosterberg, where all the wines are made, are a perfect example. 'We face south but turn into a lateral valley, best slate, water in the soil but a touch cooler than the sites directly on the river,' he explains. 'That is why we have tension in the wines.' He has also bought the vineyards of the former state domaine in the Saar in Serrig, and is recultivating them. 'I have made it my task to take the former Prussian domain back to where it once was,' he says, with great determination. Molitor is tireless. Together with Roman Niewodniczanski of Van Volxem he is also recultivating the Ockfener Geisberg, a once celebrated site which had been abandoned. The investment these two men are making in these viticultural monuments deserves much wider recognition. However, Riesling is not the only feather in Molitor's cap. In the late 1980s he was also one of the first to plant Spätburgunder in the Mosel, where this variety now shines on slate. Germany and the Mosel are lucky to have such energetic, active and untiring advocates.

Try: any of his elixir-like mature Rieslings, dry or sweet.

Weingut Martin Müllen
Traben-Trarbach
www.muellen.de

We are bound to hear more of this tiny 4-hectare estate with its holdings in the Kröver Letterlay, Kirchlay, Steffensberg and Paradies and the Trabener Würzgarten. These may not be world-famous sites but Martin Müllen, who set the course, and son Jonas, just about to finish Geisenheim, are crafting exquisite wines. Almost all their holdings are on traditional single stakes, the subject on which Jonas wrote his graduate thesis. The 20-hour cycles in their basket press allow a mix of free-run, macerated and gently pressed juices to come together. Ferments are spontaneous in old *Fuder*. The dedication they have for their sites becomes clear in the Trarbacher Hühnerberg, a site in a cooler lateral valley which received the highest grade in the 1897 classification. The site had fallen fallow but since 2000 has been painstakingly recultivated by the Müllens, who even managed to save some of the old vines. Most Rieslings are *trocken* with a few off-dry and sweet *Prädikate*. The wines are filigree and supremely balanced. A speciality is late-release Rieslings. Both current and library vintages are great value.

Try: mature Trarbacher Hühnerberg for ethereal chamomile and balm-like softness.

Weingut Paulinshof
Kesten
www.paulinshof.de

The contemporary buzzword 'sustainability' attains real significance when you realize that the first mention of this estate, a grange of the St Paulin Kirche in Trier until 1803, was in the year 936. The Jüngling family have been in charge since 1969 and farm 10 hectares of vineyards across 50 parcels in the Kestener Paulinshofberg, Paulinsberg, Herrenberg, Brauneberger Kammer (their *monopole*) and Juffer Sonnenuhr. Christa Jüngling says 'the vineyards are like family members'. Depending on vintage, whole-bunch pressing can be so slow that it constitutes skin contact; the juice is then sedimented and fermented spontaneously whenever possible in both stainless steel and *Fuder*. These wines are not the lightest; they have wonderful substance and depth, but are sinuous and subtle. They reveal their depth slowly and have a lovely savouriness. The predominantly dry styles, Christa says, are not purely a stylistic decision. Their well-ventilated sites allow for long ripening and healthy grapes so dryness is almost prescribed by the site. Great value and tons of charm.

Try: Brauneberger Kammer trocken for zesty citrus, extract and tangerine spice.

Weingut Axel Pauly
Lieser
www.wein-pauly.de

Axel Pauly came on board his parents' estate in 2004 and took over completely in 2009. He not only gave a new look to the labels, he also forged ahead with a clear-cut, stony style of dry Riesling that quickly found success, especially abroad. He pursues a snappy, pristine direction and calls his entry level wine 'Purist'. Axel worked in France, California and New Zealand but comes across as homely, almost rustic, although his wines are anything but. 'I do not want opulence,' he says as he pours his Tres Naris dry Riesling, which is bone-dry and taut, 'I want concentration but no fat.' He has 9.5 hectares in total and his main site is the Niederberg-Helden but he also has parcels in the Lieser Schlossberg. Axel has a soft spot for Pinot and farms both Früh- and Spätburgunder, which is aromatic, smoky and gorgeous – he has planted more, which has yet to come to fruition.

Try: Tres Naris Riesling trocken for utter refreshment.

> ### Mechanization equals salvation
>
> That steep-slope viticulture is back-breaking work is no surprise. In the past, mechanization was simply impossible. The second half of the twentieth century brought some relief with lighter machinery that could be hitched to a winch at the top of a slope – as long as there was access – while monorails, or *Monorackbahnen*, as they are called in German, at least facilitated easier access and transport. But the work remained cumbersome and intensive in terms of labour and cost. Mosel winemaker Axel Loersch reckons that one hectare of mechanized viticulture on flat land takes between 300–500 hours of labour per annum which can be reduced to 200 hours per year in purpose-planted vineyards. A partially mechanized steep vineyard where some machinery is pulled by winch takes around 1,000 hours per year while purely manual labour in a steep vineyard takes 1,500 hours per year. The advent of small, vineyard-specific multi-functional tracked vehicles, aka mini caterpillars, over the past decade has revolutionized steep-slope viticulture. While the machines, at roughly €150,000, are not cheap, they represent a huge leap in productivity and worker safety. Even very steep slopes can now be mechanized – without unduly compacting soil. Technical progress really has revolutionized viticulture here and ensures its survival. 'Without these caterpillars my vineyards would not exist,' attests Roman Niewodniczanski of Van Volxem, while Christian Ebert of Schloss Saarstein sees them as 'the salvation of the *Steillagen*'.

Weingut Joh. Jos. Prüm
Wehlen
www.jjpruem.com

For many, this estate embodies Mosel Riesling like no other. A visit is akin to a pilgrimage, a tasting in the genteel salon with its view across the river of the Wehlener Sonnenuhr a pinnacle of wine culture. Few have defined what Mosel stands for like this estate, both pre- and post-1971. The Prüm family, which has lived in the area since the twelfth century, were able to purchase vineyards when Napoleon secularized all church- and aristocracy-owned land to the left of the Rhine. Jodocus Prüm built the sundial in Wehlen in 1842, as well as the one in Zeltingen, which give their names to the respective vineyards. There are various Prüms in the Mosel, but it was Johann Josef Prüm who founded the estate in 1911. He was the first to live in the lovely villa in Wehlen that still houses the estate. J.J. made his name with the stellar vintage of 1921. His grandson Dr Manfred Prüm and great-granddaughter Dr Katharina Prüm run the estate today. Both hold doctorates in law but have dedicated their lives to the running of this iconic estate. Manfred took over in 1969 and was joined by Katharina in 2005. The estate does not really make dry wines but the Prüms play the entire *Prädikate*-scale with virtuosity. Selective, successive harvests are key and by now also very old vines. All ferments are spontaneous. It is especially in maturity that these wines shine with ethereal, other-worldly elegance and time-defying youthfulness. The style is marked by unusual continuity that lets Riesling shine in the concentrated facets of varying degrees of sweetness. They are not for drinking early, on the contrary. The longer you keep them, the more marvellous they get. This is true for great and lesser vintages which often surprise with crystalline clarity. They own 20 hectares in the Wehlener Sonnenuhr, the Graacher Himmelreich, the Bernkasteler Badstube and the Zeltiner Sonnenuhr. Their wines are monuments to Mosel wine culture, from the lightest *Kabinett* to the sweetest TBA. VDP member estate.

Try: a mature Wehlener Sonnenuhr Auslese from a cool vintage.

Sankt Laurentius Sekt
Leiwen
www.st-laurentius-sekt.de

Klaus Herres had slowly and quietly made a name for himself with Sekt, long before the current Sekt renaissance. His Sekts have been served at the official residence of the German Federal President, Schloss Bellevue, in Berlin, for the past twenty years. He was not given much choice when it came to taking over his parents' estate in Leiwen, 'those were different days,' he says. His home village was twinned with Mesnil-sur-Oger in one of those European village *jumellages*, and a visit from the Champenois gave young Klaus an idea. He explored, learned and experimented, making sure his short stints of work experience in Champagne were as intense as possible. He took over his family business in 1975, started making Sekt in 1978/79 and bottled his first serious Sekt in 1982. His base wines, however, were Riesling, which poses quite different challenges in vinification to the champagne varieties, so his learning curve was steep. Since then he has fine-tuned every aspect of his Riesling Sekts and has also added more traditional sparkling varieties. Ninety-five per cent of production is sparkling. He farms 6.5 hectares in Klüsserath, Köwerich, Piesport and Leiwen but also buys in grapes. Initially there was just Riesling, which still represents 45 per cent of plantings, and has now been joined by Weissburgunder, Spätburgunder, Chardonnay, Auxerrois and Elbling. His wines and local specialities are available at the Sektstuuf wine bar next door.

Try: Grande Cuvée Sponti Riesling Sekt Extra Brut – from ancient vines – for creamy freshness.

Weingut Schloss Lieser
Lieser
www.weingut-schloss-lieser.de

While the actual building of the Schloss Lieser has been fully refurbished and opened as a hotel in summer 2019, Thomas Haag has made wines in the adjacent *Weingut* since 1992. He and his wife Ute were able to purchase the estate in 1997 and have since turned it into a shining star – not only of the Mosel but of Germany. Despite being the elder son at the famous Fritz Haag estate in Brauneberg, where his younger brother Oliver is now at the helm, Thomas, along with Ute, started from scratch here. Receiving some of the family vineyards after his father's retirement helped. Today they farm 22 hectares and their sites are in Lieser and Brauneberg, amongst them the Niederberg-Helden, and the Brauneberger Juffer and Juffer Sonnenuhr as well as parcels in the Piesporter Goldtröpfchen, Wehlener Sonnenuhr, Graacher Himmelreich and most recently also in the Berncasteler Doctor. Grapes are harvested in several stages and undergo the strictest selection. The wines are fermented spontaneously and mature exclusively in stainless steel. Haag has mastered dry, off-dry and nobly sweet styles equally well and in a blind line-up of *Grosse Gewächse* from the Mosel, his always stand out with utter brilliance. If acid thrill excites you then this is an estate for you. Purity, precision, luminosity and spine-tingling completeness are the hallmarks of his style. Daughter Lara and son Niklas plan to carry on their parents' work. VDP member estate.

Try: Lieser Niederberg Helden GG for inherent coolness and blazing citrus.

Weingut Selbach-Oster
Zeltingen-Rachtig
www.selbach-oster.de

Barbara and Johannes Selbach are in the process of slowly handing over to their children, Hannah and Sebastian. The estate is known for its enduring dedication to the *Kabinett* style which is made with much conviction. The family owns 22 hectares in the Zeltinger Sonnenuhr, Schlossberg and Himmelreich, Wehlener Sonnenuhr, Graacher Domprobst and Himmelreich. Old vines, often on their own roots, dominate in their holdings and allow them the successive, staggered harvests necessary to produce a range of styles. 'Slate, coolness and clarity,' are the declared aims of Hannah Selbach. The wines are made in *Fuder*, *Halbfuder* and stainless steel and remain unfined. The beauty here is the inherent balance, from dry to sweet. The wines sit on a knife's edge with their sugar–acid precision. Exceptional value. A new tasting room on the river has been open since 2018.

Try: a mature Zeltinger Himmelreich Kabinett.

Weingut Witwe Dr. H. Thanisch, Erben Thanisch
Bernkastel-Kues
www.thanisch.com

This is one of the two estates resulting from the division of the Dr. Hugo Thanisch Weingut founded in the 1880s. The other is Weingut Witwe Dr. H. Thanisch, Erben Müller-Burggraef, also in Bernkastel-Kues, which was sold to a corporate group in 2018 but continues to make expressive Riesling and Spätburgunder. But back to this estate and its elegant classical riverside villa built in 1884. Current owner Sofia Thanisch took the helm in 1996 to continue a female tradition that has existed ever since her great-grandmother Katharina Thanisch took over the running of the estate following her husband Hugo's premature death in 1895 – when it was named Weingut Witwe, or widow, Thanisch. The German phrase *klein aber fein*, small but exquisite, is apt for this 9-hectare estate, with holdings in the legendary Berncasteler Doctor vineyard on whose wines the estate's fame is founded. There also are parcels in the Berncasteler Badstube, Lay and Graben with vines of up to 60 years old. The Doctor vineyard is special: With 3.21 hectares it is tiny – and was allowed to remain so even after the 1971 law decreed a minimum size of 5 hectares for vineyards – although it took a lawsuit to achieve this. Snow melts first in this incredibly steep south-southwest slope, water is abundant in the vineyard and its Devonian slate is so weathered that there is very fine soil as well as stone. It truly is one of the most famed sites in the entire Mosel. This historic allure means that most of the wines are exported. The Rieslings here are of infinite finesse, possessed of an almost supernatural lightness that dances like an aromatic chiffon veil in the breeze. Some of the wines are dry but the main style is off-dry. The wines really are far too affordable for what they are. Excellent value. VDP member estate.

Try: Bernkasteler Doctor Kabinett Feinherb for the merest caress of Riesling.

Weingut Daniel Twardowski
Dhron
www.pinot-noix.com/de

Daniel Twardowski's cellar might be of unprepossessing concrete in a ramshackle 1960s building but it serves his purpose well. His is an unusual project: to my knowledge this is the only estate in the entire region solely focused on Spätburgunder. Twardowski's family moved to the Mosel when he was a teenager, so wine began to figure early. He part-financed his studies by trading in old vintages of investment-grade wines and is still a rare-wine broker today. The love for Burgundy was thus established so why not grow his own wine? What was supposed to be a hobby became serious intent. Everything was to be the best for this bijou project. Vines were sourced from Burgundy, but the first plantings in 2005 fell victim to winter frost. The next lot of *fin* and *très fin* Pinots in 2006 took, and there are 3 hectares of Spätburgunder on the slate soils of the steep Dhroner Hofberg today. Yields are tiny. His approach is unashamedly Burgundian. His brokering connections give him access others can only dream of. They also allow him to purchase used barrels from illustrious Burgundian domaines. The wines ferment spontaneously and age in the cold, dripping cellar. His wines almost have cult status, and tasting through the barrels is wondrous. Twardowski gambled when he pitched his first release in 2011 at €70/bottle but his fine Spätburgunder was convincing. He makes one wine only and it usually sells out. It is a lovely, aromatic, serious but sinuous Spätburgunder – if you can get your hands on it. In 2018, a more generous vintage, there might be a second wine.

While the Mosel stands for Riesling, it does have an almost forgotten history of Spätburgunder. Twardowski's project set an important accent and is a clear statement. The world has taken note. The x in the wine's name is not a typo: it alludes to the walnuts, i.e. *noix*, that birds drop onto the hard slate to crack them.

Try: Pinot Noix for elegance and depth.

Weingut Nik Weis St Urbans-Hof
Leiwen
www.nikweis.com

Daniela and Nik Weis are the third generation of the Weis family to run the estate founded by Nik's grandfather in 1947 with vineyards that had been in the family for centuries. With 40 hectares of holdings in Mosel (17 hectares) and Saar (23 hectares) they offer Riesling's full spectrum, from dry to sweet, in classic, well-defined, brilliant styles of textbook Riesling. Each site shimmers with personality and expression. It is a wonderful place to explore the thrilling differences between the valleys: pitching the Leiwener Laurentiuslay against the Ockfener Bockstein, whether as GG or as *Auslese*, is eye-opening. After presenting a consistently impressive ten-year vertical of the site, Nik Weis managed to have the historic Layet vineyard in Mehringen classified as *Grosse Lage* and produced his first GG from the site in 2017. 'Our vintages are so different but that is exactly what I want to show,' Nik says about his wines, as he articulately explains every nuance of his sites. When he took over at home in 1997, he set his sights even higher than his father had and targeted export markets, such as the US and Asia. Nik Weis is also successful with his Riesling brand Urban which is made from bought-in grapes at a separate facility. Apart from making fabulous wines, the Weis family have also played a decisive role in preserving Riesling genetics via the vine nursery that has always been part of the estate. Today, in the capable hands of Hermann Jostock, many cuttings from ancient, ungrafted Riesling vines are selected, tested, propagated and preserved. Without the Weis nursery this genetic diversity would have been lost. Today they offer various clones and selections that Weis likens to a 'Noah's Ark of Riesling'. VDP member estate.

Try: since it is impossible to decide, both Ockfener Bockstein and Leiwener Laurentiuslay.

Weingut Weiser-Künstler
Traben-Trarbach
www.weiser-kuenstler.de

In 2005 psychotherapist Alexandra Künstler and winemaker Konstantin Weiser started their *Weingut* from scratch on the steep slopes around Enkirch. 'We came because there is very pure Riesling in the Mosel. When we arrived, it was easy to get your hands on super steep parcels. People thought we were crazy,' Alexandra remembers. Today they have

4.2 hectares in Enkirch, Traben, Trarbach and Wolf and are a team in vineyard and cellar. They deliberately chose to farm parcels with single-staked old vines to get the kind of Riesling they want. This however also meant making their lives difficult with tiny, unreliable yields. And if this wasn't challenging enough, they worked organically from the start and received certification in 2017. Yet what they craft is of an unusual, elixir-like purity. The wines ferment spontaneously in wood after skin contact. The dry Rieslings are bone-dry at very moderate alcohol levels: the Wolfer Sonnenlay Kabinett trocken 2017, for instance, came with 2 grams per litre residual sugar at 10.5% abv. This is the essence of the Mosel, captured with honesty. For some, this style is controversial, but I believe it allows us to understand both Mosel and Riesling better. Great value.

Try: Enkircher Steffensberg for ultra-light, intense saltiness.

SAAR

Weingut Cantzheim
Kanzem
www.cantzheim.eu

This bijou *Weingut* owned by horticulturists Anna and Stephan Reimann represents the contemporary Saar. A new destination like this shows how far the region has come and what its future may hold. The winery building, guesthouse and home, set on an idyllic riverbank between the towering Kanzemer Altenberg and an old arm of the river Saar, is a 1740-built Baroque manor that they restored in a fitting, contemporary style. Anna's father had bought the old manor long before anyone knew they would make it their family home, but the decision was made to create an upscale wine and gastronomy destination for the Saar in this lovely spot. There are as many visitors for the architectural details as for the wines. After the couple rescued a small plot of old vines as a hobby, Anna became the driving force and started tending 2 hectares of old vineyards in the Saarburger Fuchs site in 2015. Today there are 6 hectares across Fuchs, Kanzemer Sonnenberg and Altenberg, Ayler Kupp and Wiltinger Klosterberg. Their first proper vintage was in 2016 and the five-bedroom guesthouse opened in the same year. For the energetic, entrepreneurial Anna running her own business and *Weingut* is 'a dream come true'. It is too early to speak about wine style but the first wines, charmingly called Gärtner and Gärtnerin for the dry and off-dry versions respectively, show that tautness and finesse are central. A wonderful and promising addition to the Saar.

Try: Gärtner Riesling for slender, bright refreshment.

Forstmeister Geltz-Zilliken
Saarburg
www.zilliken-vdp.de

Despite its name, this 1742-founded estate deals with wine rather than forestry. The nineteenth-century title was added for esteem – today it is the very fine wines that are the foundation of the family's fame. Dorothee Zilliken took over from her father Hans-Joachim, or Hanno, Zilliken in 2016. Hanno, who had taken over from his father in 1981, is still involved today. Once you realize that their only holdings are 11 hectares of Saarburger Rausch and 1 hectare of Ockfener Bockstein, both classified as *Grosse Lage*, you understand why everything they do is informed by utter finesse. The south- and south-east-facing Saarburger Rausch rises to 295 metres at inclines up to 75 per cent. Its Devonian slate has inclusions of volcanic diabase. Rausch, in this case, does not refer to intoxication (as the name suggests in German) but to the sound of the stones as you clamber over them. The Ockfener Bockstein, framing Ockfen and facing south-south-east, south and south-west rises steeply to 320 metres and is of Devonian slate. Only a quarter of Zilliken's production is of dry wines, another quarter is off-dry or *feinherb* and half is nobly sweet. Zilliken refers to the phenomenon of Riesling's expressions in these unique sites as 'infinite and weightless'. One element that has a distinct influence on the indeed weightless style, regardless at what *Prädikat* level, is their cellar. Dug very deep, it remains at a constant 10°C and wet. Water drips from the ceiling, which is covered in little stalactites. Old and new *Fuder* are lined up, the new ones being seasoned for Riesling with a mix of spent lees and water for a number of years. The moisture is so high that wine does not evaporate, and the barrels remain wet and full year-round. The angels thus go thirsty but do not seem to mind. Zilliken emphasizes that the minimal oxygen-exchange the wines experience in barrel is thus even finer than elsewhere. The style Dorothee and Hanno aim for is 'utmost finesse with the lightest impression. We want intensity and length but the wines must be weightless.' This, they say, goes for an entry-level Riesling as well as a TBA. Despite farming just two *Grosse Lage* sites, they embrace the VDP pyramid, with several harvests in the vineyard constituting everything from *Gutswein* to *Grosses Gewächs*. Their wines are like veils of scented fruit and freshness. Ten, twenty, thirty or even forty years have nothing on them, they just get finer and finer. Get your hands on these treasures. VDP member estate.

Try: any version of Rausch at all.

Weingut Peter Lauer
Ayl
www.lauer-ayl.de

Florian Lauer is the fifth-generation winemaker at this 1830-founded estate, where his parents and sister Katharina are all involved. Their 11 hectares are all around Ayl: Feils, Sonnenberg, Scheidterberg, Rauberg, Schonfels, Lambertskirch and Ayler Kupp. The differences between the sites, like the fact that the Feils is on the river and benefits from solar reflection but the Kupp does not, are key to the interpretation of style. 'We allow the sites to be the conductor, we are the musicians who try to play what they prescribe,' Lauer explains. What he does, however, borders on sorcery. The wines have incredible thrill, both dry and sweet, and here is just one analytical example to make the mind boggle: a barrel sample of a 2017 Kupp Kabinett at 7.5% abv had 56 grams per litre of residual sugar and 11.3 grams per litre of total acidity. The citrus aromas can only be described as iridescent and of uncommon intensity, a marvel of lightness and sharpness. To exploit the different thermic properties of these vessels, dry wines are vinified in wood, off-dry in fibreglass tanks, sweet *Kabinett, Spätlese* and *Auslese* in stainless steel, BA and TBA in glass. Dry and off-dry wines make up 80 per cent of production; the remaining 20 per cent are nobly sweet. The Lauers have also made a name for themselves with their exquisite, late-released Riesling Sekts. It was Florian's grandfather who started this family tradition of making Sekt base and laying the wines down for a long time. Recently disgorged vintage releases in 2019 were Sekt Réserves from 1984, 1992 and 1994. These are most unusual, intense and arresting wines with unbelievable freshness. The younger Sekts are made from vines grown at the windy, cool ridges of the Lauer vineyards. They are usually harvested last, as late as November, when they are fully ripe, still totally healthy but with a very low pH – and an ideal base for expressive Sekt. Yet another marvel of what Riesling can do – especially in Florian Lauer's hands. VDP member estate.

Try: a dry GG or one of those late-disgorged Sekt Réserves.

> ### Steep slope viticulture
>
> The law of the Federal State of Rheinland-Pfalz, which includes the regions Pfalz, Rheinhessen, Nahe, Mosel and Ahr, defines vineyard steepness. A *Hanglage*, or sloping site, has a gradient of 15–30 per cent; a *Steillage*, or steep site, has a minimum gradient of 30 per cent while a *Steilstlage*, a very steep site, must have an incline of at least 50 per cent. Steepness has a direct effect on viticulture: sunlight reduces in intensity as the angle at which it hits the ground reduces from 90° to zero due to the longer distance, and a slope will compensate for this. The effect is not marked in midsummer but is significant towards the end of the growing season. Riesling with its mid- to late-ripening habit thus benefits from the autumn sunlight on steep slopes – especially during the longer day length in autumn at higher latitudes. Slopes are usually well-drained but also have higher soil moisture evaporation in summer and are prone to erosion.

Weingut Egon Müller
Scharzhof
www.scharzhof.com

Egon Müller V is the quiet but constant *éminence grise* of Saar Riesling. He lives at the Scharzhof outside Wiltingen, at the foot of the Saar's most iconic vineyard, the Scharzhofberg. It was his great-great-grandfather Johann Jakob Koch who purchased the estate and parts of the vineyard from the French Republic in 1797. Before secularization, the Scharzhof had belonged to the Benedictines of St Maria ad Martyres in Trier. When the hillside was cleared to plant vines is not certain, but it may not have been as long ago as previously supposed. In any case, at least part of it was planted to vines in the seventeenth century – the rest of it was used to grow *Lohhecken*, or oak shrub, for use in tanning. From then onwards the wine's quality was evident – reflected in the prices it fetched. To this day no other German wine has so consistently fetched such stellar, record-breaking prices. Scharzhofberger won first prizes at the World Exhibitions in Paris (1900), St Louis (1904) and Brussels (1911) and historic sources are littered with the name. All this happened under the auspices of Egon Müller I (1852–1936) whose success allowed him to build the current Scharzhof manor, in the 1880s.

What makes this 28-hectare vineyard stand out is its unusually finely weathered soil of Devonian slate, its water availability and the combination of steepness, fully south-facing exposure and constant ventilation. This ensures long, slow ripening. Comparing Scharzhofberger Riesling from various producers, both dry and sweet, is fascinating – and wine style is determined to a large degree by viticulture. To this end, Egon Müller still has many vines on single stakes, especially his oldest, ungrafted, parcel planted from 1895–1905. He owns 8.2 hectares of the Scharzhofberg and produces off-dry and sweet wines only. 'If you are convinced that a vineyard does one style especially well, then you are compelled to produce that style,' he says. Does he believe that the best Scharzhofberg wines are sweet? 'Empirically speaking, yes.' Having trained in the Rheingau, Bordeaux, California, and Japan, the Geisenheim graduate returned home to work alongside his father in 1985. He took over in 1991 and has seen the Saar's fortunes turn. Historically, the estate has exported most of its production and is no less than a German cult. The Le Gallais estate in Wiltingen with its *monopole*, Wiltinger Braune Kupp, is also part of Müller's portfolio. He also produces Riesling under the Kanta label in Australia's Adelaide Hills and cooperates with Château Belá in Slovakia. If you are lucky enough to have a Scharzhofberger or Braune Kupp, don't open them before at least a decade of bottle age.

Try: a mature vintage of Scharzhofberger Kabinett.

Weingut Stefan Müller
Konz-Krettnach
www.weingutmueller-saar.de

Stefan Müller is the third generation to run his family estate in this lateral Saar valley. It was not until 1983 that the family started specializing in wine. Today Stefan and his partner Johanna Lapinski farm 10 hectares in Krettnach and Niedermenning and have quickly won plaudits for their pristine, vivid style, which Müller describes as 'very light, honest. I aim for acidity; a bit of sweetness and low alcohol and all my work is geared towards this. We try and return to the "honest" *Kabinett* wines,' he says of his zesty, light-footed, dancing Rieslings. He also has a tiny bit of Spätburgunder, on a calcareous parcel of the Krettnacher Altenberg, which gives pure and lithe Pinot. The Rieslings, above all, deserve your attention. A young winemaking couple we are bound to hear a lot more of.

Try: Riesling Krettnacher Altenberg Trocken for perfumed zestiness.

Flurbereinigung

This unwieldy German term describes the reorganization and rationalization programmes conducted in German vineyards over the past 60–70 years. The ongoing division of vineyards according to *Realteilung* and Napoleonic law had led to a fragmentation of holdings that left many growers with scattered and tiny parcels of vines that made efficient farming impossible. Without proper roads and often just narrow stone paths, access was often difficult too, and made use of machinery impossible. Pre-1950 photographs of Mosel vineyards or the Rüdesheimer Berg (below) give an idea of just how difficult it must have been. Commune-sponsored *Flurbereinigungen* that redistributed farmers' holdings fairly and created proper access for tractors was a huge improvement. Of course, this was not always handled sensibly. The Kaiserstuhl in Baden, for instance, saw the creation of so-called 'monster terraces'. In some regions, this also led to varietal change as old vines were grubbed up and replaced with supposedly better-yielding and more efficient varieties and clones. So while *Flurbereinigung* was necessary to counteract the extreme fragmentation, it also had some unintended consequences.

The Rüdesheimer Berg in the Rheingau before Flurbereinigung *in the 1920s*

Weingut von Othegraven
Kanzem
www.von-othegraven.de

The Kanzemer Altenberg rises monumentally behind the beautiful mansion and its park. Reaching 250 metres of altitude and facing south-south-east, it looks vast both from a distance and close by and forms the chief holding of the estate. Set up in the sixteenth century this VDP-founding member received a new lease of life when Günther Jauch, a popular German TV personality and distant relative of the owning family, took over the estate in 2010. Jauch and his wife Dorothea live in Potsdam but you can find them opening bottles and pouring wine at tastings. The day-to-day work at the estate is in the hands of Swen Klinger and Andreas Barth. Othegraven owns 8.5 hectares of the heartland of the Kanzemer Altenberg and the remaining holdings are in the Ockfener Bockstein (2.5 hectares), the Wiltinger Kupp and the 4 hectares *monopole* of Wawerner Herrenberg (16 hectares in all). Klinger explains how he and Barth, both at the estate since 2004, have gradually stopped using herbicides, botryticides and insecticides and started fermenting wines spontaneously in 2006/07. 'Every year there's a step up,' Klinger says. Wild flowers have returned to the vineyard and in the cellar the wines are given 'time to unfold, to become themselves.' The wines have a certain restraint which makes them rather elegant. VDP member estate.

Try: Kanzemer Altenberg Kabinett for floral spice.

Schloss Saarstein
Serrig
www.saarstein.de

A little steam engine puffs a white cloud as it speeds past Schloss Saarstein and its vineyards, which slope steeply down to the Saar river. The illustrator for the 1921 wine label deemed it necessary to signal the easy transport links of this relatively remote region with its famous Riesling wines. Christian Ebert revived this old label, taking in the view from the Schloss, and very little has changed. Schloss and vineyards, a 9-hectare *monopole* site, are entirely recognizable, the building crowning the hill in an almost French setting of a château surrounded by vines. While the estate was built in the early twentieth century, it was Ebert's father who bought it in 1956, as a resettled farmer from the east and who managed, in 1976, to get the estate readmitted to the VDP. *Flurbereinigung* (see box, p. 144) meant that Ebert could add a little more vineyard on the Serriger Antoniusberg, where he grows Pinot Blanc, Pinot Gris and Auxerrois alongside Riesling, bringing his holdings to 11 hectares. The *monopole* Schloss Saarstein vineyard faces south-south-east, turns west and rises to 220 metres at inclines of up to 70 per cent. The soil is mainly of grey Devonian slate and brings forth nervy, fine Rieslings. Ebert exports up to 60 per cent of production and aims for a 'crystal clear' style. He achieves this with strict fruit selection and by strongly clarifying his Riesling musts. While this mostly necessitates cultured yeasts for fermentation, he also experiments with wild ferments and sometimes blends the resulting wines to great effect. One-hundred per cent stainless steel underlines the racy style. He relishes playing off Saar acidity with varying levels of residual sweetness – as elsewhere in the Saar, when juxtaposed with 9 grams per litres of acid, 20 grams per litre of sugar seems to disappear. The mature vintages are of enviable lightness. VDP member estate.

Try: a mature Schloss Saarstein GG.

Weingut Van Volxem
Wiltingen
www.vanvolxem.com

When Roman Niewodniczanski, scion of a brewing family and former management consultant, bought this old Wiltingen estate in 1999, nobody could have guessed what an enormous boost his major investment would give to the region, or what a renaissance it would unleash. His mission was singular and clear from the beginning: to return Saar Riesling to its historic glory. Niewodniczanski had amassed a collection of historic menus and wine lists, researched old literature and knew exactly what the almost forgotten potential of these once world-famous sites was. With unfailing determination, focus and drive, he started realizing his vision of creating exceptional, dry Saar Riesling. 'I want ripe, extroverted fruit; I want something voluptuous and seductive in that fruit. At the same time – and this is the most important point – I place the highest importance on lightness and digestibility,' he says. 'This is the real, great strength of the Saar: the ability to achieve high aromatic ripeness at the lowest possible alcohol. You don't get this anywhere else.' The estate director and oenologist who painstakingly has to put all this into practice, masterminding vineyards and cellar, is Dominik Völk. His task is not made any easier by the fact that all the estate's 80 hectares are on steep slopes. They include the Wiltinger Scharzhofberg, Volz and Gottesfuss, Kanzemer Altenberg, Wawerner Goldberg and Ockfener Bockstein. Niewodniczanski spent time, effort and money piecing together a substantial 14-hectare swathe of the Ockfener Geisberg as a recultivation project, together with Markus Molitor. An imposing and physically towering figure, Niewodniczanski speaks with rare articulacy but also with a determination that brooks no dissent. To crown the achievement of having made Van Volxem the biggest Saar estate, he built a new state-of-the-art winery to exacting logistical and environmental standards. While the wine has been made there since 2016, the upper part of the building, housing tasting rooms and offices, blends beautifully into the landscape and was inaugurated in summer 2019. The wines are made in time-honoured fashion with spontaneous ferments in stainless steel and wooden casks made of oak from Niewodniczanski's family's forests in the Eifel mountains. He plans to age Rieslings for a number of years in tank and barrel, as in the past, to make library releases. In the years since his arrival Niewodniczanski has moved mountains and set impetus after impetus. He frames the fortune of Saar Riesling over the past 120 years as 'the discrepancy between unbelievably rich history, great potential and abysmal catastrophe. So much lay fallow. Viticulture had almost bowed out. Today it is in the progress of recovering from this crisis.' He has played and is still playing a key part in its recovery. VDP member estate.

Try: Kanzemer Altenberg GG for chiselled brilliance and salty depth.

RUWER

Karthäuserhof
Trier-Eitelsbach
www.karthaeuserhof.com

Founded in 1335 by Carthusian monks who cleared the hill, the Karthäuserhofberg, to plant vines, this estate is an object lesson in marginality. In the lateral Eitelsbach valley of the Ruwer, just before it joins the Saar in Trier, this south-facing *monopole* of Devonian slate has never been split. While in the same family's hands since Napoleon's administrators sold it to the highest bidder in 1811, there have been ups and downs and ownership changes within the family. Now under a new management team, there is renewed energy for this ancient estate.

Renovation and restructuring envisage a wine destination, rather than the sleepy estate it is now. The Karthäuserhofberg with its 18.8 hectares is diverse enough to make very different styles of Riesling, and winemaker Sascha Dannhäuser is about to do justice to the great site potential once again. Parcels of the Karthäuserhofberg have been replanted and in order to expand, the estate has bought further vineyards in the Ruwer valley. Director Julia Lübcke hails the inherent coolness and raciness of the Rieslings. The name of their entry-level dry Riesling is apt: Schieferkristall, or slate crystal. Should you wonder why the bottles only ever sport a neck label, apparently a former owner liked to cool his Riesling in the Eitelsbach and putting the label on the neck prevented it from being washed away. VDP member estate.

Try: Riesling Schieferkristall Kabinett trocken for lightness and freshness.

Maximin Grünhaus Weingut der Familie von Schubert
Mertesdorf
www.vonschubert.com

Few estates evoke such beatific smiles of cherished Riesling memories as this ancient jewel of the Ruwer. Its first mention dates to 633 when it was gifted to the Benedictine Abbey of Sankt Maximin in Trier. Roman vine knives and shards of amphorae found in the vineyard suggest that viticulture here is even older. All vines are on the fully south-facing slope of the Grüneberg – just a little of its south-east-facing corner also planted to vines. The slope is divided tellingly according to clerical rank: the 14 hectares of the Abstberg on predominantly blue Devonian slate is the steepest part. It continues in the slightly less steep 19 hectares of the Herrenberg with more red slate and turns around to the south-east-facing single hectare of the Bruderberg on blue slate, the coolest vineyard. Abbot, canons and lay brothers thus all had their different wines from this monumental slope. The *monopole* remained in the abbey's possession until Napoleon's secularization in 1802 and has been in the hands of the von Schubert family since 1882. The wines ferment spontaneously in both stainless steel and wood, made from oaks grown on the Grüneberg. Maximin Grünhaus is synonymous with Riesling – and anyone who is lucky enough to have tasted older vintages will testify to the longevity of these brilliant, racy, luminous wines – from dry to sweet. Dr Carl von Schubert who ran the estate from 1981 and is still fully involved also planted Spätburgunder in the Abtsberg, a first little parcel in 2007, another one in 2011 – which gives elegant, sinuous reds. He has always been a thoughtful guardian of a *Weingut* that has always clung to superior quality – no matter what the rest of Germany did. He handed over to his son Maximin von Schubert in 2014. Few estates can compare in terms of history, even fewer with their wines. Maximin Grünhaus is a cultural monument, a rare treasure, and so are its thrilling Rieslings. VDP member estate.

Try: any mature Riesling.

Above: The steep vineyards of the Ahr, looking towards the east, where the Ahr river runs into the Rhine.

Below: Some of the 'monster' terraces created by *Flurbereinigung* on Baden's Kaiserstuhl.

Above: Schlossberg vineyard with Festung Marienberg, in Würzburg on the Main (Franken).

Below: Lorelei on the Rhine, the rock that launched a thousand poems (Mittelrhein).

Opposite: Hessische Bergstrasse – a vinous idyll in summer.

Above: One of the numerous sundials in the vineyards of Mosel.

Below: The dramatic upper Nahe.

Above: View onto the Rhine plain from Pfalz vineyards.

Below: Saale-Unstrut vineyards hugging the hillsides.

Above: Steep Rheingau vineyards in winter.

Below: The vineyards of the famous Liebfrauenstift in Worms (Rheinhessen).

Above: The manicured vineyards of Schloss Wackerbarth in Sachsen.

Below: Steep slopes on the Neckar in Württemberg.

Riesling at every stage of ripeness: all were picked on the same day, 18 October 2018, in a parcel of Clemens Busch's Pündericher Marienberg vineyard in the Mosel. This explains why selective harvesting, in vineyards where such conditions can occur, is key.

13
NAHE – TRIUMPH AT LAST

Someone quipped that defining the Nahe region might have been the only positive thing that came out of the 1971 German wine law. Indeed, its current outline was not defined until 1969 and its wines were usually sold as Rhine wines. Today we know the region as the home of some of the most dramatic, breath-taking and spine-tingling Rieslings, but despite a long viticultural history, until the late 1980s the region struggled with both climate and identity. Named after the river Nahe, which rises in the Saarland and runs into the Rhine at Bingen, the region is sheltered by the mountain ranges of the Soonwald, Binger Wald and Hunsrück to the north-west and the Nordpfälzer Bergland to the south-west. It is only open towards Rheinhessen and the Mainz Basin in the east where north-easterlies can bring cold spells. At a latitude of 49.8°N it is thus dry, cool to mild, and sunny. What marks the region out is its exceptional diversity of soils. This is down to the heterogeneous geology of the Saar-Nahe Basin with its volcanic activity and diverse Devonian, Carboniferous and Permian formations. Here you will find different slate formations, quartzite and volcanic rhyolite, porphyry and melaphyr as well as Tertiary sediments of gravel, sandstone and loam. Some of those rocks are dramatic like the Rotenfels, at 327 metres the highest sheer rockface between the Alps and Scandinavia; a truly breathtaking site and one of the Nahe landmarks. Underneath it is the Traisener Bastei, Germany's smallest *Grosse Lage* with 1.44 hectares. It is the Nahe and its lateral valleys of Glan, Alsenz, Ellerbach, Guldenbach and Trollbach that form the vineyard slopes. Along its course, the westernmost stretch of the Nahe valley around Monzingen can seem like the back of beyond, while the stretch from Schlossböckelheim and Bad Münster am Stein is winding and dramatic, opening up towards Bad Kreuznach, where it also gets a little warmer. Winemakers note that there can be a vegetative difference of two weeks between upper and lower Nahe.

Viticulture has Roman origins and documentation starts in the eighth century, when the large abbeys in Lorsch and Fulda recorded donations of vineyards in the area. Viticulture was widespread and a *Landesordnung*, or ordinance, from 1594 prohibited the planting of vineyards on land that could be used for edible crops. But like elsewhere the horrors of the Thirty Years' War wreaked devastation. 1669 marks the first mention of Riesling in the region: a contract orders the planting of 200 Riesling vines each year to restore war-damaged vineyards near Burg Layen. In 1688 the clearing of two hillsides near Langenlonsheim was permitted on the condition that only Riesling be planted. But these are exceptions. Most vineyards were field blends of Elbling and other more reliable croppers. As of 1794 the area was occupied by the French and from 1798 was part of the Département Rhin-et-Moselle. After Napoleon's defeat and the division of his territories during the Vienna Congress in 1815, the area was awarded to Bavaria and Prussia. The river Nahe marked the border between the Bavarian Kurpfalz in the south and Prussia in the north; the ornate Luitpold Bridge in Niederhausen is a pompous reminder of that. While the Bavarian king did not concern himself with viticulture in his distant province, the Prussians created one of their state domaines in Niederhausen-Schlossböckelheim in 1901. Records from 1907 show that more than half of Nahe vineyards were planted to field blends, but by 1921 that had shrunk to a third. Of the seven leading *Weingüter* listed for the Nahe by Frank Schoonmaker in his 1957 book on German wines, only the *Staatsdomäne*, resplendent today as Gut Hermannsberg, is still in existence. All the others folded. Tim Fröhlich of Weingut Schäfer-Fröhlich says that unless you do absolute justice to the top sites, bottle absolute quality and achieve commensurate prices, you cannot survive – and exacting vineyard work is expensive. In his view it was the creation of the *Grosse Gewächs* category in 2002 that really helped Nahe turn a corner. It had taken visionaries like Helmut Dönnhoff, Armin Diel and Fröhlich himself to keep the faith in the steep sites alive, but the GGs, Fröhlich says, 'brought a new focus' to the top sites of the Nahe, something that had not been possible in the 1980s and 1990s. It was also more difficult to ripen Riesling in the 1980s and the upper reaches of the Nahe were traditionally a source of Sekt base wines.

Pitched between Mosel, Rheingau and Rheinhessen, Nahe Rieslings are taut, expressive, sometimes marginal but always slender. There are certain parallels to the Saar where thrill, clarity, focus and poise is concerned. There is a disproportionate number of Riesling world stars in the Nahe. They do not make wine for beginners – there is a steely edge to the best of them; an utter, uncompromising purity that wows true Riesling lovers. The coolness of the climate – Helmut Dönnhoff of the eponymous estate says, 'we are cooler than the Middle Mosel and significantly cooler than the Rheingau, especially in the upper reaches of the Nahe' – chiefly spells one thing: acid. This also allows for Rieslings with residual sweetness – wonderful high-wire acts teetering deliciously between laser-acid and swirling clouds of fruit. The top estates are so exacting that their single site wines and GGs are monuments, that many *Ortsweine* are GGs in all but name.

Administratively there is one *Bereich*, six *Grosslagen* and 284 *Einzellagen*. In 2017 there were 4,225 hectares of vines, of which 1,214 hectares were Riesling, 531 Müller-Thurgau, 425 Dornfelder and 316 hectares Grauburgunder, followed by Weissburgunder, Spätburgunder and Silvaner.

Wein- & Sektgut Bamberger
Meddersheim
www.weingut-bamberger.de

Ute and Heiko Bamberger live and breathe fizz. It was Heiko's father who stopped delivering to the co-op in 1968 and started bottling his own wines. He also kick-started Sekt production with the traditional method in 1984. Young Heiko was always in tow, and had to come along on Champagne trips to translate. This was by no means the trendy idea it is today, because by then the idea of proper German Sekt was almost dead – and yet, there was the memory of the big Sekt houses sourcing their base wines in these cool reaches of the Nahe. You can taste this long experience in their hand-riddled Sekts, especially those without dosage. Sekts are made from Riesling, Pinot and even Gewürztraminer (surprisingly, this works). Age has nothing on them: on the contrary, the older Sekts are the way to go, so look out for late-disgorged releases. The fizz is so captivating that one might overlook the still wines, chiefly from the Meddersheimer Altenberg (red sandstone, Riesling and Spätburgunder) and Rheingrafenberg (red sandstone, white Pinot varieties), with Riesling from the Monzinger Frühlingsplätzchen. Heiko points out a fundamental turnaround: when he took over from his father in 1993, 85 per cent of production were wines with residual sweetness; today 90 per cent are dry. The Rieslings have a gentle side that both counters and parades their vivid freshness, they are a kind of cool comfort, not showy but convincing. The Bambergers release their Réserve category of Riesling only with some bottle age. All the wines are exquisite value.

Try: any of the zero dosage Sekts for enlivening freshness.

Weingut Anette Closheim
Langenlonsheim
www.anetteclosheim.de

Anette Closheim grew up as the fourth generation of a wine family and studied wine business and commerce. She left for the big, wide world working with premium spirits before heeding the call of her home vines. In the end, making wine and being her own woman trumped corporate structures. Rather than taking over at home, she works alongside her father and both do their own thing. His is the typically wide varietal offer while Anette has a tight, modern portfolio. Her first vintage of 2008 immediately marked her out as a young talent. Alongside the star attraction of Riesling she offers Weissburgunder, Sauvignon Blanc, Spätburgunder and red cuvées, including promising Cabernet Franc. The wines are clean-cut, aromatic and structured. A brand-new tasting room and event space makes this a real destination, showcasing an exemplary, contemporary take on an old, half-timbered building.

Try: Loirista, a subtle, oak-aged Sauvignon Blanc.

Weingut Dr. Crusius
Traisen
www.weingut-crusius.de

The Crusius family can trace their history in Traisen back to 1576. It was in the 1950s that they turned their attention fully to wine and marketed in bottle rather than bulk. Amongst their enviable portfolio of sites is the Bastei vineyard, perched between the Nahe river, a narrow road and the Rotenfels, a 327-metre sheer rockface. Both rockface and vineyard are of rhyolite on this exceptionally warm site. But they also have parcels in the Traiser Steinberg and Mühlberg (both porphyry) as well as in the Schlossböckelheimer Kupfergrube and Felsenberg (porphyry and melaphyr) and various lesser sites. Brigitta and Dr Peter Crusius, who took over in 1981, are now joined by their daughters Rebecca and Judith. Riesling comprises 60 per cent of their 22-hectare portfolio; the rest is made up of various Pinot varieties, Auxerrois and even a bit of Grüner Veltliner. Both wood and stainless steel see action. The Riesling wines are smooth and mild, the Pinots nutty and slender. The further up the Riesling scale you go, the more thrillingly steely they become. VDP member estate.

Try: Riesling vom Fels – mild, creamy and scented.

Schlossgut Diel
Rümmelsheim-Burg Layen
www.diel.eu

Few winemakers have as illustrious an education as Caroline Diel – both formal and informal. Not only did she grow up with a father who combined journalism with the management of his wine estate and published an annual German wine guide, she worked *stages* at Toni Jost (Mittelrhein), Robert Weil (Rheingau), Dr Deinhard and Rebholz (Pfalz), Ruinart (Champagne), Rippon (New Zealand), DRC (Burgundy), Vergelegen (South Africa) and Schloss Halbturn (Austria) before and after studying in Geisenheim. Her father, Armin Diel, took over his family's estate in 1987 and turned the *Schlossgut* into a groundbreaking estate that pioneered site-specific, dry Rieslings. He became regional VDP chairman and was both an influential and a controversial figure. He cast a long shadow, but Caroline has emerged as a thoughtful, exacting winemaker with a clear vision of what she wants to do. She joined the home estate in 2006 and took over fully in 2017. 'I changed a thousand little things in many small steps over the years,' she says. 'I think I have made the wines more authentic, more mineral.' Her top sites are in the Trollbachtal, a lateral valley of the Nahe, and include the south-facing stretch of Burg Layener Schlossberg and the Dorsheimer Pittermännchen, Goldloch and Burgberg. These make strikingly different Rieslings, smoky initially but revealing luminous fruit in their taut, tense structure. All the site-specific wines are made in *Stück* and *Doppelstück*. Skin contact and spontaneous ferments are the rule. Caroline's intuition shows even more in her elegant, slightly smoky Spätburgunders, aged in used *pièces* bought from Burgundy. The top cuvée, Caroline, is concentrated but very fine-boned, pure and taut. Another speciality is hand-riddled Sekt, especially those made without dosage: vivid, superfine and dangerous tonics of vintage Riesling or Pinot. Caroline's wines are as distinctive as she is herself. VDP member estate.

Try: Goldloch Riesling Brut Nature and Pinot Noir Caroline – both are elegant and addictive.

Weingut Dönnhoff
Oberhausen
www.doennhoff.com

Helmut Dönnhoff's devotion to his vineyards is exceptional. To him they are eternal treasures representing incontrovertible truth. He counts himself lucky to be able to be their guardian and steward for a while. His love for them is apparent in his wines and their pristine purity, clarity and exquisite, crystalline tension. What makes the difference is that Dönnhoff understood this when others turned their backs on those stony slopes. His grandfather started bottling wines in the 1920s, set his sights on Riesling and the course for quality. Helmut Dönnhoff took over his parental estate in 1971 when most of the best sites still belonged to patrician estates and Müller-Thurgau started trumping Riesling for a decade. It was the structural changes of the time that allowed him to purchase some of the steep vineyards that he had admired from afar. Some of his colleagues thought he was mad buying the steep sites as they expanded their Kerner on the plain. 'I did not plan it this way, it happened,' Dönnhoff says about his site portfolio. 'I saw the door was open and I could walk through. That door is closed today. I know the stories of these vineyards and I could talk through the night about each of them. That is why I write the name of the vineyard on my bottles, their provenance, because they hold the story. And these stories are what I also want to know of other wines. That is the intrinsic value for me. Wherever I go, I want to see the vineyards.' He credits his father for leaving him a very free hand and notes that ambition developed gradually. Winning prizes early on gave him confidence. 'But I've always loved great wine and was fascinated by it.' He now runs the estate with his children, Christina and Cornelius, who has made the wines since 2007. Their 28-hectare site portfolio takes in the Nahe from Schlossböckelheim to Bad Kreuznach in a wondrous geological picture book of steep sites of exceptional personality: Felsenberg, Leistenberg, Brücke, the iconic Hermannshöhle, Dellchen, Kirschheck, Kahlenberg, Krötenpfuhl and Höllenpfad. They could not be in better hands. There also is a little Weiss- and Graubugrunder and Chardonnay. VDP member estate.

Try: any Riesling at all.

Weingut Emrich-Schönleber
Monzingen
www.emrich-schoenleber.de

Frank Schönleber explains the rise of his family's estate to the Nahe's and Germany's top with the phrase 'evolution rather than revolution.' He credits his grandfather with having a feel for the best vineyards and his father Werner, who is still involved, with his quality ethos. After stints in the Mittelrhein, Rheingau and Australia and a degree from Geisenheim, Frank took over at home in 2005 and has steadily continued the fine-tuning. There is more wood in the cellar now and most ferments are spontaneous. His main sites are in Monzingen, the Frühlingsplätzchen (red sandstone, south-facing, steep), the Halenberg (south-facing, blue slate and quartzite, very steep in places), both on the Nahe, and up on the ridge above Halenberg there is Auf der Ley (dominated by pebble and quartzite, up to 230 metres). Frank says that Frühlingsplätzchen tends towards floral, filigree styles of Riesling while Halenberg offers herbal savouriness and citrus (nettle is very apparent in a wonderful *Kabinett* made from a cooler Halenberg parcel). Notable too is the painstaking clearing and recultivation of fallow parcels in the Halenberg. The wines are very pure, plump with fruit despite their slenderness but also reminiscent of wet stone. They are incisive, zesty, clear and poised. Gorgeous stuff. The attractively priced Frühtau and Halgans Rieslings are baby GGs from his two great sites. VDP member estate.

Try: Riesling Halgans for precision and tanginess.

Gut Hermannsberg
Niederhausen
www.gut-hermannsberg.de

Founded in 1901/02 as one of the Prussian State Domaines, Gut Hermannsberg's story is a paean to Prussian determination, far-sightedness and rigour. Land suitable for viticulture was bought but had to be cleared and landscaped with the aid of explosives, partially terraced and planted. Thus the Kupfergrube and the Hermannsberg were created out of a south-facing, volcanic hillside previously covered in shrub. Vast amounts of rock were broken and soil moved. Work proved so onerous that numerous prisoners were drafted in for labour – one particularly steep corner of the Kupfergrube is still known as *Mördergrube* (murderers' pit). Quality was the aim and Riesling was planted with a high density. Plantings began in 1905 and continued as more land was made arable. Research trials, in line with the remit of the domaine, started as early as 1905. The first vintage was 1907; cellar and winery were built in 1909/10 and the project was not finished until 1914 – when different challenges loomed. It was between the two world wars that the domaine blossomed. It remained state property and was run as Rheinland-Pfalz's state domaine until 1998 by which time it had lost its aura and was sold to a private investor, who had to sell again a decade later. In 2009 Jens Reidel and his wife Dr Christine Dinse, who wrote an excellent history of the estate, bought the property with the aim of doing justice to its exceptional sites and history, a huge undertaking that requires financial muscle. They installed Karsten Peter, a most intuitive, talented winemaker who knows every square inch of these extraordinary and steep slopes. Ninety-five per cent of plantings are Riesling with a token 5 per cent of Weissburgunder and Chardonnay. Their site portfolio is enviable: 30 hectares of prime sites including their *monopole*, Hermannsberg as well as Kupfergrube, Steinberg, Hermannshöhle, Bastei, Kertz and Rotenberg (up to 350 metres!) – 24 hectares immediately surround the *Gutshaus*. The complex geological composition of these sites encompasses volcanic porphyry and melaphyr, rhyolite and different kinds of slate. New plantings in the Altenbamberger Schlossberg in the Alzenz valley are also planned. 'What happens here can only be done with Riesling,' Peter says. The wines have brilliance and power, steeliness and the chiselled elegance that stems from stony, concentrated depth. They do take their time to shine but age will not wither them, on the contrary. When the Kupfergrube GG is released five years after vintage it is still a baby. For immediate gratification there is thrilling Sekt with 20 months' lees ageing – but vintage Sekts with more age are another promise of pleasure. Riesling lovers cannot miss this jewel, now revived. VDP member estate.

Try: any Riesling at all, for clarity, purpose and thrill.

Weingut Korrell Johanneshof
Bad Kreuznach-Bosenheim
www.korrell.com

Britta and Martin Korrell literally have a piece of paradise: the Bad Kreuznacher Paradies, a south-facing slope of calcareous marl and limestone on the almost freestanding Bosenberg. One of their top Rieslings grows here, as do the Weiss- and Grauburgunder and Chardonnay grapes for their top cuvée, Steinmauer (stonewall). Of Huguenot origin, the Korrell family settled in Bosenheim in 1832. Wine became the sole focus of their farm in 1970, with 5 hectares of vines. Martin, the sixth generation, who has worked in the Ahr, Pfalz and Australia, has been at the helm since 1995. Today they farm 25 hectares, half of which are Riesling, supplemented with white and red Pinot varieties. The wines are segmented into a deliberately light, dry and easy entry-level, followed by solid, clear-cut mid-segment *Gutsweine*. Above that are the *Lagenweine* from Paradies and a Riesling 'von den grossen Lagen', a blend of four classified sites in Norheim (gravel, slate), Niederhausen (melaphyr) and Schlossböckelheim (porphyry). Then there is the oak-aged Steinmauer and XX Riesling, made from 2015 onwards, a dry, late-harvest Riesling made in a *Halbstück* to mark Martin's twentieth vintage. These punch above their price. The Spätburgunder is promising, too. Great value throughout.

Try: a mature vintage of Paradies Riesling for inherent cool freshness.

Prinz zu Salm-Dalberg'sches Weingut
Wallhausen
www.prinzsalm.de

Here there is a lovely Schloss, steep vineyards and a real-live prince: Prinz Felix zu Salm-Salm is the thirty-second generation of his family to grow vines here. They've been doing this for at least 800 years without interruption – a deed gifting wine to the church on 1 May 1219 is the first documented mention. Crucially, this donated wine was from the Felseneck, a vineyard they still farm today. As the second son, Felix was not supposed to take over the wine estate but his elder brother Constantin has enough on his hands with the rest of the family's finance and forestry business. Neither was winemaking Felix's initial choice. He was already signed up for a business degree when wine became his real calling. Stints with other estates and Geisenheim followed and Felix still is hands-on, in both vineyard and cellar. Of the 18-hectare vineyard, 11 hectares are in Wallhausen (Nahe) while 7 hectares are in Bingen (Rheinhessen). The wines from both locations are made in Wallhausen and the distance is a blessing: fruit from Bingen on the Rhine at 180–190 metres comes in two weeks before Wallhausen with its Johannisberg (red sandstone) and Felseneck (green slate) vineyards that reach up to 310 metres. These sites are predestined for Riesling, as is the Binger Scharlachberg. The Johannisberg had fallen fallow: its steep slopes were hardly accessible so a communal *Flurbereinigung* in 2006 created new terraces, allowing this ancient site to thrive again. With a family history like that sustainability is a way of life: Felix's father was a pioneer of organics and one of the first to be certified. A slow but certain change is under way, with a focus on the best sites, extended lees ageing for the wine, late release for the GGs, a dedicated Sekt focus, and replanting with their own mass-selected Riesling from a 1950s vineyard. Watch this space – and read the beautiful Bible quotes on the labels. Good value. VDP member estate.

Try: Two Princes Riesling for off-dry, juicy enjoyment.

Weingut Joh. Bapt. Schäfer
Rümmelsheim-Burg Layen
www.jbs-wein.de

Sebastian Schäfer is a complete Riesling fiend. He is in his element teasing out every nuance of his sites and excels with pristine, exciting, world-class Rieslings. The family moved from selling in bulk to bottling their own wines as early as 1921, so a certain quality ethos was ingrained. But Sebastian brought unprecedented focus and a very clear vision to his 8-hectare portfolio when he took over in 2002. He added stainless steel to the old oval 1,200-litre *Stückfässer* in his cold, old 1880 cellar so that each parcel could be vinified separately. In 2007 he implemented the VDP *Guts-, Orts-* and *Lagenwein* pyramid because he wanted to be part of that illustrious group – and duly became a member in 2013. His vineyards are in the Burg Layer Schlossberg and the Dorsheimer Goldloch and Pittermännchen. These follow from east to west along the south-facing slope of the Trollbachtal, a lateral valley of the Nahe, and are conglomerates that are made up of *Tonschiefer*, quartzite, pebbles and weathered slate mixed with loam. There is also the higher altitude Rümmelsheimer Steinköpfchen (loam, quartzite, pebbles). These are his prime Riesling sites. There are no recipes: skin contact, cultured and natural yeast, *Stückfass* and stainless steel all have a role to play in these snappy, precise Rieslings. Note that the *Ortsweine* really are declassified GGs. He professes that his heart is not in reds so the little Spätburgunder he grows is made into a *blanc de noirs* still wine, purposely made from free-run juice only and one of the best I have ever tasted – not to be compared with scores of banal *blancs de noirs* across Germany. If proper, honest Riesling is your thing, this is an address to remember. VDP member estate.

Try: Riesling Kieselstein (pebble) for crisp, clean, snappy refreshment and value.

Weingut Schäfer-Fröhlich
Bockenau
www.weingut-schaefer-froehlich.de

There are two good reasons why Tim Fröhlich's wines are absolute stars in the Riesling firmament: he is a man possessed, and has the clearest vision of what he wants to achieve. With an exquisite portfolio of sites he can afford the most stringent selection. Intuition and experience play a huge part in bringing forth such stellar, brilliant, hair-raising Rieslings. As a seventh-generation *Winzer*, Tim took over at home in 1995, knowing exactly what he wanted: 'It was not about reinventing quality, rather about going back to the roots,' he says. He seems both modest and absolutely devil-may-care determined to do his own thing. He managed, when this was still possible in the 1990s, to acquire further parcels in the steep vineyards in exchange for parcels on flat land. He went from 11 hectares to 25 hectares, almost exclusively in classified sites. He has holdings in six *Grosse Lagen*: Kupfergrube, Felsenberg, Frühlingsplätzchen, Halenberg, Stromberg and Felseneck – a panoply of volcanic and slate dominated soils. He believes that 'steep and stony' is always best. There is not much cultivation, the soil is tilled minimally to let water in. He acknowledges that he has had a head-start with 25 years of well-rotted, home-made compost of manure, pomace and shredded cuttings.

He is also the high-priest of spontaneous fermentation, which his parents already practised partially. He made a clear cut and went for 100 per cent wild yeast with his first vintage – yet he emphasizes that others make brilliant wines with cultured yeasts. No chemicals, just 40°C water is used to clean in the cellar, and the same wines return to the same steel and oak vessels year after year. He favours late harvests when nights are cool which, even in warm years, he says 'returns freshness to the wines'. He employs skin contact depending on site and vintage. Ferments should be 'slow, fine and cool'. His wines are not for the fainthearted, for they are monuments to what Riesling can be. They thrill and move, are adult stuff, stony and incisive, vivid and pure. His GGs sell out but it's worth knowing that his *Ortsweine* Vulkangestein and Schiefergestein are all sourced from GG sites and represent exquisite value. The GGs only get the oldest vines, which here means at least 45 years old. There are also some white Pinot varieties, along with some Chardonnay and Gewürztraminer, and a tiny production of exquisite Spätburgunder grown on blue slate. 'Those who love Riesling inevitably must also love Spätburgunder,' he says. You can feel it in the wine. In the tasting room stands a model of a gravity-fed new winery that will have a view of the Felseneck. It will be as spectacular as the wines. VDP member estate.

Try: Felseneck GG for utter thrill.

Weingut Sinß
Windesheim
www.sinss.de

Johannes Sinß has great intuition. He might come across as shy, but this belies his sure hand when it comes to crafting sensuous and elegant Spätburgunder. Not that his Rieslings are anything but exquisite, but his Spätburgunders propel him into a different league. His family has farmed in Windesheim in the Guldental, another lateral Nahe valley, since at least 1791. Three sites dominate the offer: Sonnenmorgen, Römerberg and Rosenberg which rise to 280 metres in their upper reaches. The Sonnenmorgen (pebble and slate) and Römerberg (red sandstone) are chiefly planted to Riesling, whereas the sand, loam and pebble soils of Rosenberg are ideal for red and white Pinots. There are plans to plant more Spätburgunder on sandstone. Johannes, who trained in Geisenheim with stints in Sonoma (Williams-Selyem) and Marlborough, took over at home in 2010 and looks after vineyard and cellar. He has now been joined by his brother Markus who will focus on sales and marketing. Riesling and Spätburgunder each represent a quarter of his 8 hectares, while Weiss- and Grauburgunder each take up 20 per cent. The remaining 10 per cent are Scheurebe and Chardonnay. 'What is a great wine?' he asks. 'Gross ist, was hier gross wachsen kann,' that is, what grows into greatness here is what is great – a clear statement that all he wants to do is express his sites honestly. He does so with rare talent. The Rieslings are precise and slender with the Römerberg showing particular herbal savour. His Spätburgunders breathe purity, transparency, depth and poise. There is also lovely Sekt.

Try: Spätburgunder Windesheim -S- trocken for pure poetry.

Weingut Tesch
Langenlonsheim
www.weingut-tesch.de

Weingut Tesch has been slap bang in the middle of Langenlonsheim, or LaLo, as the locals call it, since at least 1723. Village life, however, was too cosy for Martin Tesch who left and got a doctorate in biochemistry. It was his father's impending retirement that brought him back. Thinking that his scientific background equipped him well to take over, his first vintage was in 1997. It was not winemaking but the complete overhaul of the estate which proved to be challenging. He grubbed up Silvaner, Traminer and Scheurebe but took care to preserve old Riesling plantings dating between 1948 and 1972. Experimentation characterized the following years and in 2001 the 'unplugged' concept was born. Inspired by the MTV show of acoustic music performed without amplifiers, his Unplugged Riesling was bone-dry, uncompromising and edgy – unusual at the time. This lost him 40 per cent of his German clients. But he carried on, using the newly-opened Hahn–London Ryanair route as his export launch-pad, becoming more successful internationally than at home. Today Unplugged is exported to 22 countries and represents a whistle-clean, honest, great value Riesling. 'The grapes have to be absolutely healthy because this wine is naked,' he says. It took a while to earn plaudits at home but his approach of dry wines only, made in 100 per cent stainless steel, all screw-capped, made with his own selected yeast proved a success as public taste slowly caught up with his style. In 2014 he left the VDP of which his great-grandfather had been a founding member – on good terms – because his own concept differed so much. Music still plays a part: Tesch Riesling is served by German punk rock band *Die Toten Hosen* and at heavy metal festivals. Riesling represents 90 per cent of his 22 hectares with the rest equally split between Pinot Blanc and Spätburgunder. Next to Unplugged there are clear-cut single-site Rieslings from Krone, Löhrer Berg, Königsschild, Karthäuser and St. Remigiusberg vineyards, all with real personality and worth cellaring. 'We went the way of simplification,' he says. 'We did not try to explain at all.' Yet his convictions speak clearly in everything he does. Good value.

Try: Unplugged Riesling for strait-laced refreshment.

14
PFALZ – SUNNY ABUNDANCE

There is something inherently generous about the Pfalz. Abundance insinuates itself not only in the southerly ease that lets citrus, figs, cypresses and almonds thrive but also in the local measure for wine, the so-called *Schoppen*. A *Schoppen* glass holds 500 millilitres of wine. My request for a rather civilized '*Achtele*' (125 millilitres) was met with derision: 'Wait until you're thirsty,' came the reply. Here, where pork charcuterie has been elevated to a religion, a sunny humour prevails. Nature really has favoured this region. On the left bank of the Rhine, it stretches from the Alsace border in the south to Rheinhessen in the north. Its vineyards run along the Haardt mountains, the German continuation of the Vosges, without ever getting close to the river. This wooded north–south mountain range keeps westerly winds and rain at bay and provides the slopes for the vineyards which face the Rhine plain with its mild, warm climate. The Pfalz is Germany's sunniest region. The southern Haardt from Schweigen to Edenkoben is more rugged, with more clefts to let cool air through from the west. The northern part, known as the Mittelhaardt, is more solid, so the vineyards enjoy fuller protection – which is why historically the Mittelhaardt always held the trump cards, and the Südpfalz only came into its own more recently. But it also means that the Südpfalz has more fully south-facing vineyards created by lateral valleys. The soils are very diverse. Just like Baden, the Pfalz landscape was formed by the Upper Rhine Rift around 30 million years ago (see Baden, page 59). It pushed up the Vosges and the Haardt on the western bank of the Rhine, the Black Forest and Odenwald on the right bank while breaking and folding up stratigraphic plates. Various geological formations thus come to the surface: Devonian slate and granite, Permian rhyolite and conglomerates, Triassic *Muschelkalk* and *Buntsandstein* as well as Jurassic limestone and dolomite, Tertiary marls, sands and gravels, with some areas covered by much younger, Quaternary loess. There was also volcanic activity around the Pechsteinkopf (352 metres), between Forst and Wachenheim. Magma rose and hardened to create basalt which was quarried and even carried into the vineyards, notably the Forster Pechstein, to take advantage of the dark stone's heat retention. The most famous vineyards are in the Mittelhaardt, on a stretch that takes in picture-perfect villages with half-timbered houses and cobbled streets, starting on the outskirts of Neustadt in Haardt, via Gimmeldingen, Königsbach, Ruppertsberg, Deidesheim, Forst, Wachenheim, Bad Dürkheim, Ungstein and Kallstadt. Facing east and south-east, their soils are a mix of weathered *Buntsandstein*, limestones like *Muschelkalk*, calcareous marls, clay and loam.

Remnants of a Roman wine press in Ungstein, and various other finds, prove that vines have been cultivated here for a long time. From the Carolingian era onwards, viticulture is seamlessly documented. Vines have been central to Pfalz life ever since. What is the Pfalz region today was part of Kurpfalz, the Electorate of Palatinate, but this sounds too solid – even in the late eighteenth century there were more than forty separate sovereignties in the splintered territory. Viticulture took a slight hit from the dissolution of monasteries during the Reformation, with the Kurpfalz becoming Protestant in 1556, but the Thirty Years' War caused far more serious damage. At the end of that conflict 'vineyards and forests were covered in hedges and thorns,' and the population was decimated. Even worse was to follow as Louis XIV's French troops executed their king's order to 'brûler le Palatinat' – burn the Pfalz – to the letter during the War of the Palatinate Succession (1688–97). The vineyards lay 'ravaged and devastated'. It took a century to recover but then the French returned under Napoleon's orders and occupied the left bank of the Rhine, before annexing it. In 1798 the Pfalz thus became the French Département du Mont-Tonnerre. After Napoleon's defeat most of the Pfalz then fell to the Kingdom of Bavaria, in 1815.

At the same time, a quality pioneer emerged in the form of Andreas Jordan. His family had arrived from Savoy in 1708 to repopulate the area; advantageous marriages enabled them to found a wine estate in 1718. Under French rule – freed from the yoke of tithe – Jordan turned to quality viticulture. He drained and landscaped vineyards and built protective walls, planting single varieties rather than field blends, he introduced selective harvesting and started to produce *Auslesen*. He also bottled wine as early as 1802. The wines fetched commensurate prices and were the foundation of his reputation and wealth. He used it to assemble the prized vineyards on whose quality his own and two further estates were to be built. In 1849 the Jordan holdings were split by inheritance and created three leading estates, all domiciled in Deidesheim, all in existence to this day: Geheimer Rat Dr. von Bassermann-Jordan, Reichsrat von Buhl and von Winning (formerly Dr. Deinhard). These consistently led the way in quality. While run separately, today they are once again united under the ownership of the Unternehmensgruppe Niederberger. Their considerable investment in the estates since the early 2000s has given yet another quality boost – and turned the Mittelhaardt into some of Germany's most expensive vineyard land. But back to history. The Bavarians wanted to know the lay of their new territory and ordered a survey of all agricultural land, including vineyards, which led to the *königlich bayerische Bodenklassifikation*, or royal Bavarian land classification, of 1828. The Forster Kirchenstück vineyard received the highest ranking, closely followed by other Mittelhaardt sites. Having enjoyed civil rights under the French, the Pfalz populace resented the repressive Bavarian rule and revolutionary ideas started to brew. If you are in the area, do not miss the permanent exhibition at the Hambacher Schloss. Quite apart from the views you will have across the Pfalz from this spectacular vantage point, you can see the first ever *schwarz-rot-gold* (black-red-golden) German flag, tattered, faded and threadbare. It was raised here during the Hambach Festival on 27 May 1832, the largest political manifestation of its day, demanding not only democracy, freedom of speech and a free press but also a confederate Europe.

Pfalz wines were often sold as Rhine wines – which obscured their real origin and hindered the recognition of the region. But the Bassermann-Jordans themselves worked to change that – along with the other two of the three famous 'Bs' of the Pfalz: Bürklin-Wolf and Reichsrat von Buhl. The latter's wines were used to toast the opening of the Suez Canal in 1869. By the turn of the twentieth century Pfalz wines were recognized for their quality. The German catalogue for the World Exhibition in Paris 1900 notes the quality of both Riesling and Traminer, the latter as a 'speciality' of the Rheinpfalz, as the area was then called. Notable also is that that Deidesheim and Forst wines reached higher auction prices in 1893 than either Scharzhofberger or Grünhäuser – these Pfalz villages were at the price level of lesser Rheingau villages but still far off the prices paid for top Rheingau wines. The first half of the twentieth century then saw the devastation wreaked by two world wars. Post-war the famous Mittelhaardt estates tried to cling on to their quality while the Südpfalz developed a flourishing bulk wine market exporting wines, not abroad but to the Mosel, where they were blended to beef up the meagre and barely ripe wines of the day. Varietal statistics are revealing, too: in 1964 the most planted grape variety was Silvaner, with 6,932 hectares, followed by Müller-Thurgau with 3,577 hectares and Portugieser with 3,115 hectares. Riesling only took up 2,393 hectares and Spätburgunder does not even show up in the statistics. By the 1970s most of the Pfalz was making sweetish wines – with notable exceptions of course. The wine route of the Südpfalz, the *Südliche Weinstrasse* was derided as *Süßliche Weinstrasse*, or sweetish wine route. Lone quality pioneers like Rebholz, Wehrheim and Friedrich Becker led the way in the Südpfalz. In the Mittelhaardt even estates like Bassermann-Jordan were struggling by the 1980s – not beginning their turnaround until the mid-1990s. Estates like the Knipser emerged in unsung villages like Laumersheim while Müller-Catoir, Bürklin-Wolf and Köhler-Ruprecht kept the Mittelhaardt flame alive. Today's varietal statistics tell a different story: no other German region has as much Riesling as the Pfalz and today it is also a hotspot for Spätburgunder. In 2017 there were 23,652 hectares of vines, of which 5,877 hectares were Riesling, 2,948 hectares Dornfelder, 1,968 hectares Müller-Thurgau, 1,687 hectares Spätburgunder and 1,633 hectares Grauburgunder, followed by Portugieser, Weissburgunder and Kerner. Administratively there are two *Bereiche*, 25 *Grosslagen* and 323 *Einzellagen*.

In terms of style, the best Pfalz Rieslings fit the classical ideal of proportion. Their innate symmetry is a kind of vinous golden ratio between body, texture, substance, freshness and fruit that allows for balanced, dry wines – with that sunny, generous Pfalz charm.

MITTELHAARDT AND NORDPFALZ

Weingut Geheimer Rat Dr. von Bassermann-Jordan
Deidesheim
www.bassermann-jordan.de

Founded in 1718 and at home in Deidesheim since 1783, no other estate has had such influence on Pfalz viticulture as this one. Andreas Jordan (1775–1848) was a pioneer of wine quality: he planted single varietal vineyards on sites he had drained and landscaped, and introduced selective harvests. As of 1803 he sold wines by bottle which denoted not only vintage and variety but also site – a feat since all bottles at the time were mouth-blown. Bringing such quality to market was the foundation of his reputation and wealth, which he used to assemble an enviable portfolio of vineyards. His successors, called Bassermann-Jordan since 1883, were active local and national politicians and entrepreneurs. Their progressiveness focused on quality viticulture while their influence on the national and international stage helped to make the wines from the Mittelhaardt – Traminer as much as Riesling – famous. Friedrich v. Bassermann-Jordan (1872–1959) wrote a seminal history of German viticulture, published in 1907, while his brother Ludwig helped to shape the first German wine law of 1909. In 2002 local businessman Achim Niederberger bought the estate, which has been run since 1996 by Gunther Hauck and Ulrich Mell. They farm their 49 hectares of prime sites biodynamically and have honed a style that is now as slender as it is expressive. Each site shows personality: Pechstein, Ungeheuer, Hohenmorgen, Kirchenstück and Jesuitengarten. Rieslings are fermented in both stainless steel and wood. While 90 per cent of plantings are Riesling there is also Weiss-, Grau- and Spätburgunder, along with Chardonnay. A Pfalz institution and must-visit. VDP member estate.

Try: a mature Riesling Pechstein GG, a brooding and smoky Pfalz icon.

Weingut Bremer
Zellertal
www.weingutbremer.de

This newly revived estate is not strictly in the Mittelhaardt but on the border to Rheinhessen in a cooler valley – which comes in handy. A Pinot perfectionist is at work here. The Bremer family bought this winery in 2014 while many vineyards were still leased out, so 2015 was the first vintage. The three Bremer sisters, Leah, Rebecca and Anna, hired the seasoned and internationally experienced Michael Acker to run the business and make the wines. An old hand, with a clear idea of elegant Spätburgunder and crisp Riesling, he loves the old Spätburgunder vines on solid *Muschelkalk* and the characteristic cool breeze of the Zellertal. The wind also helps to reduce disease pressure. There is also Riesling – brisk and taut – but elegant Spätburgunder takes centre stage with different soils and clones vinified separately. Very promising.

Try: Borbach Pinot Noir for aroma, structure and bite.

Weingut Dr. Bürklin-Wolf
Wachenheim
www.buerklin-wolf.de

Bürklin-Wolf has been seminal in so many ways. Like the other two of the three famous Pfalz 'Bs' (see p. 167), Bürklin-Wolf was instrumental in creating the world-class reputation of the Mittelhaardt. Unlike the other two, Bürklin-Wolf is still in family hands. Dr Albert Bürklin (1844–1924) was a member of the Reichstag, director of the theatre in Karlsruhe, president of the Weimar Goethe Society and visionary owner of this Pfalz estate. By the mid-twentieth century, things had become a little stale but Bettina Bürklin-von Guradze took over in 1990 and set about a transformation that was well ahead of its time. Yields were lowered and grapes sorted meticulously. Wines were made in an uncompromisingly dry style and as early as 1994 the single sites were labelled PC (*premier cru*) and GC (*grand cru*), according to the Royal Bavarian Classification of 1828. In 2005 the entire estate was converted to biodynamics, achieving certification in 2008 – no small feat with a total of 85 hectares across the Mittelhaardt. Ninety per cent of that is Riesling. Their portfolio of illustrious sites includes the *monopole* of Ruppertsberger Gaisböhl, a 7.5-hectare site of clay and sandstone. Their Pechstein Riesling is the stuff of legend – and there is also Ungeheuer, Reiterpfad, Hohenmorgen and Kalkofen. Italian cellarmaster Nicola Libelli makes the wines. Riesling is whole-bunch pressed, gets no skin contact and is fermented spontaneously in *Stück, Halb-* and *Doppelstück* and stays on its lees until bottling. The wines are dry and textured, a joy, paradigms of balance that will age effortlessly. In fact, older vintages are open for tasting. Tasting fees are deducted from purchases. There is also a dedicated wine shop and bar in Deidesheim. VDP member estate.

Try: Wachenheimer Gerümpel Riesling – sheer exquisiteness.

Weingut Christmann
Gimmeldingen
www.weingut-christmann.de

Rieslings from Christmann are like balm. Though they are never loud, there is something subtle and true about them that simply gets under your skin. This might have something to do with the slightly cooler aspect of Gimmeldingen and Königsbach, which are less protected by the Haardt mountains, or results from the fact that 2012 heralded a gear change of earlier harvest and shorter skin contact. The Christmanns have farmed here for generations. Steffen Christmann, also current VDP chairman, took over in 1996 and started converting to biodynamics in 2004. His daughter Sophie has been working with him for a while and joined fully in 2018. They farm 20 hectares of which 83 per cent are in classified sites, all in prime Mittelhaardt spots, among them Königsbacher Idig and Ölberg, Deidesheimer Langenmorgen and Paradiesgarten and Rupperstsberger Reiterpfad. Seventy-two per cent of plantings are Riesling, 16 per cent are Spätburgunder (partially grafted over from Grauburgunder) and 12 per cent are Weissburgunder. For the dry wines there is no botrytis tolerance at all. Hand harvest is followed by direct pressing, overnight sedimentation and fermentation starts spontaneously with relatively turbid juice. Three quarters are fermented in stainless steel, the rest in used barrels of Pfalz oak. The wines are allowed to stay on gross lees until bottling. Sophie has a particular penchant for Spätburgunder that is evident in the wines. Together with Weingut Müller-Catoir, the Christmanns have started restoring the old terraced Vogelsang vineyard above Neustadt, a site of pure *Muschelkalk* at 330 metres. VDP member estate.

Try: Riesling Idig GG for sheer serenity.

Weingut Fußer
Niederkirchen
www.mfg-wein.de

Martin and Georg Fußer have a vision. These down-to-earth brothers share an uncommon determination and almost complete each other's sentences. Their family estate grew grapes to be sold to the co-op while their father specialized in developing agrochemicals. The sons, however, had their own ideas. Both wanted to become *Winzer*, both knew they needed to do things differently. At Geisenheim they decided to do their own thing. Armed with impressive international experience they founded their own estate in 2006 and converted part of the family vineyards to biodynamics. Their first vintage was 2007. Today they have 17 hectares while the family's remaining 14 hectares – now also certified organic after a Damascene conversion on their father's part – still go to the co-op. The brothers are rightly proud to have been invited to join the biodynamic association Respekt, a circle of world-class German and Austrian estates. Clarity and focus also mean just four varieties: 60 per cent Riesling, 30 per cent Spätburgunder, 7 per cent Weissburgunder and 3 per cent Sauvignon Blanc. With sites in Deidesheim and

Ruppertsberg, both for Riesling and Spätburgunder, they show their undoubted mettle but neither of them is satisfied: they are fine-tuning every single aspect of their work. The Rieslings are zesty and pure, the Spätburgunders show welcome tension. We shall hear a lot more from them.

Try: Deidesheimer Herrgottsacker Spätburgunder for sheer elegance.

Hirschhorner Weinkontor – Frank John
Neustadt and der Weinstrasse
www.johnwein.de

What Gerlinde and Frank John have created is a little jewel. Frank John was cellarmaster at Reichsrat von Buhl from 1994 to 2003 and helped to restore the image of the estate. He founded this estate in 2002 and harvested his first fruit in 2003. There are just 3 hectares but they have been farmed organically from day one and have been certified biodynamic since 2012. Their Riesling grows on *Buntsandstein* and is fermented spontaneously in large, old barrels, sometimes with whole berries. The Spätburgunder grows on limestone and is aged in 225- and 500-litre barrels. A special string to their bow is their Riesling Sekt of exceptional finesse, gained from long lees ageing. The vaulted cellar in their lovely 1604-built house is an ideal home for the wines to become themselves. There is no stainless steel at all. These wines are precious, pure, spicy, dry and delicious. A real find.

Try: Riesling Brut 41 for taut elegance, Pinot Noir Kalkstein for translucent depth.

Weingut Knipser
Laumersheim
www.weingut-knipser.de

In 1949, Georg Heinrich Knipser was the first in Laumersheim to bottle his own wines. His sons Werner and Volker Knipser are down-to-earth and mischievous, wearing their pioneer status lightly. Trained as scientists, both speak of their learning curves and their continuing inquisitiveness. It was in the hot vintage of 1976 that they first concentrated a Portugieser ferment by bleeding off some juice. This was a key moment in their red wine thinking. It was in 1987 that the brothers won the very first edition of the *Deutscher Rotweinpreis* (Germany's first red wine competition) with a Spätburgunder. Since then they have steadily upped their game and have had more time than most to hone their art. They never stopped measuring, experimenting, questioning and their Spätburgunder, Riesling, Chardonnay, St Laurent and Syrah are amongst Germany's best. Evolution was constant: by 1985 the entire cellar only contained stainless steel but then they returned to wood. Today both wood and stainless steel are used. Their 80 hectares include the Laumersheimer Kapellenberg (sand and gravel), Dirmsteiner Mandelpfad (loess on limestone), Dirmsteiner Steinbuckel (loess and loam on limestone), Grosskarlbacher Burgweg and Kirschgarten (both loess-loam and calcareous marl on limestone). The red GGs are released with a three-year delay but there are always library releases, too, which shine with extra depth. Their entry-level wines are a joy, even more so when you consider the price. When you ask them what they want to show in their wine, Volker answers 'shape and firmness', while Werner says 'character and personality, whether the wine is light or complex.' Now their children Sabine and Stephan are part of the team. Visit, taste and be charmed by their irreverent but warm Pfalz sense of humour. VDP member estate.

Try: mature Steinbuckel Riesling and any mature Spätburgunder.

Weingut Köhler-Ruprecht
Kallstadt
www.koehler-ruprecht.com

Yet another legendary Pfalz name. This Kallstadt estate rose to the regional and German top class from the 1950s onwards, especially through its former owner Bernd Philippi, whose family had farmed here since the seventeenth century. Philippi had worked in the US and in international wine consultancy before taking over at home in 1986 – a difficult time in Germany. He honed a dry, elegant style which was highly unusual at the time. The estate was sold in 2009 (to the American Sauvage family who also own Burn Cottage in New Zealand), and Dominik Sona, who trained with Philippi, now runs the estate. He is supported by winemaker Franziska Schmitt. The chief site in their 13-hectare portfolio is the Kallstadter Saumagen, a south-east-facing site of calcareous marl where their famous Rieslings are grown. There is also some Pinot Blanc, Chardonnay and Spätburgunder. Riesling grapes without any botrytis are crushed, getting some skin contact and long sedimentation. The fairly clear juice ferments are spontaneous in *Halbstück* and the wines stay on their gross lees for almost a year, sometimes longer. Interestingly, the *Prädikate* are not given according to must weight, but to style. Quirkily, a *Kabinett* could thus have more alcohol than a *Spätlese*. But this does not detract from the fact that the wines are a picture of textured harmony, faithful records of each vintage. Their inherent balance becomes apparent with maturity. Their Spätburgunder is a find, especially the *Kabinett* which is light-footed and snappy.

Try: a mature Spätlese trocken.

Krack Sekthaus
Deidesheim
www.krack-sekt.de

This 2015-founded Sekt start-up represents the young blood enlivening Deidesheim. Three Krack brothers run the project, together with Anna Spanier; the eldest, Christian, came up with the idea while his younger twin brothers Felix and Axel were still at Geisenheim. While this Deidesheim family always had 2 hectares of local vineyards, father Krack made his living by *Lohnversektung*, that is as a service provider turning other people's base wine into Sekt, ageing and disgorging it. Sekt was thus on the youngsters' minds. Christian and Anna still work in their day jobs while their business grows, Sekt being notoriously slow and capital-intensive. They bottled their first wines in 2011 and 2012 and first disgorged them in 2015. They use no sulphur dioxide at all in their Sekts and disgorge as and when they need. Apart from using their own 2 hectares they also buy grapes from friends. In 2017 they made 30,000 bottles. Sekt from Riesling, Pinot Blanc, Chardonnay and Spätburgunder is available. Some were aged over 30 months and all have extra brut dosage. An estate to watch.

Try: Blanc de Noirs, a creamy, classy fizz full of red apple flavour.

Weingut Philipp Kuhn
Laumersheim
www.weingut-philipp-kuhn.de

Philipp Kuhn's father started bottling the wine from his 6.5 hectares in 1954. Since Philipp joined in 1991 the estate has grown to 38 hectares, spread across Laumersheim, Dirmstein, Kallstadt and Grosskarlbach. Kuhn inherited a vast range of varieties from his father and still farms a wide range but the focus is clearly on Riesling and Spätburgunder. Kuhn loves to experiment and says it's the only way to learn. 'That is the essence.' His Riesling style is whistle-clean. Grapes are whole-bunch crushed, get overnight skin contact, are pressed and are fermented spontaneously while relatively cloudy. The first Spätburgunder vines were planted in 1988 in the Laumersheimer Kirschgarten (loess-loam on limestone) replacing a plot of Huxelrebe – Kuhn refers to this site as his crown jewel but notes that Steinbuckel is equally interesting. The Spätburgunders are fermented with a portion of whole bunches and are extracted very gently. The GGs are allowed to stay on lees for two years in 40–60 per cent new oak. While opulent on the nose, the body is graceful, sinuous and bright. He also makes a charmingly floral Blaufränkisch and a gorgeous zero-dosage Pinot Sekt. VDP member estate.

Try: Spätburgunder Steinbuckel GG for spicy elegance.

Weingut Mehling
Deidesheim
www.weingut-mehling.de

Kathrin Otte has run her family estate together with Christoph Knäbel since 2014. Her parents are still involved but the two youngsters have made fundamental changes. 'A definite move away from uniformity,' is how Kathrin describes their decisions to hand-harvest, ferment spontaneously and leave the wines on gross lees. 'Now the focus is on the sites,' she says, and so it should be with 10 hectares of enviable holdings from Forst (Ungeheuer, Musenhang) all the way south to Gimmeldingen (Ölberg, Schlössel) with prime Deidesheim and Ruppertsberg spots in between. The offer of expressive, textured Riesling is rounded out with some Muskateller, Sauvignon Blanc, Weissburgunder and a rather alluring Spätburgunder. Incredible value. Certified organic since 2014. Watch this space.

Try: Riesling Forster Musenhang and Ruppertsberger Reiterpfad Spätburgunder.

Weingut Georg Mosbacher
Forst
www.georg-mosbacher.de

The Forster Ungeheuer and Freundstück vineyards immediately abut this 1921-founded estate run by Sabine Mosbacher-Düringer and her husband Jürgen. Their 22 hectares of vineyard also include parcels in the Pechstein, Musenhang, Kieselberg and Gerümpel in Forst, Deidesheim and Wachenheim. This illustrious portfolio has turned, in Sabine's own words, into Rieslings which are 'linear, rather precise, elegant. In a Pfalz context rather slender.' They show beautiful site expression, clarity and honesty. Inspired by a trip to New Zealand, they have grown Sauvignon Blanc since 1998. It thrives in their hands and proves their open, unstuffy, even cosmopolitan approach. Great value across the board. Certified organic since 2015. VDP member estate.

Try: Sauvignon Blanc Fumé, an oaked Sauvignon Blanc from their oldest vines.

Weingut Müller-Catoir
Neustadt and der Weinstrasse
www.mueller-catoir.de

This *Weingut* is one of the most beautiful in Germany. High above Neustadt, where the town gives way to vineyards, this neo-classical villa shimmers like a *Märchenschloss*, a fairy tale palace. Its wines have written Pfalz history. Founded in 1744, the estate has been one of the leading houses of the region, its twentieth-century fame cemented by cellarmaster Hans-Günther Schwarz, who characterized a pure style from 1961 onwards. He was not seduced by all the technical progress that swept through German cellars at the time, on the contrary, he refined the time-honoured methods and presented clear-cut wines long before they were fashionable. His era ended in 2002. Since then the estate has been run by Philipp David Catoir, the ninth generation at the helm, supported by cellarmaster Martin Franzen. They farm 21 hectares all around the estate and in Gimmeldingen, certified organic in 2015. Their well-known *monopole* site Im Breumel is just across the street, a *Buntsandstein* site surrounded by a perimeter wall. While Riesling takes up 60 per cent of plantings, Müller-Catoir has a reputation for aromatic whites, too, above all for Rieslaner, a 1921 cross of Riesling and Silvaner bred in Würzburg, but also Scheurebe. 'The diversity of grape varieties forms part of the Müller-Catoir legend,' says Catoir. The dry wines have elegance, lightness and depth. Their nobly-sweet wines are indeed legendary. VDP member estate.

Try: Mandelring Scheurebe Trocken for swirling clouds of tropical bliss.

Weingut Odinstal
Wachenheim
www.odinstal.de

Odinstal lies in splendid isolation. You need to switch into first gear after the tarmac stops to get up to the Pechsteinkopf, past the picturesque Wachtenburg castle. The bumpy ride is more than worth it. Ideally placed to follow biodynamic principles, which includes farming a herd of Charolais cattle, the early-nineteenth-century villa and its 5.2-hectare vineyard (6.4 hectares in total, including vineyards in the valley) are surrounded by chestnut and oak forest. Lovingly restored by Ute and Thomas Hensel, the estate sits above the crest of the Upper Rhine Rift where volcanic activity rather than the rift itself set the Triassic layers of *Buntsandstein* and *Muschelkalk* into verticals. It's windy and cool up here and Andreas Schumann, estate manager and winemaker, is free to craft exceptional, individualistic and age-worthy Riesling. There also is some Silvaner. Everything in this idyllic spot speaks of vision and farsightedness. Odinstal has been Demeter certified since 2013 and they make all their own biodynamic preparations. The wines ferment spontaneously, mainly in stainless steel, but also in wood and amphora, and most Riesling goes through malolactic fermentation, which does not stop the wines from being thrilling. The entry-level wines are called 350NN denoting the altitude of the estate and the three top Rieslings, all from the same single vineyard, are named after their respective subsoils: basalt, *Muschelkalk* and *Buntsandstein*. Prepare to be wowed.

Try: Riesling Basalt for taut pleasure.

Weingut Pfeffingen
Ungstein
www.pfeffingen.de

The Eymael family was making wine long before Emperor Ferdinand II conferred its coat of arms in 1622. With 17 hectares of vineyards around the village of Ungstein, the estate has holdings in the Nussriegel (*Buntsandstein* and loam), the Herrenberg (limestone) and the Weilberg (Terra Rossa). Here, just outside Bad Dürkheim, where the vineyards reach further into the valley and are warmer Riesling plays the leading role, with 60 per cent of plantings. Scheurebe, with 15 per cent, takes second place, and Pfeffingen is one of the best addresses for this variety in Germany. Planted in prime vineyard since the late 1950s Scheurebe is made in dry styles using the full ripeness spectrum of the aromatic, unusual but beguiling variety. There is even sparkling Scheurebe. A *stage* in Pessac-Léognan persuaded Jan Eymael to put his Scheurebe in small oak and the result is the creamy but vividly fresh Scheurebe SP, which has been made since 2009. The Rieslings have uncommon fruitiness and generosity but are bone-dry. A wonderful combination. VDP member estate.

Try: Scheurebe SP, the most intriguing dry Scheurebe ever.

Weingut Reichsrat von Buhl
Deidesheim
www.von-buhl.de

Founded in 1849 and today owned by Unternehmensgruppe Niederberger, Reichsrat von Buhl was reenergized by new management in 2013. Hiring Champagne Bollinger's ex chef-de-cave Mathieu Kauffmann was a stellar coup and a clear signal. He runs the estate together with Richard Grosche who looks after the business side. In their sixth year now, they are hitting their stride and have set this venerable house on a new path, doing justice to its impressive portfolio: 62 hectares across Forst, Deidesheim and Ruppertsberg. Alsace-born, Kauffmann clearly relishes the opportunity to work with Riesling and pursues an uncompromisingly dry, purist style. 'Precise, linear, salty, tart, dry and yet smooth,' is what he aims for. His vision is clear and executed painstakingly. He loves fermenting and maturing in *Doppelstück* for its 'efficient contact with yeast,' and all wines of *Ortswein* level and above are made this way. The wines stay on gross lees until bottling; their release is delayed by two years. He does not employ skin contact and ferments are spontaneous. He has also set new accents across the German sparkling wine landscape with his creamy, fine Sekts, both from Riesling and from classic varieties. If they are anything to go by, the single site Sekts (e.g. Pechstein) slumbering on their lees and not due for release until 2023 will mark a new era for Sekt. Most Sekt base wines are aged in tonneaux of 500 litres. Biodynamic principles rule in vineyard and cellar. If you are looking for value, the Suez Riesling (commemorating the fact that the opening of the Suez Canal in 1869 was toasted with Reichsrat von Buhl Riesling) is a cuvée of the GG Rieslings that don't make it into the final bottling. VDP member estate.

Try: Rosé Prestige Brut for exquisite creaminess; Riesling Kieselberg GG for effortless cool.

Weingut Rings
Freinsheim
www.weingut-rings.de

Before Steffen Rings joined his home estate in 2001 and decided to switch the entire production to wine, his parents also tended orchards. His brother Andreas joined him in 2008 and the pair have steered a steady course for quality ever since, while their sister Simone takes care of the business side. Their 36 hectares are in Freinsheim, Ungstein and Kallstadt, where they grow half white (Riesling, Weiss- and Grauburgunder, Chardonnay and Sauvignon Blanc) and half red varieties (Spätburgunder, Cabernets Sauvignon and Franc, Merlot, St Laurent and Syrah) – but with almost 11 hectares of Riesling and 10 hectares of Spätburgunder their priorities are clear. 'I try to put power into my wines alongside freshness, acidity and elegance,' Andreas says about his snappy wines, which are both vivid and dense at moderate alcohol levels. All wines ferment spontaneously and benefit from extended lees ageing. As of 2017 all wines are certified organic. A new cellar, finished in 2018, will serve 'to realize new ideas'. Rieslings are made in stainless steel and oak, while Spätburgunder sees less and less new wood. Clearly the brothers are only just hitting their stride. VDP member estate.

Try: Spätburgunder Kallstadter Steinacker for linear gorgeousness.

Weingut Markus Schneider
Elterstadt
www.black-print.net

Markus Schneider disrupted the status quo – not only in the Pfalz but in Germany. When he started in 1994 with just one hectare 'and no money in the bank' he knew he needed to do things differently to succeed. And succeed he did. Today he farms 92 hectares, with an emphasis on Sauvignon Blanc. Initially he broke with every Pfalz tradition in the warm soils of Ellerstadt. He made wines in Germany that tasted as though they were from the New World, gave them cool labels and everyone flocked to his door. He is a sort of involuntary wine celebrity. His wines are called Holy Moly and Tohuwabohu. His Sauvignon Blanc could easily be taken for a Marlborough wine. Nothing he does is facile, though. An almost energy-neutral, state-of-the-art winery with sufficient storage allows him to late-release wines. While he made his name with Sauvignon Blanc and gutsy red blends, Schneider does care about his Pfalz roots and also has exacting, single-site Rieslings in his portfolio, alongside Syrah, Cabernet Franc, Merlot, Chardonnay, Malbec – and even old Portugieser vines. Schneider now also has a Riesling project in the Mosel and makes wine in South Africa.

Try: Kaitui Fumé Sauvignon Blanc for creamy freshness.

Weingut Heinrich Spindler

Forst
www.weingutheinrichspindler.de

It was during vintage in California that Markus Spindler realized 'what a treasure' he had at home. This clinched his decision to carry on his family's estate, a handsome 1770 house in the middle of the picture-book village of Forst. He represents the eleventh generation, joining in 2007 and taking over in 2018. 'We've always had a clear, fruit-forward style,' he says, and notes that 'many small changes' moved him towards 'depth, substance and more precision. Finesse is the most important thing.' His 20 hectares stretch across sites in Forst (Pechstein, Jesuitengarten, Ungeheuer), Deidesheim, Friedelsheim and Niederkirchen. Eighty-three per cent are dedicated to Riesling, the rest are other whites and a little red, which he says, does not play a big role as half of it is made into rosé wines. Depending on the year, some Riesling is foot-trodden. Ferments are in both stainless steel and wood. The wines are taut, fresh, clear and great value. Certified organic.

Try: Forster Pechstein Riesling for thrill and purity.

Weingut von Winning

Deidesheim
www.von-winning.de

Few can claim to have exploded stylistic possibility like Stephan Attmann, managing director and winemaker at Weingut von Winning. His first release in 2008 of his 2007 Riesling vinified in new oak provoked, in the words of one of his colleagues, 'a shitstorm' in Germany. Attmann had slaughtered a holy cow by putting arch-German Riesling into new wood. That this produces outstanding wines is merely testament to Riesling's versatility and Attmann's talent. However, iconoclasm was not his intention. Attmann wanted to make wines 'which shine through inner depth and extract. Yes, the oak was new but I did not want to buy used barrels. I wanted the complexity that comes from wood and higher fermentation temperatures.' Whole bunches of Riesling are crushed, have skin contact and are pressed, then ferment spontaneously in wood. The GGs are exclusively in 500-litre barrels, the rest is in 500-litre, *Stück* and *Doppelstück*. The style is sonorous and channels Riesling's freshness, while accentuating its nuanced fruit. Today, newer and smaller oak is part and parcel of Germany's Riesling landscape. Eight *Grosse* and six *Erste Lagen* are vinified separately. Apart from Riesling, von Winning has also made a name with subtle, oak-aged Sauvignon Blanc and lovely Spätburgunder – altogether there are almost 78 hectares. Von Winning is one of the three Deidesheim estates that benefited from Achim Niederberger's vision and investment. Until his takeover in 2007 it was called Dr. Deinhard but was renamed to recall the estate's heyday between 1907 and 1918. The affiliated restaurant Leopold is a must when you are in Deidesheim. VDP member estate.

Try: Deidesheimer Paradiesgarten Riesling for scented elegance.

Sekt & Weingut Winterling
Niederkirchen
www.winterling-sekt.de

Martin Winterling wanted to make wine without competing with his parents-in-law. So in 1982 the idea for Sekt was born. Germany's sparkling landscape then was a desert of tank-fermented plonk, so this was a courageous idea. The Winterling family survived by opening a wine- and soil-testing lab as they slowly developed their capital- and time-intensive Sekt business. Initially they bought in grapes, and it was not until 1997 that they were able to buy their own first vineyards. These were immediately planted with Champagne clones of Spätburgunder and Chardonnay. Today they have access to 12 hectares, half owned, half leased. The focus is still on these varieties but there is some Riesling and Sauvignon Blanc and these days daughter Susanne and son Sebastian have joined the estate. While they do make some still wine, 80 per cent of production is traditional method Sekt with an output of 100,000 bottles per annum. Hand-harvest, fractional whole-bunch pressing and long lees ageing bring forth bright, expressive sparklers with wonderfully low dosage. Their aim is to grow production and keep reserve wines, a difficult challenge with smaller vintages, but 2018 should help. Certified organic. Watch this space.

Try: Reiterpfad Riesling Sekt from old vines for light-footed typicity.

Weingut Oliver Zeter
Neustadt an der Weinstrasse
www.oliver-zeter.de

You realize right away that Oliver Zeter had a taste of the big, wide world before he decided to establish this estate 2003 with his brother Christian. While the born Pfälzer trained as a *Winzer* and worked *stages* in Italy and South Africa, he spent the next decade working as a wine importer and distributor, getting to know the vineyards of the world. 'But the *Winzer* inside me was never asleep, I was always alert,' he says. He credits his time in South Africa with his life-change: 'The wines electrified me: they had an inner density without being fat, they were vibrant. That South African Sauvignon Blanc got me,' he says. Thus he started with half a hectare, of which 90 per cent was Sauvignon Blanc. Today he farms 24 hectares, from Ungstein to Pleisweiler, of which he owns 6 hectares. While his oaked Sauvignon Blanc Fumé is particularly notable, he also makes precise, savoury Riesling, brooding Syrah (in amphora), scented Viognier and bright, slender Spätburgunder. A surprising, unconventional but imaginative and delicious portfolio. His own, apt, take on his style: 'Never fat, never kitsch.'

Try: Pinot Noir Kaiserberg, Riesling Steingebiss and Syrah.

SÜDLICHE WEINSTRASSE

Weingut Friedrich Becker
Schweigen-Rechtenbach
www.friedrichbecker.de

This is one of Germany's pioneering estates for world class Spätburgunder. It was in 1967 that Friedrich Becker senior started planting Spätburgunder in Schweigen. Becker knew that his grandfather had made Spätburgunder at the turn of the century, when Spätburgunder, Traminer and Grauburgunder were the most expensive wines in the area. Becker also knew that the Kammerberg (across the border in Alsace) had been a prized site of the once very powerful Kloster Weissenburg, a Benedictine abbey. 'In the 1960s and '70s he had often visited Burgundy where the limestone soils are similar to ours,' his son Friedrich junior recounts. 'But in the 1960s from a business and financial point of view this was not a good decision. Fellow villagers thought he had lost his mind.' Not only did Becker plant Spätburgunder, he insisted on doing so in the Kammerberg, where nobody thought it would ripen. At the time the locals preferred the flat sites in the valley as they generated higher yields. It is Becker who recultivated the limestone site that rises to 250 metres which is on French soil but a German *Grosse Lage*. He started bottling his own wines in 1973, leaving the co-op bit by bit. Friedrich senior wanted to make wines like his grandfather had, 'but it took a very long time until he could support his family doing that.' He supplemented his income with pig farming and a vine nursery. Experimentation with 228-litre barrels started in the early 1980s. These new-oak-matured wines had to be sold as *Landwein* until the mid-1990s, so outlandish did they seem to the officials during the *Amtliche Prüfung*. But Friedrich persevered. These days his son Friedrich junior (whose first vintage back home was 2005) makes the wines. Their GG sites are on the Sonnenberg, through which the German–French border passes: they are all limestone dominated (*Muschelkalk*) and south-facing: Kammerberg, Sankt Paul and Heydenreich. The fruit is destemmed and crushed but a portion of stems is often added back and extraction is gentle. They mature in small oak for between 16 and 24 months and Friedrich junior says 'There is no recipe at all.' These wines take time to develop, even if they are not released until four years after the vintage. The *Erste Lage* wines from Steinwingert and Herrenwingert are more approachable. There is also Riesling, Chardonnay, Grau- and Weissburgunder across their 29 hectares. VDP member estate.

Try: Pinot Noir Steinwingert for smoky, svelte elegance.

Weingut Jülg
Schweigen-Rechtenbach
www.weingut-juelg.de

Johannes Jülg's vineyards in Schweigen straddle the border with Alsace. The 20-hectare estate was founded in 1961 by Johannes' grandparents; before that the grapes went to the co-op. It was grandfather Oskar who insisted on dry wines and it was Johannes' father Werner who started planting Spätburgunder in the early 1990s. There is still a hangover of too many grape varieties but the sights are now set on Riesling and Spätburgunder. The latter are of impressive elegance and once you realize that Johannes trained with Keller and Stodden, and at Clos des Lambrays you understand why. The vineyards are on *Buntsandstein* and calcareous marl and include the Schweigener Sonnenberg and Kammerberg (both limestone, up to 240 metres and 250 metres, respectively). When asked to express his style, the laconic winemaker says he wants his wines to show 'provenance, precision, acid and elegance'. Weissburgunder lovers will also be in heaven here. Great value.

Try: Spätburgunder Kalkmergel for vibrant juiciness.

Weingut Jürgen Leiner
Ilbesheim
www.weingut-leiner.de

Jürgen Leiner, who founded this estate a little over 40 years ago, was amongst the first in Germany to farm organically. His son Sven, who runs the estate today, switched to biodynamics and was certified in 2011. On 16 hectares he farms Riesling, Grau-, Weiss- and Spätburgunder as well as Chardonnay. He makes both conventional and natural wines – in a pure, lithe style. 'There are always possibilities,' this thoughtful young winemaker says, as he dreams up skin-fermented blends of grapes that bring forth an almost freaky saltiness or a scented *pét nat* of Scheurebe and Silvaner. It is with Sekt that he follows the most interesting and individual path. Oak-fermented reserve wines from two previous vintages are blended with fermenting, fresh must without addition of sugar or yeast and are sealed for a traditional bottle fermentation. They stay on lees for two years and emerge as very fine, super-salty brut nature Sekts of beautiful depth.

Try: Sekt 14 15 16 Brut Nature for linear freshness and depth.

Weingut Meier
Weyher
www.wein-meier.de

Georg Meier is hard-working and understated. His family estate is down to earth, in an almost self-deprecating Südpfalz fashion, but real vision shines through. This was, after all, the first estate in the village to have a proper cooling system installed in 2004. Georg joined his parental estate in 2005 after training with some of Germany's best. His Rieslings speak so much louder than he does: they are clean-cut, concentrated, steely and pure, expressing soil and site. He farms 17 hectares in Weyher, Burrweiler, Hainfeld and Rhodt. Seven hectares are dedicated to Riesling, the rest to Grauburgunder, Scheurebe, Müller-Thurgau, Weiss- and Spätburgunder as well as Merlot, St Laurent and Cabernet – a hangover from that mid-twentieth century vision of having something of everything. The offer is categorized as *Basis*, *Guts-*, *Orts-* and *Lagenwein*. The village wines, separated by soil types, already show a clean delineation of *Buntsandstein*, Rotliegendes, Granit and Schiefer. There is short skin contact, long sedimentation and fermentation in both steel and wood, with both spontaneous and cultured yeasts. The *Lagenweine* are from 30–40 year-old vines and are impressive, especially the Steinwerk Riesling, grown on granite and fermented in granite. Watch out for this promising youngster. Great value.

Try: Steinwerk Riesling for racy purity and thrill.

Weingut Oberhofer
Edesheim
www.weingutoberhofer.de

Young Pascal Oberhofer is well-placed to be ambitious. His parents own 25 hectares of vineyards in sites surrounding Edesheim, and run a small wine bar in the village. Pascal graduated from Geisenheim in 2018, trained with great German and Austrian estates and now has set his sights on bringing more drive and tension to his parents' conventional, softer wine style, and moving the entire outfit up a notch. The sandy loam soils of Edesheim favour Pinot and aromatic varieties in this regard. He and his family have big plans, also building a flash, new winery. The Oberhofers are the keepers of Germany's supposedly oldest vineyard, tending three rows of 400-year-old Traminer vines in the Rosengarten vineyard in the village of Rhodt. In 2016 the vines yielded grapes for 571 half bottles (375 millilitres) of Traminer *Spätlese*. The wine is poised, concentrated, balanced and creamy. But Pascal also works on zero-dosage Sekt and juicy Spätburgunder. Certified organic since 2011.

Try: Rhodter Rosengarten Gewürztraminer Spätlese, to drink history.

Weingut Ökonomierat Rebholz
Siebeldingen
www.oekonomierat-rebholz.de

Wine has been made in this family since 1642 but it was Eduard Rebholz, grandfather of Hansjörg, the current owner, who turned the estate into one of the leading lights of the Südpfalz. He favoured sites with poor soils that few others wanted; today these vineyards are the most prized. Hansjörg and Birgit Rebholz are no less progressive, and converted the estate first to organics and then biodynamics, with certification in 2008. Their 22 hectares across Siebeldingen, Birkweiler and Frankweiler include the Siebeldinger Im Sonnenschein, a site of *Muschelkalk* with its special gravel parcel Ganz Horn, and the Birkweiler Kastanienbusch a south-facing rhyolite elevation of up to 320 metres. But there are also sites on *Buntsandstein*. Riesling and Spätburgunder have equal top billing here, with Weissburgunder taking third place.

There is also Silvaner, Chardonnay, Gewürztraminer and Muskateller. Rebholz is an acknowledged master of precise, crystalline Riesling and beguilingly elegant Spätburgunder. Tasting the wines side by side shows how clearly every site is delineated. Even his estate Pinots unfold over their first five to seven years in bottle. Alcohol levels are moderate and purity is key. There are also delectable, long-aged, low-dosaged Sekts. Many of today's young German winemaking stars have taken in stints at Rebholz, one of Germany's leading estates. The 23-year-old Rebholz twins Hans and Valentin, still studying but already involved at home, are poised to take over. VDP member estate.

Try: Spätburgunder Förster, from 1964-planted vines, for pure poetry.

Weingut Dr. Wehrheim
Birkweiler
www.weingut-wehrheim.de

Founded in 1920 by Karl Wehrheim, this estate resolutely stuck to making dry wines. Along with Ökonomierat Rebholz, the Wehrheims were the first to sell their wine in bottle rather than bulk, from 1947 onwards, early for the Südpfalz. Karl-Heinz Wehrheim has run the estate since 1984 and his son Franz has also come on board to work alongside him. Quality seems to run in their veins since they never succumbed to planting Dornfelder or even Müller-Thurgau. Their 20 hectares, all in Birkweiler, are farmed biodynamically and are planted to Riesling, Weiss-, Grau- and Spätburgunder as well as Chardonnay, Silvaner, Muskateller and St Laurent. As early as 1976 they won a prize for dry Spätburgunder. They have 9 hectares in the Kastanienbusch vineyard alone, a fully south-facing site of rhyolite in a lateral valley, and also own part of its special Köppel parcel of *Buntsandstein*. Their slender, expressive Rieslings are destemmed and have a short maceration on skins, followed by natural sedimentation. They ferment spontaneously in stainless steel and age on their gross lees. The Spätburgunder is destemmed, getting a cold soak before fermenting spontaneously in open *cuves* before ageing in barrels made from Pfalz oak by François Frères and Stockinger. Slenderness and grace speak in every sip. VDP member estate.

Try: Spätburgunder Kastanienbusch Köppel for glorious, sylph-like juiciness.

Weingut Wilhelmshof
Siebeldingen
www.wilhelmshof.de

Barbara Roth and Thorsten Ochocki, who met in Geisenheim, joined Barbara's family estate in Siebeldingen in 2005 and took over in 2010. When her parents took over in 1975 they set the stage for sparkling wine. Both loved Champagne and both wanted to experiment, so they started with just 52 bottles – one for every Sunday of the year. Their output grew with their experience and in 1989 they bottled Germany's first *blanc de noirs* Sekt which was disgorged in 1994. Today Sekt is a firm part of the programme: all Sekts are single-vintage based and made from Riesling, Pinot Blanc and Spätburgunder. The Patina series has at least five years of lees ageing. There are 20 hectares of vines, all within 2 kilometres of Siebeldingen and Frankweiler, on *Buntsandstein* and *Muschelkalk*. Of the still wines, made from Grau- and Weissburgunder, Riesling and Spätburgunder, the reds really stand out. Good value.

Try: Patina Blanc de Noirs Brut for fine, creamy length.

15
RHEINGAU – FROM MONKS TO MERITOCRACY

'The Rhine and its vines are as inseparable as sun and light.' Thus begins Friedrich Dünkelberg's 1867 treatise on the Rheingau. While this is true for a much larger section of the river, it perfectly expresses the Rheingau's historic pre-eminence and emblematic nature. No other region has shaped the identity of German wine and therefore Riesling as comprehensively as this one. Mosel viticulture may be older; southern viticulture may be more widespread, but nowhere else can quality viticulture be traced as seamlessly as here. That nature favours this compact region is evident. It owes its existence to the Taunus mountains, which force the majestic Rhine to take a left turn on its steady south–north course from Lake Constance to the North Sea. This short stretch of river flowing east to west creates the south-facing slopes which constitute the Rheingau. It is small: from Hochheim am Main in the east to Lorch in the west is only 40 kilometres as the crow flies. Discounting the easterly outpost of Hochheim and driving from Walluf along the river to Assmannshausen you cover a mere 25 kilometres. From the riverbank to the first hills of the Taunus mountains, is a narrow band of just 3–6 kilometres where vines thrive. Enjoying the protection of the Taunus mountains to the north and benefiting from the moderating influence of the Rhine, which is wider here than at any other part of its course, predestines these slopes for the vine. The fact that the fiftieth degree of latitude runs right along the Rheingau makes it especially neat. Despite being small, the diversity of sites is great – distance from the river, altitude, aspect and the influence of lateral valleys formed by numerous almost perpendicular Rhine tributaries

(Walluf, Sulzbach, Kiedricher Bach, etc.), along with various soil types all shape a region that is anything but homogeneous. Some sites are gentle, fertile slopes, others steep, stony hillsides. The geology is diverse. At the Rheingau's western end in Lorch, Devonian slate formations dominate. In Assmannshausen, the Rheingau's historic Spätburgunder enclave, there is mica schist. The Rüdesheimer Berg, rising to 300 metres, and the elevations to its east, are dominated by quartzite; the lower-lying vineyards closer to the river are of loam, loess and clay. The notable *Brunnenlagen*, or fountain sites, of Marcobrunn, Wisselbrunnen and Nussbrunnen benefit from underground aquifers. In the east around Hochheim – which was shortened to coin the English term 'Hock' for Rhine wines – loam and calcareous marls dominate. All this happens in just 3,191 hectares of vineyard. Thus, the Rheingau was a prime spot for early settlements, positioned on the central, trans-European traffic route that is the Rhine.

Documented viticulture begins in the Carolingian era. Here as elsewhere, the church was instrumental, in this case the archbishops of Mainz, to whose powerful Electorate of Kurmainz the area belonged until it fell to Nassau in 1803. Two dates are particularly significant: the founding of the Benedictine monastery of Johannisberg in 1106 and the Cistercian Kloster Eberbach in 1136, both sites in line with their convictions: Johannisberg prominent and crowning the hill, Eberbach nestled in a forested, secluded valley. The monks cleared forest and shrub to plant vineyards and soon they were harvesting more than they needed. As early as 1162, a mere 31 years after its foundation, Kloster Eberbach owned cellars in Cologne. The abbey had its own ships and sold its wines far and wide – far more profitably than worldly merchants as the abbey did not have to pay *Rheinzölle*, the duties levied at various points on the river. It is notable that some Rheingau wines were sold under their site names very early on: Steinberg, first mentioned in 1211, and Marcobrunn, first mentioned in 1275, were amongst the first. Wine was the most important income stream for the abbey. To continue trading on this reputation demanded care in vineyard and cellar: quality viticulture was born. Economically this made sense. In 1517 vines covered only 2.8 per cent of the abbey's extended land holdings (also beyond the Rheingau) but accounted for 40.35 per cent of the abbey's income. Wine filtration through cloth is documented for 1497, isinglass for fining in 1517, sulphuring of wine in 1603. It is thus clear that the wine reputation of the Rheingau was established early. But this was not solely down to land and ready labour, to good vineyards and wines: transport and trade were equally important.

Conflict interrupted this golden wine age. Kloster Johannisberg was destroyed in the Peasants' Revolt of 1525 and dissolved in 1563. At Kloster Eberbach, Swedish troops plundered the cellars during the Thirty Years' War after the monks sought refuge elsewhere. They returned in 1635 and started repairing the damage. Viticulture remained central and various aristocratic estates made and sold wine. Since both yields and vintages were very variable, the concept of *Cabinet* wines emerged: from the best sites and vintages, these were kept separate in small *Cabinet* cellars and sold for cashflow in weaker vintages. The first documented *Cabinetkeller* dates to 1716 at Schloss Vollrads. In Kloster Eberbach's *Cabinetkeller*, first mentioned in 1730, wines aged for up to 23 years were noted as fetching higher prices. They cost at least 40 per cent more but 'after maturation between 6 to 18 years, a few particularly good barrels fetched 300 per cent more than their initial harvest price.' The premium region thus had its super-premium product: *Cabinetwein.*

The year 1716 marks another important event. Konstantin von Buttlar, Prince Abbot of Fulda bought the ruined monastery of Johannisberg, and began building a Schloss, turning his attention to the profitable Rheingau business of viticulture. He enlarged the vineyards from 14 hectares to almost 19 hectares and replaced what had been field blends with 293,950 Riesling vines in 1720/21. While historians today cast doubt on whether this was exclusively Riesling, since the abbey also bought Muscat and Orléans, this is a huge number. The fact that seedlings were available suggests that Riesling was already widely present. Vines were sourced in Rüdesheim, Erbach and in Flörsheim am Main. Stefan Doktor, current director of Schloss Johannisberg, suggests that a series of severe winter frosts starting in 1729 further cemented Riesling's regional predominance, due to the variety's relative hardiness. But still, the wines were not sold as 'Riesling', rather, as they had been in the past, as 'Johannisberger'. Slowly but surely Riesling emerged as the quality variety of the region. By 1867, Riesling covered 92.8 per cent of vineyards around Eltville, 42.4 per cent around Rüdesheim and 66.2 per cent around Hochheim. Silvaner, Orleans, Elbling and field blends are also mentioned. Riesling was planted in the best sites where it would ripen. Dünkelberg's treatise wistfully notes that due to the late-ripening nature of Riesling, 'Rheingau viticulture will always remain a lottery.' Notably, Schloss Johannisberg bottled single-vineyard Riesling as early as 1775 – when most of Germany's wine was still made by serfs from field blends. As of the eighteenth century, the story of Rheingau and Riesling are thus intertwined. When

Riesling arrived and how much it had to do with the earliest reputation of the Rheingau will remain conjecture. Occasionally botrytized grapes had been harvested[20] but it was not until 1775, when the delayed arrival of a courier carrying the permission to harvest forced a late harvest of botrytized grapes, unexpectedly yielding an 'extraordinary' wine, that the idea of selective harvesting took hold and spread. By the early nineteenth century it was common Rheingau practice and became the basis of the terms *Spätlese* (late harvest) and *Auslese* (selection).

The Rheingau's reputation was to rise further. Napoleon's pan-European antics spelled change: Kloster Eberbach was secularized in 1803 and fell to the house of Nassau. Schloss Johannisberg was given to the Austrian Emperor's minister for foreign affairs, Fürst Metternich-Winneburg in 1816. Metternich, the House of Nassau and other aristocratic estates could afford to keep an eye on quality. Their pan-European connections ensured exposure and their wines, increasingly sold by auction, fetched spectacular prices. By the mid-nineteenth century Rhine wines graced many aristocratic tables and international wine lists. After the Duke of Nassau backed the wrong side in the Austro–Prussian War of 1866, the Rheingau became Prussian. For the vineyards this was only a slight hiccup. The Ducal Domaine of Nassau at Kloster Eberbach became the *Königlich Preussische Staatsdomäne*, or royal Prussian State Domaine. Riesling was king, but with the Prussian establishment of a state domaine in Assmannshausen, Spätburgunder from that village, where it had had a presence since the fifteenth century, became Germany's only red wine with national reputation. It was suggested that a classified vineyard map should be drawn up for the 1867 World Exhibition in Paris. While the map was not published in time for the event – where Rhine Rieslings were showered with accolades – it turned out to be the first site classification of German vineyards. A historian notes that the map 'would vividly show the new lords in Berlin that they now held sway over a region whose century-old wine culture trumped everything that had hitherto developed in viticulture, including the left bank of the Rhine with its regions of Mosel and Saar.' Rhine Riesling was the best and most expensive still white wine in the world[21].

This was to remain the case until the First World War. The war and interwar years were hard. Once the Nazis assumed power, precious Rhine wines secured foreign exchange – and became popular with the totalitarian

20 Overripe/botrytized grapes were harvested in 1753, 1757 and 1760 in the Rheingau.

21 'There are no purer nor better made white wines in the world than the finer growths of the Rhine,' wrote Henry Vizetelly in *The Wines of the World, Characterized and Classed*.

elite. Post-war rebuilding was slow but the aristocratic estates (Langwerth von Simmern, Graf Eltz, Graf von Schönborn, Schloss Reinhartshausen) and the State Domaine clung on to their historic vineyards and prestige. In the 1950s they were still spoken of with awe but their wines became increasingly sweet in the 1960s and 1970s, lacking Riesling's essential spine. Relying on past glory no longer worked. The new German wine law of 1971 simply appropriated what had once been the pride of the Rheingau: the old term *Cabinet* was misappropriated into *Kabinett*; the other *Prädikate* so inextricably linked to the selective harvesting of Riesling were now a function of must weight only, no longer linked to style but to measurable sugar ripeness at harvest. By the 1980s it was hard to sell German wine at home and the Rheingau had been robbed of its *raison d'être* and spirit. The first stirrings of reborn quality came in 1984. Under the auspices of a few leading estates like Weingut Georg Breuer, Schloss Vollrads, Weingut Robert Weil and Kloster Eberbach, the Charta group was founded. It promulgated a dry style of Riesling that would go with food; an almost revolutionary idea at the time. These dry 'Charta-Wines' slowly paved the way for what were to become the *Erste Gewächse* in 1992 and the *Grosse Gewächse* in 2002. Charta was the first Riesling quality movement to emerge after Germany's glycol scandal of 1985. Robert Weil, of Weingut Wilhelm Weil, calls the founding of Charta 'a real departure' that linked quality to site rather than must weight. It was also in the Rheingau that the *Verband Deutscher Prädikatsweingüter*, or VDP, started its private classification of vineyards. The Rheingau thus always led the way in terms of Riesling. Today it is no longer alone at the top. Other regions have managed to surpass all but its best estates. The criticism still stands that too many mediocre Rheingau estates are VDP members and there are still too many vineyards whose true potential is not fully expressed. All the more reason for the Rheingau youngsters to show their mettle. When it comes to characterizing Rheingau Riesling, Wilhelm Weil of Weingut Robert Weil says: 'Rheingau Riesling is not the most delicate, fruit-exalted wine of the Mosel, neither do we reach the power of the Pfalz in this climate; but we can make absolutely balanced Rieslings that really show their site. They shy away from extremes. I see Rheingau as the most aristocratic growing region for Rieslings of finesse, elegance and shapely balance.'

Note: as of the 2018 vintage, there is a new designation of Rheingau *Grosses Gewächs*, or RGG for short, that is outside the VDP. This is possible because Rheingau is in the federal state of Hessen, where the term *Erstes Gewächs*, or *premier cru*, was written into state law as a vineyard classification. This has now been amended to *Grosses Gewächs*. RGG decrees that the wines have to be from a classified vineyard, from hand-harvested Riesling or Spätburgunder with a maximum yield of 50hl/ha. This shows how successful the VDP's strategy was in establishing this term which, ultimately, cannot legally be restricted to VDP members. How pleased the VDP is about others riding piggy-back on their achievements is another question. It demonstrates how Germany is moving, albeit slowly, towards the idea of a provenance-based idea of thinking.

Remarkably, the hectarage has been fairly constant: in 1900 there were 3,021 hectares, in 1964 2,647 hectares, in 1990 3,117 hectares and in 2000 3,219 hectares. Administratively, there is one *Bereich*, 11 *Grosslagen* and 129 *Einzellagen*. In 2017 there were 3,191 hectares of vines, of which 2,498 hectares were Riesling and 388 hectares Spätburgunder.

Wein- und Sektgut Barth
Hattenheim
www.weingut-barth.de

The Barths have been making Sekt since 1992 – but have made wine for much longer. They first started bottling, rather than selling in bulk, in 1956. In 2009 Christine and Mark Barth joined the estate, taking the helm in 2017, and have taken the Sekt to new levels. Their 20 hectares around Hallgarten and Hattenheim have been certified organic since 2013 and include the Hattenheimer Hassel, Wisselbrunnen and Schützenhaus, the Hallgarter Jungfer, Hendelberg and Schönhell as well as Oestricher Lenchen and Doosberg. Depending on site conditions, the fruit is destined either for still or sparkling wine or both. Sekt represents approximately a third of production and Mark Barth has helped to create the VDP Sekt statute. The Barth Sekt style for single-site Riesling is rich: the grapes are harvested with considerable ripeness for Sekt and thus express much varietal character, their effervescence a wonderful counterpoint to a golden roundness that is in no need of dosage. Tasting Hassel still wine and Sekt side by side is an enlightening exercise; there is also Pinot Sekt. The basic Sekts get 24 months on lees, and all are hand-riddled. This is one of the few houses that manages to make a convincing red Sekt from 100 per cent Spätburgunder. The still wines are elegant, too. Lovely tasting room. VDP member estate.

Try: Riesling Hassel Vintage Brut Nature for apricot-scented freshness.

J.B. Becker
Walluf
www.jbbecker.de

J.B. Becker is something of a cult estate for both Riesling and Spätburgunder. Founded by Jean Baptiste Becker in 1893, the estate is run today by the luxuriantly moustached Hajo Becker who took over in 1971. He has been true to his honest, clear style ever since, supported by his sister Maria and now also by his wife Eva. The wines wear no make-up, Rieslings are spontaneously fermented in large, old wood and get lots of time on lees. Becker is proud of the fact that his vivid Spätburgunders have never seen a barrique. In fact, it was Jean Baptiste who was the first to plant this variety in the eastern Rheingau, as early as 1905. The 12.8 hectares of organically farmed vineyards include the Wallufer Walkenberg, Berg Bildstock and Oberberg as well as sites in Eltville, Rauenthal and Martinsthal. Seventy-six per cent of production is Riesling, 2 per cent is Müller-Thurgau and the rest is Spätburgunder. There is something pure, bright and fresh-faced about the wines. The Rieslings go from properly light, dry *Kabinett* via *Spätlese* trocken to sweet *Spätlese*. What you get is site and vintage. The estate is known for its back catalogue. Each price list contains late releases at ridiculously affordable prices. An excellent place if you want to taste great, mature Rheingau wines. Their garden on the Rhine is open for picnickers from April to October, so long as they buy a bottle. A great spot.

Try: any of these lovely wines, white or red.

Bibo Runge
Hallgarten
www.bibo-runge-wein.de

This small, 2014-founded *Weingut* is a rather recent outfit amongst all the ancient estates, but an interesting one. Winemaking veteran Walter Bibo, formerly cellarmaster at Schloss Reinhartshausen, started with a business partner, Kai Runge, hence the name, but Markus Bonsels has since taken Runge's place. Bibo says that they are in a 'consolidation phase' with their current 4.5 hectares of vineyard (mostly Hallgarten: Jungfer, Schönhell, Würzgarten). They like making Riesling in time-honoured fashion: crushed grapes get long skin contact and go into a basket press; the juice then settles in stainless steel before fermenting in wood. Ferments are spontaneous and slow and the wines are allowed to undergo malolactic fermentation if they want. This results in textured, spicy, deeply gastronomic wines. Their small, modern cellar in Hallgarten has various barrel sizes and is distinctly low-tech. 'We are a small estate,' Bibo says, 'we don't need to copy what already exists, we just want to go our own way.' The wines are a blend of sites and are called Revoluzzer, Hargardun (old name for Hallgarten) and Romantiker, as a homage to the Romantic poets and writers who stalked the Rheingau in the early nineteenth century. They also make some lovely Sekt.

Try: Riesling Hargardun for spice and texture.

Bischöfliches Weingut
Rüdesheim
www.bischoefliches-weingut.de

Owned by the Bistum (bishopric) of Limburg and known as Pfarrgut Rüdesheim until 1985, this estate cultivates the parish vineyards of Rüdesheim and Eibingen. Most church parishes throughout the Rheingau still own vineyards, which are usually leased to local *Winzer*, but here the diocese carries on making wines. Peter Perabo, who until 2007 was winemaker at the Krone in Assmannshausen (see Wegeler, page 213) and still consults there, is cellarmaster and Pinot expert. Unassuming, he prefers to let his wines speak, and they tell of exacting work in the vineyard and cellar. The site portfolio is enviable: Riesling from the Rüdesheimser Berg Rottland, Berg Roseneck, and Berg Schlossberg Katerloch and Ehrenfels. Spätburgunder comes from Rüdesheim and the Assmannshäuser Hinterkirch. The wines are given time and true brilliance emerges. The Rieslings are crystalline, the Pinots of unusual elegance. Great value, too. The adjacent Pfarrkirche Eibingen is built on the site where Benedictine abbess and mystic Hildegard von Bingen founded an affiliate abbey.

Try: Assmannshäuser Pinot Noir 'S' for elegance.

Weingut Georg Breuer
Rüdesheim
www.georg-breuer.com

Bernhard Breuer was the dynamic modernizer in the Rheingau of the 1980s. One of his obituaries called him the 'spiritus rector' of the region. He helped to shake off the dusty image of the region with its backward-looking aristocratic estates. He had advocated site classification and dry styles ahead of his time and sadly died far too young, in 2004. His daughter Theresa runs the 34-hectare estate today and has honed a very distinctive style that unites the seemingly contradictory virtues of slenderness with textural richness and beautiful, herbal aromatics. Her vineyards are chiefly in the steep sites of the Rüdesheimer Berg and in Rauenthal – two village wines are made which show the different subsoils. Some wines are released late and show what Rheingau Riesling can be if you allow wine and winemaker to evolve. If you are after primary fruit flavours, these wines are not for you. One of the iconic Breuer wines is 'Terra Montosa', a blend of Berg Rottland, Roseneck, Schlossberg and their *monopole* Rauenthaler Nonnenberg, which has become the calling card of the estate. The entry-level wines are called 'Sauvage' and are earthy, dry and textural. The top wines are sensational. Like Theresa they have no frills, are strait-laced, come with lots of hinterland and shine with honesty. There also is sinewy, fine Spätburgunder and late-disgorged, zero-dosage vintage Sekt. An unmissable estate.

Try: Berg Roseneck Riesling for heady herbal tisane notes and endless length.

Weingut Chat Sauvage
Geisenheim-Joahnnisberg
www.chat-sauvage.de

It is courageous to dedicate a Rheingau wine estate solely to the production of Spätburgunder and Chardonnay, but that is exactly what Hamburg entrepreneur Günter Schulz did when he established this *Weingut* in 2001. Auctioning off his Burgundy collection financed the building of the winery where the one-woman dynamo that is Veronika Schöttle now makes the wines. The 8 hectares include parcels in the Assmannshäuser Höllenberg, Lorcher Kapellenberg and Schlossberg, Rüdesheimer Drachenstein and Johannisberger Hölle. The steep sites offer schist, quartzite and loess-loam soils and the wines are made in the image of Burgundy. The Pinots, with their firm and fine tannins, mature for 18 months in French oak and take a while to come out of their shell – but that is not a problem since Chat Sauvage also sells older vintages.

Try: Rüdesheimer Drachenstein Spätburgunder for grip and backbone.

Weingut Dr Corvers-Kauter
Oestrick-Winkel
www.corvers-kauter.de

This family was the envy of the entire Rheingau when, early in 2018, it received the lease of the prestigious 15-hectare site portfolio of the once grand Langwerth von Simmern estate. This comes in addition to their 12 hectares of prime sites in the Rüdesheimer Berg (Drachenstein, Roseneck, Rottland, Schlossberg) and the Assmannshäuser Höllenberg. Now they also have Rauenthaler Baiken, Erbacher Marcobrunn and Hattenheimer Nussbrunnen to complete a stellar portfolio spanning the entire Rheingau spectrum. Brigitte and Dr Matthias Corvers have been joined by their oenology graduate son Philipp who despite his youth already has international experience under his belt. The entire estate seems energized and wins plaudits for its much clearer, snappier, tauter style in Spätburgunder and Riesling. The wines are exquisitely pure and expressive. The 2018 vintage was their first with the added sites which posed a logistical challenge, but they seemed undaunted and spirited. 'We want to move ahead and have set all levers for top quality,' Philipp says. Dr Matthias Corvers had written his thesis on organic farming, the estate has been certified since 2012 and the new vineyards are in conversion. They use a basket press for Riesling and let all their juices settle naturally for 48 hours before fermentation. The wines are whistle-clean and properly dry. Their single-site wines are taut and deserve bottle age; their village wines are an ideal calling card for their elegant style. We shall hear a lot more from this family.

Try: Riesling Drachenstein for utter freshness, Assmannshäuser Spätburgunder for sheer poetry.

Kloster Eberbach – Hessische Staatsweingüter und Staatsdomäne Assmannshausen

Eltville
www.kloster-eberbach.de/weingut/

Founded in 1136 by Cistercian Abbot Ruthard in direct filiation with Clairvaux Abbey, the site had already served as a former Augustan chapter and Benedictine monastery. Kloster Eberbach is central to Germany's wine history, and exceptionally well preserved. The monks liked the secluded valley and from 1170 onwards started to enlarge the vineyard that became the famous Steinberg, a south-south-west facing slope of loam rising to 270 metres. It has been a *monopole* ever since and was first mentioned by name in 1211. Around the year 1500 the abbey owned property far and wide, extending as far as Mainz, Bingen, Oppenheim and Bad Kreuznach. It is estimated that vines only covered 3 per cent of the land but accounted for 40 per cent of the abbey's income. But prosperity would not last. The sixteenth century meant peasant revolts, poor harvests and conflicts that destroyed some of the riches. Swedish troops in the Thirty Years' War plundered not only the cellars but also the precious library. Monks did not return until 1635 and stayed until secularization in 1803, when the estate fell to the House of Nassau. Quality viticulture was revived and Kloster Eberbach became one of the stars of the Rheingau, with its Steinberg wines fetching record prices – especially those from the *Cabinetkeller*, which had existed here since at least 1730. After the Austro–Prussian War of 1866 the Dukes of Nassau lost their lands and the Ducal Domaine became the Royal Prussian State Domaine and has remained in official hands ever since. Today it is owned by the Federal State of Hessen, which runs the Hessische Staatsweingüter here at Kloster Eberbach as well as the Domaine at Assmannshausen, dedicated to the production of Spätburgunder. A new winery is dedicated to the Steinberg alone. The vineyard holdings are impressive: Steinberg, Rauenthaler Baiken, parcels in the Rüdesheimer Berg and Marcobrunn. Kloster Eberbach's unparalleled library of old vintages is a treasure. I have tasted Rieslings going back to the early twentieth century and have been blown away. They are exquisite, a testament to site and winemaking as well as to Riesling's legendary longevity. More recent vintages have lacked precision but with Katharina Puff, a young, internationally trained oenologist at the helm as of the 2018 vintage we may see the sites return to their absolute glory. In terms of German wine culture, this is a site of pilgrimage: the beautiful setting, the old cellar and the ancient architecture are a must visit. There's even something for film buffs: scenes from Umberto Eco's *Name of the Rose* were filmed here as well as trailers for TV's *Game of Thrones*. There is a wine and gift shop, a hotel and restaurant, and guided tours and concerts are also on offer. VDP member estate.

Try: Riesling Wiesbadenenr Neroberg trocken for snappy juiciness.

August Eser
Oestrich-Winkel
www.eser-wein.de

Désirée Eser, Freifrau zu Knyphausen, and her husband Dodo Freiherr zu Knyphausen run Désirée's parental estate, founded in 1759. They represent the tenth generation and are a team in vineyard, cellar and admin. They farm 11 hectares in sites from Rüdesheim to Rauenthal and have parcels in 21 illustrious sites, 17 of which are vinified as single-site wines. Ninety per cent of their plantings are Riesling plus the local curiosity Roter Riesling and some Spätburgunder. Eighty per cent of what they make is dry, but they also have a strong track record for *Auslese*. They produce two GGs but concentrate on what they call their 'mid segment' – solid and well-priced estate and village wines offering great value with clean and clear site expressions. Wines are mostly vinified in stainless steel (one-third in 40- to 50-year-old barrels). The house style is linear without being edgy: Dodo calls it 'classic' and it is. VDP member estate.

Try: Riesling Rauenthaler Rothenberg for lean, herbal zestiness.

Weingut Joachim Flick
Flörsheim am Main
www.flick-wein.de

Beharrlichkeit und Mut, tenacity and courage, is Reiner Flick's motto. This is fitting: he extended the 3.5 hectares of his family estate to 20 hectares while also renovating an ancient mill from 1318, where his estate is now based. Flick is located in the eastern Rheingau on the river Main but also has vineyards in Lorch. His chief site is the Nonnberg, with heavy argillaceous marl, prized for its water retentive qualities. Flick owns a bit of Anglo-German history. In 1845 Britain's Queen Victoria visited Hochheim – home of the famous 'Hock'. She and her German husband Prince Albert were taken to see some vineyards. In honour of the visit the then-owner renamed her favourite vineyard 'Königin-Victoria-Berg' in 1850. Four years later, in 1854, on Victoria's thirty-fifth birthday, a Queen Victoria memorial was unveiled. To this day a depiction of it graces the ultra-retro label of the Riesling – which has been served to several members of the British Royal family since. The Flick wines express the juicy ripeness of the eastern Rheingau with vivid fruit. Of his Königin-Victoria-Berg Riesling Flick says it is 'a Riesling you can give to non-Riesling drinkers,' so opulent is it with peach and stone fruit. The Nonnberg, on the other hand, shows herbal savouriness. VDP member estate.

Try: F. vini et vita Riesling, the entry-level wine, for fleshy, juicy peach.

Eva Fricke
Eltville
www.evafricke.com

Fricke's way to wine was unusual but determined. As the child of two doctors in northerly Bremen, wine was not an obvious choice, but an internship at a winery in South Africa sealed her fate. Fricke trained in Geisenheim but also in Bordeaux, Spain and Australia. It was while working for J.B. Becker in Walluf that she decided she wanted to make her own wine, and her next employment contract, with Josef Leitz, contained a clause that would allow her to do just that. She made her own first wine from the Lorcher Krone vineyard in 2006 and took the plunge of running her own estate full-time in 2011. With slow but steady investment she grew her business. As of 2019 she farms 13 hectares of which she owns 1.5 hectares outright. Her sites are around Lorch, in the western Rheingau, where quartzite-laced slate predominates. She has eschewed herbicides and pesticides since 2006, started farming organically in 2011 and became certified in 2017. She employs skin contact, slow pressing and a long, slow, cold sedimentation. The wines start fermenting spontaneously before being inoculated in stainless steel. Her wines are clear-cut, zesty and elegant. Her top sites are Lorchhäuser Seligmacher, Lorcher Krone and Schlossberg. There are some vineyards in Kiedrich and Eltvile, too.

Try: Riesling Verde for playful, citrussy lightness.

Jörnwein – Joern Goziewski
Geisenheim
www.joernwein.de

Jörn Goziewski makes wine in the Rheingau and in Thüringen, where he was born. He started his own estate in 2015 and hires a part of an old cellar in Geisenheim to make fairly off-piste wines. He has just 1.3 hectares but in exquisite sites: the Rüdesheimer Berg Rottland, Rosenbeck, Drachenstein and Schlossberg as well as the Winkeler Hasensprung and Johannisberger Hölle. He divides his time between Thüringen, where he teaches agriculture and farms a small field blend vineyard, and the Rheingau, where he does all the work himself. Some of his wines are fermented on skins in his radically low-tech cellar. He uses both stainless steel and *Stück*. The wines have individuality and backbone. A lovely, uncompromising but compelling take on Rheingau Riesling and Spätburgunder.

Try: Gutswein Riesling for orange-peel fragrance and pepperiness.

Weingut & Gutsausschank Hamm
Oestrich-Winkel
www.hamm-wine.de

When Karl-Heinz Hamm took over his parental estate he wanted to keep it small so he could do all the work himself. He started converting the vineyards to organics in 1977 and has been certified since 1990. His daughter Aurelia, a Heilbronn graduate, joined the estate in 2015 and is one of the dynamic youngsters of the region. She is clearly in her element working with the fruit from the Winkeler Dachsberg, Jesuitengarten and Hasensprung. Her younger brother Julius is at Geisenheim but the siblings love to shake things up, like starting a *pied de cuve* in the vineyard to capture native yeasts. The wine style is rounded but fresh. There is a lovely courtyard in which to enjoy the wines on summer evenings. Eighty per cent Riesling, 20 per cent Spätburgunder. VDP member estate.

Try: Riesling Ortswein Winkel Alte Reben for lovely balance.

Henkell Freixenet
Wiesbaden
www.henkell.com

Henkell is a powerhouse of global fizz. It was founded by Adam Henkell in Mainz in 1832 and has produced Sekt since 1856, at the time exclusively from French base wine. It cemented its place in the late nineteenth and early twentieth centuries through innovative, at the time ground-breaking, marketing. Consolidation meant that Henkell now owns many of the big German Sekt names, e.g. Kupferberg Gold and Söhnlein Brilliant, allowing it to service all market segments. The Henkell Group, privately owned by the Oetker family, owns Alfred Gratien Champagne, Gratien & Meyer in the Loire, Freixenet in Spain, Mionetto in Italy and numerous sparkling wine houses in eastern Europe and Scandinavia. It also runs and has stakes in various distribution companies across the globe – it really is one of the world's sparkling wine giants. As a jewel in the crown it also owns Schloss Johannisberg (see page 203). Initially the entire production was bottle-fermented, but in the 1960s Henkell was amongst those who pioneered the Charmat method. They will not release production figures but their 48-million-bottle storage capacity gives you an idea. Its main brand in Germany, the high-volume Charmat-method *Henkell trocken*, made from European base wines, is the market leader in 'premium' Sekt, i.e. retailing above €6.00 (in Germany you can buy a bottle of Sekt, including *Sektsteuer*, sparkling wine duty, of €1.02 per 750 millilitres for as little as €3.00). *Henkell trocken* also is Germany's most exported Sekt. Another well-established brand is tank-fermented Fürst von Metternich Riesling Sekt. Henkell owns and distributes the traditional method Menger Krug brand. These Sekts are rounder, riper, fuller bodied, a deliberately different style. There also is vintage-dated, traditional method Sekt under the Fürst von Metternich brand which is made exclusively from Riesling base wines grown at Schloss Johannsiberg. It's worth tasting. A visit is recommended just to see the visionary 1909 headquarters, still in use today. In tune with the rising interest in all things sparkling, Henkell opened a 'Sektmanufaktur' in 2017. Here visitors can blend their own base wines and have the result aged for them. There are tours, tastings and events and a shop that sells every wine made in the global Henkell portfolio.

Try: Fürst von Metternich Riesling Jahrgangssekt – from Johannisberg grapes.

Schloss Johannisberg
Geisenheim
www.schloss-johannisberg.de

Few estates are as pivotal to German wine history as Schloss Johannisberg. The Schloss itself sits atop the Johannisberg vineyard, exactly on the fiftieth degree of latitude. Initially founded as a Benedictine monastery in 1106, Schloss Johannisberg represents 900 years of viticulture. The monastery was destroyed in the Peasants' Revolt of 1525 and officially dissolved in 1563. The Prince-Abbot of Fulda bought the estate in 1716. He extended the vineyards and ordered the planting of Riesling in the years 1720/21 – thus the enduring marriage of Rheingau and Riesling was first formalized. At Schloss Johannisberg, the first mention of *Cabinet-Wein* dates to 1779, that of *Auslese* to 1787. As Napoleon swept through Europe, the ensuing conflicts brought several changes in ownership. Everyone wanted 'the pearl of the Rheingau' but it eventually fell to the Austrian emperor, who gave it to his foreign minister, Fürst Metternich-Winneburg, in 1816. Metternich's astuteness and quality measures ensured fame and top prices for Johannisberg wines.

Historic records testify how much care was taken in vineyard and cellar. As early as 1830 Fürst Metternich decided that each bottle was to be signed by the cellarmaster as a sign of authenticity. The Schloss itself was bombed in an air raid in August 1942, leaving only its vaulted cellar intact. It was not fully rebuilt until 1964. In 1987 the estate was bought by the Oetker family who also own Henkell Freixenet and still produce a Sekt made from Riesling grown exclusively on the estate. The Johannisberg vineyard itself, facing south-east, south and south-west, rises from 100 to 181 metres at a gradient of up to 45 per cent. The bedrock is quartzite covered by a layer of loess and loam. Of its 35 hectares, 17.85 are classified as *Grosse Lage*. Schloss Joahnnisberg today farms 45 hectares, including surrounding vineyards. A new winery came into operation for the 2018 harvest. Stefan Doktor who runs the estate today says: 'A single site and one grape variety are a blessing and a curse.' He brings a very clear, clean, straight line to the wines which are, as in the past, colour-coded: Silberlack (silver) stands for the dry Riesling GG, bronze is a dry, light Riesling, red is *Kabinett* (a new, snappier style as of 2018), green is *Spätlese* (made exclusively in a sweet style since 2007); pink is *Auslese*, pink/gold is BA and blue is *Eiswein*. Until recently gold used to be TBA but Doktor is working on a dry Riesling above the GG so that bronze, silver and gold are always dry. VDP member estate.

Try: Riesling GG Silberlack for snappy slenderness.

Weingut Kaufmann
Hattenheim
www.kaufmann-weingut.de

Eva Raps and Urban Kaufmann are poster children for mid-life career change. Swiss-born Kaufmann had established himself as one of the best cheesemakers in Appenzell, Switzerland, while Eva Raps spent 17 years working for and eventually running the VDP. The couple met while Kaufmann was searching the length and breadth of Germany for a suitable wine estate to buy. Both shared the same dream: becoming *Winzer*. They took over the Hans Lang estate in Hattenheim in 2013 and operated under this name for a while but are now known under the Kaufmann name – with a distinct, whistle-clean and clear-cut style of Riesling and elegant Spätburgunder. Neither of them denies that all this was a huge challenge and a steep learning curve, but you also see that there are no regrets. It is a pleasure to see them thrive. They farm 20 hectares which include the Hatteneheimer Wisselbrunnen, Hassel and Schützenhaus as well as the Hallgarter Jungfer and Schönhell. Seventy per cent of production is Riesling, followed by 15 per cent Spätburgunder plus a little Weiss- and Graubugunder and Chardonnay. There is always some Swiss cheese to be had alongside the Riesling and numerous gastronomic soirées are hosted by Kaufmann and Raps, who are as exacting as they are modest. VDP member estate.

Try: Tell Riesling for full-fruited, slender refreshment.

Weingut August Kesseler
Assmannshausen
www.august-kesseler.de

August Kesseler is one of Germany's Spätburgunder pioneers. Born in 1958, he started out with just 2.5 hectares; today he has 33 hectares.

He built his estate while holding down a job as a winemaker, while an open mind, good friends and travel allowed him to taste the great Pinot Noirs of the world. He thus had an idea of what Spätburgunder, the traditional variety in Assmannshausen, was capable. In the 1980s when even the State Domaine in Assmannshausen, once the high temple of Spätburgunder culture, had started making wines with residual sweetness, Kesseler pioneered a different approach. Treating Spätburgunder from the Höllenberg with respect, he once again gave structure, bite and shape to this ancient Pinot site. Two parcels of vines from 1939 and 1940 are particularly precious. The wines ferment in open-top *cuves* in a 1792 cellar, hewn straight into the schist of the Höllenberg. Fruit is destemmed; all parcels are vinified separately and hand punched. The wines mature in French oak. Since 1996 Max Himstedt has been cellarmaster, now assisted by Simon Batarseh, as Kesseler himself slowly bows out. The acquisition in 2016 of sites in Hattenheim, Erbach, Eltville and Kiedrich shifted the Riesling proportion from 50 to 75 per cent. The vineyard portfolio incudes sites in Lorch as well as the Rüdesheimer Berg Schlossberg and Roseneck. The wines are sumptuous and bold and are best after a few years of bottle age. They present the vintage characters beautifully. Cuvée Max is a 'second wine' from the classified sites. The Rieslings are juicy and peachy. VDP member estate.

Try: Spätburgunder Assmannshäuser Höllenberg, preferably with some age.

Peter Jakob Kühn
Oestrick-Winkel
www.weingutpjkuehn.de

Peter Jakob Kühn is the eleventh generation of his family to make wine in the Rheingau, yet he and his wife Angela have struck a new path. Having taken over the family estate in 1978 with 7 hectares, they stopped using mineral fertilizer and herbicides in the early 1990s. 'Within that decade we really felt a difference in the soil,' Angela remembers. As of 2001 no more cultured yeasts were used in the cellar and between 2002 and 2004 biodynamic practices were adopted; Demeter certification followed in 2009. Since then the estate has become a leading light of the Rheingau with utterly convincing, savoury, pure and age-worthy Rieslings. Today they farm 20 hectares: from those close to the river like St Nikolaus to the Oestricher Klosterberg and Hallgarter Hendelberg with their elevation. Their temperature and soil differences make tasting here an object lesson in Rheingau sites. Doosberg, Lenchen, Klosterberg, Hendelberg, St Nikolaus and Jungfer are bottled as single sites. 'The power has to exist in the vineyard before it can show its influence in the cellar,' Angela says. They aim for relatively late harvests and employ skin contact and very slow press cycles with just one to two turns in a 12-hour period, a method that allows for relatively clear juice, which is then fermented spontaneously without further sedimentation. Stainless steel, *Halb-*, *Doppel-* and simple *Stück* are used and the wines stay on their gross lees for extended periods – some of the GGs get up to three years. This results in supremely textured and bone-dry wines. Both their children, Sandra and Peter Bernhard, have now joined the estate. It may sound strange to hear down-to-earth Rhinelanders like Angela and Peter Jakob speak of the love they have for their vineyards, but one sip of their wines is all it takes to make you see. What an experience. VDP member estate.

Try: Riesling Doosberg GG for balm-like texture, utter freshness and deepest herbal savour.

Weingut Künstler
Hochheim am Main
www.weingut-kuenstler.de

The story of the Künstler family is remarkable: with a history in winemaking in Moravia going back to at least 1648, they had to leave everything behind in 1945. Franz Künstler arrived in Germany as a refugee and found winemaking work in the Rheingau. He founded the estate in 1965 and his son Gunter, who had worked alongside his father since 1988, took over in 1992, turning it into a lighthouse of the eastern Rheingau. Hochheim is special: it is on the river Main, just before it runs into the Rhine at Mainz-Kostheim. Its vineyards are the south-facing slopes of the last few kilometres of the Main valley. It is warmer here and the soils are relatively rich. Almost 80 per cent of the Künstlers' 37 hectares are planted to Riesling, 12 per cent are Spätburgunder and the rest are mixed whites. The sites include the famous Hölle (heavy argillaceous marl, up to 110 metres), Reichestal (gravelly, sandy loam on calcareous marl up to 100 metres), Domdechaney (loess-loam, marl, up to 110 metres) and the Kirchenstück (loess-loam, marl, up to 120 metres). There are also sites in the Rüdesheimer Berg. The wines used to have more opulence, especially the Rieslings from the Hölle, but now a new finesse has crept in that gives the wines tension. That Gunter Künstler is a master of Riesling is well known, that he has been on a very thoughtful quest with Spätburgunder less so. The wines are of exquisite elegance and show a questioning, intuitive winemaker at his best. Comparing Spätburgunder from Reichestal with those from the Assmannshäuser Höllenberg, where Künstler also has sites, is a great illustration of the opposite poles of the Rheingau. In Künstler's hands these wines reach exquisite expression and age effortlessly. VDP member estate.

Try: Hochheimer Reichestal Spätburgunder for spice and absolute poise.

Weingut Laquai
Lorch
weingut-laquai.de/

The Laquais were seventeenth-century immigrants from Burgundy, hence the French name. Since 1990 brothers Gundolf and Gilbert Laquai have been at the helm of what their father created after the Second World War. At that time they had 3 hectares and an old half-timbered house with an old cellar, today they have a more spacious building in the Wispertal and 25 hectares, all on steep slopes in Lorch. A new winery will be built in 2019. They are to be commended for reviving more than 10 hectares of fallow vineyards on upper slopes, which had fallen into disuse but are now prized for their cool winds. Some vineyards were terraced, at immense expense and effort, but it makes cultivation easier. Naturally the focus is on Riesling but there also is Spätburgunder, Weissburgunder, Auxerrois and even Cabernet Sauvignon. The next generation is poised to take over. The wines are solid, savoury and promising, the single-site Rieslings sing.

Try: Riesling Lorcher Schlossberg Erstes Gewächs for slender zestiness.

Weingut Josef Leitz
Geisenheim
www.leitz-wein.de

Josef Leitz's family estate was just 3 hectares when he took over in 1985 as a very young man. His work turned it into one of the Rheingau's biggest and most successful estates, at 43 hectares. Most of these are on the Rüdesheimer Berg: Schlossberg, Rottland, Roseneck, Magdalenenkreuz, Ehrenfels, Katerloch and more, including the Kaisersteinfels, a parcel at the top of that famous slope at 280 metres which he painstakingly recultivated, restoring its old drystone walls. Leitz crafts beautifully expressive wines but his success is due in no small part to his innovatively labelled wine brands, made from bought-in fruit from an additional 70 hectares: there is the Eins, Zwei Dry as well as the Dragonstone Riesling. These are his calling cards, especially in export markets where he sells far more than in Germany. But Leitz remains refreshingly down to earth. His love for the Rüdesheimer Berg is evident: seeing a poorly cultivated parcel pains him, speaking about his plots he makes it clear that he loves every single vine. There is a tiny amount of Spätburgunder but Leitz's heart belongs to Riesling. His *Grosse Gewächse* are in the top league and are now released two years after the vintage. To advertise this he has appropriated and modified Audi's slogan to 'Vorsprung durch Reife' (the edge conferred by maturity). His Magic Mountain Riesling is a cuvée from the steep, classified sites and great value. VDP member estate.

Try: mature Berg Roseneck Riesling for ethereal, herbal savour.

Weingut Mohr
Lorch
www.weingut-mohr.de

Jochen Neher and his wife Saynur Sonkaya run this 7.5-hectare estate on the slate, schist and quartzite soils of Lorch and Assmannshausen. Their sites are Lorcher Krone and Schlossberg, Bodental-Steinberg and Assmannshäuser Höllenberg, some of them notably steep. Founded in 1875, the estate has been certified organic since 2011. While there is some Muskateller, Silvaner, Scheurebe and Weissburgunder, the focus is decidedly on Riesling and Spätburgunder. Both are made in a pristine, clear and wonderfully understated style. Here you can also taste Riesling made from the oldest vines in the Rheingau. *Flurbereinigung* means that most Rheingau vineyards are now around 40 years old, but Mohr owns a parcel of Riesling in the Lorcher Schlossberg which was planted in 1934. The wine is exquisitely aromatic, slender and scented. The genetic material is being propagated and preserved. Turkish cookery courses are also on offer.

Try: Spätburgunder Assmannshäuser Höllenberg Alte Reben for beautiful depth.

Weingut Prinz
Hallgarten
www.prinz-wein.de

While this 9.2-hectare estate was not founded until 2004 it is already spoken of in hushed tones – especially when it comes to the wines from the Hendelberg, an elevated site of weathered slate at up to 300 metres where Riesling would not have ripened thirty years ago. Fred Prinz and his family grow Riesling and Spätburgunder here. The other sites – Hallgarter Jungfer, Schönhell and Frühernberg – have just Riesling. The vines have been farmed organically since 2009 and were certified in 2012. But Prinz is no greenhorn – he was cellarmaster at various prestigious Rheingau estates before taking the plunge with his own. Most Rieslings are made in stainless steel, are whole-bunch pressed and ferment spontaneously without sedimentation. They are filigree and racy. The Spätburgunder is tender and pale, scented and structured. Only the 'Reserve' sees new wood; the Hendelberg is all the better for being matured in used wood only. There is also a little Sauvignon Blanc and Traminer. VDP member estate.

Try: Spätburgunder Hendelberg for finesse and aroma.

Weingut Prinz von Hessen
Johannisberg
www.prinz-von-hessen.de

This is not just a fancy name. This 47-hectare estate is really owned by the Landgrafen and Prinzen of Hessen, who also run stud farms and hotels. Since late 2018 Bärbel Weinert has been at the helm, taking over from Dr Clemens Kiefer. Riesling accounts for 93 per cent of plantings and there is a smidgeon of Pinot Blanc, Spätburgunder and, unusually, Merlot. This was one of the first estates in Germany to grow Scheurebe (Dr Georg Scheu's son was manager here). More than 70 per cent of their holdings are on classified sites, the two most important are Winkeler Hasensprung and Winkeler Dachsberg, an elevated site of up to 200 metres that has really come into its own with climate change. *Dachs* means badger and some are still resident, as are the bees, kept for biodiversity. In homage to a former prince who made his own silk, mulberry trees have been planted. (Next to oak and acacia, there even is a mulberry barrel in the cellar.) Most wines are fermented in stainless steel but there is also wood, an amphora and a clay egg. Look out for the one-third skin-fermented, oak-matured Dachsfilet Riesling from the core parcel and the oldest vines in the Dachsberg. The style is quietly confident. VDP member estate.

Try: Riesling Dachsfilet for structure and poise.

German *vinifera* crossings – Scheurebe and co.

In the late nineteenth century, with the wine industry reeling from the damage inflicted by mildew and phylloxera, an official commitment to research and improvement was evident. The remit was initially followed by the Prussian state domaines and followed by vine breeding programmes set up by the various regional vine research institutes in the mid-twentieth century. The aim was to create new grape varieties by crossing *Vitis vinifera* grapes. Huxelrebe, Reichensteiner, Bacchus, Faberrebe, Optima, Ehrenfelser, Helfensteiner and Scheurebe were all attempts to create vines for a pre-climate change Germany which would ripen in the relatively cool climate and also bring stable yields. This was a laudable and even necessary aim. However, intraspecific crossings were a game of patience and luck: you cross two vines and hope for the best. You raise them and observe them for a number of years to see which traits they have inherited from each parent vine and then see whether they perform as desired.

Amidst this host of famous and infamous German *Vitis vinifera* crossings of the twentieth century, Scheurebe enjoys unusual standing. It seems like a fluke, a genuine stroke of luck amongst its stablemates, emerging with a distinct personality. Belatedly named after its creator Georg Scheu (1879–1949), director at the vine research institute in Alzey, Rheinhessen, Scheurebe's true identity was only established recently. Initially, it was believed to be a crossing between Silvaner and Riesling, and some older textbooks still state this. Robinson, Harding and Vouillamoz refer to this theory in their book *Wine Grapes*, but while it confirms Riesling as one parent it states that the other remains unknown. Silvaner turns out to be Scheurebe's grandparent rather than parent. Urban Krieg, researcher in charge of breeding at the DLR research centre Rheinhessen-Nahe-Hunsrück[22], who is now tasked with preserving and researching Scheu's and other crossings, confirms that Scheurebe's other parent is Bukettrebe. Bukettrebe, listed as Bukettraube in *Wine Grapes*, is in turn a nineteenth-century crossing by a private breeder in Franconia between Silvaner and Schiava Grossa (or Trollinger, as it is known in Germany). According to Krieg, Bukettrebe and Silvaner can hardly be told apart ampelographically and he suggests that this is how the initially assumed but wrong parentage gained currency. Krieg credits Dr Erika Maul of the Julius-Kühn-Institute, the German Federal Research Centre for Cultivated Plants, with establishing the true parentage.

---

22 Dienstleistungszentrum Ländlicher Raum, research centres run by the Federal State of Rheinland Pfalz in several regional hubs.

> In any case, Scheurebe, still known as Sämling (seedling) 88 in Austria, was crossed and grown from seed in 1916. It distinguished itself by its resistance to chlorosis which made it suitable for the calcareous soils of Rheinhessen, its earlier lignification than Riesling, its relative resilience to early autumn frosts as well as its ability to clock up 10–15° Oechsle more than either Riesling or Silvaner even in cool October days. Scheu is also reported to have prized the fine aroma of the grape, not as blowsy as Muscat but more intense and as fine as Riesling. It also became clear that the variety was so vigorous that it had to be planted with less density and two canes rather than one. In 2017 there were 1,404 hectares of Scheurebe in Germany, most of it in Rheinhessen, followed by the Pfalz, Franconia and Nahe. The earliest statistic I can find dates to 1964 when there were just 342 hectares of Scheurebe, rising to 1,772 hectares in 1972; to 3,669 hectares in 1979; to 3,781 in 1991 and back down to 3,606 hectares in 1995 and 2,948 in 2000. This decline shows that whoever grows and makes Scheurebe today does so out of conviction, out of a fascination with those heady, almost freaky aromatics, paired with killer acidity and wonderful light-footedness.

Klosterweingut Abtei St Hildegard
Rüdesheim
www.abtei-st-hildegard.de/klosterweingut

Sister Thekla is a trained *Winzerin* and helps to run the 7-hectare wine estate that belongs to this Benedictine abbey. Sitting in the hills above Rüdesheim, it was founded in 1900 and finished in 1904. Dedicated to St Hildegard of Bingen, who founded an abbey at Rupertsberg near Bingen and later Eibingen, now part of Rüdesheim, this spiritual community represents the link to the local saint. The abbeys were all dissolved during the secularization in 1803; this abbey is a modern-day revival. St Hildegard considered wine to be 'the blood of the earth that is in the soil, just as blood is in man and has a kind of unity with the blood of man,' so it is only fitting that this tradition was revived here. Initially the abbey was endowed with just one hectare of vineyard, for the nuns' use. A cellarmaster makes the wine but Thekla is fully involved in the vineyards which include the Rüdesheimer Klosterberg, Bischofsberg, Magdalenenkreuz and Drachenstein around Rüdesheim, as well as the Assmannshäuser Hinterkirch, where Spätburgunder is grown. The bottles, which depict Hildegard's artworks, are sold in the abbey's giftshop and by mail order. The 45 sisters currently at the abbey also get to have a glass on Sundays and holidays. 'This place is heavenly,' Sister Thekla says, with great conviction. The wines are easy, fruity and approachable.

Try: Hildegardis Scivias Riesling Spätlese for rounded, rich, sweet fruit.

Sekthaus Solter
Rüdesheim
www.sekthaus-solter.de

Verena Solter who founded this Sekt house with her husband Helmut in 1988, is now supported by the talented young winemaker Sabrina Schach who looks after vineyards and cellar. Helmut, who passed away in 2013, was a Francophile and, unusually for a man of his generation, had spent part of his training in Champagne. He and Verena built their own business as *Lohnversektung*, i.e. offering a full service turning other estates' base wines into traditional method Sekt, with all the specialized knowledge, storage and equipment this takes. Bit by bit they bought their own vineyards. Today they farm 8 hectares of which 2 hectares are owned outright and the rest is leased. Their sites are in the Geisenheimer Rothenberg, Berg Roseneck and Assmannshäuser Höllenberg. They set out from the start to make traditional method Sekt when the word itself was still terminally uncool. 'Initially we drank most of it ourselves,' says Verena, who always looked after the admin side of the business. They grow Riesling, Chardonnay and Spätburgunder and make very fresh, creamy, expressive Sekts. Their single-site, long-aged vintage Sekts are particularly expressive, as is the Pinot Cuvée 'H' Reserve. Of particular note is their brut nature Chardonnay – with low dosage a plus point in general. They deserve to be much more widely known.

Try: Rüdesheimer Berg Roseneck Riesling Réserve brut for creamy vigour.

Weingut Spreitzer
Oestrich-Winkel
www.weingut-spreitzer.de

Andreas Spreitzer and his brother Bernd took over their 1641-founded family estate in 1997 and have taken it to the top. Most of their sites are around Oestrich-Winkel (Jesuitengarten, Doosberg, Lenchen, Wisselbrunnen) with newer acquisitions around Hallgarten. They own a total of 25 hectares including their *monopole*, Rosengarten, a sandy, gravelly site close to the river, which in 1971 was subsumed into the Lenchen site and is seen as its heartland. Separately, they also make Eisenberg, another parcel subsumed into Lenchen. Ninety-five per cent of plantings are Riesling, the rest is Spätburgunder. Two-thirds of production is dry; the rest is equally divided between off-dry and nobly sweet. Andreas is the winemaker and aims to express fully ripe but taut, crystalline wines at moderate alcohol levels – doing this with aplomb across the board from Gutswein to GG. Key to this high-wire act is canopy management, with fewer leaves, to reduce photosynthesis. This way the grapes develop aromatically while clocking up less sugar. Vinification happens both in steel and wood. Try before you buy at their spacious, light-filled *Vinothek*. VDP member estate.

Try: Riesling Ortswein Hallgarten 'Buntschiefer' for slender spiciness.

Sektmanufaktur Schloss Vaux
Eltville
www.schloss-vaux.de

This Sekt house has quite a history. Founded 1868 in Berlin, the company moved its headquarters to Metz in Lothringen (Lorraine) once it had become German in 1871, to take advantage of the light Lorraine base wines for their Sekt manufacture. This is where they picked up the name Château Vaux – but history conspired against them and the Rheingau has been their base since 1920. After an interlude where Sekt was made by the Charmat method, the house turned its attention back to the traditional method in 2000, a change rung in by Nikolaus Graf von Plettenberg, who joined in 1998 and still runs the company. Schloss Vaux managed to be in the right place just as Germany turned its attention back to proper Sekt. Over the past five years it has upped its game tremendously. The estate grows 20 per cent of its own grapes and buys the remaining 80 per cent from vineyards that farm according to their sparkling base specifications. They are particularly strong in a mid-segment that offers solid quality at very affordable pricing, but that does not stop them from making some very special, longer aged cuvées. Their mature Riesling Sekts from single sites are a joy, their Rosé Resérve, with a minimum of 36 months on the lees, is delicious too.

Try: Rheingau Rosé Resérve brut in magnum for creamy bliss.

Schloss Vollrads
Oestrich-Winkel
www.schlossvollrads.com

Schloss Vollrads is one of those venerable, aristocratic estates that helped to shape the Rheingau's reputation. It was here that the first documented *Cabinetkeller*, a small, separate cellar for the best *Cabinet* wines, was built in 1716. You can visit this cellar and marvel at how small it is:

really only the most precious wines had room to mature for years. For generations, since 1097, the *Schloss* was home to the counts of Greiffenclau. The last, Erwein Graf Matuschka-Greiffenclau, was one of the first great ambassadors for dry Riesling in the 1980s, when German wine was at its lowest ebb. His father, Richard, was instrumental in reviving Rheingau viticulture after the privations of the First World War. The Greiffenclau line ended sadly in 1997 when the estate, crippled by debt, had become too much for the owners. It is now owned by the Nassauische Sparkasse, a local savings bank, which has run it ever since. The winery, with its 80 hectares of vineyards, is part of the business along with a restaurant and event space. The wines are clear and clean but could do more to express the potential of the sites. Nonetheless a visit to this historic estate is a must. VDP member estate.

Try: Riesling Kabinett Feinherb for summery ease.

Weingut Wegeler and Weingut Krone
Oestrich-Winkel and Assmannshausen
www.wegeler.com and www.weingut-krone.de

The Wegeler-Drieseberg family owns three estates: one Wegeler estate in the Rheingau, one in the Mosel and the venerable Weingut Krone in Assmannshausen. The Wegelers are descendants of German Sekt aristocracy, the Deinhard family, from Koblenz, but the Sekt business was sold to Henkell in 1997. Today the focus is on elegant Rieslings from Rheingau and Mosel and, since 2007, also Spätburgunder from Weingut Krone in Assmannshausen. The Rheingau estate owns 43 hectares across the region, 'from Hallgarten to Rüdesheim,' as Dr Tom Drieseberg notes, with an enviable portfolio of *Grosse Lagen*. 'We make classics, we are quiet,' is how he fittingly describes the elegant house style, which is executed with great consistency by cellarmaster Michael Burgdorf.

One of their true treasures is the Geisenheimer Rothenberg which is where their famous brand Geheimrat J Riesling was initially sourced. Today it is a *Grosse Lagen* blend. Geheimrat J was a ground-breaking wine when it was first released in 1985 – one of the first properly dry, high-quality Rieslings of the modern era at a time when sweetness was all. It was one of the trailblazers that opened hearts and minds for what were to become the *Grosse Gewächse*. That 10–15 per cent of Rheingau production is devoted to Sekt is more than a nod to the family's history. The top cuvée here is also called Geheimrat J. Like its still counterpart, it was ahead of its time as a traditional method brut Riesling Sekt. It is based on *Grosse Lagen*, spends five years on lees and is dosed with mature, sweet Riesling which gives the wines supreme varietal allure. Weingut Krone owns 5 hectares of up to 60-year-old vines in the Assmannshäuser Höllenberg. Wegeler became partners in the business in 2007 and have owned it outright since 2014. The wines are made in the old cellar, hewn into the schist in 1860. Their top wine, called Juwel, is a concentrated, firm Spätburgunder. The Mosel estate also has 13 hectares in the best sites. Wegeler Vintage Collection is the name given to a coveted series of library releases of mature Riesling. The family is also engaged in vineyard recultivation, including on the Rüdesheimer Drachenstein. VDP member estate.

Try: Rothenberg GG with a few years of age for poise and freshness.

Robert Weil
Kiedrich
www.weingut-robert-weil.com

There is plenty of real blue blood in the German wine world, but this estate, founded in the 1870s by the Weil family, is something like wine aristocracy. Its wines, the favourites of Kaiser Wilhelm II, rose to the highest ranks of Rheingau Riesling in the late nineteenth and early twentieth century. His imperial majesty's approval meant that Weil Riesling was soon served in various royal European households and fetched exorbitant prices. That quality ethos was never lost. Its current director, Wilhelm Weil, joined his home estate in 1987 and took over just as his father sold it to the Japanese Suntory conglomerate in 1988. In 1991 Wilhelm Weil once again became co-owner, and has been firmly at the helm ever since. He extended the estate's holdings to 90 hectares and is thus one of the Rheingau's largest operators. While his single-site wines, both dry and sweet, have been at the forefront of German Riesling for decades, there is also widely distributed simple Riesling. The chief site is the Kiedricher Gräfenberg, first planted in 1109, an elevated, steep site of mica schist rising to 230 metres. Then there is the Turmberg, also mica schist, up to 240 metres, and the Klosterberg, of slate, mica schist and gneiss, up to 260 metres. Elevation and ventilation give the wines their inherent tension and steeliness. Only Riesling is grown. Exactitude in vineyard and cellar leads to absolute precision in the wines. Stylistic continuity is also a given: estate manager Clemens Schmitt has been part of the team since 1988, like his father before him. One of the best addresses in the Rheingau. VDP member estate.

Try: anything mature for a taste of that Rheingau aristocracy.

Wine auctions

Wine auctions have played an important part in German wine history. Rheingau wines were sold via auction from the 1840s onwards. Each estate held its own auction. Commissionaires, merchants, hotel and inn owners would come to taste the wines and then bid for them. In the 1880s, as Mosel wines became ever more popular and important, estate owners got together to arrange for collective auctions in Trier. Noting how effective these collective auctions were for the Mosel, Saar and Ruwer estates, and reading in the headlines the record prices generated, the Rheingau estates also decided to bundle their efforts and held their first collective auction on 12 June 1897. Today the tradition lives on in the annual auctions held by the VDP in Rheingau, Mosel, Nahe and Ahr. Highlights in Germany's wine calendar, they are preceded by tastings of the auction wines, rare, special bottlings which often fetch stellar prices.

16

RHEINHESSEN – MORE THAN A SEA OF VINES

With 26,617 hectares, Rheinhessen is Germany's largest wine region. Of 136 communes, 133 make wine. Some of them have more hectarage than Germany's smaller regions. Framed by the Rhine on its eastern and northern confines, it borders the Pfalz to the south and Nahe to the west. Worms and Mainz are its ancient and populous poles in south and north. Its soft hills and diverse soils have been a fertile ground for vines ever since Roman times. Rheinhessen is vast and diverse, it refuses to be shoved into a neat little box, so let's dissect this veritable sea of vines.

Thirty-five million years ago what is now Rheinhessen was an inland sea within the Mainz Basin. Its Tertiary sediments created most of today's soils, i.e. limestones, along with sand, marl, clay, loam and gravel, which cover much older formations. These only come to the surface at certain points, like Permian rhyolite on the Roter Hang (or Red Slope), Devonian quartzite in the Binger Scharlachberg or volcanic ridges in the west. For the most part, Rheinhessen wine country is hilly and gentle with large areas covered by loess. The only steep slopes are those of the Roter Hang. Rheinhessen is sheltered: the mountain ranges of Hunsrück, Taunus, Odenwald and Nordpfälzer Bergland keep cold winds and rain clouds from west, north and east at bay. These sunny, dry and fertile conditions have always favoured viticulture. The Romans, with their fortifications in Mainz and Bingen, recognized this and vines have flourished ever since. In the early Middle Ages, Charlemagne established a *Kaiserpfalz* in Ingelheim and monastic settlements furthered viticulture. Rheinhessen then saw the ascendancy of two powerful electorates that dominated the area: Kurmainz in the north, and Kurpfalz in the south. Mainz, Bingen and Worms were significant medieval wine trade hubs on the Rhine.

Lying to the left of the Rhine, often seen as the natural frontier between France and Germany, Rheinhessen was borderland and therefore often contested. Villages were pillaged in the Thirty Years' War, and the War of the Palatinate Succession meant that Worms was razed to the ground by French troops in 1689: 'Destroyed is the splendour of the medieval town with its twelve mighty gates, its sixty turrets, fifty churches …'. The same source notes that the French 'followed the order of their king to destroy the Palatinate so thoroughly' that almost every vine and tree was burned. But viticulture revived. Napoleon occupied the area in 1792 and annexed it in 1798. This meant fundamental change as feudal order gave way to Napoleon's *Code Civil*: the division of church and state, the creation of civic rights, the end of serfdom, secularization of church estates. What is Rheinhessen became part of the French Département Mont Tonnerre and its free citizens could bid for and buy vineyards that had belonged to the church. But freedom did not last. After Napoleon's defeat the victors carved up the spoils and today's Rheinhessen was born: in 1816 it fell to the Grand Duke of Hesse and was German once again. Viticulture continued to thrive. The German catalogue for the 1900 World Exhibition in Paris states an area of 11,717 hectares under vine for the region – by 1925 this had grown to 13,209 hectares. Silvaner was the chief grape variety, Liebfraumilch was already a brand name (see box, page 230) and Riesling was confined to the best sites.

In the second half of the twentieth century, abundance was easier to achieve than ripeness. With a ready market for Liebfraumilch, Rheinhessen was settled with the image of cheap bulk wine. It became a winner in the 1971 wine law and the then prevailing spirit of rationalization and technical advancement. While there were 16,441 hectares of vines in 1964, by 1979 there were 25,389. Its soft hills lent themselves to industrialized, mechanized viticulture. This worked in the 1970s and '80s but by the 1990s it no longer added up – the tide had turned in Germany.

Having gathered pace in the 1990s, the quality revolution gained strength in 2001 with the 'Message in a Bottle', a group of a few young winemakers determined to lift Rheinhessen out of its cheap and sweet image. They were fed up with being labelled as 'world-class tractor drivers with poor winemaking skills. All of a sudden really good wines were made,' says Jochen Dreissigacker, one of the group alongside Klaus Peter Keller, Daniel Wagner and Philipp Wittmann. Germany was ready for them and they became the cool kids with due media attention. These youngsters have grown up and so has their movement. It is now called Maxime Herkunft Rheinhessen which translates as 'Maximum Provenance Rheinhessen'. Members agree to work within the VDP's three-tier-system of *Gutswein*, *Ortswein* and *Lagenwein* and commit to restricted yields and late release. All Rheinhessen VDP members are also Maxime members, abiding by stricter statutes. Maxime Herkunft now has 90 members, but they only represent 7 per cent of Rheinhessen's vineyards.

The varietal statistics also reflect this schizophrenia: of 26,627 hectares in 2017, 4,648 were Riesling; 4,292 were Müller-Thurgau, followed by 3,365 hectares of Dornfelder. A decade earlier, in 2007, those statistics were: 4,320 hectares Müller-Thurgau, 3,769 hectares Riesling, 3,444 hectares Dornfelder. So change is afoot – but old structures take time to break down. Varietal diversity is a Rheinhessen hallmark: Scheurebe, Spätburgunder, Chardonnay and Sauvignon Blanc all thrive. Philipp Wittmann says: 'Our aim is that this heterogeneous region should define itself via provenance.' Standing above the Morstein, you see that there are still rows of Dornfelder planted in this iconic Riesling vineyard. Wittmann says: 'The greatest story here is the vineyards, and it is astonishing that not everybody has understood this yet.'

Note that the wine region of Rheinhessen is in the Federal State of Rheinland-Pfalz, not in Hessen. Administratively, it has three *Bereiche*, 24 *Grosslagen* and 432 *Einzellagen*.

RHEINFRONT: ROTER HANG

The Red Slope is a 5-kilometre escarpment of Permian *Rotliegendes*, a reddish sandstone, one of Rheinhessen's oldest soils, which was pushed to the surface and laid bare along the left bank of the Rhine during the Upper Rhine Rift. A note of caution here: *Rotliegendes* is a term often used carelessly by winemakers to describe reddish soils, whether they are from this era or not, equally erroneously they are often referred to as 'red slate' – this is not slate but compressed sandstone. The Red Slope is one of the most striking vineyard formations in Germany. Its vineyards, about 170 metres high, from north to south, Rothenberg, Pettenhal, Hipping and Ölberg, drop steeply to the river. They look east and south-east, with sites like the Brudersberg turning gradually more south. They face the morning sun and benefit from the thermic stability of the Rhine. Johannes Hasselbach of Weingut Gunderloch says: 'Between Rothenberg, Pettenthal and Hipping the soil changes minimally in structure,' what changes is aspect and altitude within the vineyards.

St Antony Weingut GmbH & Co. KG
Nierstein
www.st-antony.de

Change is afoot at St Antony, which has made wine since 1920 and today incorporates the historic estate of Heyl zu Herrnsheim. St Antony changed hands several times but has been owned since 2005 by the Meyer family, who hired the talented Felix Peters in 2006 to be manager and winemaker. Peters converted the estate to organic, then to biodynamic methods. Demeter certification followed in 2018. Of their 40 hectares, 32 hectares are in the Roter Hang: Pettenthal, Orbel, Ölberg, Hipping and their *monopole* Zehnmorgen. While most Rieslings are from *Rotliegende* soils and show the characteristic herbal savouriness, the Zehnmorgen *monopole* of heavy, calcareous marl has the oldest Riesling vines on the estate, giving a very textured wine. Steel tanks, *Halbstück*, *Stück* and *Doppelstück* barrels are used. Riesling parcels in Pettenthal are vinified in partially new, steamed barrels (228 litres) and present an elegant synthesis of gentle wood and Riesling thrill. Peters is known for his inspired idea to plant lower-lying, less steep, Rhine-facing central parcels of the Pettenthal vineyard to Blaufränkisch vines from massal selections from Burgenland, Austria. Peters explains. 'It was important for me to reinterpret these important, old sites,' he says. Peters knew that Blaufränkisch relished the relative heat, could withstand disease pressure and would express the Red Slope. All the wines – red and white – have seamless balance. As of the 2018 vintage new winemaker and partner Dirk Würtz has taken over. VDP and Maxime Herkunft Rheinhessen member estate.

Try: Blaufränkisch Lange Berg for gossamer tannins.

Weingut Gunderloch
Nackenheim
www.gunderloch.de

Gunderloch is one of the stalwarts on the Red Slope. To many, Rothenberg Riesling and Gunderloch are synonymous. Today Johannes

Hasselbach, the sixth generation to make wine here, is at the helm. His parents Agnes and Fritz Hasselbach doubled the size of the estate and Fritz took the nobly sweet Rieslings of the Rothenberg to their greatest heights. Johannes was not an immediate convert to wine, it took *stages* abroad to show him what a treasure he was heir to. He made his first wines at home in 2012 and took over fully in 2016. He farms 26 hectares on the Red Slope, 12 hectares of which are steep sites; Riesling represents 80 per cent of plantings. There are also vineyards on the plateau towards Nierstein, where he grows Weissburgunder, Grauburgunder, Sauvignon Blanc and 'as a private pleasure' some Spätburgunder. His most important site is the Rothenberg where the topsoil is thinnest, followed by Pettenthal and Hipping. Hasselbach remembers how he always perceived the Rothenberg as a hot site; now, making the wines, he says he understands the 'tension between the cold downwinds and the warmth of the site' and seems to have found 'a cooler vein'. With exacting work in the vineyards he aims for ripeness at 90–91° Oechsle. Johannes reintroduced large, used wood in ferments after long skin contact. Hasselbach also rejoices dancing on the tightrope between acid and sweetness in his sweet *Prädikatsweine*. His dry Rieslings have that herbal spiciness the red soil seems to impart, some have elusive petrichor aromas. VDP and Maxime Herkunft Rheinhessen member estate.

Try: Rothenberg GG and Rothenberg Auslese to understand the scale of what is possible.

Weingut Louis Guntrum
Nierstein
www.guntrum.de

If you are looking for Rheinhessen wine somewhere in the world, you are likely to find a bottle of Louis Guntrum. The family has made wine since 1648 and started exporting as early as 1867. Since 1909 they have been settled in Nierstein where, in 1924, they built the villa on the Rhine housing Rheinhessen's largest vaulted cellars. Konstantin Guntrum took over in 2003 and continues to travel the world. He owns 11 hectares of vineyards on the Roter Hang, including parcels in Hipping, Orbel and Pettenthal as well as in the Oppenheimer Sackträger (loess and calcareous loam). Sixty per cent are planted to Riesling with Pinot Blanc and Noir, Scheurebe and Silvaner making up the rest. It is in the entry level that lots of Riesling fun can be had for little money but move up the ladder and savour the famous spice of those Red Slope vineyards too. Watch out: Guntrum also has a library of old vintages and features regular late releases.

Try: Riesling Orbel GG for citrus and herbal savouriness.

Weingut Fritz Ekkehard Huff
Nierstein-Schwabsburg
www.weingut-huff.de

Christine Huff, her Kiwi husband Jeremy Bird-Huff and her father Fritz Ekkehard farm 8.5 hectares in Nierstein and Schwabsburg. They have choice parcels in the Roter Hang, like Pettenthal and Orbel, and also in the Schloss Schwabsburg which has *Rotliegende* soils but is cooler, and in the limestone sites of Paterberg. Christine, who trained with Klaus Peter Keller and Aldinger, and added a stint in Burgundy after finishing Geisenheim, has made the wines since 2010. She introduced even lower yields, spontaneous ferments and shifted the focus from cellar to vineyard. Forty per cent of plantings are Riesling, 30 per cent are red and white Pinot varieties and the rest are aromatic whites. Christine's wines are filigree and show great depth at restrained alcohol levels. They are a purist pleasure. You wish Christine and Jeremy were less modest and made a little more noise about their fabulous wines. Excellent value. Maxime Herkunft Rheinhessen member estate.

Try: Riesling of course but also the dry Scheurebe Greenbird for vivid nettle and lime.

Weingut Kühling-Gillot
Bodenheim
www.kuehlingandbattenfeld.com

Carolin Spanier-Gillot is amongst that band of young winemakers who piloted the reassessment of Rheinhessen across Germany. Her parents started on the path to quality in 1970, when they took over and started assembling the portfolio of sites on the Roter Hang by selling lesser sites. When Carolin took over in 2002 there were 7 hectares, today there are 20 hectares which have been certified organic since 2008. There are parcels in the Rothenberg, Pettenthal, Hipping and Ölberg as well as in the Oppenheimer Sackträger and Kreuz. One parcel in the Rothenberg has ungrafted (*wurzelecht*) Riesling vines planted in 1934 which are vinified separately and make the GG. Carolin also recultivated an overgrown parcel of old Riesling in the Ölberg, while her parcel in Pettenthal is the steepest in Rheinhessen. In 2006 Carolin married Hans Oliver Spanier of Weingut Battenfeld-Spanier (see page 224). They united their operations in 2007 but keep the brands of each estate separate. Riesling makes up 75 per cent of plantings. The wines are made by her husband at his estate, employing spontaneous ferments, large old barrels and long ageing on gross lees to bring out salty, intense expression. Carolin says: 'That is the interesting thing. Having the two estates, one in the Wonnegau limestone soils, one on the Red Slope, with all wines made in one cellar, by the same winemaker and one handwriting, without fining or filtration. You get such differences. Starting from *Gutswein* all the way to the GGs.' Her *Ortsweine* are called Quinterra and already give you a taste of what is possible. VDP and Maxime Herkunft Rheinhessen member estate.

Try: Petthenthal for smoky savour, Ölberg for utter concentration.

Weingut Schätzel
Nierstein
www.Schaetzel.de

The Schätzel family have made wine for the past 650 years, including over 120 years at the Roter Hang. Current owners Carolin and Kai Schätzel have shaken everything up. Kai is a business graduate, noting that 'an objective education is a family principle.' He returned home to his estate in 2008 and started questioning everything, especially the style of the dry wines, which he says had 'too much alcohol'. Thus began his counter-culture, slowing everything down in the vineyard. He shortened his canopy to have lower yields without green harvest and ensured that all the grapes were in the shade. 'This allows us to make wines like they were made 100 years ago. The most fortuitous thing is that the vines adapt. We have reached a new paradigm: few, small grapes with thick skins.' His GGs thus have 11.5% abv while a new, old style of *Kabinett* at 7% abv is once again possible. Whole bunches are foot trodden before macerating for up to six days; gentle pressing and spontaneous ferment in wood follows with unsettled juice. The wines stay on their gross lees until bottling. The dry wines sometimes remain on their lees for 2–3 years. *Kabinetts* are bottled early, 'primary fruit does not play a role here,' he says. He has also been experimenting with no-sulphur wines for white and red blends, but his Rieslings have minimal sulphur anyway: 'I want to explore the boundaries of stability,' he says. His *Kabinetts* are a huge hit with their inherent, juicy, vivid lightness. They are far too easy to drink. His work shows that steep, stony slopes can meet the challenge of climate change. VDP and Maxime Herkunft Rheinhessen member estate.

Try: Riesling Hipping GG for bone-dry, elixir-like depth.

WONNEGAU AND WORMS

This is the sunny southern end of Rheinhessen, home to vineyards like Morstein, Hubacker, Bürgel and Kirchspiel. They are on various formations of limestone but have only regained their reputation in the past 30 years with climate change. Although of historic importance, they had become marginal by the early twentieth century. The entry for the village of Westhofen in the official 1927 guidebook reads: 'Clean table wines up to medium quality of good, racy character.' That for Monzernheim says: 'The wines will do, now and again they are good.' By comparison, the entry for Nackenheim, on the Red Slope, reads, 'Amongst the very best of Rheinhessen wines.' That for Nierstein, 'The wines have world renown.' Klaus Peter Keller, who played a large role in putting the Wonnegau back on the map, reminds us that while site potential was great – his Dalsheim vineyards were valued possessions of Kloster Lorch in the eighth century – in the cooler period during Riesling's heyday and until climate change in the 1980s the 'average temperatures often were too low' for grapes to ripen.

Weingut Battenfeld-Spanier
Hohen-Sülzen
www.kuehlingandbattenfeld.com

Weingut Battenfeld-Spanier, founded in 1992, started farming organically on day one. It is run with conviction and determination by Hans Oliver Spanier, called HO, who introduced biodynamic methods in 2003. His vineyards are in the dry, sunny limestones of the Wonnegau and in the cooler reaches of the Zellertal. His sites are the Frauenberg in Nieder-Flörsheim, a south-facing but exposed limestone slope rising to 250 metres, the Schwarzer Herrgott, a sloping, south-facing site on a limestone plateau and the Kirchenstück in Hohen-Sülzen, south-south-west facing with loess and loam covered limestone. Here he crafts outstanding Riesling and toned, spicy Spätburgunder. 'I want to make a kind of red Riesling,' HO says about his Spätburgunders. Since 2006 he has been married to Carolin Gillot of Weingut Kühling-Gillot in Bodenheim (see page 222). He is the winemaker and the wines of both estates are made in the Hohen-Sülzen cellar. Pristine fruit is fermented spontaneously in wood and ages slowly on gross lees. VDP and Maxime Herkunft Rheinhessen member estate.

Try: Spätburgunder Kirchenstück GG for purity and poise.

Weingut Dreissigacker
Bechtheim
ww.dreissigacker-wein.de

Jochen Dreissigacker's story exemplifies Rheinhessen's wine revolution. His new, white, state-of-the-art winery, finished in May 2018, is visible from afar. Built into the vineyard to exacting standards of wine production it is reported to have cost millions. It is site potential and confidence made manifest. 'We are in an incredibly long-term business. The decisions I make today will be important for my children,' he says. This also means sustainability. His vineyards have been certified organic since 2007. When 38-year-old Dreissigacker first trained as a tax accountant his parents deemed it a much better career path than *Winzer*. But eventually Dreissigacker trained with Klaus Peter Keller and took over the parental estate. Dreissigacker's new winery has three presses in order to have slower press cycles with longer maceration. Long lees ageing is the rule. *Lagenweine* are only released three years after harvest. In 2010 he started holding wines back for late release. Dreissigacker's focus is clearly on dry Riesling. Bechtheim has soils mostly of clay, weathered limestone and sandy loess and is very warm with budburst and harvest about a week earlier than in neighbouring Westhofen. The prime site is Geyersberg, a south-facing, protected, warm site of sandy loess, calcareous marl and clay. The Geyersberg Rieslings reflect the warm site and its limestone subsoil with nuances of honey and chalk. Dreissigacker farms 38 hectares but also buys in grapes. His site portfolio includes Geyersberg, Rosengarten and Hasensprung in Bechtheim and Morstein, Kirchspiel and Aulerde in Westhofen. Maxime Herkunft Rheinhessen member.

Try: a mature vintage of Geyersberg Riesling for length, limestone and precision.

Weingut Oekonomierat Johann Geil I. Erben GbR
Bechtheim
www.weingut-geil.de

Johannes Geil-Bierschenk is determined and motivated. As the current chairman and founder member of the Maxime Herkunft Rheinhessen movement you can read both impatience and passion in his sentences. 'It is time we did something, we cannot wait for change to happen – because quality is what counts,' he says. He exports widely and describes his own style of wine as fruit-forward. Indeed, his estate wines – Riesling, Weissburgunder, Spätburgunder, Scheurebe and Silvaner – grown mostly around the village, are squeaky clean, expressing the sunshine of Bechtheim. His Geyersberg Riesling speaks of golden ripeness and honeyed richness. His unusually fruit-driven and rounded Frühburgunder, not made every year, almost owes its style to the new world, but such is the sunshine of Bechtheim. He owns 35 hectares but grapes are also bought in for a separate project. His stylistic aim is simple: 'I do not want one-dimensional wines but complexity. I want people to drink more than one glass.' Maxime Herkunft Rheinhessen member.

Try: Bechtheimer Riesling S for sheer intensity and juiciness.

Weingut K.F. Groebe
Westhofen
www.weingut-k-f-groebe.de

Fritz Groebe is modest and understated. He is the eighth generation of his family to make wine in Westhofen and has a fine portfolio of sites: Westhofener Aulerde, Morstein and Kirchspiel, as well as Rotenstein and Steingrube. There is something quiet and calm about him that also pervades his wines. Seventy-five per cent of his plantings are Riesling, with some Silvaner, Scheurebe and Pinot varieties. Rieslings are fermented spontaneously in *Stück, Halbstück* and *Doppelstück*, mature in an old, vaulted cellar and take their own sweet time. 'To make the wine myself and to live with the rhythm that nature dictates is my greatest joy,' he says of his 8.5 hectares. The way he speaks about his vineyards, walking along Aulerde and Kirchspiel, shows that there is no artifice in his approach, only conviction: 'I make originals, not copies,' he explains. His Rieslings are exceptionally pure, long-lived and ridiculously good value. As a young *Winzer* in the early 1990s Groebe visited Burgundy often and trained with Clerget in Pommard. This gave him the idea of planting and making Spätburgunder at home. In spring 2018 I tasted a 1992 bottle that had been whole-bunch fermented and aged in oak. It gave me a glimpse of what could have been. At the time the wine had to be declared as *Tafelwein Rhein* and did not really sell. Groebe, who had been much ahead of his time, grubbed the vines up. Today world-class Spätburgunders grow alongside the Rieslings in the limestone soils of the Wonnegau. It shows what a visionary Groebe is – and how much he understands without ever trumpeting about it. VDP member estate.

Try: Westhofener Riesling for exquisite purity, Alte Reben for a flirtation with residual sugar.

Weingut Gutzler
Gundheim
www.gutzler.de

Unusually for the Wonnegau, the Gutzlers have more Spätburgunder than Riesling, with 43 per cent of their 16 hectares planted to the former. Riesling takes second place with 30 per cent. Their sites are spread across Westhofen (Morstein, Brunnenhäuschen), Gundheim and Dorn-Dürkheim, a great advantage in case of hail. They also have a parcel of Riesling in the Wormser Liebfrauenstift Kirchenstück. Christine and Michael Gutzler, who took over in 2003, run the estate and, until his untimely death in 2017, were supported by Michael's father Gerhard. He had started the quality drive, grubbing up crossings and returning to traditional varieties. Father and son built their barrique cellar with a natural stone floor and recovered bricks to preserve natural humidity for their Spätburgunder. Gerhard, the quiet pioneer, made many trips to Burgundy and Champagne to learn and absorb. 'I grew up with this idea of quality,' Michael says. 'I want to make things even more precise.' Michael has made the wines since 2003 and fine-tunes his approach to bring expression to each site: the warmth of the Kirchenstück is as evident as the coolness of Morstein in his Rieslings; the Brunnenhäuschen Spätburgunder is filigree and fine boned. Great value. VDP member estate.

Try: Dorn-Dürkheimer Silvaner from 85-year-old vines.

Weingut Keller
Flörsheim-Dalsheim
www.keller-wein.de

It is most refreshing that the two undoubted superstars of German wine, Julia and Klaus Peter Keller, are completely down-to-earth. Not only are they behind Germany's most sought-after dry Riesling, their legendary G-Max, they also make dreamlike Spätburgunder and cultivate some vines in the Mosel (a parcel of 100-year-old vines in Piesporter Schubertslay) and in Norway. Their estate has been a *Kaderschmiede*, a kind of elite training unit, for many of the rising stars of German winemaking. Few winemakers can say that they have put their vineyards on the map, but the Kellers can. Klaus Peter's parents (his mother Hedwig was from the Mosel) were ahead of their time, green harvesting as early as 1972/73. Their styles were mainly off-dry and sweet. Julia and Klaus Peter focus on dry. Klaus Peter's first vintage at home, after Geisenheim and stints in Burgundy and South Africa, was in 2001. 'Julia und ich lieben Riesling,' Klaus Peter says. 'Julia and I love Riesling, it is our main thing, and we love Spätburgunder, and the aromatic varieties …' While this may sound simple it is the very root of everything they do. Without love they could not have taken their work and their wines to such heights. There is not an aspect that they have not thought through. They have high planting densities of 7,500–8,000 vines per hectare and insist on hoeing by hand. Every parcel of their 18 hectares has an individualized concept. There are no recipes. That goes for skin contact, fermentation and maturation vessel, be it steel, wood or concrete. Their site portfolio includes the Dalsheimer Hubacker (loess and marl on limestone), the Westhofener Aulerde, Morstein Kirchspiel and Brunnenhäuschen, which contains the Abts Erde parcel as well as parcels in the Niersteiner Pettenthal. Their Spätburgunder grows in the Dalsheimer Bürgel (terra fusca) and in the Niederflörsheimer Frauenberg (limestone). Whatever Julia and Klaus Peter turn their hands to, the wines will have brilliance, backbone, character and finesse. If you want to read superlatives, read tasting notes for their wines. Even their most playful wine, their Scheurebe Kabinett, is an eye-opener. You may not get your hands on G-Max but the GGs are still affordable and worth every penny; the entry-level wines are a steal.

A word on their G-Max: the grapes are always from the same parcel of old vines on limestone bedrock but where exactly remains undisclosed. The name is a composite of wine names that is a homage to a grandfather and a son. They first made it in 2001 with the aim of making a superlative dry wine, principally for their own use. When they shared it with friends the secret was out and it became a commercial release with limited numbers. VDP member estate.

Try: simply anything.

Weingut Liebfrauenstift
Worms
www.liebfrauenstift.com

It is a strange sight to see an expanse of fenced vineyard in a residential townscape, yet the vineyards were here long before the houses. Vines have been documented here for 400 years, tended by the Capuchin monks of the Liebfrauenkirche. They surround the 'church of our dear lady', built 1267–1465 and heavily damaged, like all of Worms, in 1689, before being rebuilt. The infamous Liebfraumilch originated in this vineyard (see box, page 230). Its fame was already documented in the seventeenth century and it turned into one of the defining stories of German wine. This happened with the help of wine merchant P.J. Valckenberg who bought the vineyards in 1808. It was only in 2016 when Wilhelm Steifensand, descendant of the Valckenbergs, sold the trading company but retained the original vineyards that the Weingut Liebfrauenstift was founded. Steifensand and his wife Dr Katharina Prüm, of the famous Mosel estate Joh. Jos. Prüm, installed Heiner Maleton as estate manager and winemaker, and he immediately converted to organic farming methods. He wants to do justice to this site, which lies on a former riverbed of the Rhine. Loess and *Rotliegendes* cover a layer of sand and river gravel. The vineyard, protected within the city, is warm and classified as a *Grosse Lage*. There are new Riesling plantings. The first vintage was made in 2016, a dry, entry-level Riesling called Stiftswein and a single-site wine called Liebfrauenstift-Kirchenstück Riesling. Both wines show the ripe stone-fruit notes the vineyard is known for. It will take time but under the auspices of Steifensand, Prüm and Maleton the story of 'our dear lady' will come full circle.

Try: Liebfrauenstift-Kirchenstück Riesling.

Sekthaus Raumland
Flörsheim-Dalsheim
www.raumland.de

Volker Raumland has fizz in his veins. It was a Sekt project during his Geisenheim days that infected him and prompted him in the 1980s to start helping half of Germany make Sekt with his mobile bottling unit. His own first Sekts, made from bought fruit, came out in 1986. When in 1990 he and his wife Heide-Rose managed to buy an estate in Flörsheim-Dalsheim that came with vines, they started out on their own, producing nothing but Sekt and forging a path of uncompromising quality. In charge of their own vines, nothing stood in the way of their dream. Today they own 10 hectares of vines, planted mostly to Spätburgunder and Chardonnay, in sites like Dalsheimer Bürgel (where loess and marl sit on limestone) and Kirchenstück in Hohen-Sülzen (loess and loam on limestone). Two Sekts are named after his daughters,

Marie-Luise and Katharina, who have plans to come on board; his top rosé is named after his wife. Long lees ageing and restrained dosage are the hallmarks of his sparkling wines, which have won countless accolades. They are creamy, fresh, elegant and age-worthy. Above all they show what is possible in German Sekt. The Raumlands have played a key role in Germany's Sekt renaissance.

Try: any vintage-dated Sekt for creamy, sophisticated freshness.

Liebfraumilch

The story of the infamous Liebfraumilch, a byword for cheap, sweet, headache-inducing plonk, is the story of German wine come full circle. It was an Englishman who reported from his German travels in 1687 that there was a famous wine in the town of Worms of which the saying went that it was 'as sweet as the milk of the holy virgin.' Offered by the town to passing dignitaries, it was the wine grown by the Capuchin monks in the vineyards surrounding the Liebfrauenkirche, or Church of Our Dear Lady, in Worms – or at least in vineyards where the spires of that church cast their shade. Devastation came in 1689 when Worms was razed to the ground, but the fame remained and vines flourished again. The name Liebfraumilch starts appearing with frequency in the municipal records of the late eighteenth century. When all church estates were secularized following French occupation, the vineyards, clearly delineated as 'Liebfraumilch' and 'Liebfraustift', were auctioned off, in 1808. One of the purchasers was wine merchant Peter Joseph Valckenberg (1764–1837). This Dutchman had settled in Worms, where he founded his wine business in 1786 – it is still going strong today. Three elements coincided: the historic fame of the wine, which must have been based on real quality, the rising reputation and prices of Rhine wines and its international availability. It was Valckenberg's son Wilhelm (1790–1847) who travelled widely and managed to sell Liebfraumilch to 'Charles Dickens, Baron Rothschild, the Bishop of Canterbury [sic]' as well as to customers in 'Sweden, Belgium, France, Spain, Portugal, Austria ... Singapore, New York, Cincinnati, Veracruz, Valparaiso.'

With such reputation, demand soon outstripped supply and various other producers started to sell wine under the Liebfraumilch name. As soon as German law created protected brand names in 1909, Valckenberg created Germany's first wine brand, 'Madonna' Liebfraumilch. What happened in 1910 was more critical: the Worms Chamber of Commerce found that 'in consequence of the many decades during which reputable traders have made somewhat free and unrestricted use of the name, and the resultant wide distribution as a renowned wine of quality – the name of Liebfraumilch applies exclusively to Rhine wines of good quality and delightful character.' This opened the floodgates. Liebfraumilch, which until then had at least been loosely connected to Worms and its Liebfrauenkirche, now lost connection not only to Worms but also to Rheinhessen.

The term Liebfraumilch was thus first defined as 'Rhine wine of good quality and *lieblich* character' (i.e. slightly sweet) in 1910. The name itself always enjoyed legal protection, but not the concept. In 1971 the Federal State of Rheinland Pfalz stated that '*Qualitätswein* from white wine grapes may be called Liebfraumilch,' so long as it was made predominantly from Riesling, Silvaner or Müller-Thurgau, without stating a variety on the label, with grapes originating in the regions of Nahe, Rheinhessen or Rheinpfalz and residual sugar not exceeding one-third of total alcohol. This was loose already and was to be made even more so: by 1983 the definition included Rheingau and residual sweetness was capped at *halbtrocken*, i.e. 18 grams per litre. By 1995 it was defined as having a minimum of 70 per cent of either Riesling, Silvaner, Müller-Thurgau or Kerner and residual sweetness was capped at *lieblich*, i.e. 45 grams per litre.

It is easy to sneer but Liebfraumilch was a huge success. In 1929 H. Sichel & Söhne in Mainz coined its brand Blue Nun. This and various other Liebfraumilch brands, usually not distributed in Germany, were best sellers in the UK, the US, Scandinavia and Canada. Supported by advertising campaigns, they treated non-wine drinking cultures to a semblance of continental sophistication. Popularity peaked in the early 1980s. The damage was done: Germany was tainted with the cheap and sweet image and lost market share. Today sales of generic Liebfraumilch are either dead or in terminal decline.

Valckenberg still trades in Worms. Through all the years it clung on to the precious vineyards it had bought in 1808 and made a real Liebfrauenstift Riesling. Its managing director for many years, Wilhelm Steifensand, a descendant of P.J. Valckenberg, sold the Valckenberg trading company but retained the actual vineyards in 2015. His Weingut Liebfrauenstift (see page 228) owns 11.5 hectares of the 13-hectare vineyard that surrounds the church. Under estate manager and winemaker Heiner Maleton the vines are now farmed organically. A first vintage was made in 2016, a simple Stiftswein Riesling and a Riesling from the Liebfrauenstift-Kirchenstück. Thus, in the twenty-first century, the original Liebfraumilch comes full circle as a dry Riesling from a single, classified site. The fifteenth-century sandstone Madonna in the garden must be pleased.

Weingut Bianka & Daniel Schmitt
Flörsheim-Dalsheim
www.schmitt-weingut.de

Bianka and Daniel Schmitt have chosen an uncompromising path of natural wine in the contemporary sense of the word. They met when Bianka, an oenology graduate from Budapest, came to work in Rheinhessen in 2012. In 2017 they took over Daniel's parental estate of 16 hectares which has been farmed organically since 2007 and was certified biodynamic in 2012. An Alsace visit to the estate of Patrick Meyer set them on their stylistic path. 'When you are in love you are open and creative,' Bianka notes. They still have the broad varietal spectrum typical of Rheinhessen but want to focus on Riesling, Pinot varieties and some aromatics. They export 90 per cent of production. Wines are vinified on skins in open *cuves* or amphorae, with some wines aged in wood. Their Riesling has a creamy, structured expression, their Silvaner is spicy and slender, their Weissburgunder savoury. They know what they are doing, and their styles, while not mainstream, are whistle-clean, bone-dry and delicious. They are a determined, energetic couple and an asset to the Rheinhessen winescape.

Try: Erdreich for structure and complete salty savouriness.

Strauch Sektmanufaktur GmbH
Osthofen
www.strauchsektmanufaktur.de

'I have always preferred Sekt to still wine,' says Isabel Strauch-Weißbach. She and her husband Tim Weißbach, from a neighbouring village, got together in Geisenheim where she majored in business, and he in winemaking. They took over Isabel's family estate in 2001 and embarked on an overhaul not only of equipment but also of style: the focus is on extended lees ageing and low dosage. There is a zero dosage, zero sulphur Sekt from Pinot Blanc: 'That's what we like to drink,' they say, almost in unison. The vineyards are certified organic and viticulture is geared to Sekt production. Hand harvest and fractional pressing is a given. There is long-aged *Rieslingsekt* with the softest mousse and a mere 2.7 grams per litre of dosage, and a *blanc de blancs* of Silvaner and Chardonnay. They push the envelope with a traditional method orange Sekt: skin-fermented Grauburgunder matured in barrique, aged for 48 months and disgorged without dosage. 'We only produce what we like to drink,' is their motto. They farm 25 hectares, mostly on the Mettenheimer Michelsberg and other sites in Osthofen and Mettenheim.

Try: Riesling 40 Monate Extra Brut Bio for finest foam and honeyed evolution.

Weingut Wechsler
Westhofen
www.weingut-wechsler.de

Only when the big city lights of Berlin had lost their allure did former TV producer Katharina Wechsler return home to Rheinhessen. She started thinking about moving in 2009 and came home in 2011. Her family always had a wine estate but her parents produced grapes and sold wine in bulk. Wechsler, with her Berlin years under her belt, came to wine with a different set of eyes than your average Rheinhessen kid. She has old Riesling vines in Kirchspiel, Morstein and the *monopole* of Westhofen's smallest *Einzellage*, Benn. She has Müller-Thurgau, Huxelrebe, Scheurebe and white Pinot varieties. While she turned a very serious hand to her dry Rieslings and Silvaners, she makes the no longer fashionable Huxelrebe and Müller-Thurgau into a fizzy, fun wine called Fräulein Hu; at 11% abv it is a hit in Hamburg and Berlin wine bars. She knows how to play in different registers. 'Stylistically I have arrived, now I am working on precision,' she says. Maxime Herkunft Rheinhessen member.

Try: Silvaner Westhofener Alte Reben for slender, weightless, dry refreshment.

Weingut Weedenborn
Monzernheim
www.weedenborn.de

Gesine Roll's 22 hectares are neatly split: one third is Sauvignon Blanc – amongst the best in Germany – one third is Riesling and one third is a trio of Weiss- and Grauburgunder and Chardonnay. Monzernheim sits on a on a plateau at 232 metres and is Wonnegau's highest elevation. 'This really works for the wines I make: taut, lower abv, elegant, filigree,' she says. She took over her family estate in 2008 and her parents still help. After training in the Pfalz (at Bassermann-Jordan) and South Africa (at Vergelegen) she also gained a business degree. It takes character to throw one's weight behind Sauvignon Blanc in such legendary Riesling country, but Roll has demonstrated that this works: 'Sauvignon Blanc is as demanding as Riesling. I see great potential for it in Germany, it works well on calcareous soils.' Her sites are in Westhofen, Monzernheim and Dittelsheim. Her Chardonnay grows above the top edge of the Morstein and combines utter freshness with a creamy core. Her Kirchspiel Riesling is a gloriously citrussy rendition of elegance. Her entry-level Sauvignon Blanc speaks vividly of nettle, her SB Réserve, fermented in 225-litre and 500-litre barrels can easily take its place next to Pessac-Léognan and the Steiermark. Watch out for this talented woman. Maxime Herkunft Rheinhessen member.

Try: Sauvignon Blanc Terra Rossa for leafy perfume and lovely texture.

Weingut Weinreich and Natürlich Weinreich
Bechtheim
www.weinreich-wein.de; www.natuerlichweinreich.de

Brothers Marc and Jan Weinreich have run their organically certified 20-hectare estate since 2009 and have since streamlined the usual Rheinhessen varietal excess. Many of the aromatic varieties have found a home in their natural wine project, Natürlich Weinreich, which they have run separately since 2016. Marc was smitten with natural wines from the start, but he describes his brother Jan as a moderating influence to his own extremism – even though he comes across as thoughtful and curious. Their natural wines are spicy, smooth and dry. They set a new impetus, even if they baffled some local folk. For the 'conventional' Weinreich wines, Marc's aim is to emphasize freshness, precision and slenderness – absolute dryness helps to show site typicity. His *Ortswein* Bechtheimer Riesling from the cooler Hasensprung and the warm Geyersberg sites is crisp and lithe, with mouth-watering lemon and snappy verve. The Lagenwein Riesling, also from Hasensprung, majors in citrus freshness but has an added dimension. I am sure we will hear more from these enterprising brothers. There also is a guesthouse. Maxime Herkunft Rheinhessen member.

Try: Tacheles for a fragrant, skin-fermented take on Bacchus, Kerner and Silvaner.

Weingut Wittmann
Westhofen
www.weingutwittmann.de

Philipp Wittmann has become a legend in his own lifetime. He took over from his progressive parents in 2004 (they introduced organic farming when this was still unfashionable, Philipp introduced biodynamic farming in 2004) and has been fully in charge since 2007. 'But we live this as a family,' he is keen to stress. He owns 30 hectares but also runs the separate label 100 Hügel from bought-in fruit. His own vineyards, all in Westhofen, are farmed biodynamically: Aulerde (south-facing, warm, loess and loam on limestone), Kirchspiel (clay and marl on weathered limestone), Brunnenhäuschen (like Kirchspiel but with more iron oxide) and finally Morstein (calcareous clay marl on limestone). These vineyards are all in one ridge running east to west, just south of Monzernheim's plateau. They slope from about 270 metres to 90 metres. While these vineyards do not look spectacular, what makes them exceptional is below ground. There are further sites in Bechtheim and Gundesheim. Morstein was mentioned as early as 1282, but Wittmann notes that wines from these exceptional sites were often sold under the far more famous name of Nierstein. Seventy per cent of plantings are Riesling, 20 per cent are Weissburgunder, 'a grape variety that adapts wonderfully to our area,' he says. There also is Silvaner and Chardonnay – he has planted Spätburgunder in his Höllenbrand vineyard but no wine has been made yet. 'But I see myself as a white wine winemaker,' he notes. His Riesling vines were selected in the Pfalz, Alsace and Saar to achieve genetic diversity. His aim is to make textured, precise, long-lived wines. 'It is all about provenance. I am not speaking about fruit, I am interested in what happens afterwards.' His Rieslings have an alluring saltiness that draws you in, as well as purity and an inherent coolness. He is amongst Germany's best. VDP and Maxime Herkunft Rheinhessen member estate.

Try: Any of his Rieslings for extended, saline freshness and thrill.

BINGEN, INGELHEIM, MAINZ, NORTH- AND WEST- RHEINHESSEN

The central part of Rheinhessen is the Selztal. The river Selz runs into the Rhine near Ingelheim and traces the valley around the Mainzer Berg. 'We see the Selztal as the cool north of Rheinhessen,' says Stefan Braunewell of Weingut Braunewell. Tobias Knewitz, of the eponymous Weingut, points out that harvest in Ingelheim starts ten days later than in Bechtheim, one of the warmest villages in the Wonnegau.

Vineyards are mainly on the hillsides and plateaus, ridges of the former seabed; the flat lowlands are planted to other arable crops. The 1927 guidebook entry for Essenheim suggests its wines are suited for Sekt production; the Appenheim entry says 'light wines'. Bingen had a trump card with its Scharlachberg, the south-facing slope of the Rochusberg. Ingelheim on the Rhine had a long tradition for Spät- and Frühburgunder. In western Rheinhessen, volcanic formations of porphyry and melaphyr come to the surface, former islands in the inland sea. Yet the story is no different: Gernot Achenbach in Wöllsheim remembers that in the 1980s vines often would not flower until July. Daniel Wagner in Siefersheim says his grandfather still made base wines for Sekt producers – it was much cooler then – 'steely' is how the old guidebook characterized the wines.

Weingut Achenbach
Wonsheim
www.weingut-achenbach.de

While three generations help to run this estate in the cool, western edge of Rheinhessen, Frank and Constanza Achenbach are its fresh-faced current winemakers. The youngsters met when they both worked a vintage in New Zealand, Constanza being a wine graduate from Chile. They joined Frank's family estate in 2014 and are in the process of putting their stamp on proceedings. Father Gernot had laid the groundwork, starting with just 2 hectares in 1980, which have grown to 22 hectares today. Seventy per cent of plantings are white and are the typical mix of Riesling, Pinot varieties and aromatics. The reds are Spätburgunder, Frühburgunder and St Laurent. Their sites are in Siefersheim and Wonsheim. It is obvious that the young couple has many ideas and that the older generation gives them rein. 'I want to make wine without fear and with feeling,' Constanza says. 'We want to give our wines time,' continues Frank. It is lovely to see Chilean spirit and Rheinhessen realism combine. They are using skin contact and spontaneous ferments in wood to hone their style and there is a clear desire to give more profile to their sites and some of their old-vine treasures. Their wines are honest, clear-cut and expressive.

Try: St Laurent Uralt, a gorgeously Pinot-esque red from 70-year-old vines.

Weingut Simone Adams
Ingelheim
www.adamswein.de

Dr Simone Adams is a complete Pinot nut. She also is a scientist and hunter. Her father's unexpected and untimely death in 2010 prompted Adams to leave her research post in Geisenheim and return to Ingelheim where her family has made wine since 1832. Spätburgunder has always been part of the programme in this *Rotweinstadt*. The only condition she set on her return was to do everything her own way. 'It meant learning very fast,' she remembers. It also meant building a new, modern cellar in 2013. Since then she has made a name for herself with fine, nervy Spätburgunder. Her vision includes whole-bunch ferments and her top wine, Kaliber 48 (her hunting reference), was fully whole-bunch fermented. The other Spätburgunder bottlings also have various degrees of whole-bunch fermentation. There is also Grauburgunder, Weissburgunder, Chardonnay and a tiny bit of Riesling and Viognier. She has 10 hectares of which 4.5 are planted to Spätburgunder. Some are in the upper reaches of the Ingelheimer Pares, Horn and Sonnenhang, with its 'Auf dem Haun' parcel. Her Pinots, which are great value, are already speaking for her. Watch this space.

Try: Spätburgunder Auf dem Haun for inherent freshness and brilliance.

Weingut J. Bettenheimer
Ingelheim
www.weingut-bettenheimer.de

Jens Bettenheimer returned to his parental estate in the narrow lanes of old Ingelheim in 2005. His family has made wine here since 1710. After nine months in Marlborough, New Zealand, he returned with an open mind and various ideas. He farms almost 15 hectares on various sites: the Ingelheimer Horn, Täuscherspfad and Sonnenhang, all southwest-facing sites on the Mainzer Berg, Appenheimer Hundertgulden and Egelspfad – predominantly limestone sites which works well for his Pinot-heavy offering. There are Pinots Blanc and Gris, Chardonnay, Silvaner and Riesling as well as Spät- and Frühburgunder. He is in the process of building a new winery in the Sonnenhang, is looking to expand but not in a rush to do so. He works organically but is not certified and tries to ferment as much as he can spontaneously, using

Stück, Halbstück and tonneau. He ferments Silvaner in granite and skin-ferments his Grauburgunder Aurum. He also has a rare talent for Frühburgunder which is lovely, tender and translucent. Maxime Herkunft Rheinhessen member.

Try: Schlossberg Frühburgunder for perfume and spice.

Weingut Bischel
Appenheim
www.weingut-bischel.de

Christian and Matthias Runkel are an ambitious pair of young winemakers. Both made sure they trained with leading lights at home and abroad and set about refining what their parents had built. Their grandparents already made wine, but their parents founded the *Weingut*. They farm about 20 hectares in the Binger Scharlachberg, Appenheimer Hundertgulden and Siefersheimer Heerkretz, so their portfolio gives you the best of Rheinhessen. Just 15 per cent of production is red wines (Spätburgunder and a little Frühburgunder), and 35 per cent of their sites are dedicated to Riesling, followed by Weissburgunder, Grauburgunder and Silvaner. They work organically but are not certified. They set store by judicious skin contact, spontaneous ferments and vinification in both stainless steel and wood. Their intuition brings out the lovely spice notes of the Scharlachberg. Great value. VDP and Maxime Herkunft Rheinhessen member estate.

Try: Binger Riesling for juicy, spicy citrus fruit.

Weingut Braunewell
Essenheim, Selztal
www.braunewell-wein.de

Father Axel and sons Stefan and Christian Braunewell are a team of allrounders. 'Everyone does everything,' Stefan says, going on to explain that his forebears were Huguenots who came to this Protestant village in 1655 in the largely Catholic area around Mainz. Stefan's grandfather started bottling wines in 1967 when the estate was still a mixed farm. Today the family's focus is on 26 hectares of wines in the calcareous terra fusca soils of the Essenheimer Teufelspfad (190–230 metres), the Klopp parcel in its higher reaches has very poor limestone soils. This is where Riesling and Grauburgunder grow. They also have vines in the Elsheimer Blume, a steep, terraced site of calcareous marl with Spätburgunder and their oldest Riesling vines, planted in 1976. Grauburgunder and Riesling make up 30 per cent of plantings each, followed by 20 per cent Spätburgunder, 10 per cent white aromatic varieties and 10 per cent Syrah, Merlot and Cabernet Franc. Stefan relishes the natural acidity of his wines which the higher elevations and the constant breeze bring. The wines put fruit and freshness into focus, the Spätburgunders are rounded and cherryish in style, almost in an international vein, but full of freshness. The family is building a new cellar, store and tasting room, so this will be a Selztal destination. Maxime Herkunft Rheinhessen member estate.

Try: Spätburgunder Teufelspfad for dark, brooding fruit with an edge.

Sektmanufaktur Flik
Mainz
www.flik.de

Rüdiger Flik is sensible. When he trained with Baden Spätburgunder legend Bernhard Huber, looking after the Sekt base wines was one of his jobs. This gave him the desire to produce his own Sekt. Once he had Geisenheim under his belt in 2011 he asked Huber for some used barriques and started with three barrels of base wines, 'just for pleasure and friends'. Of course he could not stick to this and his project grew. In 2016 he was able to move his production to an old Mainz estate and could start farming his first hectare of Spätburgunder and Chardonnay vines. To finance this he hangs on to a full-time job so he does not need investors and can grow at his own pace. So far, he has only released vintage Sekts which spend a minimum of 16 months on the lees. But fear not, he also has some top stuff slumbering in his cellars. For now, there are bright, fresh-faced Sekts with promising creaminess. One more face in Germany's increasingly colourful and exciting Sekt landscape.

Try: Blanc de Noirs for easy elegance.

Weingut Knewitz
Appenheim
www.weingut-knewitz.de

Since brothers Björn and Tobias Knewitz took over their parental estate in 2009, they have earned plaudits for their brilliantly pure, snappy and bright Rieslings. Both trained as *Winzer* and have international *stages* under their belt. Their father started the estate in 1968 with 4 hectares. Today they farm 20 hectares but have made a clear cut: until 2007 the estate grew 28 grape varieties. The brothers have reduced this to 45 per cent Riesling, 20 per cent Weissburgunder and 20 per cent Chardonnay with some Spätburgunder, Silvaner and Sauvignon Blanc. 'Riesling plays first fiddle,' Tobias says, and it could not be more evident in the wines. Their sites are in the Appenheimer Hundertgulden, Eselspfad and Goldberg, Nieder-Hilbersheimer Steinacker and Honigberg. They are mainly of calcareous loams and marls on limestone but have proportions of iron ore. The Hundertgulden vineyard is their key site, first mentioned in 1143 in a deed from Kloster Disibodenberg. The wines show an uncommon freshness and purity. There is something effortless about their depth and brilliance, something taut and vivid. What is even better is their incredible value. These brothers will be stars. Maxime Herkunft Rheinhessen member estate.

Try: Gutsriesling for total refreshment and Riesling DNA – their calling card.

Weingut J. Neus
Ingelheim
www.weingut-neus.de

This 1881-founded Spätburgunder house was rescued from obscurity and decline when it was bought by the local Schmitz family in 2013. It is their plan to return it to its former glory. To achieve this they hired Julien Meissner, who makes the wine and looks after the vineyards, and Lewis Schmitt, on the commercial side. They joined in 2015 and 2016, respectively, and make a promising team. Meissner says the idea is 'to reinterpret Spätburgunder without ever forgetting that we are in Ingelheim, Rheinhessen.' They have big boots to fill as Neus was once a leading estate. Its founder, Josef Neus, even made his own clonal selection. Today 80 per cent of their 12 hectares are planted to Spätburgunder; the rest is Pinot Blanc, Chardonnay (watch out for this!), Riesling and Silvaner, with a tiny bit of St Laurent and Frühburgunder for rosé. The vineyards are on the sandy loams of the Mainzer Berg and the heavier loams of Westerberg – both have limestone bedrock. What Meissner and Schmitt present of their maiden vintages is exciting. The Spätburgunders show immense purity, an acidic backbone and the perfume that results from fruit harvested *à point*. They use some stems and dial back on new oak. They have also announced the exciting prospect of Sekt. What a wonderful addition, or rather readmission, to Germany's Pinot landscape. VDP and Maxime Herkunft Rheinhessen member estate.

Try: Spätburgunder Alte Reben from 60-year-old vines for gorgeous perfume.

Weingut Riffel
Bingen-Büdesheim
www.weingut-riffel.de

Carolin and Erik Riffel are proof that you need neither tattoos nor abundant beards to be cutting edge. The pair met at a wine tasting in 1999 and planned their dream winery on their honeymoon. When Erik had taken over his parental estate in 1991 there were just 2 hectares. Together they took this to the next stage with a new winery that was finished in 2007. They farm 17 hectares of vineyards today, spread around Bingen with a substantial parcel on the Scharlachberg which gets its name from the high iron-oxide content of its topsoil on quartzite bedrock. It is a majestic slate fault that falls to the Nahe river, which forms the border between this northern part of Rheinhessen and the Nahe region, rising to 220 metres and first mentioned in 1248. Their house style is whistle-clean, wonderfully pure and incredible value. This is as evident in their zesty *Gutswein* as in their impressive single-site Riesling from Scharlachberg, a GG in all but name. In 2014 they started experimenting and were amongst the first to produce *pét nat* in Germany. Skin-fermented Silvaner is a new paradigm in the orange category. Maxime Rheinhessen Member. Certified organic since 2009 but now working with biodynamic practices.

Try: Gutswein Scheurebe trocken, which is subtle but sassy.

Michael Teschke
Laurenziberg near Gau-Algesheim
www.weingut-teschke.de

There is nothing conventional about Michael Teschke. This uncompromising libertarian openly admits that he has created his own little world up here. You pass flourishing orchards and gardens *en route* to Laurenziberg, a hamlet on one of Rheinhessen's three holy hills, sites of early Christian worship. At 240 metres, the Laurenziberg affords views of the Nahe valley to the west, and the Rhine to the north, the Rochusberg partly obscuring the view of the Rheingau on the opposite bank. The soils are sandstone sediments, calcareous loams and marls. Teschke, who resists every mould, describes his winemaking style as 'naïf'. Looking at his calloused hands, his almost childlike fascination with the wildlife, his unintentionally lyrical statements, this unusual term seems apt. Far from being some latter-day hippy, he says he is the product of a 'Prussian' upbringing, and trained as a soldier. His grandparents and parents had moved to the farm as resettled refugees from the east after the Second World War and eventually bought it in 1956. Teschke took over in the late 1990s, trained as a *Winzer* in 1995 and has developed a very individual way of working, treasuring his Silvaner vines, planted in the 1960s. 'This is my hill, I know every clod of earth,' he says. His vineyards are in stark contrast to the neat, machine-harvestable rows in neighbouring plots, where the brown death of glyphosate is so apparent. But he refuses the labels of organic and biodynamic farming. He makes *Landwein*, so he does not require the official *Amtliche Prüfnummer*. His Silvaner 'Erster unter Gleichen' (first among equals) is whistle-clean, slender and profound. One-third of his production is natural wine without added sulphur. All his ferments are spontaneous, the wines are made in stainless steel and used oak. He farms 6.5 hectares and is a keen observer of nature, taking joy from every nuance of the season – and defying every convention. Rheinhessen is lucky to have him.

Try: Blauer Silvaner for purity and transparency.

Weingut Thörle
Saulheim, Selztal
www.thoerle-wein.de

Brothers Johannes and Christoph Thörle surprised themselves as much as the international wine world when their Spätburgunder from the Saulheimer Hölle won first place in a blind line-up of international Pinot Noirs in London in 2011. Since then they have raised their game yet further, still supported by their father Rudolf. They farm 28 hectares around Saulheim in the Selztal and have three chief sites: Probstey, a very exposed, south-facing site at around 120 metres; Schlossberg, a west-facing, well-ventilated site of heavier marl that catches Rhine winds and rises to 220 metres; and Hölle, a south-facing, protected slope of limestone rising to 240 metres. The family always grew vines but had just 1.75 hectares in the 1970s, expanding to 9 hectares by 2000 and 28 hectares today. Fifty per cent are planted to Riesling, 25 per cent to Spätburgunder and the remaining quarter is Silvaner, Weissburgunder and Sauvignon Blanc. The brothers have a clear aim, and work steadily towards it. They set store by finesse and substance and favour a lean, bone-dry style. They achieve this by exacting standards in vineyard and cellar. The wines are whistle-clean, precise and expressive and have enough confidence not to lean on too much oak. On the contrary, they rely on inherent concentration. It is impossible to say what impresses more: the snappy, zesty, salty Rieslings or their seductive, chiselled Spätburgunders. Excellent value. Maxime Herkunft Rheinhessen member estate.

Try: Spätburgunder and Riesling Ortsweine – as a most exquisite calling card.

Weingut Wagner-Stempel
Siefersheim
www.wagner-stempel.de

Daniel Wagner is a purist, a quiet man in a quiet corner of Rheinhessen. Old volcanic and rhyolite formations, once stony islands in Rheinhessen's prehistoric sea, are his fascinating vineyard soils. Wagner describes this part of Rheinhessen as 'undiscovered, untouched and wild. Hard to farm but compelling.' He took over in 1992, when the estate had just 7 hectares of vines. Wagner expanded this to 25 hectares (certified organic since 2008) and has taken his estate to the very top in Germany. In his easy, self-deprecating manner he refers to himself as the 'janitor'. Fifty per cent of his plantings are Riesling, 20 per cent Weissburgunder, followed by Silvaner, Scheurebe, Sauvignon Blanc and – as a hobby – some Spät- and Frühburgunder. Wagner's chief sites are Siefersheimer Heerkretz (an exposed, south-east and south-west-facing volcanic reef of rhyolite and melaphyr, up to 280 metres), Siefersheimer Höllberg (south-south-east facing, rhyolite, up to 220 metres, warmer than Heerkretz) and Binger Scharlachberg (south-facing, quartzite, up to 220 metres). Here he grows exceptional, world-class Rieslings of breathtaking purity. It was Wagner who really put the Heerkretz on the international map and recultivated various fallow parcels over the years. The Heerkretz wines are crystalline and brisk, the Höllberg wines are alluringly tangerine-fruited. Both wines are slender, taut, and precise. Both sites are combined in the 'Porphyr' Riesling – a steal. This is a Riesling experience that cannot be missed. The same clarity pervades his other wines. You simply must visit: the 1840s manor has a gorgeous cobbled courtyard with an ancient chestnut tree in the centre and the tasting room is under the elegant vaulted ceiling of the former stables. VDP and Maxime Herkunft Rheinhessen member.

Try: Porphyr Riesling for purity and thrill.

17
SAALE-UNSTRUT AND SACHSEN – ADDITIONS FROM ANOTHER GERMANY

Saale-Unstrut and Sachsen (Saxony), respectively the most northerly and easterly regions, stretch German viticulture to a latitude of 51.5 degrees in the north and almost to the Polish border in the east. With the reunification of Germany in October 1990 (it had been divided since 1949), these two regions located in the former German Democratic Republic (GDR) – a clear misnomer – brought the total of German wine regions to 13. The GDR with its Stalinist socialism and collectivized agriculture had not been kind to viticulture. A Sachsen winemaker remembers: 'There was simply no diversity. The state-owned co-op in Meissen made just one wine: Müller-Thurgau. All the individuality that characterizes a wine landscape was gone.' He also remembers the turbulent weeks and months following the collapse of the old regime, the process of returning collectivized, state-run agriculture to private ownership and of integrating these two regions into the existing German wine law in 1990: 'There was a gold-rush atmosphere. It was the zero hour. You had no administration, nothing. There were many compromises. It was chaotic. Notwithstanding that, we made wine. We evolved alongside the authorities.' Some vineyards that had been confiscated by the state between 1945 and 1949 were restituted to their previous owners, or their heirs, who could then farm or sell them. Vineyards could also be bought from the *Treuhandanstalt*, a public trust agency established in 1990 and tasked with privatizing all the property of the now defunct state. The events of 1990 were cataclysmic and the change these wine regions witnessed and lived through is immense. Looking at the ancient vineyards now, forty years of socialist management seem like a mere intermission. Thirty years after the reunification, they thrive once again. The resilience of people and land is simply remarkable.

SAALE-UNSTRUT – SCATTERED JEWELS

This far north it is only in choice spots that vines will flourish: like the south-facing slopes lining the Unstrut river for the 20-something kilometres from Memleben to just outside Naumburg where it joins the Saale. This much larger river, likewise, flows past a few select spots from Bad Sulza in the south to Merseburg in the north. This at least is the heartland of Saale-Unstrut. The region straddles three *Bundesländer*: Thüringen, Sachsen-Anhalt and Brandenburg. Do not expect a sea of vines, vineyards are few and far between, scattered like jewels across a large area. Some, like the Saalhäuser, are sheltered suntraps, others, like the terraced Freyburger Edelacker, cling spectacularly to a steep curve of the Unstrut. There are also vineyards just north of Jena and outside Weimar in the southernmost part of this region and west of Halle in the area of the Mansfelder Seen (Mansfeld Lakes). The northern extreme is on the river Havel in Werder, just west of Potsdam, at a latitude of 52°N! With just four small vineyards it really is a lone outpost. Geologically the area is dominated by Triassic formations of *Muschelkalk*, loess and loam with some *Keuper* and *Buntsandstein* present in parts. Just how choice the Saale-Unstrut sites are is evident in their long history. The first documented mention of viticulture was thought to date to a 998 deed from emperor Otto III gifting a vineyard to the Benedictine abbey of Memleben. However, just as the region was celebrating its millennial anniversary of viticulture in 1998, another source was found that pinned the year to 973. One of the oldest named vineyards is the Pfortenser Klöppelberg, first documented in 1154, planted by the Cistercians of Pforta Abbey, founded in 1137. How deeply viticulture is ingrained becomes evident in Naumburg's Gothic cathedral. In the mid-thirteenth century an anonymous stonemason, known only as 'Master of Naumburg', carved vine leaves, buds and grapes into the stone in exquisite, naturalistic detail. His sculptures of the cathedral's founders seem to be a proto-feminist statement. The women have such expressive, modern faces: Margravine Uta with her haunting gaze, Margravine Reglindis with her encouraging smile. The menfolk next to them pale in comparison. But back to wine. The Medieval Warm Period allowed viticulture to spread to an estimated 10,000 hectares in the area. A decree from emperor Charles IV from 1350 allowed all citizens in the area to own vineyards. Cooling climate and the Reformation, with its dissolution of monasteries, set viticultural decline in motion. When phylloxera hit the area in 1887 there were just 600 hectares of vines left. The nineteenth century saw a second, tentative viticultural flowering by way of Sekt with the foundation of various smaller *Sektkellereien*. By 1849 there were 43 of them. One *Sektkellerei*, Kloss & Foerster, founded in 1856, survived both world wars, the Third Reich and the GDR and became one of Germany's biggest Sekt brands: Rotkäppchen (i.e. Little Red Riding Hood). Only a small proportion of the nineteenth-century Sekt base wines were sourced locally as Saale-Unstrut vintages were unreliable. Today only an infinitesimal part of Rotkäppchen's production is from Saale-Unstrut vineyards.

With just 100 hectares of vines in 1918, viticulture was almost usurped by other crops. After the First World War in 1919, the loss of Lorraine to France prompted the government to move its antiphylloxera research station from Metz to Naumburg. This led to the establishment of trial vineyards, but by the 1930s just 'three dozen hectares' remained in the area. After the Second World War the area was under Soviet occupation. With the foundation of the GDR in 1949 viticulture initially took a back-seat. New plantings were made in the 1960s and the VEB, or *Volkseigener Betrieb*, the state-owned winery in Naumburg-Bad Kösen (today Landesweingut Kloster Pforta), was mainly engaged in bottling wines from Bulgaria, Romania and Yugoslavia (as it was then). Rotkäppchen, meanwhile, moving from traditional method via the transfer method to Charmat, just like its western counterparts, became a model factory, pumping out socialist Sekt. In the fierce 1986/87 winter a horrendous frost killed more than half of the vines. There was no nursery in the east which could have supplied the replacement vines needed but somehow, via Moravia and other connections, Austrian Zweigelt vines could be imported – and Zweigelt found a new home here.

Administratively, there are three *Bereiche*, four *Grosslagen* and 47 *Einzellagen*. In 2017 there were 772 hectares of vines (almost doubled from the 390 hectares in 1990), of which 114 hectares were Müller-Thurgau, followed by Weissburgunder (108 hectares), hailed by many as the most important variety for the region, and Riesling (69 hectares) – but there is a vast array of varieties. Viticulture is revived and flourishes but climate remains a challenge. 'The region is marginal,' says Klaus Böhme of the eponymous estate. 'I am not talking about heat summation or hail storms but about winter frosts where temperatures go as low as -20°C. This is where the greatest danger lies.' In 2010 eight estates got together to form 'Breitengrad 51' (latitude 51), an association that promotes the region and sticks to the quality pyramid of *Gutswein, Ortswein, Lagenwein*. Every year they make one communal wine, called Allerhand, an easy-drinking, light white which embodies their sunny optimism.

Weingut Klaus Böhme
Laucha an der Unstrut
www.weingut-klaus-boehme.de

The small farm on the river Unstrut has been in the family for more than 300 years and vines always were a part of it. It was a quirk of the law that the vineyards legally remained the family's cadastral property despite the wholesale liquidation of private farms in 1960. This quirk turned into opportunity when Klaus Böhme was able to reclaim his half hectare in 1990 and start his own *Weingut*. 'I turned my hobby into my job and was at just the right age to do that,' he says. His first commercial vintage in 1994 featured Silvaner, Weissburgunder, Müller-Thurgau, Riesling and Portugieser – still the core of his offer. Today he farms 13 hectares in ten parcels on ten different *Einzellagen*. The Dorndorfer Rappental, a south-south-west facing *Muschelkalk* site, and the Burgscheidunger Veitsgrube, south-facing with deep clay soils, are bottled as single sites. He eschews herbicides and mineral fertilizers and aims to apply for organic certification, the first in Saale-Unstrut. His whites are fragrant, bright and fresh. His top Riesling is called Bergstern.

Try: Bergstern for Unstrut Riesling expression.

Weingut Born
Höhnstedt
www.weingut-born.de

Elisabeth and Jochen Born are young parents and winemakers: Elisabeth looks after the vineyards while her husband, imported from Württemberg, makes the wines. Ninety per cent of their 8.5 hectares are on the Höhnstedter Kreisberg (*Buntsandstein*), the rest on the Höhnstedter Steineck. Elisabeth's family was allowed to keep some vineyard land but had to deliver all the fruit to the co-op during GDR times. Her father, Günter, an electrical engineer, tended the vines as well as he could, made some wine as a hobby in glass balloons and in 1991 was the first in the village to start a private *Weingut*. Bit by bit he added small parcels of vines and replanted them. Those were tough days and young Elisabeth did not immediately fall in love with wine, but changed her agronomy studies in Halle to viticulture in Geisenheim. There she met Jochen and the couple then worked in New Zealand and South Africa. They returned home and have run the estate since 2010. Elisabeth loves her Weissburgunder, Jochen his Riesling, both are avid experimenters. Their wines are whistle-clean, the whites are pure, the reds are vivid and smooth. 'We have the chance to make very honest wines,' she says and that's just what they do. Watch this space. Breitengrad 51 member estate.

Try: Riesling Höhnstedt Buntsandstein for precision, Steillage Portugieser for gentleness.

Winzerhof Gussek
Naumburg
www.winzerhof-gussek.de

André Gussek is a veteran of Saale-Unstrut winemaking. He was the last cellarmaster of the state-owned co-op in Naumburg and today uses the former site of the viticultural research station as his base. He remembers the supply issues of the socialist *Materialwirtschaft* with its shortage of cork, bottles and labels well but has happily turned to quality winemaking. In 1993, when the co-op was finally wound down, he was able to apply to buy land and has since run his own estate, initially with just 1.8 hectares. These days he has a cellarmaster, Hella Päger, and his sons Thomas and Stefan have also joined the company. Today they farm 12 hectares, spread over the *Muschelkalk* sites Naumburger Steinmeister, Naumburger Sonneck, Naumburger Göttersitz and, much further upstream on the Saale, the Kaatschener Dachsberg. This last vineyard holds a treasure: a parcel of 1927-planted Silvaner vines whose grapes are vinified and bottled separately each year. The wines are rounded and mellow, a little old-school perhaps, but they have concentration and a lasting aftertaste. Breitengrad 51 member estate.

Try: Naumburger Steinmeister Riesling for extract and roundness.

Weingut Hey
Naumburg
www.weinguthey.de

Matthias Hey farms 5 hectares in the Naumburger Steinmeister and Naumburger Sonneck vineyards; he owns half of them and leases the other half. Half of his production is Riesling, the rest are Weiss-, Grau- and Spätburgunder, Silvaner and Zweigelt. Hey was a pupil at the Kloster Pforta boarding school and while his parents were visiting him, they came across an old, steep, overgrown vineyard and bought it in 2001 in order to cultivate it as a hobby. They restored the drystone walls in the steep site and young Matthias was so taken with viticulture that he decided to study it in Geisenheim, where he graduated in 2005. He followed this with stints in Friuli and Abruzzo before returning home in 2007. He founded his estate in 2008 with the one hectare of vineyard his parents had re-cultivated. 'It was the best decision I ever made,' he says, acknowledging that 'it was only possible by everyone in the family pulling together.' He is enthusiastic: 'Saale-Unstrut is a region which had to reinvent itself. And we are in the middle of doing just that. We have to discover this for ourselves.' His wines are fresh and experimental, with great backbone. Some of the whites are partially fermented on skins. Watch this youngster! Breitengrad 51 member estate. VDP member estate.

Try: Zweigelt for wonderful structure.

Landesweingut Kloster Pforta
Naumburg
www.kloster-pforta.de

If any estate encompasses the entire history of the region it is this one. Its wine shop is still on the site chosen by the Cistercians in 1137 as they founded the Abbey Sanctae Mariae ad Portam, or Kloster Pforta. Before the Reformation the abbey owned 167 vineyards, amounting to 260 hectares across 62 villages. In 1540 Moritz, Duke of Saxony dissolved the monastery and established a school which exists to this day. Björn Probst, managing director, says the *Weingut* was always in the hands of the state: whether that was the feudal lord, the Prussian state, the German Reich or the GDR. In GDR times it served as state-run co-op, made some local wines but mainly bottled foreign wines and cranked out wine-based fruit cocktails. Since 1993 it has been owned by the federal state of

Sachsen-Anhalt and now makes much of its monastic past. The modern winery is just across the Saale river from the old abbey. With 50 hectares of vineyards it is the region's largest estate. Its sites include the Pfortenser Klöppelberg (*Muschelkalk*), Naumburger Paradies (loam), Saalhäuser (*Muschelkalk*), Gosecker Dechantenberg, the oldest terraced site of the region (*Buntsandstein*) and the Eulauer Heidelberg (loess-loam). Probst, who came on board in 2017, is a dynamic manager and wants to turn Kloster Pforta into the leading estate of the region, knowing 'how much potential slumbers in these sites'. He is also active in the Breitengrad group, which he sees as a 'quality offensive necessary due to the remoteness of the region.' While local sales are strong, he knows he needs to sell nationally and internationally. The fact that he has allowed cellarmaster Christoph Lindner to invest in a granite vessel and in 1,200-litre *Doppelstück* barrels shows the direction of travel. The wines are expressive, slender and vivid. There is much to look forward to. Breitengrad 51 member estate.

Try: Gosecker Dechantenberg Riesling for fragrant tangerine notes.

Weingut Uwe Lützkendorf
Naumburg
www.weingut-luetzkendorf.de

The Lützkendorfs are an old *Winzer* family in Naumburg and have long owned the Hohe Gräte vineyard in Karsdorf on the Unstrut, a site classified as *Grosse Lage* by the VDP. It is a spectacular south-south-west facing site on a limestone escarpment. Uwe Lützkendorf is the man who picked up where his forebears had left off when they had to give up their own vineyards under GDR rules. Uwe's father was cellarmaster at the state winery in Naumburg (today Landesweingut Kloster Pforta) so he decided to study fermentation and drink technology at Berlin's Humboldt University, graduating in 1990. He worked at a large winery and a co-op in the west but when the family vineyard land was restituted in 1991, he started making wine. Apart from the Hohe Gräte, where 90 per cent of his 9-hectare vineyards are, he also farms a parcel on the Freyburger Edelacker which he replanted completely in 1998. Textured Weissburgunder with chalky complexity is his strong suit, even though he also grows Riesling, Traminer, Gutedel, Spätburgunder and Zweigelt. Lützkendorf is a history buff and excellent raconteur and his wines have much of his own strait-laced honesty and real character. VDP member estate.

Try: Weissburgunder GG Hohe Gräte.

Weingut Pawis

Freyburg-Zscheiplitz
www.weingut-pawis.de

Bernard Pawis caught the wine bug from his parents, who had 0.15 hectares of vines. Like all owners of small vineyards, they had to deliver the fruit to the co-op. Pawis apprenticed as a *Winzer* at Schloss Wackerbarth in Sachsen, then continued with horticulture at the University of Erfurt. After the collapse of the GDR Pawis decided to go west and did not return home until 1998. His parents had founded a *Weingut* in 1990 with just 0.5 hectares and ran a small *Strausswirtschaft*. Pawis's mind, however, was set on quality. Success came quickly and he and his wife Kerstin managed to buy or lease parcels in the best sites: the terraced Freyburger Edelacker, of weathered *Muschelkalk*, Freyburger Mühlberg, Zscheiplitzer Himmelreich and Naumburger Sonneck. In 2005 Pawis took on another vast project, with the purchase of the ruined former grange of a Benedictine abbey in Zscheipliz. Today it is a real destination, with tasting rooms and a restaurant. Do not miss its 500-year-old well: it is 90 metres deep and wonderfully spooky. Today the family farms 16 hectares in total. Unusually 35 per cent are planted to Riesling – the wines are zesty and taut. Next up is Weissburgunder which, he says, 'is very important for this region, I could not imagine my estate without it.' The entry-level wines are light and bright, made from aromatic varieties. There is bottle-fermented Sekt as well. VDP member estate.

Try: Gewürztraminer for real freshness and Zweigelt for suppleness.

Rotkäppchen Sektkellerei

Freyburg
www.rotkaeppchen.de

Founded in 1856 as Kloss & Foerster, the name Rotkäppchen, or Little Red Riding Hood, has been in use since 1894. The *Sektkellerei* has survived much adversity and today is Germany's leading entry-level brand of Sekt, selling fizz for as little as €3.99 (even less when on special offer). These tank-fermented wines are distributed across Germany and made from pan-European base wines. Kloss & Foerster was a favourite brand of Kaiser Wilhelm II, helping to popularize the brand in military circles. The house weathered the world economic crisis and the Second World War, was turned into a socialist model factory in GDR times and was once again privatized in 1993. In 2002 the company merged with the old Sekthaus Mumm in Eltville, and in 2003 it bought Geldermann in Baden, creating a sparkling wine powerhouse with enviable brand equity. Today the Rotkäppchen-Mumm *Sektkellereien* owns a portfolio of wine and spirits brands. The historic site in the centre of picturesque and cobbled Freyburg boasts a five-floor-deep cellar and offers daily tours and tastings. Here you can also taste a range of bottle-fermented Sekts – the Weissburgunder Sekt is made from local grapes.

Try: Mocca Perle for its sheer exoticism: a sweetish, creamy, coffee-flavoured Sekt.

SACHSEN – THE PLEASURE PRINCIPLE

Germany's most easterly region runs along a majestic stretch of the Elbe river. From quaint Pillnitz just south of Dresden, past Radebeul and Meissen, it follows the river for about 50 kilometres before petering out in the old wine village of Diesbar-Seußlitz. Its vineyards, mostly looking west and south-west across the river, have turned their face towards the sun in knowing, eternal optimism. Do not let the northerly latitudes confound you – 51.0°N in Pillnitz, 51.5° in Zadel – these steep slopes were made for wine. Where other regions come across as wild or remote, majestic or pastoral, Sachsen (Saxony) appears like an extended pleasure ground. You can barely move for *Lustschlösser,* pretty pleasure palaces, set in beautiful parkland. Despite the manicured parkland there is nothing effete about Sachsen. On the contrary, its humour and language have remained deliciously earthy. The pleasure principle seems to have been anchored in Saxon DNA for a while: in 1491 Saxons applied for and received a special papal dispensation to use butter in their Stollen, initially a meagre bread for the pre-Christmas fast, turning it into the rich Christmas confection it is today. No-one, however, did more to cement the region's reputation for opulence than the absolutist Kurfürst August der Starke ('the Strong', 1670–1733), Elector of Saxony. His family had form in living it up, but he took celebration and debauchery to a whole new level. One commentator aptly dubbed him the 'Bacchus of Baroque'. He is also responsible for the architectural splendour that is Dresden, bombed to smithereens in 1945 and painstakingly rebuilt, and the establishment of the world-famous porcelain manufacturer in Meissen. Today August's lifestyle is a source of regional pride and various festivities keep his spirit alive.

> ### Goldriesling
>
> Despite hailing from Alsace where this variety was crossed in 1893, today Goldriesling is celebrated as a Saxon original. That's probably because there are 28 hectares of it here – more than anywhere else in the world. One of its parents is Riesling, the other has yet to be identified. It flowers late and ripens early – so is a relatively safe bet in this deeply continental climate, where winters can be long. It makes easy-drinking, fragrant wines.

The first documented mention of viticulture in Sachsen comes relatively late. It dates to 1161 and concerns a vineyard in Meissen. Like elsewhere, viticulture was initially down to monastic settlements spread beyond the Elbe valley during the Medieval Warm Period. In 1401 Margrave Wilhelm I created the vineyards around Hoflößnitz, still in existence today and a *Weinbergsordnung*, or vineyard charter, from 1588 detailed the vineyard work to be performed throughout the year. It is estimated that there were 5,000 hectares of vines before worsening climatic conditions and the Thirty Years' War started the decline. The early seventeenth century saw official favour from the elector which led to the terracing of the first vineyards between Meissen and Hoflößnitz. By the late eighteenth century frost, poor harvests and almost constant warfare meant many vineyards were given up. When phylloxera hit in 1887 it almost sounded the death knell for the vineyards. Nonetheless, the first replantings with grafted vines started in 1905. A state domaine was founded in 1927, giving rise to new plantings. This continued during the Second World War, when the forced labour of French and Russian prisoners of war was used. By 1945 there were 67 hectares of vineyard. From 1958 Schloss Wackerbarth served as headquarters of the state domaine, turning its attention to Sekt production, with base wines sourced elsewhere. This revived a tradition begun by Sektkellerei Bussard in 1836. The 1970s and 1980s saw new plantings so that by 1989 there were 310 hectares. Today Sachsen's vineyards are once again resplendent and pleasure is writ large. August the Strong would be pleased.

Today there are 497 hectares in Sachsen, two *Bereiche*, four *Grosslagen* and 17 *Einzellagen*. Müller-Thurgau is the leading variety, followed by Riesling, Weissburgunder and Grauburgunder, but there also are 28 hectares of Goldriesling (see box, above). In 2018 there were only 37

Winzer making wine full-time. Sachsen soils are varied. Weathered granite and syenite rocks are partially covered with loess, loam and sands. Syenite is a hard, igneous rock. At a latitude of 51.0°N to 51.5°N, and 13.7°E, Sachsen's climate is deeply continental. Due to the exposure of the vineyards and the high number of sunshine hours, ripening grapes is not a problem. The chief danger is winter frost.

Weingut Karl Friedrich Aust
Radebeul
www.weingut-aust.de

There is something childlike in Karl-Friedrich Aust's excitement as he climbs around lankily in his vineyard terraces on the Goldener Wagen in Radebeul. He has done so since early childhood as his parents had a parcel of vines here. Born into an artistic family and coming of age just as political upheaval spelled huge change, he decided to train as a stonemason at Cologne Cathedral. After his father's untimely death, Aust's mother wanted the family tradition to continue and Aust set about tending the few vines in their possession. The weather taught him a bitter lesson in the winter of 1996, when it started snowing during harvest. Nonetheless, he resolved to grow grapes and make wine, starting his own estate in 2001 with his family's half hectare in the Goldener Wagen. Today he has 6.5 hectares in the Goldener Wagen and other sites and is a man possessed. His estate is housed in one of Radebeul's oldest buildings, the Meinholdsches Turmhaus. It has a tiny clocktower and the bright peal of its bell tolls the hour. Above it is a weathervane dedicated to the goddess Fortuna, 'She watches over everything,' Aust says, 'she is wayward but says that everything will be all right.' Restoration of the crumbling drystone walls is an ongoing project, and according to Aust his 'life's task'. He grows 80 per cent whites (Riesling, Kerner, Weissburgunder, and others) and 20 per cent Spätburgunder which is elegant, crunchy and vivid. His entry-level line is fittingly called Genussmensch, or hedonist. Aust is one of Sachsen's real originals, as are his wines. The newly renovated *Gartensalon* is a lovely backdrop for celebrations while the restaurant (check opening times) makes a virtue of local simplicity.

Try: Genussmensch Weiss for joyful lightness, and Spätburgunder for poise.

Weingut Frédéric Fourré
Radebeul
www.weinbau-fourre.de

This vivacious Parisian fell in love with a local ballet dancer, moved to Dresden and ended up staying. He worked as a sommelier before founding his *Weingut* in 2007. He part owns, part leases his 2.5 hectares, which include small terraces in the Goldener Wagen vineyard, and treasures the up to 60-year-old vines he found there. He grows Gutedel, Kerner, Scheurebe, Müller-Thurgau, Traminer and Weissburgunder, and manages to tease out much character. He is a deft hand when it comes to cuvées, one of which is called Chimäre de Saxe.

Try: Scheurebe for utter freshness and fragrance.

Weingut Kastler Friedland
Radebeul
www.kastlerfriedland.de

Both Enrico Friedland and Dr Bernd Kastler came to wine via property. They both moved to the Dresden area for work and found that each of their houses came with some vineyard land. Both decided to farm the vines and grow grapes. Their paths crossed when they met at the local growers' association, and embarked on their common project. They are a rather different but well-suited pair, witty and self-deprecating. Their motto is 'to make Elbe Valley wines for explorers'. With a motley mix of varieties – think Riesling, Bacchus, Kerner, Scheurebe, Silvaner, Regent and Muscaris – on just 4 hectares, in sites like the Goldener Wagen, Steinrücken and Johannisberg, as well as in Cossebaude across the Elbe, they offer an approachable, fruit-driven style that perfectly encapsulates their enthusiasm.

Try: Silvaner for aroma and slenderness.

Sächsisches Staatsweingut Schloss Wackerbarth
www.schloss-wackerbarth.de

Schloss Wackerbarth is yet another palace in a picturesque vineyard setting, a baroque château built in 1728 for August Christoph Graf von Wackerbarth, a minister at August the Strong's court. With its pretty Belvedere, a pavilion set centrally on a hillside terrace, the entire park sits within the terraced vineyards of Radebeul. State-owned and making Sekt during GDR times, the estate has served as Sachsen's state domaine since 1992. It has been thoroughly renovated and turned into a tourist destination and *Erlebnisweingut*, or experience winery, including a shop, restaurant and event space with a full roster of tastings, guided tours and concerts. The Staatsweingut farms 104 hectares, in its house vineyard, the Wackerbarthberg, amongst others, as well as in the Goldener Wagen, Paradies, a *monopole*, and Heinrichsberg. A quarter of their vineyard is classified as *Steillage*. They also own a field blend parcel within the Goldener Wagen, planted in 1956, which is vinified separately each year. The wine style at the Schloss has become increasingly refined over the years. Depending on harvest point and style the wines can be quite full-bodied, testament to the amount of Saxon sunshine these vineyards can absorb. There are aromatic whites and Rieslings as well as reds. Sekt is an important part of the business. Set aside some time for your visit – there is much to explore.

Try: Pinot Brut Nature Sekt for Saxon *esprit* and Riesling from the cooler Protze parcel within the Goldener Wagen.

Weingut Schloss Proschwitz
Meissen
www.schloss-proschwitz.de

With just above 80 hectares of vineyards, Schloss Proschwitz is Sachsen's largest private wine estate. It is also the ancestral home of the zur Lippe family, where wine has been made for the past 800 years. Georg Prinz zur Lippe's family lost everything under Soviet occupation in 1945. As aristocrats his parents were seen as enemies of the people and had to flee west. A cruel clause of the law meant that while small estates were restituted to their rightful owners after 1990, owners of estates above 100 hectares were not entitled to compensation, so Prinz zur Lippe had to buy back his ancestral land piece by piece. He moved east in 1990, his wife, Prinzessin Alexandra, following shortly after. Their vineyard purchase contract meant that they had to deliver their first harvest in 1990 to the local co-op. Since they had no equipment, Prinz zur Lippe trucked their 1991 harvest to his relatives, the Castell family in Franken, to be vinified. Today the zur Lippes can look back on almost 30 years of adventure, risk-taking, renovation, investment and hard work. Winemaking is in the hands of South African winemaker Jacques Du Preez, in a modern winery in Zadel which comes with an adjoining guest house and distillery. The Schloss itself is used for events and concerts. There are two vineyard sites, both *monopoles*, both of loess- and loam-covered granite and syenite: Schloss Proschwitz and, across the Elbe,

Meissener Kloster Heilig Kreuz. They grow Riesling, Müller-Thurgau, Elbling, Weissburgunder, Goldriesling and Traminer but the estate is deservedly winning ever more plaudits for its elegant Spätburgunders. Sekt is an increasingly important and delicious part of the programme. VDP member estate.

Try: Spätburgunder GG for spice and body.

Weingut Klaus Zimmerling
Dresden-Pillnitz
www.weingut-zimmerling.de

Visiting this winery is like entering another world. Few places are as enchanted, enchanting or unusual. Eye-catching female figures, hewn by Malgorzata Chodakowska, Klaus Zimmerling's sculptor wife, sit strikingly above the entrance of the winery. Further statues, placed throughout, create a serene, dreamlike atmosphere. The entire setting is perfect: the cellar sits at the foot of the 170-metre-high Rysselkuppe mountain, whose south-south-west facing, terraced slope of weathered granite is the *Königlicher Weingarten*, or royal vineyard, created in the early nineteenth century for Saxon King Friedrich August II. Trained as an electrical engineer but in love since student days with fermenting any fruit he could get his hands on, Zimmerling is an accidental winemaker, with some winery experience from Nikolaihof in the Austrian Wachau.

The tale of Zimmerling and Chodakowska's meeting and how they revived this treasure of a vineyard is one of perseverance, hard work, fate and serendipity. They arrived in 1992 and started with 1.5 hectares, which have now become 4 hectares, and created something very special. Zimmerling grows Riesling (40 per cent), Grauburgunder, Weissburgunder, Roter Traminer and Gewürztraminer. There is also Spätburgunder, exclusively for Sekt. Zimmerling's wines are rich and singular in style, rounded and almost unctuous. Yields are low and demand is high, so wines are sold in 500-millilitre bottles. The next aim is organic certification. 'For me, making wine is the noblest form of agriculture,' Zimmerling says. 'You are not just growing something, there is a second step of refinement that brings such joy to people and creates a completely individual product, which subsumes climate and soil, even oneself. What my wife does with her sculptures, I do with my wine.' VDP member estate.

Try: Super Natural Zero Dosage Spätburgunder Sekt for delicious idiosyncrasy.

18
WÜRTTEMBERG – SOUTHERN PROMISE

Unknown artists carved the Old Testament story of the drunken Noah into the choir stalls at Maulbronn Abbey. He slumbers in the vines, clutching grapes in his hand. He could be a metaphor for this region: viticulture is so deeply ingrained but parts of it need to be shaken awake. While Württemberg's winelands have northerly and southerly outposts in the Tauber Valley and Lake Constance, respectively, most viticulture is concentrated in two climatically favoured areas: Heilbronn and the Zabergäu, known as the lower-lying *Unterland*; and around Stuttgart and the Remstal, where vineyards rise to 400 metres, sometimes even higher. Vines line the lovely valleys along the winding loops of the rivers Neckar, Rems, Enz, Jagst and Kocher. On its south–north course from Tübingen via Esslingen, Stuttgart and Ludwigsburg to Heilbronn, the Neckar wound its way through the Triassic layers of *Muschelkalk*, *Keuper* and various sandstones (see box, page 271) to create majestic vineyards, and so did its tributaries, albeit to a lesser degree. Some of these historic sites are precipitously steep and terraced but sadly their names are virtually unknown. Mundelsheimer Käsberg, Hessigheimer Wurmberg and Roßwager Halde are as spectacular as any Mosel vineyard, yet nobody wrote their names on wine labels a hundred years ago – and few do today. While Württemberg has unique selling points others can only dream of, in their red varieties of Lemberger, Trollinger and Schwarzriesling (see box, page 262) – their potential is only partially fulfilled. No other German region is so schizophrenic. The top wines easily stride the world stage but the vast majority of production is still banal. With the headquarters of Porsche, Daimler and Bosch, Württemberg is a hotbed of manufacturing progress, yet much of its wine industry is stuck in the past. 'The whole world comes to Stuttgart to buy technology,' one young winemaker said, 'but the deals are toasted with wines from Italy and Spain.' Stuttgart has one of Germany's wealthiest demographics, yet suburban placards proclaim dumping prices for locally grown wines. But a few lonely pioneers have blazed a trail and energetic youngsters are working to clear Württemberg's reputational deficit. This did not come about by chance.

Württemberg's first documented mention of viticulture was in 766. Initially, the vine spread with monastic settlements and, helped by the Medieval Warm Period, reached its greatest extent in the sixteenth century. Stuttgart alone had 1,271 hectares in 1594. Württemberg's wines had their heyday before the Thirty Years' War when they were shipped in barrel both up and down the Neckar as far afield as England, the Netherlands, Vienna and Hungary. The area was shared between ecclesiastic and worldly powers, amongst them the Duchy of Swabia, which became the County of Württemberg in the thirteenth century. Where Württemberg differs from other parts of Germany is in its land-ownership structure, defined by *Realteilung*, the equal division of inheritance among all children. Commonplace even before then, it was enshrined in one of Duke Christoph of Württemberg's all-encompassing new laws for church and state in 1555. This led to a much earlier fragmentation of landholdings than elsewhere. The seventeenth and early eighteenth century were dominated by conflict, above all the Thirty Years' War, which left a decimated population and a quarter of the previous vineyard land. Survival was all and villages had large communal wine presses. Their use was tightly regulated as an instrument of feudal control and the collection of tithes. Once the County of Württemberg had become a post-Napoleonic Kingdom in 1805, various efforts were made to encourage quality viticulture, but nobody addressed the structural problems. The *Kelterbann*, a feudal law which made the pressing of wine an exclusive privilege of church and aristocracy, had existed in various regions during the Middle Ages. In many Württemberg communes, however, it was not abolished until the early nineteenth century, when the *Keltern*, or wine presses, became village property and their use continued. You can still see old *Kelter* buildings in Stetten, Besigheim and Fellbach today. Such communal presses were not conducive to quality winemaking. Sites, usually field blends anyway, were co-fermented, sometimes under the open sky, sometimes with immense delay, leading to spoilage. A wine-wise observer commented in 1837 on new wine presses in Mundelsheim: 'They are in such accordance with quality improvement as the abolition of the death penalty is with the building of gallows.' A 1910 overview of German wine villages still lists copious amounts of *Schillerwein*, the pinkish wine resulting from co-fermenting red and white varieties (see box, page 34). Even in the early twentieth century, once fermented, wine was still sold there and then, at the *Kelter*, in bulk to innkeepers and wine merchants who often had the wine farmers over a barrel. These structures explain the strong tradition of viticultural co-operatives, the earliest being founded in the 1850s.

But there is another aspect. The nineteenth century also brought industrialization. Places like Stuttgart boasted a ready workforce whose tiny land holdings did not require full-time farming. Vineyard owners thus earned a living in the factory, but clung on to their vines and delivered their grapes to the *Winzergenossenschaft*. The extra money was welcome but rarely the chief income. This worked well while thirsty Swabians drank these wines – demand was such that virtually all was consumed locally. Vineyards expanded from 5,825 hectares in 1964 to 11,264 hectares in 2000. But most co-ops missed the turning tide of quality in the late 1990s and kept producing quantity. As co-op members' livelihoods did not depend on wine sales there was no incentive to change what ticked over nicely. But overproduction of poor wine is no longer profitable. Litre-bottles of off-dry Trollinger-Lemberger blends retail for €3.60 in supermarkets to this day. This is where these varieties and Württemberg got their bad name. Ownership structures are similar today with 67.4 per cent of Württemberg vineyards belonging to co-op members – those gloriously steep and terraced sites among them. The agricultural premiums paid to those who still farm the steep slopes, according to Erbgraf zu Neipperg, are 'nothing but sad measures to keep a dying thing alive.' As more and more co-ops struggle with their outdated business model young winemakers strike out on their own. Pioneers like Gert Aldinger, whose family never joined a co-op, showed the way in the late 1980s, along with Haidle and Ellwanger. Rainer Schnaitmann, who left the co-op in 1997, followed suit. In 2002 five ambitious young winemakers founded the 'Junges Schwaben' movement and many more youngsters now snap at their heels. At last there is much excitement in Swabia. About time, too. Stuttgart still boasts 423 hectares of vineyards, amongst them the terraced and beautifully named Canstatter Zuckerle, or 'little sugar'.

Lemberger, Trollinger and co. – Württemberg's red tradition

Unusually for Germany, in the nineteenth and twentieth centuries Württemberg predominantly grew red grapes. Even today 68.7 per cent of plantings are red. Chief amongst them with 2,160 hectares in 2017 is Trollinger – the German name for Schiava Grossa, whose origin is thought to be in the Alto Adige, Italy. There is no record of how and when it arrived in Württemberg but mentions of the variety are numerous from the second half of the seventeenth century onwards. It is prized for its large, juicy berries with their ability to bring generous yields. These make it suitable as a table grape, known as Black Hamburg. It brings good must weights even at high yields. Erbgraf zu Neipperg says that 'Trollinger is talked about as a high-yielding variety without inherent quality,' when its qualities are simply different from those of other red grapes. Trollinger, even when fully ripe and made from restricted yields, will never make a full-bodied red. It is a gentle, nimble, pale wine which has much to recommend it, especially if you want easy, everyday drinking. In this respect it is probably Germany's most misunderstood grape variety. Especially today, when contemporary cuisines look for subtle wines, Trollinger can be a winner – and there are some signs of this happening. Jens Zimmerle of Weingut Zimmerle in Korb is a fan: 'Trollinger belongs to our history and our presence and is firmly rooted in our lives. The mistake was to try and turn Trollinger into something it was not. I believe that Trollinger has a great future if we make it as it should be made: as a light-bodied red with lovely berry notes, not dominated by wood but as a wine for the table that charms with its lightness and its aromas of berry and bitter almond. If you have tasted everything there is in the world, you will realize how unique Trollinger is. There is something playful, something open about it.' What is churned out by the cooperatives is thermovinified and mostly off-dry. Fermented on its skins to dryness, from lower yields, Trollinger has immense southern charm.

Lemberger's story is very different. Not that anyone knows much more about its arrival in Württemberg. It is the same grape as Austrian Blaufränkisch and Hungarian Kékfrankos and there is a legend that it was introduced by the Neipperg family through their close links to Habsburg – and it has an excellent track record in the Neipperg vineyards. Then there is the theory that it came with Austrian settlers who repopulated the area after the Thirty Years' War. Be that as it may, initially Lemberger was no success. It only took hold in the lower-lying Unterland around Heilbronn. It demands good sites and gave superior wines only in good years. It was very susceptible at flowering and did not provide reliable yields. Neipperg remembers that before climate change Lemberger barely reached 80° Oechsle, or 10.7 per cent potential abv. This made it neither a popular nor a wise choice. Yet a few die-hards believed in it. In 1925 just 6.5 per cent of Württemberg's vines were Lemberger, compared to 28.1 per cent of Trollinger. In 1964 there were a mere 350 hectares but by 1995 there were 900 hectares and today there are 1,718 hectares. Climate and recognition were the two factors for change. It was first planted in the cooler Remstal in the late 1980s. At the same time, Gert Aldinger experimented with international varieties. He had tasted full-bodied reds abroad and wanted to attempt something similar at home. He was permitted to plant foreign varieties as a trial but that necessitated a local variety for comparison. So he planted Lemberger alongside Merlot and Cabernet Sauvignon and treated them all exactly the same. This was the game changer. 'Reducing yields was the crux,' Aldinger emphasizes. 'Along with that that came climate change. Had I tried these varieties in the 1970s I would have failed. But I have to say for the winemakers of my generation in this region the international grapes were significant. They opened our minds.' Thus the potential of Lemberger became apparent in the late 1980s. The last time Aldinger planted any international varieties was in 2000. He also notes that his Bordeaux-style-blends opened doors that usually would have remained closed for a Württemberg winemaker, so dire was the reputation of the region. Many co-ops still thermovinify Lemberger into a limp red, but made properly it has structure, backbone and longevity. Today Lemberger is Germany's spicy, full-bodied yet sinuous secret. It is slightly more slender than its cousins from Burgenland or Hungary, and often has a lovely floral overtone with the tell-tale pepper note. It is Württemberg's brooding, dark treasure.

Württemberg also adds a small footnote to the chapter of the Pinot family. Mentions of 'Clevner' or 'Clävner' are numerous and usually refer to a member of this family; in Württemberg this may have been Frühburgunder (see box, page 53) but none of it is left today. It also hints at historic Pinot presence. What plays a distinct role and is vinified as red wine today is Schwarzriesling, or Müllerrebe, aka Pinot Meunier. There are 1,418 hectares of it in Württemberg but sadly much of it is made into rather indifferent, light red wine. In 1928 a grape breeder in Heilbronn discovered a mutation of Pinot Meunier which

> was isolated and propagated and got the name 'Samtrot', or velvet red. It has slightly thicker skins than Spätburgunder, with larger berries, good acidity and higher must weights. While Spätburgunder itself only ever had a minor role, it is now the fifth most-planted variety with 1,324 hectares – a downright explosion compared to the 61 hectares in 1964. The variety excels in the limestone and *Keuper* soils.
>
> The grape breeding centre in Weinsberg is also responsible for some red crossings: in 1929 it successfully crossed Portugieser and Lemberger to create Heroldrebe; in 1931 it crossed Frühburgunder with Trollinger to make Helfensteiner. In 1956 August Herold crossed these two to create Dornfelder. In the white department they crossed Trollinger and Riesling, also in 1929, to create Kerner. Weinsberg also boasts further reds which were bred chiefly for their colour – probably to pimp the gallons of pale, thermovinified Trollinger. These include the 1970/71 Cabernet Sauvignon–Lemberger crossings that were named Cabernets Cubin, Doria, Dorsa and Mitos as well as the 1971 Lemberger-Dornfelder crossing Acolon. Thankfully there is no longer any real need for these.

Administratively, Württemberg has nine *Bereiche*, 17 *Grosslagen* and 210 *Einzellagen*. In 2017 there were 11,360 hectares of vines of which 2,160 hectares were Trollinger, 2,120 hectares Riesling and 1,718 hectares Lemberger.

STUTTGART AND REMSTAL

Weingut Aldinger
Stuttgart-Fellbach
www.weingut-aldinger.de

Brothers Hansjörg and Matthias Aldinger forge ever further ahead on the quality course their grandfather Gerhard set and father Gert defined. It was their ancestor Bentz Aldinger who planted the first vines in Fellbach all the way back in 1492. The estate grew from a *négociant* business but since 1973 only home-grown grapes have been used. The family has 28 hectares, their most famous sites are Fellbacher Lämmler and Untertürkheimer Gips, warm, south- and south-west-facing sites of *Gipskeuper*. The Lämmler lies higher and gets cooler air at night, its base is of coloured marl, the upper parcels are of *Stubensandstein*. Gips has the poorer soil and the GGs from this vineyard are called 'Marienglas', after the compressed gypsum crystals that can be found in the soil. In the late 1980s, Gert Aldinger was amongst the first to plant international grape varieties like Cabernet and Merlot. These in turn taught him the potential of his indigenous grapes, especially Lemberger. He proved that powerful reds could be made in Württemberg and was a lone pioneer. His sons have dialled back the power to show how far you can take elegance. Gert says: 'Where Merlot and co. showed what was possible with Lemberger, it is now Spätburgunder that shows the new path for Lemberger. Now it is about earlier harvest, transparency and depth.' Lemberger is nuanced and perfumed, Spätburgunder is elegant, cool and snappy, made partially with whole bunches. But there is more: their gorgeous brut nature vintage Sekt, from grapes grown in the Gips vineyard, is amongst Germany's best and their Trollinger Sine is seductive. Great wines from great people. Among Germany's best. VDP member estate.

Try: Aldinger Brut Nature Sekt for sheer joy.

Weingut Beurer
Kernen im Remstal
www.weingut-beurer.de

Jochen Beurer's name is synonymous with Riesling. He has forged an uncompromising and unusual style which shows how versatile this variety is, how expressive it can be in different hands. The Beurer family delivered grapes to the co-op before Jochen started making the wine in 1997 after training with, amongst others, Elisabetta Foradori in Italy. He started fermenting everything spontaneously in 2003, the vineyards have been certified biodynamic since 2008. Of his 13 hectares in Stetten, 60 per cent are planted to Riesling. The rest is Sauvignon Blanc, Spätburgunder, Lemberger, Zweigelt and Trollinger. His sites are Pulvermächer (*Keuper*, up to 370 metres), Mönchberg (*Schilfsandstein* up to 250 metres) and Häder (*Bunte Mergel*, up to 360 metres). The Rieslings are named after soil types rather than sites. Low canopies allow Beurer to harvest as late as October even in warm years and Riesling is harvested late at full ripeness – and health. This is followed by long periods of skin contact, spontaneous ferment, often also full malolactic fermentation. This results in Rieslings that are surprisingly moderate in alcohol but very rich in texture. Although rich, they are not fat, creamy and mellow. They need bottle age to show their true and fascinating face but get full marks for personality. In 2011 Beurer planted a 'museum vineyard' in a parcel of the Pulvermächer with a field blend of 17 different historic grape varieties. Grapes like Honigler, Hängling, Fütterer, Urban and Eicheltraube give an idea of the former biodiversity of co-planted vineyards. In the reds both bone-dry Trollinger and sinuous, savoury Lemberger are wonderful. Junges Schwaben member. VDP member estate.

Try: any Riesling at all.

Weingut Bernhard Ellwanger
Weinstadt-Großheppach
www.weingut-ellwanger.com

The Ellwanger family's roots reach far back into Remstal history and reveal a real wine dynasty (also see below). They can document their local presence back to 1514, since when wine has been part of their lives. Of this branch of the family, Bernhard and Ingrid Ellwanger started marketing their own wine in 1975. When Sven Ellwanger, a founding member of Junges Schwaben, and his wife Melanie took the estate over in 1999 they had 17 hectares of vineyards. In 2003 he was joined by his sister Yvonne and today they preside over 32 hectares with a mind-boggling 25 varieties. While this might be just a little too much in other hands, here it is testament to an untiring curiosity and an avid desire to learn. Riesling and Sauvignon Blanc (which they pioneered here) play first fiddle in the whites, Lemberger, Spätburgunder and Trollinger in the reds. What is striking is that these wines are not smooth or easy – they all have an intriguing edge. There is inherent freshness and tension but also a naked honesty. Bottle age transforms them – Ellwanger is knowingly playing the long game. Like his colleagues, he utilizes the altitude of his vineyards, up to 430 metres, for the freshness. Sauvignon Blanc loves the loam and *Stubensandstein* soils up there. Spätburgunder from 45-year-old vines from the Großheppacher Steingrüble shines with savouriness and unusual elegance. Junges Schwaben member.

Try: Syrah from Großheppacher Klingenberg for sexy impact, Fumé Blanc for utter balance.

Weingut Jürgen Ellwanger
Winterbach, Remstal
www.weingut-ellwanger.de

There is a running joke that this branch of the Ellwanger family (see page 266) are the last winemakers before Moscow. This is down to the fact that Winterbach used to be the easternmost commune to grow wine in the Remstal. In his time, Jürgen was a trailblazer. Taking over from his father in 1965, he was amongst the first to plant Lemberger and later the very first to plant Zweigelt, Syrah and Merlot. He was also a founding member of the HADES, a small group of Württemberg estates who pioneered and defended the use of barriques in red winemaking, starting in 1986 when the *Amtliche Prüfung* still viewed new, small barrels as atypical and too exotic. Today the 26-hectare estate is run by sons Jörg and Felix who took over in 2006 and two-thirds of production is red. The easterly Hebsacker Lichtenberg and Linnenbrunnen vineyards, both south-south-west facing *keuper* sites, have proved themselves to be exquisite for elegant, long-lived, floral and layered Lembergers and elegant Spätburgunders; the Schnaiter Altenberg for finely proportioned Riesling. If you want stunning Lemberger, this is the right address. VDP member estate.

Try: Ortswein Hebsacker Lemberger for floral charm.

Weingut Gold, Weinstadt-Gundelsbach
Remstal
www.weingut-gold.de

The setting of Weingut Gold is beautiful: a vaulted cellar underneath an old inn on a wooded hill makes for a gorgeous tasting room and event space. The brand-new winery and cellar, functional but still under construction, is hidden below ground. Forest surrounds everything and its cold airstreams, once a disadvantage, are a boon today, giving the wines lightness and acidity – a bonus for Leon Gold's passion for fine fizz. This is helped along by lower canopies and vineyards that make the most of the available altitude. Leon Gold founded the estate in 2014 and launched himself in 2015 with the strikingly labelled 2013 and 2014 vintages. 'I started with little more than a pair of secateurs,' he explains. He does not hail from a wine-growing family but trained as *Winzer* and *Techniker* nonetheless; doing this at biodynamic estates had a lasting effect. All his vineyards are farmed organically and according to moon phases; certification is underway. It was his wife's grandfather's vineyard that started him out. Now he has 10 hectares under vine. In the new cellar stoneware vessels ferment away and some of the reds are foot-trodden for gentle extraction – so we can look forward to experimental styles. He has adopted the familiar pyramid of *Guts-*, *Orts-* and *Lagenwein*. Riesling, Zweigelt and Spätburgunder are his focus. The latter, along with Pinot Meunier, is central to Gold's big Sekt ambitions. The only thing the promising fizz needs is more time on lees. A thoroughly convincing undertaking full of delicious (and effervescent) promise.

Try: Sekt Cuvée Ida Marie brut for freshness, Ortswein Riesling for purity.

Weingut Karl Haidle
Stetten, Remstal
www.weingut-karl-haidle.de

Moritz Haidle took the helm at this estate in 2014. Full of ideas and energy, he is pushing boundaries with Riesling – but that is in his veins. In 1949 his grandfather Karl Haidle was amongst the first in the region to bottle his own wines, and his father Hans made headlines as a red wine 'revolutionary' in the local papers for being amongst the first to plant Lemberger in the cool Remstal. The stocky ruin of Yburg castle, depicted on the Haidle label, stands in the Stettener Pulvermächer vineyard that rises right behind the house. This south-west-facing site of marl, weathered *Keuper*, *Kiesel-* and *Schilfsandstein* is one of Württemberg's most famous Riesling sites, and for Moritz his 'holy vineyard'. He also has parcels in the Mönchsberg and Häder sites and further afield. The biggest changes Moritz, who trained in Burgundy and California, has rung in were conversion to organics, earlier harvests, spontaneous ferments and less or no new wood for the reds. Moritz also got rid of some less glamorous varieties and replanted with Riesling and Lemberger. Half of plantings today are Riesling. The site expressions range from creamy and round (Häder) to snappy and taut (*Schilfsandstein*). The same site-specific breadth exists in his very elegant Lembergers. Stay tuned for world-class wines. Certified organic since 2017. VDP member estate.

Try: Lemberger Stettener Häder for purity and spice – and amazing value.

Weingut Markus Heid
Stuttgart-Fellbach
www.weingut-heid.de

With a Fellbach family history dating back to 1699, Markus Heid is unassuming but as convincing as his wines. In 1996 Heid took over at home, where his parents marketed their own wines. Trollinger represented 70 per cent of production then. Today he has 12 hectares in Fellbach, including Lämmler, Schnait and Stetten where he farms part of the Pulvermächer vineyard. Initially he made bigger, bolder, more powerful wines but now he says he wants to make 'German reds with spiciness, with acid, with savouriness.' He likes his wines to have an 'addictive' quality and that is exactly what you get with the lovage savouriness and beautiful purity of his Spätburgunders and Lembergers. He also has juicy, spicy Syrah, St Laurent and Trollinger. For white he has Riesling (ripe, spicy, textured and rounded), Sauvignon Blanc and Silvaner. Sekt also plays an increasing role. Nothing here is superficial or obvious, there is something calm, collected and utterly convincing at work. Among the region's best. Certified organic since 2009. VDP member estate.

Try: Pinot Noir Fellbacher Goldberg, gloriously pure and addictive indeed (not to mention great value).

Kessler Sekt
Esslingen am Neckar
www.kessler-sekt.de

Founded by Georg Christian Kessler in 1826, this is Germany's first and oldest Sekt house. Born in Heilbronn, apprenticed as a merchant, the highly Francophile Kessler joined Veuve Clicquot in Reims as an accountant in 1807. Young Kessler had been able to tap new export markets during Napoleon's Continental System, which curtailed the vital British trade for the Champagne house, so just three years later, in 1810, Mme Barbe-Nicole Clicquot, the widow herself, made him manager of her house. By 1815 he was a partner in the business. Kessler was a born entrepreneur and while also founding a bank and two cloth mills, he started experimenting with German sparkling wine. This resulted in him founding the first German Sekt house in Esslingen in 1826 and prompted his return to Germany. By the 1830s he was exporting 'Sparkling Neckar' to Russia, England and the US. Kessler Sekt was also served aboard the Graf Zeppelin 1929 round-the-world flight. It became a popular and successful German Sekt brand and remained so well into the 1970s.

If the company has a new lease of life today, it is down to the vision and courage of Christopher Baur. This Esslingen-born businessman heard of the company's insolvency in 2004 and managed a buy-out with other investors in 2005. In 2013 he partnered with the Italian Cavit co-op from Trento, where most of Kessler's base wines (Chardonnay and Spätburgunder) are now sourced. Still housed in a most handsome half-timbered thirteenth-century tithe house on Esslingen's picturesque market square, an iconic German Sekt brand is thus preserved. Right now, about 50 per cent of Sekt is made by the transfer method, over 30 per cent is made by traditional bottle fermentation and just under 20 per cent is made in tank (the Kessler Gold brand). A new facility outside town and investment in the tithe house cellars will enable Kessler to return to 100 per cent bottle fermentation. The company has set a clear course for quality. It is a pity for such a Württemberg icon that its base wines are sourced abroad. The local co-ops, with their existing vineyards of Schwarzriesling (Pinot Meunier) and Riesling, missed a trick and an opportunity here. The Sekts are clean and crisp. Don't miss Kessler Karree – a wine bar, and tours through the historic building.

Try: Riesling Réserve 2015 – Sekt made from Riesling grown in the Maulbronner Eilfingerberg.

Weingut Klopfer
Weinstadt-Großheppach, Remstal
www.weingut-klopfer.de

Christoph Klopfer knows exactly what he wants. He says, 'My generation wants to show the sites and we are no longer shy about it. We know that we are as good as other regions. We make wines with real provenance. My generation has seen the world, we taste differently.' His parents Dagmar and Wolfgang founded the estate in 1986 by leaving the co-op. Christoph, who trained at the Neustadt campus, at Bassermann-Jordan in the Pfalz and the Okanagan in Canada, made his first full home vintage in 2013. He refers to his 15 hectares of vineyards as 'still very diverse,' hinting that he wants to specialize. While he makes remarkable Riesling, his heart beats for Lemberger and Spätburgunder. 'It is difficult to give a new face to Lemberger,' he says of the struggle with Lemberger's image problem in Germany, 'but in the long run it is better. Württemberg and Lemberger just go together.' Across the board his wines are moderate in alcohol but strong on expression. He makes the most of the differences that his sites afford him in terms of soil, aspect and altitude. His most prized site is Kleinheppacher Greiner, a steep site of *Bunte Mergel* from whose 32-year-old Lemberger vines Klopfer fashions a most elegant, layered wine. Watch him, there is star potential. Certified organic.

Try: Lemberger from Kleinheppacher Greiner, with some bottle age.

> ### Trias
>
> The *Schichtstufenlandschaften*, or 'tiered layer landscapes', of the Triassic era (250 to 200 million years ago) dominate the regions of Franken and Württemberg. Its trinity of *Buntsandstein*, *Muschelkalk* and *Keuper* gave the name to a geological age which was characterized by alternating periods of desertification and flooding. The lowest stratum, *Buntsandstein,* was created as the Germanic Basin was sedimented with layer upon layer of sand and debris, getting its red colour from iron oxide and its black colour from manganese. Ten to fifteen million years later the area was flooded by the Tethys Ocean which brought algae, oysters and other crustaceans. As the waters receded and re-flooded, several layers of marine sediment called *Muschelkalk*, literally fossil limestone, were deposited. Another ten to fifteen million years later periods of tropical moisture and dryness took turns. This allowed ferns, equisetums and conifers to thrive. Both fresh- and seawater flooded and receded, and the remnants of flora and marine fauna were deposited as layers of *Keuper*. All three formations have various subdivisions: Lower, Middle and Upper *Buntsandstein;* Lower, Middle and Upper *Muschelkalk*, as well as *Knollen-, Gips-* and *Lettenkeuper* and *Bunte Mergel*. Confusingly, some layers of *Keuper* are also called sandstone, like *Kiesel-, Schilf- and Stubensandstein*. The Upper Rhine Rift 30 million years ago distorted the layers and created faults, raising some areas and lowering others. In Franken all three main formations are present, in Württemberg it is mostly *Muschelkalk* and *Keuper*. Triassic formations also come to the surface in Baden and the Pfalz.

Weingut Knauß
Weinstadt-Strümpfelbach
www.weingut-knauss.com

Andreas Knauß is one of Württemberg's new stars. He trained with Hans and Anita Nittnaus in Austria before taking over at home from 2003. This estate was founded by his father in 1995 with just 0.5 hectares. Today there are 18 hectares, all within a 3-kilometre radius of the winery, and 65 per cent of plantings are red. Andreas started the conversion to organics and was certified in 2018. He makes the most of the altitudes in the Schnaiter Altenberg (up to 380 metres, *Schilfsandstein*) and the Beutelsbacher Sonnenberg (420 metres, *Stubensandstein*). Knauß knows exactly what he is doing in crafting wines with moderate alcohol but wonderful depth. There is texture, expression, purity and freshness, old vines help in this respect. This goes for pristine Riesling, luminous Spätburgunder and silky Lemberger. Watch out for this determined young man and his gorgeous wines. Great value.

Try: Lemberger Schnaiter Altenberg for silkiest elegance.

Weingut Rainer Schnaitmann
Stuttgart-Fellbach
www.weingut-schnaitmann.de

In 1997 Rainer Schnaitmann released his first vintage with his own name on the label. Before that his family, with 600 years of viticultural tradition in Fellbach, had been members of the local co-op. With lower yields and new oak, he quickly became the new Spätburgunder wunderkind of Württemberg. Today he has 26 hectares of vineyards across 165 different parcels in Fellbach, Uhlbach and further into the Remstal in Schnait. When he started out, he says the Lämmler vineyard stood for 'sweetish Trollinger', so he had to think of a name for his wines and used the old parcel name Simonroth which is used to this day for his fine reds. It would have been easy for him to rest on his laurels and continue in his initial, more powerful style but for the ever questioning, ever experimenting Schnaitmann this was never an option. He has continued to push the envelope. 'You have to want it. Wanting it comes from knowing what is possible,' he says about his evolution. Today his Spätburgunders, grown in the upper reaches of the vineyards beyond 300 metres, have a wonderfully wild, poetic but elegant streak. Even Lemberger is made using 100 per cent whole bunch and old vine Trollinger goes into magnum without sulphur. His Rieslings, some of which undergo full malolactic fermentation are bursting with fruit. Evoé!, after the joyful exclamation of classical bacchantes, denotes his entry-level rosé and white as well as a brut nature Sekt. Vineyards are farmed organically. He continues to be amongst Württemberg's best. VDP member estate.

Try: Spätburgunder GG Lämmler for exciting silkiness.

Weingut Albrecht Schwegler
Korb, Remstal
www.albrecht-schwegler.de

If you tasted the Schwegler wines blind, you'd immediately know you are in the most capable hands, but would you know you're in Württemberg? This relatively young estate stands out stylistically and steers its path with confidence, conviction and gusto. Andrea and Albrecht Schwegler founded the estate in the 1990s and, unusually at the time, had explored New Zealand and South Africa. They also prized quality above quantity and wanted to vinify reds in barrique. In the mid-80s, before founding the estate, they started with just 0.64 hectares and planted Zweigelt, Lemberger and Merlot. The idea was to sell mature wines only and indeed, current (red) releases are at least three years old. Their son Aaron, with Swiss, Californian and Kiwi experience under his belt, took over with his wife Julia in 2011 and now there are 12 hectares of international and indigenous reds (including Cabernet Sauvignon) along with Riesling and Chardonnay across 80 parcels. The whites are sold under varietal names, the reds are all oak-aged blends. It starts with the impressive, Trollinger-based D'r Oifache which is local dialect for 'the simple one' but there's nothing simple about it. It continues with polished Beryll, Saphir and Granat. The plush, exacting style could be described as 'international' but the finesse, freshness and ingenuity remain totally Swabian. In the best years Solitär is made. Granat enjoys cult status with lovers of powerful wines.

Try: the peppery, bone-dry Rosé or really mature vintages of Granat.

Weinmanufaktur Untertürkheim
Stuttgart-Untertürkheim
www.weinmanufaktur.de

This Stuttgart co-op with its 95 hectares of vineyard and 85 members (only 40 of which are active) is a success story. In 2002 its members unanimously decided to turn their fortunes around by focusing on quality rather than quantity. Amidst a sea of indifferent co-op blends sold cheaply in litre-bottles, the members knew their survival depended on it. Like every co-op, they make a broad range of wines, still in off-dry styles too, but under the watch of Dr Stefan Hübner the lines are clear-cut and prices affordable without being cheap. The offer is skewed towards the mid- and premium range. Cellarmaster Jürgen Off, modest but devoted to his work, started here in 1987. It was he who steered this ship throughout its changing course – to his great credit he has never stopped being curious. The results of his experiments are fabulous: bone-dry and spicy orange wine or golden Graubugunder which spent four years on lees. But rounded Riesling and barrel-aged Spätburgunders are good, too. If only more co-ops had management and cellarmasters like this. In Stuttgart at least two others have followed their example: Collegium

Wirtemberg in Rotenberg and Weinfactum in Bad Canstatt. The other Württemberg co-op with a proven quality record is Cleebronn-Güglingen (www.cleebronner-winzer.de) in Cleebronn/Zabergäu.

Try: Orange, a skin-fermented blend of Chardonnay and Grauburgunder Sur Lie for spice and joy.

Weingut Wöhrwag
Stuttgart-Untertürkheim
www.woehrwag.de

Hans-Peter Wöhrwag is a cosmopolitan. Any provincial shackles there might have been were shaken off a long time ago, yet he is Swabian to the core. Having grown up in his family's estate and trained with Bürklin-Wolf and Salwey, he branched out into banking and his very early, if not to say premature success in share speculation allowed him to expose his young palate to some of the world's finest wines. He could have worked in Napa but decided to follow in the footsteps of his family, who had left the local co-op in 1962 – but distinctly on his own terms. Hans-Peter was one of the first in Württemberg to make dry Riesling in an elegant style (cool ferment, clarified juice) in the early 1990s. The fact that his oenologist wife Christin is from the Rheingau helped, of course. The Wöhrwags, including kids Johanna and Philipp, farm 20 hectares today; unusually for Württemberg 50 per cent of that is Riesling, another 10 per cent are Weiss- and Grauburgunder, Sauvignon Blanc and Muskateller. With reds the focus is on Lemberger and Spätburgunder. Most of the vineyards are in the Untertürkheimer Herzogenberg, a slope of *Gipskeuper* with parcels classified as both *Erste* and *Grosse Lage*. The Goldkapsel Riesling, always dry and precise, reflects each vintage beautifully with lots of verve and texture and is great value. But the reds, most recently in Philipp's hands, are sublimely elegant. The only pity is that you will have to buy these – amongst Württemberg's best – in Stuttgart as almost nothing is exported. VDP member estate.

Try: Lemberger GG for floral scentedness and finesse.

Weingut Zimmerle
Korb, Remstal
www.zimmerle-weingut.de

It was current owner Jens Zimmerle's father who left the local co-op to start his own estate and distillery. Jens, with experience at top German estates and in Bordeaux, took over 8 hectares of vineyards and 2 hectares of orchards in 2008. Today there are 16 hectares of vineyards, which were certified organic in 2015. Sixty per cent of the sites are on the steep *Keuper*, *Schilf-* and *Kieselsandstein* slopes of the west- and south-facing Korber Sommerhalde and Steinreinacher Hörnle, which reach 400 metres. They are exposed most beautifully, allowing vistas across Stuttgart and as far as Ludwigsburg, and are home to Lemberger, Trollinger, some international reds, Spätburgunder, Chardonnay and Riesling, with a little Sauvignon Blanc and wonderfully scented, fresh Viognier. Altitude and aspect allow each variety to be in the perfect spot, making the most of the west-facing higher parcels for sun-kissed white with inherent coolness but also a high parcel of supremely pure Lemberger. 'Rehabilitating Lemberger is the task of my generation,' says Jens, whose wines across the board are of immense purity with a light, inspired touch – and great value.

Try: berry-tastic Trollinger, Lemberger Korber Berg for absolute poise.

UNTERLAND AND ZABERGÄU

Weingut Dautel
Bönnigheim
www.weingut-dautel.de

Christian Dautel is one of Württemberg's bright young talents. With experience in Australia, Oregon, Austria, South Africa and Burgundy he returned home and continued what his parents Ernst and Hannelore Dautel had built. Despite the self-deprecation, the easy, southern humour and the twinkle in his eye that he shares with Christian, Ernst Dautel is a revolutionary and pioneer. Insatiable curiosity, determination – often against the grain of local tradition – and hard work turned a mixed farm with 3 hectares of vines into one of the ground-breaking estates of Württemberg. He made his first wines in 1978 and when Ernst cut off half his fruit for a green harvest in 1984, his father was horrified. By the mid-1980s he was experimenting with barriques. He even put Riesling in barrique, which had to be sold as *Tafelwein*, but a 1993 tasted in 2018 stood up magnificently. Family holidays were always taken in wine regions: the Dautels always liked looking beyond their sphere. Christian returned home in 2010 and took over fully in 2013. He cannot imagine not making Riesling and is a master in teasing out the different soils while preserving zesty, bright freshness. It is with his reds that he pushes subtlety and elegance. Oak is dialled back with larger formats such as 300 litres and 500 litres and less new wood. Lemberger is spicy and slender, Spätburgunder silky and aromatic. There are 16 hectares today. Lemberger comes from the Cleebronner Michelsberg (*Bunte Mergel*, up to 385 metres), Spätburgunder from the Schupen parcel in the Bönnigheimer Sonnenberg (*Gipskeuper*, 280 metres) and the Oberstenfelder Forstberg (*Bunte Mergel*, up to 360 metres). Riesling comes from the steep *Schilfsandstein* of the Steingrüben and the even steeper *Muschelkalk* of the Besigheimer Wurmberg on the river Enz. The best thing: Christian has only just begun. VDP member estate.

Try: Schupen Spätburgunder for nuanced beauty.

Weingut Drautz-Able
Heilbronn
www.drautz-able.de

Markus Drautz and his wife Stéphanie de Longueville-Drautz have taken over at this Heilbronn-based estate, which Markus's late father Richard turned into one of Württemberg's best estates in the 1980s and 1990s. Markus has been on board since 2006. Viticulture goes back centuries, but it was only in the post-war years that the family focused solely on wine. There are 16 hectares of vineyards with the Heilbronner Stiftsberg (*Mergel*, *Gipskeuper* and *Buntsandstein* up to 300 metres) and Neckarsulmer Scheuerberg (*Gipskeuper*, up to 260 metres) the main sites. Depending on aspect and altitude, the Stiftsberg is home to Lemberger, Trollinger, Riesling and Sauvignon Blanc. Its Hunsperg parcel brings particularly zesty Rieslings. In Neckarsulm both Spätburgunder and Lemberger shine. While Riesling and creamy Sauvignon Blanc are wonderful, it is with the reds that Markus manages to combine power with elegance and a huge portion of charm. This is particularly true for the Lembergers. But he can also go all out on power with Jodokus, a barrique-matured blend of Lemberger with Merlot and Cabernet Sauvignon. Of particular note is Samtrot, a local mutation of Pinot Meunier, vinified as a red wine. Drautz, who wrote his thesis on the ageing potential of the variety, is a specialist and turns it into an elegant, rounded red that shows off the beautiful *sous bois* notes of the Pinot family. All the wines age beautifully and we shall see where Stéphanie's and Markus's experimentation will lead. A very solid offer and good value. VDP member estate.

Try: Samtrot HADES from an older vintage for pure Pinot charm.

Weingut Eisele
Hessigheim
www.weingut-eisele.de

This small winery is in the most perfect spot: wherever you turn you see the vertiginously steep, terraced vineyards of Hessigheim as they drop down to a loop of the Neckar. Alexander Eisele has made the wines since 2011 and took over in 2013. His parents founded the estate in 1989 with 0.2 hectares of vineyard but currently there are 9.5 hectares, of which 1.5 hectares are in the steep *Muschelkalk* terraces of the Hessigheimer and Besigheimer Wurmberg. Seventy per cent of production is red: Trollinger and Lemberger take the lead but there is also Zweigelt, Merlot, Cabernet Sauvignon and Cabernet Franc. The whites are Riesling, Chardonnay and Sauvignon Blanc. The whites have fragrance and freshness and benefit from long lees ageing and subtle use of wood. The reds are elegant and juicy. Eisele has a very good hand for blends, both red and white, but he also wants to pay respect to Trollinger which is so often just used as a workhorse grape. Here it is vinified spontaneously after a cold soak and aged in old barriques – and makes a lovely wine. The wines are tiered into *Gutsweine*, *Terroirweine* as a step up, Edition Eisele above that, from older vines, and the top segment is the S-Linie. All of them are far too cheap for the work that goes into them, making them excellent value. Certified organic.

Try: Trollinger Edition Montis Casei for a different take.

Weingut Herzog von Württemberg
Ludwigsburg
www.weingut-wuerttemberg.de

The Dukes of Württemberg have holdings in many historic sites of the former kingdom. The iconic Riesling site of the Stettener Brotwasser is their *monopole*. The Maulbronner Eilfingerberg, once created by the Cistercians, is largely farmed by them alone but they also have parcels in the Untertürkheimer Mönchberg, Mundelsheimer Käsberg, Hohenhaslacher Kirchberg and the Gündelbacher Steinbachhof. All the fruit is vinified at a modern winery at Schloss Monrepos in Ludwigsburg, a former hunting lodge. Until 1980 the wines were made in the Altes Schloss in the centre of Stuttgart. While the ducal family's businesses also include property, forestry and agriculture, the wine estate has been run by Michael Herzog, Duke of Württemberg since 1997. The wines are made by oenologist Moriz Just who joined in 2012 after working in South Africa,

Australia and France. Their joint aim is to let the sites speak. To this end they have made some changes in vineyards and cellar and work increasingly with spontaneous ferments. Clarity and transparency increasingly creep into the wines under Just's direction. Forty-two per cent of the 40 hectares are planted to Riesling, 20 per cent to Lemberger, 9 per cent to Trollinger and 7 per cent to Spätburgunder. These traditional varieties are very important to Herzog, who admits that a lot has changed, especially in the past decade, after a period in the 1980s and 1990s that he describes as a 'standstill'. 'We are reclaiming our rightful place,' he says. The sights are now set to quality and clarity. Michael Herzog loves the linearity and finesse of Brotwasser Riesling but as a passionate hunter and consumer of venison is also fond of Lemberger and Spätburgunder. There is a small wine shop at the Schloss. VDP member estate.

Try: Maulbronner Eilfingerberg Lemberger for elegance and grip.

Wein- und Sektgut Hirschmüller
Lauffen am Neckar
www.weingut-hirschmueller.de

Wiebke Krüger and Tobias Hirschmüller met in Geisenheim and knew they wanted to do their own thing. They both went to California to do a *stage*, Krüger at Williams Selyem, Hirschmüller at Flowers. As Krüger hails from Hannover there were no vineyards in her family but Hirschmüller's parents always grew grapes for the co-op. In 2013 the youngsters founded their *Weingut* with half a hectare that his parents let them farm. Now they have expanded to 5 hectares, which they lease from old local *Winzer* who are retiring. They make their wines in a rented barn. Lauffen with its loess-covered *Muschelkalk* soils is a village where Schwarzriesling, aka Pinot Meunier, has a long tradition. The couple knew they wanted to focus on Sekt. But since quality fizz has a long lead time, they also make still whites and reds with the aim to do more Sekt as cashflow allows. The Pinot Meunier Blanc de Noirs from their first vintage (2013) shows great promise, a still Pinot Meunier red from 1968-planted vines is also impressive. The couple is the youngest generation of Württemberg winemakers shaking things up. 'We are still getting to know all our vineyards,' Hirschmüller says. 'All the different sites used to disappear in the big blends of the co-ops.' We have much to look forward to once they hit their effervescent stride.

Try: Perlage Sekt Extra Brut for Swabian verve.

Weingut Neipperg
Schwaigern
www.graf-neipperg.de

Karl Eugen Erbgraf zu Neipperg took over his family's ancient estate in 1978 and rang in fundamental changes. Once he had finished his degree in agronomy, he added a few semesters at Geisenheim and made the estate, which also includes arable farming and forestry, into one of Württemberg's best. His father had expanded the vineyards, but it took Karl Eugen to return to the dry, skin-fermented Lemberger for which the estate had been renowned. The family has owned vineyards here since the thirteenth century but Erbgraf Neipperg distinguishes between owning vineyards and making wine. Wines have been made and bottled at the estate since the early twentieth century. While there is a lovely theory that links the Neippergs' close ties to the house of Habsburg to the arrival of Lemberger in Württemberg, there are no records to prove this. Nonetheless the immediate area has been a consistent Lemberger pocket since at least the late nineteenth century. Today Neipperg stands for consistently elegant Lemberger, taut Riesling and seductive Spätburgunder. Winemaker Bernd Supp has clearly mastered his brief. The wines are quiet and unshowy but they do get under your skin. Lemberger in particular is fragrant, with violet and white pepper and true to each vintage. The two top sites are the Schwaigerner Ruthe (*Keuper*, up to 300 metres) and the Neipperger Schlossberg (weathered *Keuper* and *Schilfsandstein*, just over 300 metres). There is also the Dürrenzimmerer Mönchsberg (*Keuper*, up to 270 metres) which always brings sinuous, scented Lemberger. Wood from their own forests is used for their barrels. A clone of Lemberger, notable for its low yield and high quality, has been selected in the Erbgraf's vineyards – he calls this genetic material his 'true treasure'. Lovers of dry Muskateller are also in for a treat. VDP member estate.

Try: an older vintage of Lemberger from Schlossberg or Ruthe for depth and spice.

Weingut Roterfaden
Vaihingen an der Enz-Roßwag
www.weingutroterfaden.de

Olympia Samara, from Thessaloniki, and Hannes Hoffmann, from sleepy Roßwag, met in Geisenheim. The winemaking couple then managed to work in Napa and Sonoma, respectively. They then worked and studied in southern France. Stints in South Africa and Austria (with Dorli Muhr and Claus Preisinger) followed and the couple could easily have carried on their peripatetic winemaking – but they wanted to have a project of their own. So they test-drove a vintage at Hannes's home, where his grandparents' farm had 0.5 hectares of vines in the steep, dry-walled *Muschelkalk* terraces of Roßwag, on a loop of the river Enz. They vowed to work exactly to their biodynamic standards and insisted it would just be a trial. It must have gone well, since the Roterfaden (red thread) estate was founded in 2015. They were Demeter certified in 2018 and remodelled the old barn into a winery. The initial scepticism of his grandparents has by now turned into beaming pride – even if some neighbours still think that wild flowers have no place at all in an orderly vineyard. Olympia and Hannes have 2 hectares today, one on the terraces, one on the plateau. They grow Lemberger, Spätburgunder and Riesling and classify everything as *Landwein*. Riesling is harvested with stonking freshness, foottrodden and left for some time on its skins. It stays on its gross lees until bottling. Pinot and Lemberger are fermented with some whole bunches and stay on their skins for four weeks with minimal extraction so you get gorgeous berry in the Pinot and crunchy cherry in the Lemberger. Sulphur additions are minimal and happen just before bottling. What a coup for Roßwag to have snared them.

Try: Riesling for irresistible saltiness and the reds for vivid tenderness.

Weingut Steinbachhof
Vaihingen an der Enz
www.steinbachhof.de

The beautiful, half-timbered Steinbachhof, an old grange of Maulbronn Abbey, was first mentioned in 1178. It lies in peaceful isolation in a forest clearing and used to belong to the Dukes of Württemberg, who sold it to the Eissler family in 1848. They have farmed here ever since and in the past sold the grapes of their 2.5 hectares to the co-op. Ulrich Eissler founded the *Weingut* in 1999 and made the wines from 2000–14. By 2010 he had expanded the vineyard to 10 hectares. However, a new event location business that makes the most of the beautiful setting meant that he has now halved the vineyards, hiring the engaging and talented Ambra Terrazzan, a wine graduate from Trentino, to make the wines. The 5 hectares are planted to Riesling, Lemberger, Trollinger and Pinot varieties in red and white. The vineyards are in the neighbouring villages on *Keuper*, *Mergel* and *Stubensandstein*. Ambra loves teasing out the sweet spot between residual sugar and freshness in the whites, while the reds are all dry. Fruit and sheer drinkability are to the fore – a winning strategy as the farm is a popular wedding venue.

Try: Lemberger Drei Sterne for lovely balance and precision.

Weingut Wachtstetter
Pfaffenhofen
www.wachtstetter.de

Rainer Wachtstetter is a quiet genius. The origins of the *Weingut* are in the Gasthaus Adler, an inn, where home-grown wines had been part of the offer since 1820. This meant that the Wachtstetters never joined a co-op. Rainer Wachtstetter, who runs the estate today, has made the wines since 1987 after his father founded the estate in 1985 in order to sell bottled wines. Rainer, a very thoughtful, modest man, remembers that lowering yields put them miles ahead of the competition in the late 1980s. He says that it took him a while to hone his own style but he worked uncompromisingly towards quality. With his wife Anette he farms 20 hectares of vines on the Pfaffenhofener Hohenberg of which the base is *Gipskeuper* and the upper reaches are *Schilfsandstein*. Certain Hohenberg parcels are singled out as Mühlberg (Riesling), Ochsenberg (Lemberger) and Gaisberg (Spätburgunder). The *Schilfsandstein* contains glauconite, so the top Riesling, Lemberger and Spätburgunder are called Glaukós. The Riesling grows at up to 290 metres and Wachtstetter says he loves 'a certain phenolic and tannic structure in his Rieslings.' But it was with Lemberger that he made his name. These wines are of exceptional elegance with a density, aromatic intensity and sinuous tannins. He also makes a Lemberger from a windy, exposed knoll which is toned, peppery and dew-fresh even after a decade in bottle. But such is his exactitude that Grauburgunder here is structured, snappy and elegant while Trollinger Alte Reben has an unusual but fitting edge of new oak. Wachtstetter is a treasure hidden away in a rural backwater, but more than worth the journey. Junges Schwaben member. VDP member estate.

Try: any of the Glaukós range.

GLOSSARY

Alte Reben. Old vines – not a legally defined term.
Amtliche Prüfung. Official quality control testing for *Qualitäts-* and *Prädikatswein*.
Bereich. District; wine regions are divided up into *Bereiche*.
Bundesland. German federal state, plural: *Bundesländer*.
Buntsandstein. Sedimentary, iron-rich sandstone, Triassic formation – see box, page 271.
Burg. Castle.
Doppelstück. See *Stück*.
Erste Lage. VDP vineyard classification equivalent to *premier cru*.
Federweisser. Partially fermented must/grape juice. You will find this advertised on improvised signs in wine villages around the time of the harvest, usually alongside *Zwiebelkuchen*, or onion tart. Be warned: it is easy-drinking but dangerous stuff.
Feinherb. Not a legal definition but a useful, nuanced term, best translated as 'off-dry'. It describes a wine that often finishes dry-ish but is not in the legal definition of 'trocken'. It speaks to subtlety and the flavour-enhancing and balancing properties of very slight sweetness which works so well with Riesling's prominent acidity.
Fuder. Typical 1,000-litre, round, large Mosel barrel.
Gallization. A process invented and promulgated by Heinrich Ludwig Lambert Gall (1791–1863) in which grape must is chaptalized/enriched not with dry sugar but sugar solution, i.e. sugar dissolved in water. This has the added benefit of diluting acid.
Geisenheim. Germany's foremost viticultural college.

Gemischter Satz. Field blend, i.e. varieties grown in the same vineyard to be co-harvested and co-fermented.

Gewann. Named parcel/plot of land, *lieu-dit*, often superseded by 1971 zoning.

GG. See Grosses Gewächs.

Gipskeuper. Triassic formation – see box, page 271.

Grosse Lage. VDP vineyard classification equivalent to *grand cru*.

Grosses Gewächs. Top category of the VDP quality pyramid for still wine. A *Grosses Gewächs*, or GG, denotes a wine from a single vineyard classified as *Grosse Lage* in the VDP classification. Made according to VDP's regulations on variety, yield, etc.

Gutswein. Literally estate wine, but also lowest level of VDP quality pyramid for still wines.

Halbstück. See *Stück*.

Halbtrocken. Legally defined term denoting a wine with a maximum of 18 grams per litre of sugar.

Hayflowers. *Heublumen* – mixture of seeds, flowers and grasses, sieved from hay and used for medical purposes. Tasting term describing the ethereal lift of mixed, wild herbs

Kaiserpfalz. Temporary seat of the imperial court of the Holy Roman Empire.

Kellerei. Big *négociant* business that buys in grapes to make wine.

Keuper. Triassic formation – see box, page 271.

Lagenweine. Literally wine from a named site, but see also *Ortswein* and *Gutswein*.

Landwein. Defined in German wine law – requires no *Amtliche Prüfnummer* – see box, page 82.

Lettenkeuper. Triassic formation – see box, page 271.

Lieblich. Legally defined term denoting a wine with a maximum of 45 grams per litre of sugar.

Monopole. A single vineyard in sole ownership.

Muschelkalk. Triassic formation – see box, page 271.

Nassverbesserung. See Gallization.

Oechsle. Measure of must weight, i.e. sugar content and therefore ripeness of grape juice/must. After Ferdinand Oechsle (1774–1852) who invented a calibrated hydrometer to measure the specific gravity of sugar in grape must.

Ortswein. Literally village wine, but also mid-level of VDP quality pyramid for still wines.

Pièce. Burgundian small barrel of 228 litres.

Pied de cuve. Yeast starter culture.

Realteilung. Legal system describing the equal split of inherited property between all children.

Rotliegendes. Both a term for geological age (Permian) and a catch-all term used by many growers to describe reddish soils.

Schaumkalk. Porous cellular limestone.

Schichtstufenlandschaft. Triassic topography – see box, page 271.

Schilfsandstein. Triassic formation – see box, page 271.

Schloss. German term for château or castle, but note that castle is also *Burg*.

Sektkellerei. Large sparkling wine producer/factory, plural *Sektkellereien*.

Staatsweingut. State domaine, i.e. owned by a federal state.

Steillage, Steilstlage. Steep sites of minimum gradient (respectively) 30 per cent and 50 per cent. See also box on page 142.

Strausswirtschaft. The widespread, historic practice of opening the winery temporarily to the public in order to serve home-grown wine in an informal atmosphere alongside regional food.

Stubensandstein. Triassic formation – see box, page 271.

Stück, also Halbstück and Doppelstück. *Stück* is the typical 1,200-litre, oval barrel of the Rheingau, a *Halbstück* is 600 litres and a *Doppelstück* is 2,400 litres.

Süss. Legally defined term denoting a minimum of 45 grams per litre of sugar.

Süssreserve. The addition of sterilized, unfermented grape must to fermented dry wine before bottling in order to make it sweet.

Techniker. Advanced professional qualification following on from *Winzer*.

Trocken. Legally defined term denoting a wine with a maximum of 9 grams per litre of sugar.

Weingut. Wine estate, winery.

Weinfest. Wine party: every village seems to have one. Expect wine, sausages and local specialities in a very informal atmosphere.

Winzer, Winzerin. The German term for vigneron, i.e. a person who grows, makes and sells wine. It is also the name of the profession you attain after Germany's structured vocational training.

Winzergenossenschaft. Viticultural cooperative.

Winzerlehre. Formalized apprenticeship within Germany's dual vocational system.

Wurzelecht. German term for ungrafted, i.e. vines on their own roots.

BIBLIOGRAPHY

Where quotes are in English from German sources, the translation is the author's own.

Adelmann, Raban, Die Geschichte des Württembergischen Weinbaus, *Schriften zur Weingeschichte*, Nr 8, Wiesbaden, 1962
Ahrwein e.V., *Stein & Wein an der Ahr*, Bad Neuenahr-Ahrweiler, not dated
Aldinger, Gerhard, *Mein Leben mit den Reben*, (self-published) Fellbach, 2000
Aldinger, Gerhard, *Weinbauchronik*, (self-published) Fellbach, 2000
Allgemeine Hotel- und Gastronomiezeitung, Großer Verlust für Deutschlands Weinwelt, Stuttgart, 28 May 2004
Anon., 'Die Nasse Hand', *Der Spiegel*, Hamburg, 30/1961
Anon., 'Immer wieder anders sein', *Der Spiegel*, Hamburg, 5/1971
Anon., 'Klebrige Spuren', *Der Spiegel*, Hamburg, 45/1980
Anon., 'Gepanschter Wein: "Schön rund und ölig"', *Der Spiegel*, Hamburg, 31/1985
Anstett, Peter R., *Kloster Maulbronn*, Deutscher Kunstverlag, Munich-Berlin, 1996
Arntz, Helmut, 'Aus der Geschichte des Deutschen Weinhandels', *Schriften zur Weingeschichte*, 13, Wiesbaden, 1964
Arntz, Helmut, 'Frühgeschichte des Deutschen Sektes I', *Schriften zur Weingeschichte*, 80, Wiesbaden, 1987
Arntz, Helmut, 'Frühgeschichte des Deutschen Sekts II', *Schriften zur Weingeschichte*, 82, Wiesbaden, 1987

Arntz, Helmut, 'Frühgeschichte des Deutschen Sektes V', *Schriften zur Weingeschichte*, 89, Wiesbaden, 1988

Arntz, Helmut, 'Die Geschichte der Sektkellerei Kloss & Foerster-Rotkäppchen', *Schriften zur Weingeschichte*, 111, Wiesbaden, 1994

Bach, A., Butt, S., Hallet, T., et al., *Die Wissenschaft vom Bier*, WDR, Cologne, 1996

Badischer Weinbauverband e.V., *Tätigkeitsbericht 2018*, Freiburg, 2018

Bassermann-Jordan, Friedrich von, *Geschichte des Weinbaus*, Zweite Wesentlich Erweiterte Auflage 1923, Frankfurter Verlags-Anstalt AG, Frankfurt, 1975

Baumann, Reinhold, *Zwölf Jahrhunderte Weinbau und Weinhandel in Württemberg*, Schriften zur Weingeschichte, 33, Wiesbaden, 1974

Bayerische Landesanstalt für Weinbau und Gartenbau, *Boden und Wein*, Veitshöchheim, 2015

Bayerische Landesanstalt für Weinbau und Gartenbau, *Sachgebiet Weinrecht, Rebsortenverteilung im bayerischen Weinbau*, Veitshöchheim, 2018

Berry, Charles Walter, *Viniana*, Constable & Co. Ltd., London, 1934

Biewer, Ludwig, *Das Wappen von Rheinhessen*, Weinbruderschaft Rheinhessen, Weinbrief, 2015

Borchardt-Wenzel, Annette, *Kleine Geschichte Badens*, Verlag Friedrich Pustet, Regensburg, 2011

Braatz, D., Sautter, U., Swoboda, I., *Weinatlas Deutschland*, Hallwag, Munich, 2007

Bronner, Johann Philipp, *Der Weinbau in Süddeutschland*, Viertes Heft, Winter, Heidelberg, 1837

Bronner, Johann Philipp, *Die Bereitung der Rothweine*, Verlag Heinrich Ludwig Brönner, Frankfurt, 1856

Bronner, Johann Philipp, *Die Teutschen Schaumweine*, Akademische Buchhandlung von C.F. Winter, Heidelberg, 1842

Bundesanzeiger Verlag GmbH, Bundesgesetzblatt, accessible at https://www.bgbl.de, for all legal texts 1949–present

Bungert, Karl-Heinz, '"Heilige Berge" sind Wahrzeichen', *Allgemeine Zeitung*, 7 January 2016

Christoffel, Karl, *Durch die Zeiten strömt der Wein, Die Wunderbare Historie des Weines*, Cram, De Gruyter & Co, Hamburg, 1957

Daten und Fakten zum Weinmarkt 1990, Deutscher Weinfonds, 1991

Deckers, Daniel, *Es blühe der Steinberg, Kloster Eberbach*, Tre Torri, Wiesbaden, 2015

Deckers, Daniel, *Frankenweine der Besten Art, Bürgerspital Würzburg*, Tre Torri Verlag, Wiesbaden, 2016

Deckers, Daniel, 'Gerbstoff, Geist und Bouquet, Wein und Zeit', *Fine Magazin Deutschland*, 2/2012

Deckers, Daniel, *Im Zeichen des Traubenadlers*, Verlag Philipp von Zabern, Mainz, 2010

Deckers, Daniel, *Kiedricher Auslese, Der Riesling-Weingut Robert Weil*, Tre Torri Verlag, Wiesbaden, 2013

Deckers, Daniel, 'Luscious, seductive, innocent: the perception of Hocks and Moselles in the nineteenth century', lecture, Internationales Rieslingsymposium, Kloster Eberbach, 2017

Deckers, Daniel, 'Massstäbe Gesetzt', *Fine Weinmagazin*, 4/2018

Deckers, Daniel, 'Sangria von der Saale', *Fine Weinmagazin*, 1/2018

Deckers, Daniel, 'Versonnte Weinstadt?', *Fine Weinmagazin*, 1/2013

Deckers, Daniel, 'Von Hoher Kulturhistorischer Bedeutung', *Fine Weinmagazin*, 1/2011

Deckers, Daniel, *Wein Geschichte und Genuss*, Verlag C.H. Beck, Munich, 2017

Deutsche Stratigraphische Kommission, *Stratigraphische Tabelle von Deutschland 2002*, Deutsche Geoforschungszentrum, Potsdam, 2002

Deutsches Weininstitut GmbH, *German Wine Manual*, Bodenheim, 2018

Deutsches Weininstitut GmbH, *Deutscher Wein Statistik 2018/19*, Bodenheim, 2019

Dinse, Christine, *Geschichte der Königlish Preussischen Rieslingdomäne Gut Hermannsberg*, Gut Hermannsberg, Niederhausen, 2012

Dohm, Horst, *Sekt Zwischen Kult und Konsum*, Verlag & Druckerei D. Meininger, Neustadt, 1981

Donath, Günter and Richter, Frank, *Gärten aus Stein, Die Pflanzenwelt des Naumburger Meisters*, Michael Imhof Verlag, Petersberg, 2015

Dornfeld, Immanuel, *Die Geschichte des Weinbaus in Württemberg*, Cohen und Risch, Stuttgart, 1868

Dünkelberg, Friedrich Wilhelm, *Der Nassauische Weinbau*, Verlag von Chr. Limbarth, Wiesbaden, 1867

Endriss, Gerhard, 'Der Badische Weinbau in Historisch-Geographischer Betrachtung', *Schriften zur Weingeschichte*, 14, Wiesbaden, 1965

Fadani, Andrea, 'Landwirtschaft in Baden und Württemberg in den letzten 200 Jahren, Die Landwirtschaft im Blick der Kunst', *Nützliche Natur*, Beuroner Kunstverlag, Beuron, 2011

Fiedler, Siegfried, *Der Markgraf, Carl Friedrich und seine Zeit*, Markgräflich Badische Museen, Karlsruhe, 1981

Fisch, Jean and Rayer, David, 'Vineyard Classification – The Classification before the Classification', *Mosel Fine Wines*, 39, January 2018

Gieler, P. and Konrad, H., 'Die Frucht, die aus der Kälte kam', *Deutsches Weinbaujahrbuch 2011*, Verlag Eugen Ulmer, Stuttgart, 2011

Goerges, Josef, *Der Rotweinbau an der Ahr*, Adolph Kirfel Buch- und Kunstdruckerei, Ahrweiler, 1928

Goldschmidt, Franz, *Deutschlands Weinbauorte und Weinbergslagen*, Verlag der Deutschen Weinzeitung, Mainz, 1910

Graichen, G. and Hammel-Kiesow, R., *Die Deutsche Hanse*, Rowohlt, Hamburg, 2015

Gunzelmann, Thomas, 'Fränkische Terrassenweinberge als Denkmale – Geschichte und Bedeutung', transcript of a lecture delivered for a seminar on 'Trockenmauerbau in Weinbergsterrassen', 7 August 2007 in Klingenberg

Haeger, John Winthrop, *Riesling Rediscovered*, University of California Press, Oakland, 2016

Hägermann, Dieter, *Karl der Große*, Rowohlt Verlag GmbH, Hamburg, 2003

Hahn, Helmut, *Die Deutschen Weinbaugebiete*, Geographisches Institut der Universität Bonn, Bonn, 1956

Heitmann, Patrick *et al.*, *Die KHS Historie*, KHS GmbH, Dortmund, 2019

Hessischer Weinbauverband, *Die Rheinweine Hessens*, Philip von Zabern Gmbh, Mainz, 1927

Hoffmann, Kurt, '1100 Jahre Spatburgunder in Bodman am Bodensee', *Schriften zur Weingeschichte*, 73, 1985

Holthöfer, Hugo, 'Deutsche Gesetzgebung über Wein', extracted chapter from *Handbuch der Lebensmittelchemie, Siebenter Band Alkoholische Genussmittel*, Verlag von Julius Springer, Berlin, 1938

Huber, Elfriede C., *Vergleich von Steillagen-Mechanisierungsformen im Weinbau*, Masterarbeit, Technikhochschule Mainz, 2015

Illert, Friedrich, *Liebfraumilch, Aus der Geschichte eines berühmten Weins*, Erich Norberg, Worms, 1961

Irsigler, Franz, *Die Privatisierung des Scharzhofes zu Beginn des 19. Jahrhunderts*, Universität Trier, 2015

Junglas, Wolfgang, 'Laudatio auf Armin Diel', Weinpersönlichkeit des Jahres 2017, held 19 Oct 2017, Mainz

Koch, F.W. and Stephanus, H., *Die Weine im Gebiete der Mosel und Saar*, Verlag von Heirich Stephanus, Trier, 1898

Koch, Hans-Jörg, *Wechselwirkungen zwischen Weinbaugeschichte, Weinrecht und Weinkultur*, Geschichtliche Landeskunde, Band 40, Institut für Geschichtliche Landeskunde, Mainz, 1993

Kocks, Hans-Hermann, *375 Jahre Weingut Witwe Dr. H. Thamisch Erben Thanisch*, Bernkastel, 2011

Kramp, Mario, *Napoleon, Der Kaiser Kommt!*, Görres Druckerei & Verlag, Koblenz, 2004

Krasenbrink, Josef, 'Hildegard von Bingen und der Wein', *Binger Geschichtsblätter*, 20, Folge, Bingen, 1998

Krebiehl, Anne, 'Scheurebe The Way of the Crossing', *The World of Fine Wine*, 63, 2019

Krebiehl, Anne, 'Pinot Noir: Cracking the Clonal Code', *The World of Fine Wine*, 55, 2017

Krebiehl, Anne, 'Genius Loci Scharzhofberg', *The World of Fine Wine*, 52, London, 2016

Krebiehl, Anne, 'An Almost Identical Twin with a Distinct Personality', *World of Fine Wine*, 47, 2015

Krebiehl, Anne, 'Balancing Act', *The Drinks Business*, London, November 2014

Krebiehl, Anne, 'Of Soil, Yeast, and Petrol: Groundbreaking Studies of Riesling's Multifarious Delights', *The World of Fine Wine*, March 2014

Krebiehl, Anne, 'The New Saxony', *The World of Fine Wine*, 46, London, 2014

Kriege, Wilhelm, *Der Ahrweinbau*, Paulinus-Druckerei, Trier, 1911

Küppers, Heinrich, 'Rheinland-Pfalz, der Wein und Europa 1970–1990', *Geschichte Im Westen*, 2012

Landesamt für Geologie und Bergbau Rheinland Pfalz, *Gute Gründe für Rheinhessenwein*, Rheinhessenwein e.V., Alzey, no date stated

Langenbach, Alfred, *German Wines and Vines*, Vista Books, London, 1962

Linsenmaier, Otto, 'Der Trollinger und seine Verwandten', *Schriften zur Weingeschichte*, 92, Wiesbaden, 1989

Loeb, O.W. and Prittie, Terence, *Moselle*, Faber and Faber, London, 1972

LVWO Baden-Württemberg, 'Klone von Ertragsrebsorten', *Referat Rebenzüchtung*, März 2010

Maltmann, Alex, *Vineyards, Rocks and Soils*, Oxford University Press, Oxford, 2018

Meier, Robert, *Fürst Löwenstein: 400 Jahre Wein und Geschichte*, Wertheim, 2011

Mertes, Peter Josef, *Zukunft für Vergangenheit, Begleitschrift zur Saar-Mosel Karte*, Stadtbibliothek-Stadtarchiv Trier, 2004

Mesenhöller, Mathias, 'Ein Kind der Revolution', *Merian Rheinhessen*, November 2015

Ministerien für Wirtschaft und Umwelt Rheinland-Pfalz, *Weinbergsböden in Rheinland-Pfalz*, Mainz, 2013

Monz, Heinz, 'Ludwig Gall, Retter der Moselwinzer oder Weinfälscher', *Schriften zur Weingeschichte*, 57, Wiesbaden, 1981

Muhl, Servatius, *Der Weinbau an Mosel und Saar*, Verlag von C. Troschel, Trier, 1845

Müller, Karl, *Geschichte des Badischen Weinbaus*, Moritz Schauenburg, Lahr, 1953

Neigenfind, Rulf, *Die Zwei Leben des Georg Christian Kessler*, Lane Books, Paris, 2012

Nickening, R. and Rückrich, K., *Zahlen-Daten-Fakten 2008 DWV-Statistik zur Internationalen Weinwirtschaft*, Deutscher Weinbauverband, Bonn, 2008

Ossendorf, Karlheinz, 'Sancta Colonia als Weinhaus der Hanse', *Schriften zur Weingeschichte*, 116, Wiesbaden, 1996

Peukert, Jörg, 'Der Freyburger Weinbau vom 16. bis zum 18. Jahrhundert', *Schriften zur Weingeschichte*, 132, Wiesbaden, 1999

Pigott, Stuart, *Wine Atlas of Germany*, Mitchell Beazley, London, 1995

Presse- und Informationsdienst der Bundesregierung, *Tatsachen über Deutschland*, Societäts-Verlag, Frankfurt, 2000

Prössler, Helmut, 'Koblenz 2000 Jahre und der Wein', *Schriften zur Weingeschichte*, 107, Wiesbaden, 1993

Rausch, Jakob, 'Die Geschichte des Weinbaus an der Ahr', *Schriften zur Weingeschichte*, 10, Wiesbaden, 1963

Reichsgesetzblatt, Jahrgang 1930, Teil 1, Weingesetz vom 25 Juli 1932

Reichsgesetzblatt, Jahrgang 1932, Teil 1, Verordnung zur Ausführung des Weingesetzes vom 16 Juli 1932

Rheinhessenwein e.V., *Rheinhessen Himmel und Erde*, Nünnerich-Asmus Verlag & Media, Mainz, 2015

Rheinisches Landesmuseum Trier, *2000 Jahre Weinkultur an Mosel-Saar-Ruwer*, Trier, 1987

Robinson, Jancis and Harding, Julia, *Oxford Companion to Wine*, Fourth Edition, Oxford University Press, Oxford, 2015

Robinson, J., Harding, J., Vouillamoz, J., *Wine Grapes*, Penguin, London, 2012

Schäfer, Rainer, 'Besessen von Grossem Wein', *Fine Das Weinmagazin*, 03/2014

Schäpers, Maria, 'Heilmittel für Körper und Seele: Heiligenverehrung, Schenkungen für das Seelenheil und Klostereintritte im Rheinland der Karolingerzeit', Portal Rheinische Geschichte (rheinische-geschichte.lvr.de), accessed 20 May 2019

Schmid, J., Manty, F., Lindner, B., *et al.*, *Geisenheimer Rebsorten und Klone*, Geisenheimer Berichte 67, Geisenheim, 2009

Schmitt, Conrad, *Die Weine des Herzoglich Nassauischen Cabinetkellers*, Verlag Paul Parey, Berlin, 1893

Schmitt, Friedrich, 'Geschichte des Weinbaus an der nahe', *Schriften zur Weingeschichte*, 148, Wiesbaden, 2004

Schoonmaker, Frank, *German Wines*, Oldbourne Press, London, 1957

Schreiber, Georg, *Deutsche Weingeschichte*, Rheinland-Verlag, Cologne, 1980

Schruft, Günter, 'Die Geschichte der Veredelung des Weinbaus auf Vulkanböden Im Kaiserstuhl', Schriften zur Weingeschicte, 186, Wiesbaden, 2015

Schulze, Hagen, *Kleine Deutsche Geschichte*, dtv, Munich, 2015

Sichel, Peter M.F., *The Secrets of My Life*, Archway Publishing, Bloomington, 2016

Sommerfeld, Hubertus, 'Kaiser Karl IV und der Wein', *Sachsen-Anhalt Journal*, Ausgabe 4, 2016

Staab, Josef, '500 Jahre Rheingauer Klebrot', *Schriften zur Weingeschichte*, 24, Wiesbaden, 1971

Staab, Josef, 'Die Zisterzienser und der Wein', *Schriften zur Weingeschichte*, Wiesbaden, 1987

Staab, J., Seeliger, H. R., Schleicher, W., *Schloss Johannisberg Neun Jahrhunderte Weinkultur am Rhein*, Woschek Verlags GmbH, Mainz, 2001

Stadtarchiv Worms, Weinhandelshaus/Familie P.J. Valckenberg GmbH (Dep.) (Bestand) https://www.deutsche-digitale-bibliothek.de/item/BDJG2TONDESHIVIGPFHWW74FSI5RNEUS

Strache, Wolf, *Das Moselbuch*, Deutsches Verlagshaus Bong & Co., Berlin, 1937

Troost, Gerhard, 'Zur Geschichte der Weinfiltration', *Schriften zur Weingeschichte*, 79, Wiesbaden, 1986

Ufer, Peter, *Perlender Genuss, Sektgeschichten aus Sachsen*, Sächsisches Staatsweingut GmbH, Radebeul, 2016

Vizetelly, Henry, *The Wines of the World, Characterized and Classed*, Ward, Lock & Tyler, London, 1875

Volk, Otto, 'Quellen und Forschungen zur spätmittelalterlichen Weinbaugeschichte', *Weinbau, Weinhandel und Weinkultur*, Institut für Geschichtliche Landeskunde an der Universität Mainz e.V. (online)

von Plessen, Marie-Louise, *Navigation und Verbauung, Der Rhein – Eine europäische Flussbibliografie*, Prestel Verlag, Munich, 2016

Weber, Andreas Otto and Dohna, Jesko, *Die Anfänge der fränkischen Weinkultur, Geschichte des fränkischen Weinbaus*, Volk Verlag, Munich, 2012

Wege zum Wein, Weinbauverband Saale-Unstrut e.V. Gebietsweinwerbung, Freyburg, 2016

Weinbau in Sachsen, Geschichte, Pressemappe Weinbauverband Sachsen, Meissen, 2018

Weinbauverein Ahrweiler, *Brochure: Der Weinbau an der Ahr und die Winzergenossenschaften, ca. 1900*, Landesbibliothekzentrum Rheinland-Pfalz www.dilibri.de

Witt, Otto, *Amtlicher Katalog der Ausstellung des Deutschen Reichs*, 1900

Wurzer-Berger, Martin, *Warum Eberbach?*, Kloster Eberbach, Tre Torri, Wiesbaden, 2015

Zamora, M.C., Goldner, M.C. and Galmarini, M.V., 'Sourness-Sweetness Interactions in Different Media: White Wine, Ethanol', *Journal of Sensory Studies*, November 2006

INDEX

Achenbach, Constanza 236
Achenbach, Frank 236
Achenbach, Gernot 236, 237
Acker, Michael 169
Acolon 264
Adams, Simone 237
Adenauer, Konrad 122
Adeneuer, Frank 50
Adeneuer, Marc 50
Affenthaler 61
Ahr valley 32, 33, 45, 47–57
Albert, Prince 200
Aldinger, Bentz 264
Aldinger, Gerhard 264, 265
Aldinger, Gert 261, 263, 264, 265
Aldinger, Hansjörg 264
Aldinger, Matthias 264, 265
Alfred Gratien Champagne 202
Alice, princess 36
Alter Fränkischer Satz 87, 88
Amtliche Prüfung 74, 82, 83, 183, 242, 267
Arnold, Peter 104
Assmannshäuser 31–2
Association of German *Naturwein* Auctioneers (VDNV) 11, 18
Attmann, Stephan 180
auctions, wine 216
August der Starke ('the Strong') 253, 254, 256
August Eser 199–200
Auslese 10, 13, 14, 23
Ausoniuis 119
Aust, Karl-Friedrich 255
Austro–Prussian War 6, 192, 199

Auxerrois 68, 70, 73, 135, 145, 155, 207

Bacchus 13, 17, 97, 210
  Baden 66
  Franken 87, 99, 100
  Sachsen 256
Baden 32, 33, 34, 45, 59–83
Baden, Carl Friedrich von 60, 66, 76, 81
Badische Bergstrasse 62, 64
Badisch Rotgold 34
Baltes, Benedikt 33–4, 51, 101–2
Bamberger, Heiko 153–4
Bamberger, Ute 153–4
Barth, Andreas 145
Barth, Christine 194
Barth, Mark 194
Bassermann-Jordan, Friedrich v. 169
Bassermann-Jordan, Ludwig 169
Bastian, Fritz 113
Batarseh, Simon 205
Baur, Christopher 269
Bayreuther Festspiele 36
Becker, Eva 195
Becker, Friedrich, junior 182, 183
Becker, Friedrich, senior 73, 182–3
Becker, Hajo 195
Becker, Jean Baptiste 195
Becker, Maria 195
Beerenauslese (BA) 10, 13–14, 23
Benedictines 4
  Ahr valley 48
  Franken 86
  Mosel 142, 148

Pfalz 182
Rheingau 190, 198, 203, 211
Saale-Unstrut 246, 252
Benzarti, Sandi 72
Bercher, Arne 70–1
Bercher, Martin 70–1
Bergsträsser Winzer e.G. 107
Bernard of Clairvaux 4
Bertram, Julia 34, 50, 51, 102
Bettenheimer, Jens 237–8
Beurer, Jochen 265–6
Bibo, Walter 195
Bibo Runge 195–6
Bickel, Carmen 88
Bingen 217, 218, 235–43
Bingen, Hildegard von 196
biodynamic farming
    Baden 77
    Franken 95, 97, 101
    Mosel 126, 127, 129
    Pfalz 169–72, 177, 178, 184–6
    Rheingau 205
    Rheinhessen 220, 224, 232, 235, 241
    Württemberg 265, 267, 280
Bird-Huff, Jeremy 222
Bischöfliches Weingut 196
Bismarck, Otto von 4
Black Hamburg 262
blanc de blancs 232
blanc de noirs 34, 51, 101, 160, 187
Blankenhorn brothers 63
Blauer Silvaner 97
Blaufränkisch *see* Lemberger
Blue Nun 231
Bocksbeutel 85, 88
Bodensee 63–4
Böhme, Klaus 248, 249
Bonsels, Markus 195
Born, Elisabeth 248–9
Born, Günter 249
Born, Jochen 249
botrytis 9, 23, 28, 29, 44
    Franken 93
    Mosel 126, 130
    Pfalz 171, 173
    Rheingau 192
Brandner, Niko 108
Braunewell, Axel 238
Braunewell, Christian 238
Braunewell, Stefan 235, 238–9

Breisgau 62, 67–70
Breitengrad 51: 248, 249, 251
Bremer, Anna 169
Bremer, Leah 169
Bremer, Rebecca 169
Breuer, Bernhard 196
Breuer, Theresa 196–7
Bronner, Johann Philipp 31
Bukettrebe 210
Bundesrepublik 11
Burgdorf, Michael 214
Bürgerspital zum Heiligen Geist 89
Burkhardt, Laura 102
Bürklin, Albert 12, 170
Bürklin-von Guradze, Bettina 170
Busch, Clemens 125–6
Busch, Johannes 126
Busch, Rita 125–6
Buttlar, Konstantin von 191

Cabernet 184, 265
Cabernet Cubin 264
Cabernet Doria 264
Cabernet Dorsa 264
Cabernet Franc 77, 80, 101, 154, 179, 239
Cabernet Mitos 264
Cabernet Sauvignon 264
    Ahr valley 55
    Baden 75, 78
    Pfalz 179
    Rheingau 207
    Württemberg 263, 273, 276, 277
Cabinet 10, 11, 13, 20
Capitulare de villis 4
Capuchins 229, 230
Carolingians 3, 4, 86, 112, 166, 190
Carthusians 147
Castell-Castell, Fürst Ferdinand zu 99
Castle Kastenholz 48
Catoir, Philipp David 176
Celts 3
Champagne 35–6
Chaptal, Jean Antoine 120
chaptalization 120
Chardonnay
    Ahr valley 52
    Baden 65, 68–74, 77, 79, 81–2
    Franken 89, 95, 102, 103
    Hessische Bergstrasse 108
    Mosel 135

Nahe 156, 158, 162
Pfalz 169, 173–4, 179, 181, 183–4, 186
Rheingau 197, 204, 212
Rheinhessen 219, 229, 232–3, 235–7, 239–40
Württemberg 269, 273, 275, 277
Charlemagne 3–4, 31, 64, 217
Charles IV 247
Charles the Fat 64
Charmat method 202, 213, 247
Charta 16, 18, 193
Chasselas *see* Gutedel
Château Belá 143
Chenin Blanc 66
Chodakowska, Malgorzata 258
Christmann, Sophie 171
Christmann, Steffen 19, 22, 171
Christoph, Duke of Württemberg 260
Churfranken 86, 101–4
Cistercians 4, 31
   Baden 69
   Franken 86, 96
   Rheingau 190, 198
   Saale-Unstrut 246, 250
   Württemberg 277
classification 18–20
   Mosel 120
   Pfalz 167, 170
   Rheingau 192, 193
Cleebronn-Güglingen 274
Clicquot, Barbe-Nicole 269
climate change 23, 24, 41–5
   Mosel 122
   Riesling 41, 43–4
   Spätburgunder 31, 32, 41
   Württemberg 263
Closheim, Anette 154
Clotten, Franz Josef 120
Cluniac Reform 4
Code Civil 6, 112, 119, 218
Collegium Wirtemberg 273–4
cooperatives
   Ahr valley 48, 51–4, 56
   Baden 61, 64, 76, 82
      Breisgau 68
      Kaiserstuhl 63, 70, 72–4
      Markgräflerland 77
   Franken 91, 93, 99, 101
   Hessische Bergstrasse 107
   law 15

Nahe 153
Pfalz 171, 182, 183
Saale-Unstrut 248–50, 252
Sachsen 245, 257
Württemberg 261–3, 265, 269, 270, 272–4, 278–81
Corvers, Brigitte 198
Corvers, Matthias 198
Corvers, Philipp 198
Crémant 37, 38
Crusius, Brigitta 154
Crusius, Judith 155
Crusius, Peter 154
Crusius, Rebecca 154

Dagobert, King 3
Dannhäuser, Sascha 147
Dautel, Christian 275–6
Dautel, Ernst 275
Dautel, Hannelore 275
Degen, Alberich 96
Deinhard 36, 112
Demeter 177, 205, 220, 280
Deutscher Bund (German Confederation) 6
Deutscher Rotweinpreis 172
Deutscher Sekt 38
Deutscher Wein 14, 16
Deutscher Weinbauverband 24
Deutscher Zollverein 48, 61
Deutsches Reich (German Empire) 4, 6, 120, 121
Diabetikerweine 22
Dickens, Charles 230
Diel, Armin 152, 155
Diel, Caroline 155
diethylene glycol scandal 122, 193
Dinse, Christine 158
Doktor, Stefan 191, 203–4
Domina 87, 99
Dönnhoff, Christina 156
Dönnhoff, Cornelius 156
Dönnhoff, Helmut 15, 20, 152, 153, 156
Dornfelder 52, 55, 153, 168, 219, 264
Drautz, Markus 276
Drautz, Richard 276
Dreissigacker, Jochen 219, 225
Drieseberg, Tom 214
Dünkelberg, Friedrich Wilhelm 10, 18, 191
Du Preez, Jacques 257
Dutch War 60

Ebert, Christian 133, 145–6
Ebrach Abbey 86, 96
Echter, Julius 90, 100
Edelbeerenauslese 10
Ehrenfelser 210
Eicheltraube 266
Einzellagen 14–15
Eisele, Alexander 277
Eissler, Ulrich 280–1
Eiswein 10, 13–14
Ekkehard, Fritz 222
Elbling
    Baden 61
    Franken 88
    Mosel 117, 119, 121, 123, 135
    Nahe 152
    Rheingau 191
    Sachsen 258
Ellwanger, Bernhard 266
Ellwanger, Felix 267
Ellwanger, Ingrid 266
Ellwanger, Jörg 267
Ellwanger, Jürgen 267
Ellwanger, Melanie 266
Ellwanger, Sven 266
Ellwanger, Yvonne 266
Embricho, bishop 94
Enderle, Sven 67–8
Erste Gewächse 193
Erste Lage 19, 38–9
Eser, Désirée 199
Espe, Hansbert 69
Eva Fricke 200–1
Eymael, Jan 177

Faberrebe 210
fakes 16
Federal Republic 11
Fendant *see* Gutedel
Ferdinand II, Emperor 177
First World War 7, 21, 121–2, 193
Fischer, Ulrich 29
Flick, Reiner 200
Flik, Rüdiger 239
Flurbereinigung 63, 144, 208
Foradori, Elisabetta 265
Forstmeister Geltz-Zilliken 140–1
Fourré, Frédéric 256
François Frères 186
Franco–Prussian War 6, 120–1

Franken 33, 45, 85–105
Fränkischer Rechen 87
fränkisch trocken 87
Frankish empire 4
Franzen, Martin 176
Frauer, Nikolas 90
Freixenet 202
Fricke, Eva 200–1
Friedland, Enrico 256
Friedrich August II 258
Fröhlich, Tim 152, 161
Frühburgunder 53, 264
    Ahr valley 50–6
    Franken 98, 103
    Mosel 132
    Rheinhessen 226, 236–8, 240, 243
    Württemberg 263
Fulda, Prince-Abbot of 25
Fulda Abbey 86
Fürst, Paul 33, 102–3, 105
Fürst, Sebastian 103
Fürstbischöflicher Hofkeller 94
Fürstlich Castellsches Domänenamt 96, 99
Fußer, Georg 171–2
Fußer, Martin 171–2
Fütterer 266

Gall, Ludwig 120
gallization 11, 12, 16
Gault Millau Weinführer 17
Geil, Peter 99
Geil-Bierschenk, Johannes 225–6
Gelber Silvaner 97
Gemischter Satz 77
Georg I zu Castell-Remlingen, Graf Wolfgang 96
German Confederation (*Deutscher Bund*) 6
German Democratic Republic (GDR) 245–8, 250–2, 256
German Empire (*Deutsches Reich*) 4, 6, 120, 121
German Wine Growers' Association (*Deutscher Weinbauverband*) 24
Geschützte Geografische Angabe 17
Geschützte Ursprungsbezeichnung 17
Gewanne 19
Gewürztraminer 27, 153, 162, 186, 258
Gillot, Carolin 222–3, 224
glycol scandal 122, 193
Goethe, Johann Wolfgang von 86, 111

Gold, Leon 267–8
Goldriesling 254, 258
Götze, Alexander 79
Gouais Blanc 25
Goziewski, Jörn 201
Graf Zeppelin 76, 269
Gratien & Meyer 202
Grauburgunder
   Ahr valley 54
   Baden 61
      Badische Bergstrasse 64
      Breisgau 68, 70
      Kaiserstuhl 70–5
      Markgräflerland 78, 79, 81, 82
   Badisch Rotgold 34
   Franken 92
   Hessische Bergstrasse 107
   Mittelrhein 114
   Nahe 153, 156, 158, 162
   Pfalz 168
      Mittelhaardt and Nordpfalz 169, 171, 179
      Südliche Weinstrasse 182, 183, 184, 186, 187
   Rheingau 204
   Rheinhessen 221, 232, 233, 237, 238–9
   Saale-Unstrut 250
   Sachsen 254, 258
   Württemberg 273, 274, 281
Greißl-Streit, Petra 108
Griebeler, Peter 126–7
Griebeler, Ulrich 126–7
Griesel & Compagnie 108, 109
Groebe, Fritz 226–7
Grosche, Richard 178
Grosse Lage 18, 19, 38–9
Grosses Gewächs (GG) 18, 23
Grosslagen 14–15, 17
Grüner Silvaner 97
Grüner Veltliner 155
Grünfränkisch 77
Grünhaus, Maximin 123
Guntrum, Konstantin 221–2
Gussek, André 249
Gussek, Stefan 249
Gussek, Thomas 249
Gutedel 76
   Baden 60, 61, 63, 75, 77–9, 81, 82
   Franken 88
   Saale-Unstrut 251
   Sachsen 256

Gut Hermannsberg 152, 157–8
Gutswein 18, 23
Gutzler, Christine 227
Gutzler, Gerhard 227
Gutzler, Michael 227

Haag, Lara 135
Haag, Niklas 135
Haag, Oliver 135
Haag, Thomas 135
Haag, Ute 135
Habsburg empire 60, 279
HADES 267
Haeger, John Winthrop 21, 25, 27
Haidle, Hans 268
Haidle, Karl 268
Haidle, Moritz 268
Haller, Robert 89, 96
Hallgarten, Fritz 7
Hambacher Schloss 167
Hamm, Aurelia 201–2
Hamm, Julius 202
Hamm, Karl-Heinz 201
Hanglage 142
Hängling 266
Hanseatic League 5
Harding, J. 210
Hasselbach, Agnes 221
Hasselbach, Fritz 221
Hasselbach, Johannes 220–1
Hau, Johann Baptist 63
Hauch, Gunther 169
Heger, Joachim 61, 71
Heger, Rebecca 71
Heger, Silvia 71
Hehle, Johannes 52
Hehle, Wolfgang 52
Heid, Markus 268–9
Heigel, Klaus-Peter 100
Heine, Heinrich 111
Helfensteiner 210, 264
Helios 92
Hemingway, Ernest 59
Henkell, Adam 202
Henkell Freixenet 202–3
Henkell Group 36, 37, 202–3, 214
Hensel, Thomas 177
Hensel, Ute 177
Herold, August 264
Heroldrebe 264

Herres, Klaus 134
Herrmann, Lukas 100
Herzog, Michael 278
Hesse, Grand Duke of 218
Hessische Bergstrasse 107–9
Hessische Staatsweingüter 199
Heuft, Thilo 94
Hey, Matthias 250
Hildegard of Bingen, St 211
Himstedt, Max 205
Hirschhorner Weinkontor – Frank John 172
Hirschmüller, Tobias 278–9
history 3–7
    Ahr valley 48–50
    Baden 60–4, 67, 70, 76, 81
    Franken 85, 86–7, 96, 99
    Liebfraumilch 230–1
    Mittelrhein 111, 112
    Mosel 119–22
    Nahe 152, 159
    Pfalz 166–7, 168–9, 176
    Rheingau 189, 190–3, 203, 213, 215
    Rheinhessen 217–18, 230–1
    Riesling 25–6
    Saale-Unstrut 246–7, 250
    Sachsen 253–4, 256
    Sekt 35–7
    Spätburgunder 31–2
    Württemberg 260–1, 266
Hock 190, 200
Höfer, Carsten 89–90
Hoffmann, Hannes 279–80
Hofmann, Alois 104–5
Hofmann, Jürgen 104–5
Hölderlin, Friedrich 111
Holy Roman Empire 4–6, 60, 99
Honigler 266
H. Sichel & Söhne 231
Huber, Bernhard 65, 68, 69, 239
Huber, Julian 34, 68–9
Hübner, Stefan 273
Huff, Christine 222
Huxelrebe 13, 17, 175, 210, 233

Immich family 127
Ingelheim 235–43
inverted sugar syrup scandal 122

Jauch, Dorothea 145
Jauch, Günther 145

J.B. Becker 195
JJ Söhnlein 36
Joh. Jos. Prüm 21, 123, 133–4
John, Frank 172
John, Gerlinde 172
Jordan, Andreas 166–7, 168–9
Jörnwein – Joern Goziewski 201
Jost, Cecilia 113–14
Jost, Peter 112, 113
Josten, Frank 54
Josten, Marc 53–4
Jostock, Hermann 57, 138
Jülg, Johannes 183
Jülg, Oskar 183
Jülg, Werner 183
Juliusspital 90
Junges Schwaben 261, 266
Jüngling, Christa 132
Just, Moriz 278

Kabinett 13–14, 22, 23
Kaiserstuhl 61, 63, 70–5
Karthäuserhof 147–8
Kastenholz 48, 51
Kastler, Bernd 256
Kauffmann, Mathieu 39, 178
Kaufmann, Urban 204
Kékfrankos *see* Lemberger
Keller, Franz 72, 74
Keller, Friedrich 74
Keller, Fritz 74–5
Keller, Hedwig 228
Keller, Irma 74
Keller, Julia 227–8
Keller, Klaus Peter 219, 224, 225, 227–8
Kerner 13, 17, 168, 231, 255, 256, 264
Kesseler, August 204–5
Kessler, Georg Christian von 35–7, 269
Keßler, Yvonne 75
Kessler Sekt 269–70
Khrushchev, Nikita 122
Kiefer, Clemens 209
Klein, Torsten 53–4
Kleinberger *see* Elbling
Kleist, Heinrich von 111
Klingelberger 62
Klinger, Swen 145
Klopfer, Christoph 270
Klopfer, Dagmar 270
Klopfer, Wolfgang 270

Kloss & Foerster 247, 252
Kloster Eberbach 4, 5, 10, 190–3, 198–9
Kloster Fulda 4
Kloster Johannisberg 190, 191
Kloster Lorsch 4
Kloster Pforta 246, 247, 250–1
Kloster Prüm 4
Klosterweingut Abtei St Hildegard 211
Kloster Weissenburg 182
Knäbel, Christoph 175
Knauß, Andreas 271–2
Knebel, Matthias 124–5
Knewitz, Björn 239–40
Knewitz, Tobias 235, 239–40
Knipser, Georg Heinrich 172
Knipser, Sabine 173
Knipser, Stephan 173
Knipser, Volker 172–3
Knipser, Werner 172–3
Knoll, Ludwig 95
Knoll, Sandra 95
Knyphausen, Dodo Freiherr zu 199–200
Koch, F.W. 121
Koch, Gabriele 71, 72
Koch, Holger 71–2
Koch, Johann Jakob 142
Kollmann, Gernot 127
Königlich Bayrishcher Hofkeller 94
Kopp, Ewald 64–5
Kopp, Johannes 64–5
Korrell, Britta 158
Korrell, Martin 158–9
Krack, Axel 174
Krack, Christian 174
Krack, Felix 174
Krack Sekthaus 174
Kraichgau 62
Krämer, Stephan 91
Kreuzberg, Ludwig 54
Krieg, Urban 210
Krug, Joseph 35
Krüger, Wiebke 278–9
Kühn, Angela 205–6
Kühn, Peter Bernhard 206
Kühn, Peter Jakob 205–6
Kuhn, Philipp 174–5
Kühn, Sandra 206
Künstler, Alexandra 138–9
Künstler, Franz 206
Künstler, Gunter 206–7

Kuntz, Sybille 127–8
Kuntz-Riedlin, Markus 127
Kupferberg 36

Lagensekt 38
Laible, Alexander 65
Laible, Andreas, junior 66
Laible, Andreas, senior 65, 66
Landesweingut Kloster Pforta 246, 247, 250–1
Landwein 14, 16, 17
Landweinmarkt 83
Langenwein 18
Lapinski, Johanna 143
Laquai, Gilbert 207
Laquai, Gundolf 207
Lauer, Florian 20, 23, 141
Lauer, Katharina 141
law 9–23
 1892: 11
 1909: 11, 169, 230
 1930: 11–12
 1971: 12–14, 18, 24, 151, 193, 218
 classification 18–20
 Einzellagen and *Grosslagen* 14–15
 Prädikate today 22–3
 Sekt 37–8
 sweetness 20–22
 VDP 18–20
 Württemberg 260
Leflaive, Anne-Claude 79
Leiner, Jürgen 184
Leiner, Sven 184
Leitz, Josef 207–8
Lemberger (Blaufränkisch) 264
 Baden 64, 65
 Franken 89
 Rheinhessen 220
 Württemberg 259, 261–70, 272, 273, 274, 275–81
Leyen, Freiherr von 25–6
Libelli, Nicola 170
Liebfraumilch 218, 229, 230–1
Lindner, Christoph 251
Lippe, Georg Prinz zur 257
Loeb, O.W. 7
Loeb, Sigmund 7
Loersch, Alexander 128
Loersch, Axel 133
Longueville-Drautz, Stéphanie du 276

Loosen, Ernie 21, 122, 128–9
Lorelei legend 111
Louis XIV 166
Löwenstein, Cornelia 124
Löwenstein, Erbprinzessin Stefanie zu 104
Löwenstein, Reinhard 124
Löwenstein, Sarah 124
Lübcke, Julia 148
Lüchau, Hans-Jörg 52
Luckert, Philipp 97, 98
Luckert, Ulrich 98
Luckert, Wolfgang 98
Luther, Martin 5
Lützkendorf, Uwe 251
Lydtin, Ernst Georg 63

Maindreieck 86, 88–98
Mainviereck 85–6, 101–4
Mainz 217, 218, 235–43
Malbec 179
Maleton, Heiner 229, 231
Männer, Martin 75
Mark, Jürgen von der 76–7
Markgräfler 61, 63
Markgräflerland 63, 75–82, 83
Marx, Karl 120
Materne, Rebecca 125
Materne & Schmitt 125
Matuschka-Greiffenclau, Erwein Graf 214
Matuschka-Greiffenclau, Richard 214
Maul, Erika 210–11
Maxime Herkunft Rheinhessen 219, 225
Maximin Grünhaus Weingut der Familie von Schubert 119, 123, 148–9
May, Rudolf 91–2
mechanization 133
Medieval Warm Period 4, 247, 254, 260
Meier, Georg 184
Meissner, Julien 240
Mell, Ulrich 169
Melsheimer, Thorsten 129–30
Merlot 239
  Baden 75, 77, 80
  Pfalz 179, 184
  Rheingau 209
  Württemberg 263, 265, 267, 273, 276, 277
Merovingians 3, 48
Message in a Bottle 218–19
Metternich-Winneburg, Fürst 192, 203

Meyer, Patrick 232
Michael Teschke 241–2
Mionetto 202
Mittelhaardt 165, 166, 167, 168–82
Mittelrhein 45, 111–16
Molitor, Markus 122, 130–1, 147
Moll, Florian 67–8
Morio-Muskat 97
Moritz, Duke of Saxony 250
Mosbacher-Düringer, Jürgen 175
Mosbacher-Düringer, Sabine 175
Mosel 45, 117–49
Muhl, Servatius 121
Muhr, Dorli 280
Müllen, Jonas 131
Müllen, Martin 131
Müller, Christoph 114
Müller, Egon, I 142
Müller, Egon, V 21, 27, 123, 142, 143
Müller, Johannes 114
Müller, Marianne 114
Müller, Matthias 114
Müller, Stefan 143
Müllerrebe *see* Pinot Meunier (Schwarzriesling)
Müller-Thurgau 13, 231
  Baden 61, 68
  Franken 87, 94, 95, 97, 99, 100
  Mittelrhein 113, 115
  Mosel 122, 123
  Nahe 153, 156
  Pfalz 168, 184
  Rheingau 195
  Rheinhessen 219, 233
  Saale-Unstrut 248, 249
  Sachsen 245, 254, 256, 258
Münsterschwarzach Abbey 86
Muscaris 92, 256
Muscat 27, 191
Muskateller
  Baden 66, 71
  Franken 88
  Pfalz 175, 186
  Rheingau 208
  Württemberg 274, 279
Mythos Mosel 123

Nahe 45, 151–63
Näkel, Dörte 54–5
Näkel, Meike 54–5
Näkel, Werner 50, 54–5

Napoleon Bonaparte 5–6, 269
　Ahr valley 48
　Mittelrhein 112
　Mosel 119, 120, 133, 147, 148
　Nahe 152
　Pfalz 166
　Rheingau 192, 203
　Rheinhessen 218
Nassau, House of 192, 199
Nassauische Sparkasse 214
Nassverbesserung 120, 122
National Socialism 7
Natürlich Weinreich 234
Naturwein 11, 12, 13
Naumburg Cathedral 246–7
Nazism 7, 11–12, 122, 193
Neher, Jochen 208
Neipperg, Karl Eugen Erbgraf zu 261, 262, 263, 279
Neipperg, Stephan 72
Neruda, Pablo 124
Neus, Josef 240
Niederberger, Achim 169, 181
Nieger, Sven 66
Niewodniczanski, Roman 122, 131, 133, 146–7
Nittnaus, Anita 97, 271
Nittnaus, Hans 97, 271
Nordpfalz 168–82
norisoprenoids 26–7, 29
North-Rheinhessen 235–43

Oberhofer, Pascal 185
Ochocki, Thorsten 187
Oetker family 202, 203
Off, Jürgen 273
Ökologischer Land- & Weinbau Krämer 91
Optima 210
organic farming
　Ahr valley 51
　Baden 65, 68, 70, 77–9
　Franken 91, 92, 95, 98, 101
　Mosel 125, 127, 129, 139
　Nahe 160
　Pfalz 171, 172, 175, 176, 179–81, 184, 185
　Rheingau 194, 195, 198, 201, 208, 209
　Rheinhessen
　　Bingen, Ingelheim, Mainz, North- and West-Rheinhessen 237, 238, 241, 243
　　Rheinfront: Roter Hang 220, 222

　　Winnegau and Worms 224, 225, 229, 231, 232, 234, 235
　Saale-Unstrut 248
　Sachsen 258
　Württemberg 267–72, 275, 277
Orleans 77, 191
Orstwein 18
Ortenau 62, 64–7
Ortssekt 38
Österreicher *see* Silvaner
Österreichisch Weiss 96
Otte, Kathrin 175
Otto III 246

Päger, Hella 249
Palatinate Succession, War of the 60, 166, 218
Pauly, Axel 132
Pawis, Bernard 252
Pawis, Kerstin 252
Peasants' Revolt 5, 191, 203
Perabo, Peter 196
Peter, Karsten 158
Peter Jakob Kühn 205–6
Peters, Felix 220
Petit Manseng 77
Pfalz 33, 45, 165–87
Pfarrgut Rüdesheim 196
Pfortenser Klöppelberg 246
Philippi, Bernd 173
Philipps, Martin 115
Philipps, Thomas 115
phylloxera 6, 7, 210
　Franken 87, 94
　Mittelrhein 112
　Saale-Unstrut 247
　Sachsen 254
Piesporter Michelsberg 122
Pinot Blanc
　Ahr valley 55
　Baden 77
　Mosel 126, 145
　Nahe 163
　Pfalz 173, 174, 187
　Rheingau 209
　Rheinhessen 221, 232, 237, 240
Pinot Gris 28, 77, 145, 237
Pinot Meunier (Schwarzriesling)
　Baden 62
　Franken 102
　Württemberg 259, 263–4, 268, 270, 276, 278

Pinot Noir *see* Spätburgunder
Pinot Noir Précoce *see* Frühburgunder
Plettenberg, Nikolaus Graf von 213
Portugieser 264
    Ahr valley 52, 53, 55
    Franken 87, 99, 101
    Mittelrhein 113
    Mosel 121
    Pfalz 168, 172, 179
    Saale-Unstrut 248
Potsdam Zeitreihe 42
Prädikate
    botrytis 44
    law 10–16, 20, 22–3
    VDP 19
Prädikatswein 16, 17
Preisinger, Claus 280
Prinz, Fred 209
Prinz zu Salm-Dalberg'sches Weingut 159–60
Probst, Björn 250, 251
ProWein wine fair 16
Prüm, Jodocus 133
Prüm, Johann Josef 133–4
Prüm, Katharina 134, 229
Prüm, Manfred 134
Prüm Abbey 48
Puff, Katharina 199

Qualitätswein
    international equivalents 17
    law 14, 16, 17
    must weights 13–14
    VDP 19
Qualitätswein bestimmter Anbaugebiete (QbA) 12, 17, 22
Qualitätswein mit Prädikat (QmP) 12, 17, 22

Raps, Eva 204
Ratzenberger, Joachim 115
Raumland, Heide-Rose 229–30
Raumland, Katharina 230
Raumland, Marie-Luise 230
Raumland, Volker 229–30
Realteilung 260
Rebholz, Birgit 185
Rebholz, Eduard 185
Rebholz, Hans 186
Rebholz, Hansjörg 33, 185–6
Rebholz, Valentin 186
Reformation 5

Regent 97, 256
Reichensteiner 210
Reichsnährstand 7
Reidel, Jens 158
Reimann, Anna 139
Reimann, Stephan 139
Remstal 259, 263, 264–75
Respekt 171
Restzuckerbegrenzung 21
reunification of Germany 245–6
Rheinfront 219–24
Rheingau 33, 45, 189–216
Rheingold 36
Rheinhessen 45, 217–43
Rias, Diego 124
Rieger, Philipp 76, 77
Rieslaner 97, 176
Riesling 2, 25–9
    acidity 27, 28–9
    Ahr valley 50, 52, 54, 55, 56
    aroma 29
    Baden 61–3, 65–7, 70, 71
    climate change 41, 43–4
    crossings 210, 264
    flavour 26–7
    Franken 87
        Maindreieck 88, 89, 91, 93, 95, 97
        Mainviereck and Churfranken 103, 104
        Steigerwald 99, 100
        Taubertal 105
    growing conditions 26
    Hessische Bergstrasse 107, 108, 109
    history 6–7, 25–6
    law 9–13, 19, 23
    lessons for Spätburgunder 33–4
    Liebfraumilch 231
    minerality 27–8
    Mittelrhein 113, 114, 115, 116
    Mosel 117, 119, 121–3, 126, 129–39
        Ruwer 147–9
        Saar 119, 140–7
        Terrassenmosel 124, 125
    Nahe 152–63
    Pfalz 167–87
    Rheingau 189, 191–6, 198–209, 212, 213, 214, 215
    Rheinhessen 218–29, 231–43
    Saale-Unstrut 248, 249, 250, 251, 252
    Sachsen 254–8
    steep slope viticulture 142

sweetness 28–9
Württemberg 265–70, 272–81
Rieslingsekt 39
Riffel, Carolin 241
Riffel, Erik 241
Rings, Andreas 178–9
Rings, Simone 179
Rings, Steffen 178–9
Riske, Jan 55–6
Riske, Volker 55–6
Robert Weil 193, 215
Robinson, J. 210
Rodlein, Hans 88
Roll, Gesine 233
Romans 3
  Ahr valley 48
  Holy Roman Empire 4–6, 60, 99
  Mittelrhein 112
  Mosel 119, 148
  Nahe 152
  Pfalz 166
  Rheinhessen 217
rosé 34
Roter Hang 217, 219–24
Roter Riesling 199
Roter Silvaner 97
Roter Traminer 258
Roth, Barbara 187
Rothe, Manfred 92, 96
Rothschild, Baron 230
Rotkäppchen Sektkellerei 247, 252–3
Rotling 34
Rotweingut Jean Stodden 56–7
Rotweinpreis 52
Ruinart, Remy Auguste 112
Runge, Kai 195
Runkel, Christian 238
Runkel, Matthias 238
Ruwer 45, 117–22, 147–9

Saale-Unstrut 45, 245, 246–53
Saar 45, 117–23, 139–47
Saar Riesling Sommer 123
Sachsen (Saxony) 34, 45, 245–6, 253–8
Sächsisches Staatsweingut Schloss Wackerbath 254, 256–7
Sal-Salm, Constantin zu 159
Sal-Salm, Felix zu 159–60
Salwey, Konrad 63, 72–3
Salwey, Wolf Dietrich 72

Samara, Olympia 279–80
Sämling 88 *see* Scheurebe
Samtrot 264, 276
Sankt Laurentius Sekt 134–5
Sankt Maximin Abbey 148
Sauer, Horst 93, 96
Sauer, Sandra 93
Sauvignon Blanc 76
  Ahr valley 54, 55
  Baden 64, 66, 73, 77
  Franken 95, 104
  Mosel 126
  Nahe 154
  Pfalz 171, 175, 176, 179, 181, 182
  Rheingau 209
  Rheinhessen 219, 221, 233–4, 240, 242, 243
  Württemberg 265–7, 269, 274, 275, 276, 277
Savagnin Blanc 25, 96
Schach, Sabrina 212
Schaetzel, Kai 43–4
Schäfer, Andreas 52
Schäfer, Heiko 52
Schäfer, Paul, junior 52
Schäfer, Paul, senior 52
Schäfer, Sebastian 160
Schäfer, Stefan 94
Schamaun, Albert 54
Scharzhofberg 119
Schätzel, Carolin 223
Schätzel, Kai 223
Schätzle, Robert 67
Schaumwein 37
Scherer, Felix 76, 78
Scheu, Georg 209, 210, 211
Scheurebe 97, 210–11
  Baden 65, 66
  Franken 95, 100
  Mittelrhein 113
  Nahe 162, 163
  Pfalz 176, 177, 184
  Rheingau 208, 209
  Rheinhessen 219, 221, 226, 233, 243
  Sachsen 256
Schiava Grossa *see* Trollinger
schiefer 123
Schieler 34
Schillerwein 34, 261
Schlegel, Friedrich 111

Schloss Bellevue 134
Schlossgut Diel 155–6
Schloss Johannisberg 10, 25, 191–2, 202–4
Schloss Saarstein 133, 145–6
Schloss Schönberg 108–9
Schloss Vollrads 191, 193, 213–14
Schloss Wackerbath 254, 256–7
Schmitt, Bianka 232
Schmitt, Clemens 215
Schmitt, Conrad 20
Schmitt, Daniel 232
Schmitt, Franziska 173
Schmitt, Janina 125
Schmitt, Lewis 240
Schnaitmann, Rainer 261, 272
Schneider, Alexander 73
Schneider, Christoph 79
Schneider, Cornelia 73
Schneider, Johannes 78–9
Schneider, Klaus 24
Schneider, Markus 179
Schneider, Reinhold 73
Schönleber, Frank 157
Schönleber, Werner 157
Schoonmaker, Frank 32, 47, 152
Schoppen 165
Schöttle, Veronika 197
Schubert, Carl von 148
Schubert, Maximin von 148
Schug, Bernhard 128
Schultz, Hans 28, 41–3
Schulz, Günter 197
Schumacher, Paul 56
Schumann, Andreas 177
Schür, Sebastian 102
Schwarz, Hans-Günther 176
Schwarzriesling *see* Pinot Meunier
Schwegler, Aaron 273
Schwegler, Albrecht 273
Schwegler, Andrea 273
Schwegler, Julia 273
Schwörer, Christian 24
Second World War 7, 253, 254
Seeger, Thomas 64
Seitz 21
Sekt 35–9
  Ahr valley 49
  Baden 71, 81
  Franken 88, 89–90, 100, 102
  Hessische Bergstrasse 107, 108

  history 35–7
  law 37–8
  Mittelrhein 112, 115–16
  Mosel 126, 127, 129, 134, 141
  Nahe 152, 153, 155, 158, 160, 162
  origins of term 35
  Pfalz 172, 174, 175, 178, 181, 184–7
  Rheingau 194, 196, 197, 202–3, 212–14
  Rheinhessen 229–30, 232, 236, 239, 240
  Saale-Unstrut 247, 252–3
  Sachsen 254, 256, 257, 258
  styles 39
  taxation 36, 37
  Württemberg 265, 268–70, 272, 278
Sekt & Weingut Winterling 181
Sekt b.A. 38
Sekt Burkhardt-Schür 102
Sekthaus Raumland 229–30
Sekthaus Solter 212
Sektkellerei Bussard 254
Sektkellereien 112
Sektkellerei Höfer 89–90
Sektmanufaktur Flik 239
Sektmanufaktur Schloss Vaux 213
Sektsteuer 36
Selbach, Barbara 135
Selbach, Hannah 135, 136
Selbach, Johannes 122, 135
Selbach, Sebastian 135
Shakespeare, William 35
Shelter Winery 69
Sichel, Peter 7
Silcher, Friedrich 111
Silvaner 96–7, 210, 231
  Baden 61, 73, 82
  Franken 87
    Maindreieck 88–93, 95, 97, 98
    Mainviereck and Churfranken 104
    Steigerwald 99–101
    Taubertal 105
  Mosel 121
  Nahe 153, 163
  Pfalz 168, 177, 184, 186
  Rheingau 191, 208
  Rheinhessen 218
    Bingen, Ingelheim, Mainz, North- and West-Rheinhessen 237, 238, 240–3
    Rheinfront: Roter Hang 221
    Winnegau and Worms 226, 232, 233, 235
  Saale-Unstrut 248, 249, 250

Sachsen 256
Württemberg 269
Simonit & Sirch 90
Sinß, Johannes 162
Sinß, Markus 162
slate 123
Smith, Clark 28
Söhnlein 36
soil temperatures 42
Solter, Helmut 212
Solter, Verena 212
Sona, Dominik 173
Sonkaya, Saynur 208
Spanier, Anna 174
Spanier, Hans Oliver (HO) 223, 224
Spanier-Gillot, Carolin 222–3, 224
Spanish Succession, War of the 60
sparkling wine
   Schaumwein 37
   Sekt *see* Sekt
Spätburgunder 2, 31–4
   Ahr valley 47, 48, 49–51, 52, 53, 54, 55, 56
   Baden 61, 64
      Badische Bergstrasse 64
      Breisgau 68–70
      Kaiserstuhl 63, 70–3, 75
      Markgräflerland 75, 77–82
      Ortenau 65, 66, 67
   Badisch Rotgold 34
   climate change 31, 32, 41
   Franken 87
      Maindreieck 89, 91, 92, 97, 98
      Mainviereck and Churfranken 101–4
      Steigerwald 100
   Hessische Bergstrasse 107
   history 31–2
   landscape 33
   Mittelrhein 113, 114, 116
   Mosel 121–3, 126, 129, 131, 132, 135–7
      Ruwer 148
      Saar 143
   Nahe 153, 154, 155, 159, 160, 162, 163
   Pfalz 168
      Mittelhaardt and Nordpfalz 169, 171–5, 179, 181, 182
      Südliche Weinstrasse 182–7
   Rheingau 190, 192, 194–9, 201, 202, 204–9, 211–13
   Rheinhessen 219, 221, 224, 226–9, 236–40, 242, 243

Saale-Unstrut 250, 251
Sachsen 255, 258
style 33
synonyms 31, 68
Württemberg 264–70, 272–6, 278–81
Spätlese 10, 13–14, 16, 23
Spindler, Markus 180
Spreitzer, Andreas 212–13
Spreitzer, Bernd 212
Staatlicher Hofkeller 94
Staatsdomäne Assmannshausen 199
Staffelsteuer 36
Stahl, Christian 94
St Antony Weingut GmbH & Co. KG 220
Starker, Kathi 124
steep slope viticulture 142
Steifensand, Wilhelm 229, 231
Steigerwald 86, 99–101
Steillage 142
Steilstlage 142
Stephanus, H. 121
Steren, Johannes von 89
sterile filtration 21
St Laurent 173, 179, 184, 186, 236, 240, 269
Stockinger 68, 186
Stodden, Alexander 50, 56–7
Stodden, Gerhard 50, 56
Strauch Sektmanufaktur GmbH 232–3
Strauch-Weißbach, Isabel 232
Streit, Jürgen 108
Stübinger, Oscar 12
Stumpf, Matthias 88
Stumpf, Melanie 88
Stumpf, Reimund 88
Stuttgart 259, 260, 261, 264–75
Sudliche Weinstrasse 168, 182–7
Suntory 215
Supp, Bernd 279
Süssreserve 21
sweetness in wine 20–22
Syrah 81, 173, 179, 182, 239, 267, 269

table wine/ *Tafelwein* see *Landwein*
Tauberfranken 62
Tauberschwarz 87, 104, 105
Taubertal 104–5
taxation 36, 37
TDN 29
Tennenbacher Güterbuch 69
terpenes 26–7

Terrassenmosel 118, 124–5
Terrazzan, Ambra 281
Tesch, Martin 163
Tesche, Carl 49
Tesche, Karl Anton 112
Tesche & Co. Cooperation 112
Teschke, Michael 241–2
Thanisch, Hugo 136
Thanisch, Katharina 136
Thanisch, Sofia 136
Thekla, Sister 211
Thirty Years' War 5
   Ahr valley 48
   Baden 60, 70
   Franken 87, 96
   Mosel 119
   Nahe 152
   Pfalz 166
   Rheingau 191, 199
   Rheinhessen 218
   Sachsen 254
   Württemberg 260, 262
Thörle, Christoph 242–3
Thörle, Johannes 242–3
Thörle, Rudolf 242
Tischwein see *Landwein*
Traminer 10, 26
   Baden 63, 66
   Franken 88
   Mosel 121
   Nahe 163
   Pfalz 167, 169, 182, 185
   Rheingau 209
   Saale-Unstrut 251
   Sachsen 256, 258
Trautmann, Rabea 108–9
Treuhandanstalt 245–6
Triassic era 271
Trockenbeerenauslese (TBA) 10, 13–14, 23
Trollinger
   crossings 210, 264
   Württemberg 259, 261–4
      Stuttgart and Remstal 266, 269, 272, 273, 275
      Unterland and Zabergäu 276, 277, 278, 281
Tulla, Johann Gottfried 61
Tuniberg 62
Turner, J.M.W. 111
Twardowski, Daniel 137

Unterland 259, 263, 275–82
Unternehmensgruppe Niederberger 167, 178
Urban 266

Valckenberg 231
Valckenberg, Peter Joseph 229, 230, 231
Valckenberg, William 230
Valentinian 119
Verband Deutscher Naturweinversteigerer (VDNV) 11, 18
Verband Deutscher Prädikatsweingüter (VDP)
   law 18–20, 24
   Maxime Herkunft Rheinhessen 219
   Raps, Eva 204
   Rheingau 193
   Sekt 38–9, 194
Versailles Treaty 36
Vetter, Stefan 97
Veuve Clicquot 35, 269
Victoria, Queen 200
Vienna Congress 6, 120, 152
Viognier 80, 182, 237, 275
Vizetelly, Henry 76, 86, 121, 192
Völk, Dominik 146
Volkseigener Betrieb (VEB) 247
Vouillamoz, J. 210

Wachtstetter, Anette 281
Wachtstetter, Rainer 281
Wackerbath, August Christoph Graf von 256
Wagner, Daniel 219, 236, 243
Wagner, Richard 36
War of the Palatinate Succession 60, 166, 218
War of the Spanish Succession 60
Waßmer, Fritz 80
Waßmer, Martin 80–1
Wechsler, Katharina 233
Wehrheim, Franz 186
Wehrheim, Karl 186
Wehrheim, Karl-Heinz 186
Weickert, Markus 75
Weil, Robert 193, 215
Weil, Wilhelm 193, 215
Weimar Republic 7
Wein- & Sektgut Bamberger 153–4
Weinbergsrolle 15
Weinert, Bärbel 209
Weinfactum 274
Weingart, Florian 116
Weingut & Gutsausschank Hamm 201–2

INDEX

Weingut Achenbach 236
Weingut Albrecht Schwegler 272–3
Weingut Aldinger 261, 264–5
Weingut Alexander Laible 65
Weingut am Stein 95
Weingut Andreas Laible 66
Weingut Anette Closheim 154
Weingut August Kesseler 204–5
Weingut Axel Pauly 132
Weingut Battenfeld-Spanier 223, 224–5
Weingut Benedikt Baltes 101–2
Weingut Bercher 70–1
Weingut Bernhard Ellwanger 266
Weingut Bernhard Huber 68–9
Weingut Beurer 265–6
Weingut Bianka & Daniel Schmitt 232
Weingut Bickel-Stumpf 88
Weingut Bischel 238
Weingut Blankenhorn 75
Weingut Born 248–9
Weingut Braunewell 238–9
Weingut Bremer 169
Weingut Burggarten 51–2
Weingut Cantzheim 139–40
Weingut Chat Sauvage 197
Weingut Christmann 22, 170–1
Weingut Claus Schneider 78–9
Weingut Clemens Busch 125–6
Weingut Daniel Twardowski 137
Weingut Dautel 275–6
Weingut der Stadt Klingenberg 101
Weingut Deutzerhof Crossmann-Hehle 52–3
Weingut Dönnhoff 156
Weingut Drautz-Able 276–7
Weingut Dr. Bürklin-Wolf 167, 168, 170
Weingut Dr Corvers-Kauter 197–8
Weingut Dr. Crusius 154–5
Weingut Dr. Deinhard 181
Weingut Dreissigacker 225
Weingut Dr Heger 71
Weingut Dr Loosen 128–9
Weingut Dr. Wehrheim 168, 186
Weingut Egon Müller 142–3
Weingut Eisele 277
Weingut Emrich-Schönleber 157
Weingut Enderle & Moll 67–8
Weingut Erwin Riske 55–6
Weingut Familie Hoffmann 104–5
Weingut Frédéric Fourré 256
Weingut Friedrich Becker 168, 182–3

Weingut Fritz Bastian 113
Weingut Fritz Ekkehard Huff 222
Weingut Fritz Waßmer 80
Weingut Fürst Löwenstein 104
Weingut Fußer 171–2
Weingut Geheimer Rat Dr. von Bassermann-Jordan 167, 168–9
Weingut Georg Breuer 193, 196–7
Weingut Georg Mosbacher 175–6
Weingut Gold, Weinstadt-Gundelsbach 267–8
Weingut Gunderloch 220–1
Weingut Gutzler 227
Weingut Heinrichshof 126–7
Weingut Heinrich Spindler 180
Weingut Herzog von Württemberg 277–8
Weingut Hey 250
Weingut Heymann-Löwenstein 124
Weingut H.J. Kreuzberg 54
Weingut Holger Koch 71–2
Weingut Horst Sauer 93
Weingut Immich-Batterieberg 127
Weingut J. Bettenheimer 237–8
Weingut J.J. Adeneuer 50–1
Weingut J. Neus 240–1
Weingut Joachim Flick 200
Weingut Joh. Bapt. Schäfer 160–1
Weingut Joh. Jos. Prüm 21, 123, 133–4
Weingut Josef Leitz 200, 207–8
Weingut Josten & Klein 53–4
Weingut Jülg 183
Weingut Julia Bertram 51
Weingut Jürgen Ellwanger 261, 266–7
Weingut Jürgen Leiner 184
Weingut Jürgen von der Mark 76–7
Weingut Karl Friedrich Aust 255
Weingut Karl Haidle 261, 268
Weingut Kastler Friedland 256
Weingut Kaufmann 204
Weingut Keller 227–8
Weingut K.F. Groebe 226–7
Weingut Klaus Böhme 248
Weingut Klaus Zimmerling 258
Weingut Klopfer 270
Weingut Knauß 271–2
Weingut Knebel 124–5
Weingut Knewitz 239–40
Weingut Knipser 168, 172–3
Weingut Köhler-Ruprecht 168, 173–4
Weingut Kopp 64–5
Weingut Korrell Johanneshof 158–9

Weingut Krone 196, 214–15
Weingut Kühling-Gillot 222–3, 224–5
Weingut Künstler 206–7
Weingut Laquai 207
Weingut Liebfrauenstift 228–9, 231
Weingut Loersch 128
Weingut Louis Guntrum 221–2
Weingut Markus Heid 268–9
Weingut Markus Molitor 130–1
Weingut Markus Schneider 179
Weingut Martin Müllen 131
Weingut Martin Waßmer 80–1
Weingut Matthias Müller 114
Weingut Mehling 175
Weingut Meier 184–5
Weingut Melsheimer 129–30
Weingut Meyer-Näkel 54–5
Weingut Mohr 208
Weingut Müller-Catoir 168, 171, 176
Weingut Neipperg 262, 279
Weingut Nik Weis St Urbans-Hof 138
Weingut Oberhofer 185
Weingut Odinstal 176–7
Weingut Oekonomierat Johann Geil I. Erben GbR 225–6
Weingut Ökonomierat Rebholz 168, 185–6
Weingut Oliver Zeter 181–2
Weingut Paulinshof 132
Weingut Paul Schumacher 56
Weingut Pawis 252
Weingut Peter Lauer 141
Weingut Pfeffingen 177–8
Weingut Philipp Kuhn 174–5
Weingut Philipps-Mühle 115
Weingut Prinz 208–9
Weingut Prinz von Hessen 209
Weingut Rainer Schnaitmann 261, 272
Weingut Ratzenberger 115–16
Weingut Reichsrat von Buhl 167, 172, 178
Weingut Reinhold & Cornelia Schneider 73
Weingut Rieger 77–8
Weingut Riffel 241
Weingut Rings 178–9
Weingut Roterfaden 279–80
Weingut Rothe 92
Weingut Rudolf Fürst 102–3
Weingut Rudolf May 91–2
Weingut Salwey 72–3
Weingut Schaetzel 43

Weingut Schäfer-Fröhlich 161–2
Weingut Schätzel 223–4
Weingut Scherer-Zimmer 78
Weingut Schloss Lieser 135
Weingut Schloss Neuweier 67
Weingut Schloss Proschwitz 257–8
Weingut Schwarzer Adler – Franz Keller 74–5
Weingut Seeger 64
Weingut Selbach-Oster 135–6
Weingut Simone Adams 237
Weingut Sinß 162
Weingut Spreitzer 212–13
Weingut Stefan Müller 143
Weingut Stefan Vetter 97
Weingut Steinbachhof 280–1
Weingut Sven Nieger 66–7
Weingut Sybille Kuntz 127–8
Weingut Tesch 163
Weingut Thörle 242–3
Weingut Toni Jost 113–14
Weingut Uwe Lützkendorf 251
Weingut Van Volxem 131, 133, 146–7
Weingut von Othegraven 145
Weingut von Winning 167, 180–1
Weingut Wachtstetter 281–2
Weingut Wagner-Stempel 243
Weingut Wasenhaus 79–80
Weingut Wechsler 233
Weingut Weedenborn 233–4
Weingut Wegeler 214–15
Weingut Weingart 116
Weingut Weinreich 234
Weingut Weiser-Künstler 138–9
Weingut Wilhelm Meuschel 100
Weingut Wilhelmshof 187
Weingut Wirsching 100–1
Weingut Wittmann 234–5
Weingut Witwe Dr. H. Thanisch, Erben Müller-Burggraef 136
Weingut Witwe Dr. H. Thanisch, Erben Thanisch 136–7
Weingut Witwe Thanisch 136
Weingut Wöhrle 69–70
Weingut Wöhrwag 274
Weingut Ziereisen 81–2
Weingut Zimmerle 262, 274–5
Weinmanufaktur Untertürkheim 273–4
Weinreich, Jan 234
Weinreich, Marc 234

Wein- und Sektgut Barth 194
Wein- und Sektgut Hirschmüller 278–9
Weis, Daniela 138
Weis, Nik 123, 138
Weiser, Konstantin 138–9
Weißbach, Tim 232
Weissburgunder
  Ahr valley 55
  Baden 61, 70–3, 75, 78, 79, 81, 82
  Franken 100, 103
  Mittelrhein 114
  Mosel 135
  Nahe 153, 154, 156, 158, 162
  Pfalz 168
    Mittelhaardt and Nordpfalz 169, 171, 175, 179
    Südliche Weinstrasse 183, 184, 186, 187
  Rheingau 204, 207, 208
  Rheinhessen
    Bingen, Ingelheim, Mainz, North- and West-Rheinhessen 237, 238, 240, 242, 243
      Rheinfront: Roter Hang 221
    Wonnegau and Worms 226, 232, 233, 235
  Saale-Unstrut 248, 249, 250, 251, 252, 253
  Sachsen 254, 255, 256, 258
  Württemberg 274
Weissherbst 34
Wenceslaus, Clemens 25, 119
West-Rheinhessen 235–43
Wilhelm I, Margrave 254
Wilhelm II, Kaiser 36, 215, 252
wine law *see* law
Winnegau 224–35
Winterling, Martin 181
Winterling, Sebastian 181
Winterling, Susanne 181
Winzergenossenschaften see cooperatives

Winzerhof Gussek 249–50
Winzerhof Stahl 94–5
Winzersekt 37, 38
Wirsching, Hans 100
Wirsching, Heinrich 100
Wittmann, Philipp 219, 234–5
Wöhrle, Hans 69–70
Wöhrle, Markus 69, 70
Wöhrle, Monika 69–70
Wöhrwag, Christin 274
Wöhrwag, Hans-Peter 274
Wöhrwag, Johanna 274
Wöhrwag, Philipp 274
Wolber, Christoph 79
Wolf, Silke 69
World Exhibitions
  1867 (Paris) 192
  1900 (Paris) 36, 61, 121, 142, 167, 218
  1904 (St Louis) 142
  1911 (Brussels) 142
Worms 217, 218, 224–35
Württemberg 34, 45, 259–82
Württemberg, Dukes of 277–8, 280
Würtz, Dirk 220

Zabergäu 259, 275–82
Zehnthof Luckert 98
Zeter, Christian 181
Zeter, Oliver 181–2
Ziereisen, Edeltraud 81–2
Ziereisen, Hanspeter 76, 81–2, 83
Zilliken, Dorothee 140
Zilliken, Hans-Joachim (Hanno) 23, 123, 140
Zimmer, Michael 78
Zimmerle, Jens 262, 274–5
Zimmerling, Klaus 258
Zollverein 48, 61
Zweigelt 247, 250, 251, 265–8, 273, 277

9781913141554